FOUR DECADES OF POLISH ESSAYS

FOUR DECADES OF POLISH ESSAYS

Edited by Jan Kott

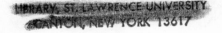
NORTHWESTERN UNIVERSITY PRESS   EVANSTON, ILLINOIS

Northwestern University Press
Evanston, Illinois 60201

These translations have been made possible (in part) through grants from the
Wheatland Foundation, New York, and the National Endowment for the Arts.

Printed in the United States of America

Library of Congress Cataloging-in-Publication Data

Four decades of Polish essays / edited by Jan Kott.
    p.   cm.
    ISBN 0-8101-0862-3. — ISBN 0-8101-0863-1 (pbk.)
    1. Polish essays—20th century—Translations into English.
    2. English essays—Translations from Polish.
PG7445.E8F68   1990
891.8'547—dc20   90-34265
                                                       CIP

Contents

Acknowledgments

Grateful acknowledgment is made to the following for permission to reprint or to translate work originally published elsewhere.

Jerzy Stempowski, "The Smugglers' Library," and "Essay for Cassandra," from *Eseje dla Kassandry* (Paris: Institut Littéraire, 1961). Translated by permission of the publisher.

Stanisław Vincenz, "An Encounter with the Hasidim," from *Tematy żydowskie* (London: Oficyna Poetów i Marlarzy, 1973). Translated by permission of Irena Vincenz.

Józef Czapski, "Paradise Lost," from *Oko* (Paris: Institut Littéraire, 1960). Translated by permission of the publisher.

Jarosław Iwaszkiewicz, "Dostoevsky," from *Petersburg* (Warsaw: PIW, 1976). Translated by permission of Maria Iwaszkiewicz.

Józef Wittlin, "Sorrow and Grandeur of Exile," from *The Polish Review* 2, no. 2/3 (1957). Reprinted by permission of *The Polish Review*.

Stanisław Ignacy Witkiewicz, "On a New Type of Play," translation © 1967 by Daniel Gerould and C. S. Durer. Reprinted by permission of the translators.

Bruno Schulz, "An Essay for S. I. Witkiewicz" and "Afterword to Kafka's *The Trial*," from *Letters and Drawings of Bruno Schulz*, ed. Jerzy Ficowski. Copyright © 1988 by Harper and Row, Publishers, Inc. Reprinted by permission of the publisher.

K. A. Jeleński, "Avant-Garde and Revolution," from *Zbiegi okoliczności* (Paris: Institut Littéraire, 1962). Translated by permission of the publisher.

Zbigniew Herbert, "Defense of the Templars," from *Barbarian in the Garden* (London: Carcanet, 1985). Translation © 1985 by Michael March and Jarosław Anders. Reprinted by permission.

Bolesław Miciński, "Portrait of Kant," from *The Polish Review* 24, no. 4 (1979). Translation © 1979 by Jadwiga Kosicka. Reprinted by permission.

Zygmunt Kubiak, "Pascal" and "From Saint Augustine," from *Półmrok ludzkiego świata* (Warsaw, 1963). Translated by permission of the author.

Andrzej Kijowski, "Postscript to Saint Augustine's *Confessions*," from *Tropy* (Poznań: Znak, 1986). Translated by permission of Kazimiera Kijowska.

Stanisław Jerzy Lec, selection from *Unkempt Thoughts* (New York: St. Martin's Press, 1962; New York: Hippocrene Books, 1990). Translated by Jacek Galazka. © 1962, 1990 by Jacek Galazka.

Jan Błoński, "The Poor Poles Look at the Ghetto," from *Polin: A Journal of Polish-Jewish Studies* 2 (1987): 321–36. Reprinted by permission of Basil Blackwell, Inc.

Gustaw Herling, "The Shadow Hour," from *Drugie przyjście* (Paris: Institut Littéraire, 1963). English translation © 1990 by Ronald Strom.

Aleksander Wat, "Reading Proust in Lubyanka," from *My Century: The Odyssey of a Polish Intellectual*, trans. and ed. Richard Lourie. © 1988 The Regents of the University of California.

Stanisław Lem, "Reflections on My Life," from *Microworlds*, © 1984 by Stanisław Lem. First published in *The New Yorker*. Reprinted by permission of Harcourt Brace Jovanovich, Inc.

Leszek Kołakowski, "Modernity on Endless Trial," from *Encounter* (March 1986). Reprinted by permission of Encounter Limited.

Jerzy Grotowski, "Performer." Published by Centro di Lavoro di Jerzy Grotowski. English translation © Jerzy Grotowski. At the request of the author, this essay has been reprinted exactly as it originally appeared.

Witold Gombrowicz, "Selections from *Diary*." Translation © 1988 by Northwesten University Press.

Czesław Miłosz, "Nobel Prize Lecture." © 1980 by The Nobel Foundation.

Stanisław Barańczak, "Tounge-Tied Eloquence: Notes on Language, Exile, and Writing," from *University of Toronto Quarterly* 38, no. 4 (Summer 1989). Reprinted by permission.

Wojciech Karpiński, "The Blazon of Exile," from *Zeszyty Literackie* 12 (1985). Translated by permission of the author.

Adam Zagajewski, "Selections from 'The Little Larousse.'" Translation © 1990 by Adam Zagajewski and Lillian Vallee, © 1990 by Adam Zagajewski. From *Solidarity, Solitude* (New York: Ecco Press, 1990). Reprinted by permission.

Adam Michnik, "Don Quixote and Invective," from *Polskie pytania* (Paris: Zeszyty Literackie, 1987). Translated by permission of the author.

Jan Kott

Introduction

During the past half century of Polish literature, poetry and the essay are the two genres that have fully developed their own distinct voices. Or to put it differently: it is in poetry and the essay that the experience of the last decades has found the most Polish and at the same time the most universal image and reflection. And it is not by accident that so many Polish poets of the period have cultivated the essay as a genre of equal importance in their creative work. Of the authors represented in this anthology, this holds true not only for Czesław Miłosz but also for Józef Wittlin and Jarosław Iwaszkiewicz, from the generation born in the previous century; for Aleksander Wat, born in 1900 between two centuries; for Zbigniew Herbert, from the generation born in the first decade of newly independent Poland; and finally for the youngest authors in this volume, Stanisław Barańczak and Adam Zagajewski, who were born after the Second World War during the first two years of the new Yalta order.

The essay and poetry always use the first person, even if this first person is hidden under many stylistic disguises. The lyrical subject in Polish poetry of the period stubbornly and repeatedly turns out to be an epic subject. I should not like to overemphasize this opposition, but if one's experience, one's destiny, and one's life are common to all mankind, then form will seem to be less important than content. And the content is man's destiny. In this image of man's fate in the Polish poetry and the Polish essay of those years, history is more frequently and more vividly present than metaphysics. Or to put it quite bluntly, even in philosophical and religious reflections, the experience of totalitarian night always makes its presence felt. If Polish poetry often speaks about the real world, the essay does it all the time. The essay gives testimony about this world through a personal story, inscribed just as the blows of a whip make marks on the skin.

The great patron of the essay is Montaigne. But the traditional English essay, and, to a still greater extent, its modern equivalent as practiced in American journalism have blurred the original, Renaissance sense of the word. The title in Polish of Boy-Żeleński's splendid translation of Montaigne's *Essays* is *Próby* (attempts, trials, endeavors). The French word *essais* comes from the verb *essayer*, to assay, to test, to try. In this testing of the world the touchstone—I must repeat it once more—is one's own destiny, one's own skin, like a hand that refuses to trust the eyes and feels the irregular surface of the wall. For that reason Touchstone, the fool in Shakespeare's *As You Like It*, deserves to be the second patron of the essay. A touchstone is something more than a means of testing precious metals. And acid is used not only for testing gold and silver. Touchstone, the most philosophical of Shakespeare's fools, free of any illusions, is a faithful companion to the daughter of the banished prince, first in her flight from a home that resembles a slaughterhouse ("This is no place, this house is but a butchery," 2.3) and then in her banishment. In yet another instance of Shakespeare's unfailing presence, which never ceases to astound me, Touchstone and the fool in *King Lear* are loyal companions to exiles. It is of course not a matter of chance that the embittered companion of exiles, Touchstone, should become the unexpected patron of the Polish essay.

Although it was not my intention in assembling this collection, the theme and experience of exile, or what in the contemporary idiom is called emigration, will appear again and again. It is present in Wittlin's "Sorrow and Grandeur of Exile" (1957), by now a classic piece; in Miłosz's Nobel lecture, delivered in Stockholm in 1980, about the heroic decision of a poet from the "other Europe" to continue writing in his native tongue; and in Barańczak's reflections—dedicated, not surprisingly, to Josef Škvorecký—on the fundamental impossibility of translating from one language into another, not only semantically, but above all emotionally. And although these essays speak about the experiences of Polish writers, they constitute only one of the most striking examples of a situation that is becoming increasingly common, almost universal, in this our second half of the twentieth century.

Romantic and modernist poets would often assert that the artist is an "exile" in his own country. And that he always remains an "alien." But this "alienation," which, like a cloak, was more often than not an artistic embellishment, has become common, everyday reality for millions of exiles, voluntary or forced, coming from homelands where "butchery" or widespread poverty reigns. The Greek *idiotes* initially signified a newcomer who could not speak the language of the natives. In this Greek sense, not only every writer but every emigrant remains mute for a long time.

By choosing emigration a writer not only accepts the condition of a mute, he also makes another much more difficult decision to cut himself off—and none of us ever knows for how long—from his own soil and from readers in his native language in his own country. And it is not accidental that for Wojciech Karpiński during his first émigré years in Paris, the model of pride and perseverance in choosing emigration was Nabokov, as is evident in the title of his essay, "The Blazon of Exile"; whereas for Adam Michnik in his essay written in prison in 1986, it was Thomas Mann who became the model for the difficult and painful decision to sever ties with and condemn one's own country once it had plunged into the darkness of hatred.

Emigration is a difficult and painful choice. But forbidding it is inhuman. In this collection of essays the aphorisms of Stanisław Jerzy Lec occupy a special place. "Open Sesame—I want to get out." Or a variation on the same experience: "I prefer the sign NO ENTRY to the one that says NO EXIT." For the Polish writer, whatever the genre he has chosen, there is no escape from the stranglehold of history.

In this anthology I have tried to avoid specifically Polish subjects in the narrow sense, such as would result from writers writing about one another. I have also tried to avoid topicality and politics in any narrow sense. But in the Polish essay of the last half century, the memory of history makes itself felt perhaps more often and certainly more clearly than it does in the reflections of writers from happier countries. It is this painful historical memory that Miłosz in his Nobel address compares to an open wound, a memory that is

"the heart of darkness of the twentieth century." In Zygmunt Kubiak's reflections on despair and faith in Pascal's *Pensées*, Nietzsche
and his "philosophizing with a hammer" make a sudden and unexpected appearance. Nietzsche's "hammer" is likewise invoked in
Leszek Kołakowski's meditations on the mythology of modernity,
of which Nietzsche was a harbinger and embittered prophet. But,
as Kołakowski points out, madness was the only cure Nietzsche
found for the despair caused by the "death of God."

The "wound of history" will reappear in reflections and descriptions apparently as far removed from present-day concerns as
Zbigniew Herbert's collection of essays about Renaissance Italy,
significantly called *Barbarian in the Garden*. In these essays delight
in the unchanging beauty of Siena is accompanied by a history of
the Templars, from the glory and violence of the Crusades to the
Templars' dispersal, imprisonment, torture, and forced recanta-
tions, followed by the final dissolution of the order. Herbert titles
his essay "Defense of the Templars."

This constantly open "wound of history" appears unexpectedly even in the seemingly radiant essay by Józef Czapski, "Paradise Lost." It seems that an art of painting obsessed with the beauty
of the body and the almost transparent luminosity of matter was "a
paradise lost" serving as an effective antidote to the cruelties of war,
occupation, forced labor, and death camps. Czapski, one of the
finest Polish painters of his generation and one of the most "luminous," was for many years an advocate of pure painting, free of all
moral obligations and consisting only of a penetrating gaze of unceasing wonder at the surface of the world. But even he, the eldest
of the living authors in the anthology, was expelled from his
paradise.

In the choice of texts I have tried to show that the Polish essay
and by extension Polish culture have always been receptive to writers and thinkers from all corners of the earth who have molded and
who continue to mold the European consciousness. For many
years Shakespeare and Molière have been quite domesticated in
Poland, but in the realm of moral and philosophical speculation,
both secular and religious, the participants in an interior dialogue
are unfailingly Saint Augustine and Pascal, with Kant a close third.
The essay by its very nature bears witness to and calls upon previous readings, but in Polish practice the time and place of reading are

not always commonplace. In *My Century* Aleksander Wat recalls how in a cell in Lubyanka prison in 1940 he read *The City of God*, Machiavelli, and Proust. He read them enthralled and intoxicated. Reading Machiavelli's letters in a Stalinist prison seems fitting, in respect to both time and place, but I myself also understand the feeling akin to hallucination that Wat felt reading Proust in a cell: my own most gripping reading of *Remembrance of Things Past* was in a hospital in the first days after my first heart attack.

It is in the very nature of the essay to have a present tense that makes it almost always seem contemporary. Not only does the essay like to invoke the contemporary, but it tries to give it shape as well. The chapter from *An Introduction to the Theory of Pure Form in the Theatre* by Stanisław Ignacy Witkiewicz is astonishingly prophetic when we consider that it was written in 1919, anticipating by almost three decades the theater of the absurd. Almost fifteen years before Artaud's theater of cruelty, Witkiewicz concluded his manifesto with the statement: "We must unleash the slumbering Beast and see what it can do. And if it runs mad, there will always be time enough to shoot it before it's too late." Witkiewicz, who had experienced the revolution in Russia, saw in 1917 how the slumbering Beast had broken loose from its chains. Forty years after Witkiewicz issued his proclamation on the theater of pure form, Konstanty Jeleński reveals, in his study of the Russian avant-gardists of the twenties, the lost illusions of the artists who had been convinced that they were creating a new art, when in fact they were seeing the final split between the avant-garde and revolution, or rather between the myth of the avant-garde and the myth of revolution.

This volume of Polish essays would be the poorer without Jerzy Grotowski, the creator of a "poor theater," whose theory and practice, and even something as difficult to grasp as his life and example, have become an inseparable part of modern theater; without Stanisław Lem, who has given science fiction a new excellence and seriousness; and finally without Bruno Schulz and Witold Gombrowicz, who almost before our eyes have become classics of twentieth-century literature.

But this volume would be seriously lacking if it failed to speak of the empty space left in Poland by the genocide of Polish Jewry. For two centuries the Hasidim differed from the rest of the Jewish

community in their distinctive dress, customs, and, most important, the fervent practice of their faith. Stanisław Vincenz recorded
the customs, legends, and pastoral myths of Huculs living in the
Carpathian Mountains in a remote southern part of ancient Poland.
I can compare his three-volume *On the High Uplands* only with
Claude Lévi-Strauss's *Tristes tropiques* in its respect and tenderness
for a culture on the verge of extinction. Like Martin Buber's *Tales
of the Hasidim*, Vincenz's essay is both a recorded memory and a
tombstone. Jan Błoński's dramatic essay, "The Poor Poles Look at
the Ghetto" (whose title comes from a poem by Miłosz, slightly
transposed), also speaks of the "wound"—shameful, closed, and
healed, but sometimes still painful—caused for Poles by the destruction of the Jews on their soil.

The anthology opens with two essays by Jerzy Stempowski,
meant as a tribute to the master of the Polish essay. Stempowski
was also the master of my youth, who taught me how to write and
how to doubt; the first I learned fairly quickly, the second only
after his death. He was also the master and perhaps the personal
model for two authors in this collection, Bolesław Miciński and
Gustaw Herling. But Stempowski has continued to be the master
for many who could not have known him personally, for the disciples of his disciples. For this reason the anthology begins with
Stempowski and closes with Adam Michnik.

Santa Monica, December 1989

TRANSLATED BY JADWIGA KOSICKA

P · A · R · T   O · N · E ·

Jerzy Stempowski

The Smugglers' Library

Which of the books read during the war impressed me most?

The simplest questions are often most difficult to answer. Reading is a complex, continuous, and fluctuating phenomenon—like life itself. During wars and upheavals, one's personal destiny and reading become only more prone to chance. My case was no different. In wartime I traveled—partly on foot—through many countries and used many libraries, both private and public. Within each country the books were different in content as well as typography. Tastes of collectors also varied from country to country, not to mention the variation in three basic kinds of readers. Some people, seduced by the demon of knowledge, read systematically, coupling one book with another. Others—like Montaigne—read for pleasure, trying a bit of everything. Still others buy famous and expensive books, though they never have time for them.

My reading was guided by what I found on my way. It included books of many varieties: bitter like wormwood and ominous—centuries-old futile prophecies of the extinction of Man and his works; light, serene books removed from any experience; books to be read at one sitting; and books to be read with pleasure only one page a week. Which were the best? Which left the most profound impression? I find no answer. All were necessary—each after its own fashion. Some concealed a surprise like a strange ring at the bottom of a dustbin. In an old guidebook to the spas of Normandy I found a couple of sentences that I would like to return to in a separate essay. In the works of the classics—supposedly familiar for years—I discovered unusual passages that previously escaped my attention. Which should I mention? Separately each brought something new and important; together they contributed to the mysterious life of the written word that has been going on for almost a hundred generations. Instead of presenting a random list of titles, I would like to talk about the wartime adventures of some particular books and about their encounters with a wartime reader.

Those who were seriously ill started to arrive at our mountain hospital shortly after Christmas. It seemed that the anxiety of the times combined with large amounts of consumed vodka cast a gloomy shadow over even the perennial feast of the new sun.

The procession was opened by two Hungarian soldiers—attempted suicides with bullet wounds in their skulls. These were followed by patients with Christmas intestinal torsions and by numerous victims of bone fractures—the result of careless lumbering. Soon there was not enough space in the hospital.

My room contained three beds. I had been staying there for five weeks, the first three of which I did not remember. There was a blackboard above my bed with the date of admission—28 October 1939—and "Diet No. 3" written in chalk. In practical terms that meant I was to be given hardly any food. My neighbors changed frequently. Only one of them left the room alive. I saw Dr. Bergman bending over the others. I watched from behind as he closed his eyes to feel with his fingers the needle penetrating the muscles, pleura, pericardium, and the ventricle. The intracardiac injection became the last sacrament of our time.

Just three days after my fever dropped the doctor started to persuade me to take walks. The first attempts were less than successful. After a few steps, without even reaching the center of the room, I returned to my bed short of breath and drenched in cold sweat. Instead of a pulse I heard some gurgling in my arteries. *Pulsus paradoxalis*, pronounced Dr. Bergman. Pneumonia left me with toxic paralysis. My legs were completely numb, and I walked on them as on artificial limbs. As the result of my diet my left kidney became loose and was turning around its axis, causing me excruciating pain. I had to keep it in place with my hand.

In the meantime snow fell and was glittering under my window.

On New Year's Eve I finally passed my walking exam. I walked the whole length of the corridor and climbed to the second floor. Dr. Bergman, who was waiting for me there, unexpectedly asked where I planned to go next. The question made me realize that there was no place to hurry to. After a painful silence I replied that I would like to return to the smugglers, that is, to the village from which the district doctor had transported me to the hospital. Dr. Bergman approved. The date of my dismissal was set for the second of January.

The distance was less than eighty kilometers, but it took a whole day and two transfers—from bus to train to bus again. The day was bright and the air freezing. It was dusk when I stopped in front of the familiar inn, whose elderly owner resembled President Kruger and possessed the unofficial title of "King of the Smugglers."

The room that I had once occupied was empty. The smugglers treated me to goulash and gave me some sweet *glühwein* to drink. They wrapped me in a sleeping bag and covered it with a pile of quilts and pillows. A small iron stove glowed in the room.

I slept no longer than an hour and woke to murmurs and whistles coming from all corners of the room. I lit a candle. The water I had left by the candlestick was solid ice rising above the rim of the glass. On the southern slopes of the Carpathian Mountains houses are built in such a way that you can almost see through the walls. The whistling I heard was wind gushing through the gaps between logs. Throughout the sleepless night frost was biting my face.

In the morning the smugglers rekindled the stove and decided I could no longer stay in that room. At night the temperature fell below minus twenty-eight degrees centigrade, and the wind was strong. It was less than minus twenty degrees centigrade inside. There was a brick house—the only one in the area—on the banks of the Cisa River less than a kilometer from the inn. It had four rooms and under the Czechs served first as a station for the gendarmerie and later as a tourist hostel. It had stood empty for several years and had the reputation of a haunted place. No one dared come near it after dark.

"How are you getting along with the devil?" asked the smuggler's son.

"Perfectly fine."

"Then you'll be comfortable there."

The smallest of the rooms had a tall iron stove installed by the gendarmes. The smugglers brought my bed, a couch, a huge pan for boiling water, a small lamp, a bottle of unrefined oil, and a huge cord of aromatic beech wood.

I was to spend the rest of the winter in that hiding place. At noon I used to walk to the inn for goulash and white *glühwein*. At night I returned to my lonely shelter surrounded by snowdrifts. One day after my arrival trains stopped running in the whole trans-Carpathian region because of freezing temperatures and snow and started operating again only thirty-five days later. I soon ran out of oil and candles. I spent my solitary evenings by the fire that was flickering behind the stove's door. My nerves were still in shambles. After depression there came silly self-pity and tears. It cost me some effort to compose myself in front of the others. Under these circumstances I could only appreciate the discretion and kindness of the smugglers. In their profession good manners forbids asking too many questions or showing surprise at any adventure. In the inn I was surrounded by their kind, unobtrusive faces. I think that in my condition any other company would have been an unbearable burden.

Some days after installing me in the haunted house the old smuggler paid me a brief visit.

"You must have been reading your whole life, and now you're going to be sad without books. I'll try to get you something to read."

On the next day a young smuggler, Andrijko, appeared with a sack on his shoulder. He put it on the floor. When the room warmed up I untied the bag and started to take out the books. The first to appear was a good edition of Horace, then the *Metamorphoses*, Virgil's *Bucolics* and *Georgics*, and some Latin poets of the Renaissance. Next there came some Spanish publications, mostly from the time of the Civil War, although they included Grácian y Morales. At the very bottom of the sack I found the English romantics—Southey, Coleridge—and also several volumes of Walter Scott, *Pride and Prejudice*, and a slightly worn copy of Spencer's *Faerie Queene*.

It was the best kind of reading for the long winter.

Where did that strange and rigorous selection come from and how did it get to the smugglers' hideout in the forest?

Obviously not every book travels so far into the mountains. Very few people carry books when they set off on a long journey on foot. It takes a consummate reader whose library contains only the best books—the sediment of many years of reading. And even he does not take just any book on the road.

I learned the story of those books only later and in fragments, since I was also expected not to ask too many questions.

The Latin books came from a small lumberyard situated down river, some distance from my house. A student of classical languages had been hiding there, disguised as a worker, during the wars and upheaval that visited the country in 1938. In his spare time he covered the margins with marks and comments. One day he disappeared as mysteriously as he arrived, leaving his meager luggage behind. He had been silent and avoided company. Nobody knew who he was or where he had come from.

"He must certainly have liked his books very much to carry them so far," said the smugglers. "Perhaps one day he will return to take them back."

The Spanish publications reached the inn by a different route. After the end of the Civil War two travelers were making their way through forests and mountains, probably trying to reach the Soviet Union. They either had to cross eastern Galicia risking encounters with the KOP* or seek passage through Bukovina, where they were likely to be arrested by the Rumanian Siguranza. The meeting with Soviet border guards could prove equally tragic. Who knows what fate they would meet and where?

In the mountains they were attacked by robbers. A leather bag with Spanish books and toiletries was of little interest to the bandits, and it was left in the woods. It remained there for several days. Apparently the travelers were more eager to reach the border than to collect their belongings.

"Who knows whether they'll like it in Russia? People say all kinds of things. Maybe they'll come back this way again," said the smugglers. "Let's keep their bag for them, just in case."

*Korpus Ochrony Pogranicza, i.e., border guards.

The story of the English books was even more intricate. In the
times when the Italians started to discover Hungary, a certain Italian aristocrat from the vicinity of Trieste conceived of the idea of
hunting bears and lynx in the Carpathian Mountains. He was rich
and apparently liked to go off the beaten track. He reached the
springs of the Cisa and bought a little cottage in the last settlement
on the edge of wilderness. He furnished it after his own taste. His
abundant luggage contained a bottle of champagne, a box of cigars,
and fifty new decks of cards. The young sportsman also seemed to
fancy books, since he brought with him a small library for rainy
days. After a couple of weeks, evidently bored with the Carpathians, he left and never returned—yet kept the house.

During the wars and upheaval the cottage was visited by German adventurers, who drank the champagne, smoked the cigars,
and played with the cards left by the Italian aristocrat while paying
little attention to the books. The story of the house was rich and
tumultuous. In recent times it was a home of an infamous and
impudent agent of the Gestapo. Part of the furniture disappeared.
One of the accidental visitors, evidently leaving the cottage with
some property, left a package of English books in the inn.

"Nobody buys a house to abandon it like that," said the smugglers. "The Italian duke will return some day and perhaps he'll be
glad to find some books among empty walls."

The smugglers were wrong. He who leaves his home in wartime rarely returns. The Italian hunter abandoned not only his cottage in the Carpathians, but also his palazzo in Dalmatia. Much
later I learned that for some time he lived as an émigré in Tessina.
Besides, the fate of the smugglers was not much different.

Only *The Faerie Queene* had no owner. It was brought by a
tourist who spent a night in a nearby lodge. He set out in the
morning, leaving his book behind. His body, mutilated by wolves,
was found only the next year. The times were already uncertain,
and no one from his family traveled to the place of his disappearance.

During wars and upheaval a reader leaves his library at home.
He takes only his favorite book, but even this book is soon abandoned in a roadside inn or at a forest crossroads. The smugglers'
library was a vivid testimony and a warning. A wartime reader

must rely first and foremost on his memory. At the end of the road he will be left only with what he remembers.

When we need it most, memory becomes a thin and fragile thread. Among great upheavals whole generations suddenly lose memory and stand in torpor, deprived of their past and not knowing which road may lead them forward.

During the months spent in the smugglers' hideout the question of memory was for me a constant source of pain. Owing to illness and exhaustion there were huge gaps in my recollection. I couldn't write to anybody because I didn't remember addresses. All the names of medicines were erased. I couldn't recall a single formula for the sulfamides which I worked with before the war and which I was fed, to little avail, in the hospital. I knew only that the name of the whole group began with "s." Sitting in the dark room I made inventories of things I remembered. These were miserably poor inventories. Music was most vivid, and it came back quite clearly with all the glare of instrumentation.

In that state of mind I hesitated for half an hour before opening Horace. Did I still remember Latin, or would this book be just a mockery of my crippled memory?

The time spent with the books was an attempt to reclaim my past—a random burrowing in dark, crumbling passages. If I were to look critically at my reading of that time, I would have to establish first what I still remember of the process, what part of it remains to me until today.

I devoted most time and attention to the *Bucolics* and *Georgics*. Both books were quite familiar to me. I often pondered about their structure and their timelessness, reflected in the stream of imitations and borrowings continuing until the present time.

In the smugglers' hideout, however, I was struck for the first time by the realistic and psychological content of the *Bucolics*. An exile departing from his native land instinctively clings to the soil, absorbs it with his eyes as if to preserve it forever in memory. He has nothing more to do there. No pragmatic thought disturbs the intensity of his contemplation. This perspective is the secret of Virgil and the source of the timeless appeal of the *Bucolics*.

This reading also affected my own plans. Until the end of 1939 I resisted the thought of emigration. I had crossed the border to avoid contact with the two occupying armies that had invaded my country. However, I was resolved to return as soon as the situation clarified and therefore stayed alone near the border. I looked upon emigration in a much more sober way than my companions in misfortune. Born in the remote eastern provinces, I was an émigré of sorts even in Poland. I knew many exiles from various countries, and in my early youth I had even met Polish refugees of 1904–5. I had a clear picture of the misery and impotence of emigration. I also knew that since the times of Saint-Evermond and Cavalier de Grammont, who left France unable to bear the bad taste of Louis XIV, émigrés (with few exceptions) never returned. Besides, I had lived for some time in the West and was sure that the new Polish emigration—unlike that of 1831—would find neither political nor moral support there. When leaving the hospital I expected to regain my strength and cross the mountains in the spring.

News from Poland wrecked my plans. I was afraid that with my poor health I would only be a burden to my friends who would have to hide me. The naked facts pushed me onto the sidetrack of emigration. In this skeptical state of mind I could not imagine achieving anything useful in Poland. I could resist fate only by trying to be myself wherever I was. I was about to move west, and I was aware that I was seeing for the last time a fragment of Eastern Europe that had been shrinking under my feet for a quarter of a century. I wanted to preserve a clear, Virgilian picture of the part still accessible to me. Therefore I planned to leave the smugglers' hideout in early spring and follow the side roads from village to village. On my way I wanted to talk to people about local customs and antiquities, as if that was the only purpose of my journey. I knew that such a mode of behavior wins friends everywhere and dispels suspicion. I calculated that Eastern Europe would not be occupied before the fall harvest, by which time I expected to cross the Italian border.

For a variety of reasons I managed to carry out only part of my plan. On my way I collected materials for a long essay on Virgil that I hope to finish and publish some time in the future.

Of the other books read in my hiding place I remember only fragments. In *The Faerie Queene* my attention was caught by a new image of the Knight of the Red Cross. Many years ago, while reading this beautiful baroque poem, I did not notice that the knight without arms was not only aloof and gloomy but also full of wrath and that he evoked fear. "Yet nothing did he dread, but ever was y'dread." It would be laughable to use this description in reference to today's officers of the Red Cross, not to mention the gentlemen from UNRRA or IRO*—the ignoble bastards of the Spenserian knight.

Cruelty and barbarity did not provoke in our generation any gesture of anger. News about executions and torture was accepted—especially in the West—with either disbelief or calm objectivity suitable for natural phenomena. Prison camps and torture are seen today by many as a new mode of existence—quite widespread in fact, and even unavoidable.

A traveling reader who carries his books only in his memory must be especially attuned to gnomic poetry—a popular genre of antiquity that was still practiced by Latin poets of the Renaissance and baroque periods. They left us many beautiful samples of this literary form. From my readings in the smugglers' hiding place I remember the following couplet about the Tiber:

> Disce hinc quid possit fortuna; immota labescunt
> Et quae perpetuo sunt fluitura, manent.

In the time of the Renaissance the Tiber ran among ruins, which have partly survived until today and have partly disappeared under new constructions. Edifices from the time of the republic and the empire, from the Byzantine revival, and from various periods of the Middle Ages one by one turned into rubble. A poet, having witnessed all that, realizes that the only durable and immutable thing is the river flowing among ruins. "Look"—he says—"what fortune can do; what was immobile is turning into dust, and what was meant for perpetual fluidity, remains."

When I read this poem in the winter of 1940 I thought about Warsaw, where only the Vistula perhaps remained unchanged. Today the same can be said about many other cities of Europe.

The longer I repeated the poem in my dark hideout, the better I saw its elegant form: the broad gesture of the introduction raising the curtain and revealing majestic ruins under the tall Campanian sky, then a whisper of the pentameter like the murmur of the Tiber

*United Nations Relief and Rehabilitation Organization and the International Relief Organization.

washing against its clay banks. If I were a poet in command of the magical power of the word, I would like to write gnomic poetry. If I were vain, I would like to be remembered as the author of such a couplet.

There was a magical element in my encounters with those books—like an enchanted table that fills itself with dishes, or a flying carpet that transports us into faraway countries. This element did not escape my attention, and I had enough time to ponder it in my hiding place.

In fact the flying carpet is but a literary metaphor for a familiar phenomenon. Every true traveler rides on his own magic carpet. He is inhibited neither by the inconveniences of his journey, nor by borders, front lines, demarcation zones, visas, passports, vast distances, or other obstacles. When we see him—thin, darkened, with his feet deformed by thousands of miles, stubbornly silent, bedazzled by the multitude of changing landscapes—we understand that hardships of the road are nothing but the price of his passion.

The flying carpet becomes a transgression against the natural order only when it falls into the hands of undeserving people who feel no compulsion to travel, who content themselves with two or three flights and then get married and lead a happy sedentary life.

There is a Middle Eastern proverb that in Levantine French reads as follows: "Qui mange du caviar noir, Dieu lui donne toujours un peu du caviar noir." By what intricate routes does tobacco reach every place where there are smokers? Similarly, hidden books are waiting for their readers in places seemingly deprived even of bread and wine: in forest hideouts, clearings, rafters' shacks, or sailors' abodes. The more discriminating his taste, the higher his demands—the more rare and beautiful reading awaits him. All he has to do is to be himself, to persist in his demands, never to give up, and to be like the Levantine caviar eater stubbornly asking his God for his favorite snack.

On the last day of my stay in the mountains I carried the bag of books back to the smugglers' inn. As far as I know the place was later ransacked many times, and its inhabitants either died a violent death or dispersed throughout the world. Who knows what fate befell the books? Soldiers and bandits plundering the inn were looking for vodka and tobacco and probably took little interest in books. Perhaps they still wait in the ruins of the inn for their reader. To the one who will find and read them—the unknown lover of Virgil and the Latin poets of the Renaissance—*salutem.*

(1948)

TRANSLATED BY JAROSLAW ANDERS

Jerzy Stempowski

Essay for Cassandra

To the shadows of L.R.

1

For the ancient Greek authors Cassandra was a symbolic figure representing the interior anguish and impotence of prophets.

In the *Iliad* she appears only as an outline. In the Homeric world, where gods take heroes by the hand and lead them to their glory or extinction, there is little place for the dialogue between prophet and people. Such dialogue belongs to the world of the republic, where the difference between the seer and the unseeing crowd becomes manifest.

Cassandra as a tragic figure is a product of the Athenian imagination that developed and fulfilled itself in democracy. Among the preserved monuments of literature the most outspoken on the subject are Aeschylus's *Agamemnon* and Euripides' *The Trojan Women*.

The daughter of Priam received the gift of prophecy from Apollo: "He battled for my love," says Cassandra about her suitor. The god with golden hair failed in his pursuits. Cassandra deluded him with promises, yet despite disappointment he respected her virginity and did not deprive her of the ability to see the future. According to Euripides, Cassandra remained Apollo's priestess until the fall of Troy, but because she did not keep her promise, nobody believed her prophecies.

From the time Helen arrived in Priam's city and the conflict between Troy and Greece began, Cassandra warned in vain of the destruction of both Troy and the house of Priam, though Homer— the bard of the Trojan War—leaves us few details.

After the fall and destruction of the city, the victorious Greeks killed all Priam's men and divided the women among themselves as slaves. Cassandra sought asylum in the temple of Pallas Athena, who sided with the Greeks, but Ajax dragged her from the altar and threw her among the Trojan women for whom the victors were drawing lots. —This scene is beautifully depicted on a vase in the Louvre.

The profanation of Athena's temple and the decision to leave the slaughtered Trojan bodies unburied marked the turning point for the Greek army. From that moment on, it encountered nothing but disaster. Thus the Greek authors demonstrate the ancient belief in the relationship between propriety and military luck. In *Agamemnon,* Clytemnestra speaks after learning of the fall of Troy: "If they respect the gods and temples of the defeated they shouldn't fear that from victors they will turn into victims." In Euripides a similar thought is expressed by Poseidon: "Only a madman depopulates and plunders cities, destroys temples and tombs worshiped as homes of the dead. He who does so creates a desert in which he'll perish."

Offended, Athena turns against the Greeks and sinks a part of their fleet on its way from Troy. Among the captive Trojan women Cassandra is given to Agamemnon—king of Argos and the leader of the Greek army. His ship reaches home safely, but the victorious king returns to die at the hand of his wife, Clytemnestra. She wants to avenge the death of their daughter Iphigenia, sacrificed by her father, who hoped to win the favor of the gods for the Greek expedition. Cassandra, who arrives in Argos with Agamemnon, is also killed by Clytemnestra.

Here the legendary Trojan part of Cassandra's story ends and the Greek chapter begins. Since the fall of Troy and the offense against Athena, Cassandra has continued to prophesy the death of the Greek leader and the calamities that will fall on his house. This part of the story, as preserved by Aeschylus, is told in a realistic manner concordant with the notions developed by Athenian democracy. Cassandra's prophecies and the reactions of her listeners are both given equal attention.

The most dramatic part of *Agamemnon* is the long dialogue between the prophet and the chorus, which represents the opinion of the majority, common sense, the conscience of righteous citizens of Argos. The dialogue begins with Agamemnon entering the palace where he will be killed in his bath. Cassandra notices the statue of Apollo of the Road at the gate and her voice rises in complaint: "Apollo, Apollo, the guardian of the roads, where hast thou led me? Into whose house?"

The chorus remarks that such lamentations do not belong to the Apollonian rite and Cassandra's behavior seems improper. The citizens know her fame as a prophet, yet conclude that their city has no need for seers.

Cassandra tells them about the crime being prepared in the palace. She does not speak in the language of abstract visions but of facts that are well known to the citizens. The chorus reacts with hostility, although it does not reject her reasoning: "Have prophecies ever brought common mortals any good news?" Later on, the citizens even show compassion and curiosity; they ask who taught her to tell the future and when that was. "Though a god, he must have loved you very much," they remark upon learning about Apollo, and they want to know whether she lived with him as his wife. Priam's daughter replies that in the old days she would be ashamed to talk about such matters. "Life of luxury begets pride," declares one of the citizens.

Sometimes the dialogue strays from the main subject, as if the citizens are trying to postpone their confrontation with reality. As they complain about the vagueness of prophecies, Cassandra tells them they will see the death of their king.

"Be quiet, unfortunate woman," replies a citizen, "let gods protect us from such events." Cassandra says: "You wish in vain. They are preparing the murder right now." Even those words, however, seem unclear to the citizens, who would like to know exactly how the murderers are going to carry out their plan.

Knowing that her death is near, Cassandra rises and approaches the gates of the palace. Again, the citizens of Argos show their compassion, advising her to run away. "Nothing can save me," says Cassandra. "What use is there for yet another hour of life?"

"The last hour has the highest value," replies the chorus sanctimo-niously. Though surrounded by citizens, Cassandra can expect no help; she is facing her fate alone. Numbers are insignificant—this thought permeates the last scenes of the tragedy.

Accompanied by the skeptical chorus, Cassandra withdraws to the gate of the palace. She smells blood, yet the members of the chorus, the *choreutai,* explain it is only blood of sacrificed animals. After bidding farewell to the crowd and begging it to bear testimony to her suffering, she enters the palace.

After Cassandra's departure, the chorus bemoans human destiny, until the cry of dying Agamemnon is heard from the palace. Even then the citizens refuse to accept the deed. The chorus—so unified in skepticism and anticipation—breaks into a dozen contending voices:

A crime has been committed. Our king's voice leaves no doubt. Friends, let's call a council. . . . In my view, let's call all the citizens to come to the rescue! All to the palace! . . . Let's run to the palace to catch the murderers. . . . I am of the same opinion: let's act! There is no time to lose. . . . Wait, this is just a beginning. A tyranny awaits our city. . . . That's because we linger and let them do as they please. . . . Even those who want to act have to think first. . . . I agree. Our words will not raise the dead. . . . What's that? Are we to bow in front of those who brought infamy upon the palace just to prolong our miserable lives? . . . Shame! It's better to die than to suffer tyranny. . . . Yes, but this cry is not a proof that our king is dead. . . . Indignation requires certainty, and we are just speculating. . . . I support that view. First we must learn what exactly has happened to the king.

Torn by contradictions, the chorus remains inactive. In the meantime Clytemnestra appears in the doorway with a sword in her hand and declares the death of Agamemnon and Cassandra. The chorus protests and orders her to leave the city. Clytemnestra defends herself, presenting various arguments, and the chorus even agrees with her. The debate continues for some time, until the queen's lover, Aegisthus, enters the stage accompanied by armed guards and warns that chains and prison food would certainly tame the citizen's uncontrolled tongues. With this threat the tragedy ends.

The Athenian version of Cassandra's story is rational, free of legendary or supernatural elements. Cassandra's prophecies are not

Cazotte's visions, but accurate analyses of known facts and their possible consequences. The suspicion with which they are met in Aeschylus's tragedy is not the result of Apollo's revenge but a characteristic typical of every Greek assembly. The author consistently underscores this thought by making the chorus as incredulous of obvious facts as of Cassandra's prophecies.

From this perspective Cassandra's tragedy appears as a perennial element of our civilization and a product of democratic mechanisms.

That is why in Aeschylus we find so many familiar characters disguised in Greek robes. The scene of the questioning by the mob, the *ochlos*, reminds us of the thoughtless and cruel crowds populating our towns, and it could have been written by Dostoevsky. After Agamemnon's death the council of citizens seems even more contemporary. If we dressed the *choreutai* in the clothes of our present-day *ochlagōgoi*—with their mustaches, glasses, and haircuts—the "various voices" of the citizens of Argos would sound strangely familiar. The contemporary democratic choruses responded with almost exactly these words to the news about concentration camps and hostile preparations of dictators. Only those who advised running immediately to the palace were in short supply.

2

Antiquity has left us with two concepts of prophecy. One of them is based on the belief in a hierarchy of supernatural forces who have access to the future and, for a small compensation, are willing to provide their clients with some useful hints. The other concept assumes rational predictability of natural processes as well as human ability to foresee probable results of actions and circumstances.

The first kind of divination was widely practiced in ancient times by various initiates operating in temples and other places conducive to contacts with the supernatural. It has survived into our times, providing steady income to various fortune-tellers, psychics, and astrologers. Today there are even fortune-telling machines. I have seen one on the top of the Eiffel Tower. My friend inserted a coin and out came a piece of paper saying: *Tu seras toujours follement aimée* (you will always be loved madly).

People resorted to this kind of augury—both in ancient and in present times—in private rather than public issues. In our personal lives our ability to foresee the future seems to be most limited. Predictability is diminished by the human power to influence events. The eclipse of the moon can be predicted with great accuracy because the possibility of our interference with that phenomenon is zero. The number of road accidents—at a given rate of gasoline and alcohol consumption—can be projected with considerable proximity, although less accurately than the eclipse. Yet the person who makes that estimation cannot predict when he himself will be run over by a car. If he knew the date, he would stay in bed the whole day, rendering his own forecast invalid. The death of a mortally ill person can be predicted with some accuracy, but only if the disease is incurable and resists medical intervention. Apart from the payment of our bills, the predictable elements of our private lives are so scarce that whoever wants to know his future rightly turns to fortune-tellers and tarot experts.

Political issues constitute a kind of gray area, subject only to approximate projections. In a republic the most important constant and predictable factor is the inertia and lack of initiative of collective bodies. It can be assumed with a high degree of probability that elections and parliamentary decisions will bring few surprises, that nothing uncommon will happen and everything will stay more or less as it was. This stability and continuity make the republic rich, and at the same time vulnerable to external circumstances. The acts of dictators seem to be more incalculable and dependent on individual initiative, but only in appearance. A dictator is a slave of the rigid mechanism of his own absolute power. His personal tastes and convictions are the least important factor.

A prophet's position in a republic is ridden with contradictions. His ability to predict corresponds to the force of mechanical factors independent of human initiative. In other words it is easier to tell the future when citizens are unable to anticipate the effects of their actions and are less likely to interfere with the course of events. The accuracy of prophecy is therefore inversely proportional to the following the prophet gains among the citizens. Caught in this contradiction, he stands before his people, helpless and often desperate. The more certain his knowledge, the greater his loneliness.

Under dictatorships the anticipation of future disasters is usually widespread, and the prophet has nothing new to say. Besides, his ability to convince is of little importance because the opinion of the majority is irrelevant. Even the most accurate projections are useless when it is too late to reverse the course of events.

3

The ability to predict future political developments does not seem to be an uncommon phenomenon. In the interwar period I heard predictions that were later fulfilled to the last detail. They never came from people in high office with access to all the necessary facts—people who were in fact expected to look into the future. The assertion that expert advice, abundant documentation, and secret reports can muddle even the simplest affairs is therefore not totally unfounded.

When I look back on those times I have an impression that in the interwar era the ability to predict the future was an obvious handicap to a political career. Today this phenomenon seems to me quite understandable. The future of Europe was dark, and whoever assessed it correctly was a pessimist—a figure who rarely finds a willing audience. Tactful people avoid sad subjects. And yet there was tragedy in the fact that for many years even the slightest effort at good will might have averted the catastrophe threatening the continent.

While remembering those prophets of doom I should start with Szymon Askenazy.

The period of his high creative powers and fame belonged to his youth in the years preceding World War I. Like Julian Klaczko, he came from a rabbinic family in Vilno. He married a rich Warsaw woman and for many years was a professor of modern history at the University of Lvov. He had hundreds of listeners, his seminar garnered eighty students who rummaged the archives of all Europe. A new, sensational book of his appeared almost every year: *Prince Józef*, *Łukasiński*, many volumes of dissertations and historical essays. In Europe, the historicism of the previous centuries was already on the decline. The most outstanding historians of the West,

F.-A. Aulard, Arthur Chuquet, Guglielmo Ferrero, could hardly find listeners and concentrated instead on small groups of disciples. Compared to them Askenazy seemed the head of a prominent school—the captain of a ship carrying excited and learned youth. It turned out, however, that this late Polish historicism was merely the product of local circumstances. Young people who in an independent country would seek diplomatic, military, or financial careers studied history and wrote sonnets in partitioned Poland.

In 1914 Askenazy traveled abroad. Upon his return to Poland he applied for the chair in history at the reborn Warsaw University. Resurrected Poland, however, was young and capricious. In 1920 the university council turned down his candidacy. Soon afterward Askenazy was nominated envoy to the League of Nations and left Poland for two years. He resigned in 1922 and returned to Warsaw, where he lived until his death in 1935.

We became close friends in the years 1928–32. At that time Askenazy lived a lonely and idle life in his apartment on Czacki Street. He had given up all scholarly work. Numerous manuscripts—some almost ready for publication—slumbered on his shelves. When in 1931 Warsaw University offered him a chair in the Department of Law, Askenazy refused. "I had twelve years to ponder my reply," he said after a visit with university representatives. "All I told them was to kiss my a—— three times." The decision seemed correct. The university's standards had been declining for several years, a result of a growing number of students interested only in immediate advantages and diplomas. The audience Askenazy had in Lvov no longer existed—in Poland or anywhere else.

Askenazy seemed a living testimony to the deep changes occurring at that time. He was tall, very thin, with a large head, very long nose, and a pair of dark, piercing, and unfriendly eyes. His tongue and his judgment were razor sharp. In the course of the years he had fewer and fewer visitors. At the end he was completely alone.

Askenazy suffered me better than the others—maybe because my own views at that time were not much different from his. I used to visit him in the early afternoons. For an hour or two he would tell anecdotes from the life of Adam Czartoryski or read fragments of some abandoned manuscript. Around five he put on his bowler—brown in winter, pearl-gray in summer—and we went for a walk. We usually strolled along Krakowskie Przekmieście, Miodowa Street, Bank Square. Askenazy would stop in front of each house and tell me what happened on the eve of the 1830 uprising: who had gathered there and what was the subject of the conversation. His oral account of the events was sometimes considerably different from the version he presented in *Łukasiński*—a picture of chaos, shameless and conflicting private interests, helplessness. Heroism rubbing shoulders with mindless egoism and provocation. It seemed that the shadow of defeat hung over the uprising from its first day. I *wrote history* ad usum delphini, *for the younger generation, whom I tried to educate, to prepare morally for the new struggle for independence,* he said. *Today one could try to tell it differently. But to whom? Who cares about such things anymore? Who could make use of this knowledge?*

On a clear summer day in 1932, having followed our usual route through the older part of the city, we entered the 3rd of May Avenue and sat on a bench. On the other side of the street foundations were being laid for some large edifice. *What are they going to build there?* I asked. *I've heard it is the National Museum,* answered Askenazy. *I wonder why people waste money and energy erecting expensive buildings in a city doomed to destruction? Why destruction?* I asked. *Just now, when we are sitting here on this bench*—said Askenazy—*I almost see German planes dropping bombs on the city.* To my skeptical remark about such prophecies he reacted emotionally: *How can you not see it? Just think for a moment. Can it be otherwise?*

I was well acquainted with the German scene at that time and the remarks that followed seemed to me quite plausible:

Only the most naive person can imagine that Poland will be waging war otherwise than on two fronts. The Germans cannot cross the border in Zbąszyń without Russians crossing it in Baranowicze. One has to take into account the simple mechanism of such events. Before striking at Poland the Germans will amass their forces and secure neutrality, or inaction, of the Western powers. One can assume, therefore, that sooner or later they will conquer the country and go as far as Baranovichi. Can the Russians wait until the Germans reach their borders? No. The most elementary precaution will dictate that they cross the Polish border as well, to occupy as much of the country as possible in order to have something to bar-

gain with, and to hold the Germans far from their borders in case of
a confrontation. Whether on that particular day the Soviet Union
will be in alliance with Germany, or with England and France, or
even with us, will have no impact on the course of events. The
crossing of the Polish border and the occupation of Poland's eastern
regions will be for Russia more urgent than any alliance.

After a pause he added:

The same mechanism will function in case of peaceful territorial
changes. If, for some reason, Poland had to cede Vilno and Lvov to
the Russians, on the same day it would have to give Silesia and
Pomerania to the Germans. After yielding Lvov and Vilno the fu-
ture existence of Poland would be possible only under German
guarantees, and the price for these guarantees will be Silesia and
Pomerania. The opposite also is true: if circumstances forced Poland
to cede Silesia and Pomerania to Germany, her future would be
possible only with Russian support, and the Russians will demand
Vilno and Lvov as their price. In fact, after such territorial losses one
could hardly speak of any sovereign existence. For the Western pow-
ers Poland is only a pawn to checkmate either Germany or Russia.
After such cuts it would lose any value for them.

Three years after this conversation Szymon Askenazy died, apparently of kidney failure. In fact he was killed by his own thoughts
and an awareness of the future nobody seemed to share. His wife
died in a Warsaw hospital in 1940, and his only daughter was murdered by the Germans.

Nobody seeks accurate forecasts from journalists—the manu-
facturers of ephemerals that turn to scrap paper with each next issue
of a newspaper. The press lost the ambition to inform long ago,
contenting itself with providing the reader with some entertainment to glaze the inevitable chaff of offical reports. Yet I have met
journalists who could produce—for private use—accurate predictions. Their personal acquaintance with political and parliamentary
circles in the countries where the future was germinating often provided them with material for precise assessment of coming events.

From the interwar period I remember several conversations
with Robert Dell—one of the last independent journalists.

I met him in Düsseldorf in 1922. The French had just occupied
Rhura. A state of "cold war"—to use the present term—had existed

between England and France for several weeks. The English were doing their best to ruin the franc and to push France into an economic predicament. Nobody knew how the Germans in Rhura would respond to French occupiers. The commander of the small occupation force, General Mangin, had initiated talks with Karol Radek, who was responsible for the German policy of Komintern. Paul-Prudent Painlevé, whom I had visited the previous week in Paris, interrupted his reading of Einstein to say that in his opinion the situation was dangerous and the occupation of Rhura seemed exceptionally risky from both a military and political point of view. France's allies were anxious. The Sudeten Germans were looking for contacts in London, hopeful of winning the support of England, which was trying to weaken France on all possible fronts, including Czechoslovakia. I met Dell in the lobby of a hotel built by Hugo Stinnes, and we made a brief review of the situation. Dell was gloomy and pale, as if he felt responsible for the madness of earthly powers:

The political order established in 1919 is already in ruins, he said. *America has withdrawn her signature. England and France are so embattled that their influences cancel each other out. Russia is not ready yet to reach for the inheritance. There is no one to defend the order of 1919. So far the Germans are in a state of chaos, yet the road stands open for them. England does not want to, and France alone cannot defend the old arrangements. The future of Europe will be decided by the Germans. It depends on the internal evolution of Germany.*

What I saw during the next days in Germany corroborated this prognosis and filled me with sickening premonitions. While looking into the future I saw only the ruins of everything upon which the world had tried to rest the harmonious coexistence of Europe after the Treaty of Versailles. At the end of December I bought a handful of gold dollars in Paris. I saved them until 1939 and was thus able to escape from occupied Poland.

I met Dell again in Geneva in the late fall of 1936. The Spanish war was in full swing, and England had managed to impose the policy of nonintervention upon France, which was struggling with internal crisis. The roles were already cast: the armored Italian division and the German air force were crushing the Spanish Republic, and the system of nonintervention bound those who could come to her rescue. Moscow had not decided yet what to do, and the press smeared the republic daily.

Dell was depressed. His independent editorials brought him nothing but trouble: he had been expelled from both Germany and France. He lived in Geneva and wrote reports from the League of Nations, about which there was already little to be said. When we were alone he started to speak:

Nothing is left of the Europe that nourished me and to which I was deeply committed. Suicide would be the only logical solution for me. If I stay alive it is for two reasons: as an Englishman I abhor extreme gestures, and at my age of sixty-seven suicide would be like breaking down an open door.

I tried to console him as best I could. In order to distract him with different matters I started to talk about the political situation. Dell interrupted:

There is nothing to talk about. The situation is clear. During the last decade or so the main goal of English policy was to reduce France to the rank of Portugal. This goal has been achieved. Having disposed of its only possible ally in Europe, England will have nothing more to say in European matters. The fate of Poland is clear. She cannot rely on the French "Portugal," and England has already backed out of her commitment.

Having noticed that his mood was deteriorating I started to develop my theory of generations. The youth brought up on the discipline of totalitarian states will start—first secretly and then openly—longing for some kind of liberalism. I quoted several examples of such reversals known in history and concluded with the following picture:

In ten or fifteen years we shall be invited to Berlin to the uncovering of Dickens's monument in Nolendorfplatz. The Prussian minister of education will recommend the works of Godwin as school reading. In the evening there will be a banquet in the Kaiserhof honoring Garrison-Villard. Lilacs will blossom on all the squares of Charlottensburg. We will joyfully drink light beer with raspberry syrup, surrounded by kind and liberal Germans.

Dell listened to me with a smile, squinting his eyes like a man who looks for a pretext to distance himself from his own thoughts. Then he started to cloud over again:

As all the English in my generation, I was a Germanophile throughout my life. The last years have cured me of this weakness. There will be no peace in Europe until fire falls from the sky and burns down the place called Germany.

That evening Dell must have been "inspired," as they say about prophets, because even "fire from the sky," which at the time seemed only a biblical metaphor, turned out to be real.

I heard strikingly accurate forecasts even during the turmoil of war, when everything seemed possible and there was no point of reference for any plausible assessment. In the summer of 1940 there was talk about the inevitable conflict between the German military circles and the dictator. It was reasoned that in the case of German victory the generals would be exterminated, as they were no longer useful. In the case of defeat they would be executed by the victors. As long as they commanded a victorious army they would grasp at an opportunity which could not be repeated.

At that time I met a high-ranking Swiss officer, a man of exceptional intelligence, who through his family connections and education was thoroughly acquainted with the society of German generals. When I asked him about this theory, he replied:

Don't let yourself be deceived by that balderdash. The leaders of the Germany army are at present the best craftsmen of war who exist, and they can even win. To overthrow a dictatorship, however, quite different talents are needed—especially character, which hardly any of them can boast. Nothing will come of that. However, it seems quite possible that they will be hanged.

When I recall this conversation today, I am struck by the word "hanged." In 1940 no one would use it in reference to military people, who were customarily executed by firing squad. The word "hanged" has a visionary concreteness that surpasses the boundaries of theoretical calculation.

In the interwar period there was also no lack of written prophecies. Surrealist literature provides many examples. Its true sense, muddled by the critics, escaped the attention of general readers. When in the years 1939–40 I watched masses of fugitive crowds gathering in various countries on river banks and seacoasts I recognized the climate of Georges Ribemont-Dessaignes's novel *Les frontièrs humaines.* The sight of columns of cars with mattresses on top recalled "the second manifesto of surrealism": *Partez sur les routes. Semez les enfants au coin du bois* (Take to the roads. Loose the children on a forest edge).

What often strikes me in prophecies of such concreteness and accuracy is the simplicity, dryness, even poverty of their premises. I keep thinking about a prophecy fulfilled only in part, which I heard from Mahmud Tarzy in 1923.

Tarzy's character requires some explanation. Afghanistan is a mountainous country bordering on one side with India, on the other with Russian Turkestan. Abdur-Rahman, the last emir of the first period of independence, used to say about this situation: "I am like a swan in a pond. On one bank a Bengali tiger walks, on the other—a Siberian bear. I am in the middle and the water is quite shallow." When in 1882 the government in Petersburg proposed to rectify the border in Pamirs, the emir got frightened and gave up sovereignty of his country to the British protectorate. In 1917 two Afghans—Weli Khan and Mahmud Tarzy—traveled to Moscow and stayed there for a year and a half watching the revolution. Having decided that in the next couple of years nothing threatened Afghanistan from the north, they returned to their country, overthrew the emir, and enthroned Amanullah, who was to gain some prominence later. Without much delay Amanullah declared war on England and eventually won recognition of independence for Afghanistan. Soon afterward the new emir married Mahmud Tarzy's daughter. After that time Weli Khan and Tarzy rotated as commander of the Afghan army and president of the government. In 1923 Mahmud Tarzy went to Europe, and after an extensive tour of Italy, France, and England he settled in Paris as his country's ambassador. I have visited him there several times in the company of my Muslim friends.

Weli Khan was a short man with a face like the moon beaming with satisfaction. Mahmud Tarzy was taller, more slender, his skin was dark like tanned leather. He had a black beard, walked with downcast eyes, and seemed to harbor dark premonitions. On one occasion he explained the difference in appearance between his prominent colleague and himself:

Have you ever talked to Weli Khan face-to-face without wit-nesses, or have you only seen him in the company of other Afghans?
I replied that I had never had the opportunity to see him alone.
If you had, he would have appeared less rapturous. With us a smile and the appearance of satisfaction is a sign of politeness. In order to elevate someone to the top, people have to contribute their money and bear humiliation and troubles. They would be worried to see their emir unhappy and their sacrifices in vain.
He reached into his drawer and took out a photograph of Weli Khan surrounded by a group of Afghans:
If you take a close look, you'll recognize the rank of each one of them. The faces of those of the lowest rank show keen attention and readiness to serve. Those higher up emanate the readiness to serve, but also confidence that their service will be well rewarded. The one on the top looks somehow above the heads of the others and seems to see Muhammad's Paradise.
Mahmud Tarzy was not only a experienced man but also one accustomed to looking at human matters from a grand perspective. Taking advantage of his buoyant mood, I asked what his impression of Europe was and how he saw her future.
Nothing good, he replied. *If the Europeans occupied themselves with raising goats, like us, they could perhaps look to their future with hope. Yet the administration of such great riches and complex enterprises requires a certain degree of intelligence which I can hardly find here. Therefore I think that Europe faces unprecedented disasters and you all will perish shamefully like slaughtered animals.* After a pause he added: *I like the English more than the others. They are no wiser, but have more money.*
Many years have passed since that conversation. I remembered Mahmud Tarzy's words when I witnessed the incredible discipline of human anthills. On the order of mad dictators, or equally lunatic democratic governments, whole nations marched in step toward inevitable and quite predictable disasters. Nobody tried to think independently, nobody even tried to escape, unless carried by the fleeing crowd. Changes that occurred in Europe—which used to be the main laboratory for critical thought—are so profound that we do not notice our grotesque behavior which amazed the Afghan mountaineer.

4

In the last decade all those, beginning with Jacob Burckhardt, who saw the future with clarity were sad. They carried the burden of their loneliness and the uselessness of their knowledge. In my youth, accurate predictions could bring limited personal gains. To-day even those possibilities are closed off. Prudence dictates that we run from a place that is about to be struck by lightning. But where? War and chaos can start in any place. The last war was started in the remote provinces of Europe—in Spain. The dictators even considered starting it in South America. There is no place to run. The few countries that can claim some stability guard their privileges and close their borders to strangers. Besides, the modern state with its regimentation of life can give the exile no asylum that would be worthwhile. There is no place to run, and no reason.

The ability to predict the future is useless to those who do not see its significance. Within the present social framework it is of no use to the seer either. It is an unbearable burden—heavier today than ever before. Why should one bother with auguries? One of my friends in politics told me long ago:

After forty years of experience I reached the conclusion that common sense and thoughtfulness are the most serious handicaps in our lives.

Will the gift of seeing future events still visit our chosen ones, despite its total ineffectiveness?

This question makes me think about a certain conversation in a laboratory I attended as a student. I once brought there a novelty of the time—a book by Louis Blaringhem about sudden mutations in plants and animals. My professor, and the head of the laboratory— a learned physiologist and a member of numerous scientific socie-ties—took an interest in the book and read it that evening. The next morning he asked:

You have studied history. Don't you think that historical civiliza-tions were also products of some mutations, like those described by Blaringhem? Everything we know seems to point in that direction. Every new civilization was the fruit of several generations working under favorable circumstances and revealing abilities unknown to their ancestors. The same comes to my mind when I think about the advancement of the natural sciences. The abilities necessary in our laboratory work were developed only recently, and there is no evidence that they ever existed before.

He sighed and continued:

The conclusions are rather ill-boding. Varieties based on mutation are not very durable and are subject to rapid regression. One day we may wake up among idiots unable to understand anything we have created with so much exertion and ingenuity.

In a narrow sense his predictions were fulfilled ten years later when, during the political purges in Germany, he was expelled from the university and deprived of the possibility of doing research.

Almost all the people mentioned here are dead. The talent to predict the future certainly does not favor longevity. Even I, only the listener, did not avoid my share of difficulties. On the other hand it is clear that today discipline and patience will not suffice. If Europe, ruined by so many insanities, is to avoid annihilation, her population must learn to foresee more accurately the results of its actions, and it can no longer afford to ignore those who possess this gift. For the older ones it is almost insignificant. Yet I am thinking about people of the younger generation, who have their whole lives in front of them. Who among them will be ready to put on the robe in which Cassandra addressed Apollo: "In this gown of a prophet you have put me to ridicule in front of your enemies."

(1930)

TRANSLATED BY JAROSLAW ANDERS

Stanisław Vincenz

An Encounter with the Hasidim

The purpose of my essay—which was initially conceived more modestly, as an oral report for a small circle of German friends—was to stress the importance of those active individual and even local aspects of Hasidism which have received little attention in the existing literature on the subject. Since I am familiar with those aspects from personal experience, I think that even though I am not Jewish, I am at least partially qualified to speak about a movement that is so deeply rooted in Jewish history; of course, some basic questions could be raised whether I am entitled to do so. I am of the opinion—contrary to the still widely held view—that denominational and traditional affiliation, in the case of feelings as intimate as religious ones, does not preclude objectivity but on the contrary facilitates understanding and sharpens our senses more than inner coldness, indifference, and aloofness. I feel authorized to speak on the subject because these are things I know from my native land in the eastern Carpathians, and since childhood I have seen and experienced much. So these are matters not unfamiliar to me, although describing them requires more of an effort on my part than would the usual traditional introduction to any religion whatsoever. The presence within me of personal experiences and images serves as a kind of guarantee that the traits I am discussing are not derived from my reading and that I do not confuse them with the traits of any other, somehow related mysticism.

Furthermore, I should point out two other difficulties: First, in the course of its history until very recently Hasidism was a religion of the poor. That was actually the source of its real power, as it required of its adherents, for prayers and the observance of holidays, a conversion, a genuine rising above, a detachment from the wretched bustle and prosaic chores of everyday life. For people who have never been really in need, this point of departure of Hasidism is difficult to grasp. The Hasidim were poor, simple, and naive not only in the material but also in the spiritual sense. For highly educated people immersion in the passion of prayer and religious ecstasy, without falsifying them, is doubly difficult. It is truly astonishing how often a certain kind of theology is present in the Hasidic consciousness, but since the Hasidim are imprisoned in their daily occupations and activities, hardly ever can they dedicate themselves to serious study; instead images from their ordinary everyday world become elevated to the level of religious symbols. Thus their entire humble life becomes a kind of unending call to God. This is a world almost totally inaccessible to a mind formed by books. But anyone with an open heart, capable of understanding spontaneity and the welling up of living sources, will look with sympathy at the experience of the Hasidim, finding nothing there to cause surprise.

Second, it is misleading, or at least inaccurate, to define, as is often done, the main principle of Hasidism as pantheistic. Hasidism does not eliminate or falsify the Essence of God. If anything, Hasidism stresses the presence of God, which, as Dante put it, is not solely confined—"non circonscritto"—to the heavenly spheres.

The pessimism of the Cabala, its renunciation of life, its harsh asceticism, are well known. Undoubtedly these views also have their origin in the uninterruptedly terrible fate of Jewry throughout history. God has constantly been called on, even experienced mystically—but from the viewpoint of radical pessimism God has always been distant from the affairs of this world. But did the Hasidim ever have any external causes for optimism? Absolutely never. Unable to escape from hard work and poverty, they often did not even have the time to observe the Sabbath in accordance with the precepts of their rabbis. If anyone has ever really tasted the bitter fruits of poverty and a total lack of independence in their daily life, it was those Jewish petty artisans and merchants, traders, waggoners, farm lessees, and shepherds. In old Russia, during the reign of Nicholas I, an anecdote had it that the more the authorities tormented the Jews with harsh taxation and persecution, the less time they had for crying and complaining: in the end their only defense was laughter, and laugh they did; the authorities had to admit that their harshness totally failed to accomplish its purposes. That would be symbolic of Hasidic life. Lack of education and of the satisfaction that the exact fulfillment of ritual rules brings to the faithful did not succeed in dimming their awareness of God's presence; the daily life of the Hasidim was experienced in different ways as a symbol of that presence. Cast deep into the abyss of the diaspora, they never forgot that they were God's children. In fact, the diaspora strengthened their resistance and became a source of joy because they found in it the treasure of their ancient heritage: *Mer hoben ja inzern Tate in Himl* (We have our Father in Heaven): the Hasidic chant in Yiddish provides a consolation.

To give that transformation, so long in the making, proper expression, form, and word, there was need for a great prophet and religious reformer. Polish Jewry found such a master in the rabbi Israel ben Eliezer, known as the Baal Shem Tov, literally "the Master of the Divine Name," that is, the name of God. In the middle of the eighteenth century, when the Jews were gripped first by faint hope and then by disillusionment, despair, and hopelessness, the Baal Shem Tov found the magical key that for thirsting souls opened the new way of the Hasidim, that is, of people full of good will, devout and compassionate. The history and teachings of Hasidism are interesting in many ways, but the legend that surrounds it is probably still more important. The legend is a testimony to concrete experience, and it is worth stressing that these legends, these orally transmitted words of the Baal Shem Tov and his followers, have here and there been kept alive to this very day in individual families, among the Jews and among the Catholic peasants as well.

The name *Hasid* has appeared repeatedly in the history of Jewry. When the venerable Mattathias rebelled against the king's command and ordered his sons and brothers, the Maccabees, to act in accordance with the Agreement their forefathers had made with God, the Hasideans (as they were then called) came out of their caves in the wilderness and joined the revolt. Eventually the priests among them quarreled perhaps with the heirs of the Maccabees, but there is no doubt that those Hasideans regarded themselves as zealous observers of the Law and in their feeling of ritual purity held themselves scrupulously at a distance from their unclean enemies.

Almost the exact opposite can be said about the Polish Hasidim—and their enemies lost no time in doing so. They were considered heretics because of their ignorance and lack of education. (I myself have heard the expression *am horetz,* which literally means a "man of earth," or an illiterate peasant.)

The term *Hasidim* reappears at the beginning of Christianity. This time it is applied to those small, poor, and very honest artisans, scattered throughout the length and breadth of the Roman Empire, who for the Apostle Paul are the basis and the nexus of his thought, especially in Greece. These "Hasidim" can more easily be compared with their Polish counterparts than can their biblical predecessors, or, more precisely, with that group of Jews which in the eighteenth century became the setting for the development of Polish Hasidism, except that the latter, after all the atrocities connected to the uprisings by the Ukrainian Cossacks, were even poorer and more helpless. (The Jews in eastern Poland temporarily lost even their fixed settlements and led the precarious life of wanderers.) And to an even greater degree than those poor wretches in the Roman Empire, these Polish Jews had need of consolation from their spiritual masters, not only in the form of sermons but also in the form of miraculous signs. What sort of a magical key did the Baal Shem Tov have, then?

First of all, there was his orthodoxy, and this cannot be stressed enough. His appearance came at a time when the authority of tradition and custom was unconditionally accepted. On the other hand, a turning away from ascetic practices, rigorous fasting, and an all-too-pedantic formalism was something new and liberating that the poor and unlettered followers of the Baal Shem Tov embraced enthusiastically. But what gave the Baal Shem Tov's activity its special power was his confidence in God, the joy springing from this confidence, and the knowledge that to the pure in heart God is attainable by many paths.

Certainly a rigid explication of doctrine and dogma was not of great consequence to the Hasidim. Their wretched social position as well as their lack of education protected them from any denominational pride. Nonetheless, we find in Hasidism a notion, clearly Platonic in origin, that served almost as a basic tenet: The world is in "exile" in that it can be imagined as flowing out from God and therefore constantly moving away from him. All creatures and all humans can be likened to falling and expiring sparks. The duty of the Hasidim, humble men of good will, is to stir up these sparks with love and compassion, to inflame them, and to send them back to God. This basic requirement of participating in wandering through understanding and compassion explains the atmosphere of tolerance that characterizes Hasidism more than any other Jewish Orthodox group. And yet their fervently impatient search for God was so unusual that it called forth vigorous criticism on the part of the *mitnaggedim,* who were proponents of old rabbinical piety. At a conference held in Brody in the middle of the eighteenth century dangerous clashes took place. "Put on a garment of vengeance," the *mitnaggedim* urged, "against those who during prayer, instead of keeping their eyes downcast, and their senses raised upward toward God, have the audacity to seek Him with frantic gestures and challenging glances!" Anyone who has had an opportunity to see, even in our own times, the ecstasy that the Hasidim reach while dancing and praying will confirm this observation and will understand why the proponents of more moderate and reserved behavior considered it a challenge.

That was not the end of the accusations: the Hasidim allegedly greeted the holy Sabbath with wild dances, forgetting the whole world around them, including their own duties; supposedly they drank vodka after prayers—much too much at times; and apparently one of their rabbis maintained that sitting together and drinking vodka was just like studying the Torah. The Hasidim responded that their opponents say their prayers without any warmth, thus rendering them ice-cold, as though they were conducting a wake; whereas the hearts of the Hasidim grow inflamed during prayer and that is why a living human being must drink vodka. The following psychological explanation can also be adduced: if a person forces himself to pray with excessive seriousness, the tempter opposes the prayer with equally excessive strength and disturbs it with "alien thoughts." If, on the other hand, after prayer a person refreshes himself in a friendly, sociable manner, if he drinks to the health of his fellow man, the tempter thinks that it is a vain pastime, loses interest in it, and the prayer rises toward heaven joyous and unobstructed.

This controversy explains the opposition to Hasidism, not only of the rationalists—that is, the strict, exacting Talmudists—but also of such subtle and highly spiritual mystics as Rabbi Elijah of Vilno (1720–97), who considered the Hasidic teachings to be a distortion of the Cabala. Rabbi Elijah signed a petition that called for imposing a ban on the Hasidim. The split between these two factions frequently was the cause of discord within a family. For example, the kind-hearted Hasidic rabbi Leib of Sasov, a friend of all creatures, men and beasts alike, who was also loved and respected by non-Jews, had a father bitterly opposed to the Hasidim. For years the father could not forgive his son for choosing the Hasidic way, and what is more, he apparently kept a "vicious rod" ready for his son's return as an instrument of fatherly punishment. The father's name was Rabbi Jacob of Brody, a town known as the center of the opposition to the Hasidim. It was even said that the opponents had a permanent meeting place ironically nicknamed the "Hasidim Sztibełe" (the Hasidic room).

The Baal Shem Tov succeeded in deflecting the attacks of the conservatives in two ways. First of all, he declared that he himself did not want to believe, or to force others to believe, in any way other than in strict accordance with tradition. He did not pass over a single word of Scripture, or a single traditional custom. Next he physically got out of the reach of his opponents by wandering in the forests and the Carpathian highlands far beyond Brody. He became a hermit, appearing with his wife at his side here and there along the rivers Prut and Czeremosz, living now in a forest inn, now in a cave. The names of certain places are repeatedly mentioned, and the persistence of these traditions allows us to assume that he actually spent some time in many if not all of these places. One such place, Jasienov on the Czarny (Black) Czeremosz, is known to me personally on the basis of direct oral tradition.

Of course, the authenticity of this tradition could be challenged on the grounds that these legends came into existence only when the Jewish settlements had begun to go higher into the mountains, and this happened quite late—for example, along the banks of the upper Czeremosz only at the beginning of the nineteenth century. The Hucul tradition is undoubtedly much older and must rely on its own memory, without any Jewish mediation. The Huculs, shepherds long settled in the mountains who speak Ukrainian and profess the Greek Catholic faith, limit themselves primarily to local and family traditions, telling—even when the story is mystical in nature—of the heroic shepherds, peasants, and robber chieftains of their mountain homeland. Their heavens are also populated with such figures. Undoubtedly some elements have been taken over from the legends of the ancient Slavs—for example, the many apocryphal tales and folk songs coming partly from the Balkan Peninsula, partly from the Ukraine. But the Huculs certainly were not interested in what was happening among the Jews in far-off places in relatively recent times. Therefore they could pass on information only about what they had heard in their own village or in a nearby community. Such information was stubbornly preserved and passed on to future generations.

Since childhood I too have heard many stories about the Baal Shem Tov, especially about how he lived in Jasienov with a Hucul family named Fedieczkowi, who looked after him kindly and nursed him when he was sick. The direct descendants of that family, who still referred to that tradition, lived in the village of Krasnojila, not far from Jasienov. Another account gives the name of a forest cave (*surduk*) on the left bank of the Czeremosz in which the hermit Baal Shem Tov lived in his wandering days, and the name of the mountain spring in which he bathed.

Historiography tends to dismiss as legend everything that has not been recorded in writing. Of course, some stories may have been brought by the Jews at a later point and incorporated into the local tradition; similarly, legendary mythopoetic embellishments of a tale can easily be recognized. But the core of the tradition—as has already been pointed out—belongs to the treasury of the Huculs' memory, the memory of a people who have lived in one spot for centuries; the untouched mountain landscape and the specific legendary lore of the local shepherds serve to define in an unmistakable and indelible fashion the atmosphere of the tales about the Baal Shem Tov. Especially characteristic of these tales is their connection with the robber chieftain Oleksa Dobosz, a figure who, above and beyond the mythical traits he has acquired with the passage of time, exists in the written court proceedings of the eighteenth century. Whereas in other localities the Jews despised those who lived by violence, whether they were Cossacks or robbers, oddly enough Dobosz plays a wholly sympathetic role in the oral

Hasidic tradition as the defender of the poor and the weak and even as the Baal Shem Tov's personal friend.

Written history has little to say about the Baal Shem Tov's years as a hermit, and so we must be content to follow the more or less believable traces left us by legend. One legend, for example, which undoubtedly grew up in connection with his abortive journey to Palestine, relates how the Baal Shem Tov on his way from Jasienov to Safed took an underground passage under a mountain known as the Pysanyi Kamien (the Painted Rock) and returned by the same route. Other legends recount how, sitting in his lonely cave, he pored over voluminous tomes—this information has the authentic ring of an oft-repeated "eyewitness" account. The legend goes on: the Baal Shem Tov is said to have left behind in the mountains a book that was given to him by God. They say that for many years after, mountain explorers looked in vain for that book in the forests and gorges. According to an interpretation that could be of more recent date, that book was written by God himself.

These legends clearly show how spontaneous was the Hasidim's love for nature as the creation of God. The history of the emergence of Hasidism can perhaps be characterized in the following way: it flew out of a cramped room into the vast expanses of the world in order to find its essence in the solitude of forests and mountains, and then went back again to form a new community. Once awakened, love for nature took root and proved to be a long-lasting and mighty force among the believers, in accord with the Master's command: to awake through the power of love all the divine sparks now scattered and extinguished. Many proofs of this are to be found in any number of Hasidic tales. According to one tale, as a young man Rabbi Zusya of Annapol (who died in 1800) so disliked the house of study (yeshiva) that he went out into the forest to meditate there. Another story, attributed to Rabbi Eisik of Zydachov, informs us that young Zusya could foretell the future by listening to the rustling of the trees.

Most colorful are the tales about the Baal Shem Tov's great-grandson, Rabbi Nachman of Braclav. They tell of the solitary life he led far from any human settlements and of the huts he built on the shores of distant lakes. Even Nachman's bent for asceticism was secondary to his overpowering love for nature. To describe the depth and fervor of this experience, Martin Buber found these

beautiful words: "In the meantime God watches over the experiencing person from every tree and is familiar with each herb."

In this fashion those paupers, who owned absolutely nothing
and lived as it were on the margin of Jewry, were suddenly exposed
to living nature, which had been closed to them for centuries. The
Master of the Divine Name led them out of their cramped rooms,
walls, and streets into the world of living creatures.

The Baal Shem Tov's inner transformations, attested to by the
oral tradition, can best be grasped in the context of their external
landscape. An old Buddhist maxim says, "Great things happen
when men and mountains meet together." And so it is with the
solitary wanderer and hermit Baal Shem Tov, who owes many of
his spiritual discoveries to the forests and mountains. He foresaw
such a meeting with nature, longed for it, and finally achieved it,
not without a struggle. The typical Jewish inhabitant of a small
town—who in keeping with his station in life could not bear
arms—would never have exposed himself to such danger, terrified
at the very thought of so many wild beasts and bands of robbers
roaming the countryside. But that was no obstacle for a man like
the Baal Shem Tov. Yet even he must have found it difficult to
cover the vast distances between isolated settlements. By the eighteenth century there are references to rabbis permanently residing
in Kuty (Kitew in Yiddish) and Kosov, both located on the Czeremosz River. The Baal Shem Tov was married to a sister of Rabbi
Gershon of Kuty, so he obviously had to travel from Brody, located to the north of Lvov (Lwów), to Kuty, which was almost on
the Rumanian border. According to an oral tradition from the eighteenth century (written reports about the administration of lands
on the upper Czeremosz go back only to the nineteenth century)
the Baal Shem Tov had leased from the dominion in Jasienov a
country inn located on the "Plac" (Square). Today the distance
between Kuty and Jasienov by a new road linking the two towns is
forty kilometers, but the old route, which probably went around
the cavern and along the Sokolska Skata (Cliff), must have been
much longer.

Legend has it that the Baal Shem Tov lived in a cave with his
wife before his illumination and that every day his wife wheeled a
barrow full of clay to town to sell to the local brick maker. After
they rented the inn in the mountains, the wife usually stayed home,

while her husband would wander for days on foot. He must have traversed the long road from Jasienov to Kuty and back again many times in order to visit the local house of prayer for the solemn holidays or to call upon his wife's family. Here we have to keep in mind that the way of life then was quite different from what it is today. In the forests and highlands of the eastern Carpathians agriculture was scarcely practiced, and the main occupations were cattle breeding and hunting. Consequently the diet consisted mainly of game and dairy and grain products, such as barley and buckwheat, supplemented by maize polenta. Even today bread and cakes are baked only for holidays. Goods indispensable for everyday use were transported from the valleys up to the high mountains by a breed of especially hardy and surefooted packhorses without which it would have been impossible to mount the steep and perilous paths. The climate is harsh, with blizzards in winter and violent storms in summer. So it is understandable that the Baal Shem Tov avoided the clothes Jews wore in the small towns and instead dressed in simple peasant garb and a sheepskin coat, which he never took off and kept secured with a piece of rope tied around his waist. And in that simple garb the image of the wanderer and hermit has been preserved in the people's memory.

As far back as memory goes, there have always been many isolated cottages and huts whose inhabitants have led a secluded life cut off from other people and the world. Even today it is customary for shepherds to spend the summer with their flocks in the mountain pastures, and the winter in snowbound *zymarki* (huts) far from their native villages. In such isolated places man is obviously exposed to dangers that he would scarcely face in society. I have met people who told me that they had seen the devil in various shapes. Constantly threatened by magic and the world of evil spirits, people would try to protect themselves by learning magical practices and attempting to apply them. Such practices included the "living fire," the "living water," and the "living word," that is, magic spells and incantations. Evil spirits can appear in the most varied shapes, depending on a person's receptivity. For example, it sometimes happpens that young men are possessed by "forest women," and the sufferings that result from these often pathological states grow so extreme as to be unbearable. So it is understandable that in such circumstances the victims have greater confidence in the magic formulas than in their confessors. In this case the advice is to avoid the subject of woman in one's conversations. For obvious reasons an individual man is far more likely to fall prey to the evil powers present in nature. But evil finds a field for action not just in the helplessness of the solitary individual; it finds it to a much greater extent in the readiness of the human spirit to embrace evil so as to use it to exert power over his fellow man. As the eminent Swiss historian Jacob Burckhardt says, "Power is always evil." It is interesting to note that these mountain regions have always been densely populated by formidable sorcerers; they have used their magical powers not only to avenge themselves on their enemies but also to gain control over other creatures and to torment them. These sorcerers were enormously feared, since magic could produce effects at great distances, and they were masters of the most ingenious means of inflicting pain and death, which they had no scruples about using. They represented an invisible, nay, an untouchable power against which even the clergy was helplesss; the sorcerers never opposed the Church openly, but only in secret, and thus were able to avoid any counterattacks. Their hunger for power did not stop short at any crime, including sacrilege. For that reason all pastoral attempts aimed at saving their hardened and depraved souls must have proved absolutely useless.

On the other hand, precisely this unconstrained way of life, unhampered by convention, made it possible for such a solitary people to have much greater freedom in their dealings with all creatures living in nature. They were able to participate directly and intensely in the life and sufferings of all creation and with religious veneration called this life "everything that breathes." This deep harmony with nature is best illustrated in the attitude of Nachman of Braclav, the great-grandson of the Baal Shem Tov. Of Nachman, Martin Buber writes that he could not sleep in a newly built wooden house; he had the feeling that lying among fresh planks was exactly like lying among corpses, because he believed that the soul of a tree is murdered when it is prematurely cut down. Not long ago a certain Hucul working as a woodcutter for a large lumber company confessed to his priest that he felt that cutting down trees was a form of mass murder committed on innocent beings.

It is worth recalling another essential characteristic of these mountain dwellers: their love of dance. Their rare gatherings are celebrated especially joyously; frequently they dance all night long, even after putting in a whole day of hard work. The first detailed description of Hucul dances is found in Baltazar Hacquet's *Neueste physikalisch-politische Reisen,* published in Nuremberg in 1794 (some forty years after the Baal Shem Tov's sojourn in the mountains). The way of life and the customs of these mountain dwellers have remained almost unchanged until the present day.

The return of the Baal Shem Tov from his mountain solitude to the life of the new community and the beginnings of his spiritual leadership have not been recorded, but they can easily be pieced together. From childhood he displayed an interest in teaching: they say that he taught prayers and songs to school children with unbounded love and patience. The new community that he founded after years as a hermit was figuratively, if not literally, a community of children. So after all the years of solitude and isolation, the Baal Shem Tov devoted all his energy to the community and lived with his spiritual children in close intimacy. "Mit simche, Yidelech, mit simche lomir im dinem!" (In joy, O Jews, in joy serve him!)—this song characterizes the atmosphere of exaltation and love that filled the hearts of the early Hasidim.

We should avoid the error of explaining the phenomenon of Hasidism and its emergence by means of the folklore of the land. To my mind, "folklore" is a totally inappropriate and presumptuous formulation; instead it would be better to talk of "the traces of an ancient, particularly archaic religious culture." The Baal Shem Tov was spiritually well armed—he was famous as a maker of protective magic charms, above all of amulets that drove away sickness and demons, and these amulets were always signed only by him. In the eyes of Orthodox Jews it would have been a glaring abuse if such amulets were to prove effective through the use of the Holy Name of God; many who had tried something similar had been excommunicated as heretics. But for all that, the Baal Shem Tov kept up his "personal" battle against demons and did not fear either the devil or sorcerers. In this connection it is worth mentioning that the magical practices used in urgent cases of need by the Christian Huculs and the Hasidic Jews were fundamentally the same. I was once a witness to the interchange between village Jews and Huculs concerning a crime committed by a certain sorcerer who had cast a demonic spell, and to my astonishment, I discovered that all those present not only knew how that particular spell worked but also had the same name for it. In almost poetic terms they were talking about the possibility of sending back the spell, which they imagined as a kind of magic spear. (In the language of the Huculs such a sending back is called *obertyn*.)

The question naturally arises whether and to what extent there was any influence of Christianity on the origin of Hasidism. In a poem written in Yiddish by Nuchim Bomze of Sasov, a Jewish boy standing by the wall of a Christian cemetery listens as though enchanted to the sound of Christian prayers coming from a church. Such was the force of attraction that emanated from either the joyousness or the strong feeling of those prayers. Or perhaps it was the powerful childlike confidence of the simple peasants in their God that impressed the Jewish Hasidim so deeply, because it closely resembled their own religious feelings? But there seems to be little possibility of any direct influence here, nor of the influence of the Cabala or of Christian Neoplatonism. We must not forget that for several thousand years Jews have been observing their religious rituals within the family, and that it has mainly been the family that has preserved and transmitted the tradition. It is interesting to note that despite the supposedly conservative tendency of the Talmudists, the Hasidim were more firmly rooted in the tradition; they were, so to speak, the incarnation of orthodoxy, and that is why they were less susceptible to deviation than was the rationalist current. In Vilno, which was the center of Jewish learning, two celebrated deist tracts were published, written by rabbi-scholars, one a Talmudist, the other a Karaite. Translated into Latin, these tracts were later acclaimed by Voltaire. A Hasidic text, it is safe to say, could not have achieved such recognition from dissenters. The rationalists were threatened by their high level of general education itself, and thus they became uprooted in a relatively short time. In Poland it was a frequent occurrence for the descendants of educated rabbis to convert to Catholicism. The fact that the Hasidic movement was almost free of such conversions should be regarded as a unique phenomenon in the history of religion. For this reason some Polish and French works on the subject characterize the Hasidim as "reactionary forces."

It is impossible to overlook the existence of common traits shared by Hasidism and the Franciscan order. The similarity can undoubtedly be explained by the decisive influence of the poor and uneducated element in both; it should not be forgotten that the teachings of the Baal Shem Tov were based on a conscious opposition to an erudition that exhausted itself in scholastic and logical subtleties. Humility was the key factor in Saint Francis's creed. Essential to Hasidism was a totally changed attitude to the animal world, a feeling of compassion for all of creation—an approach that was foreign to the hitherto existing religious sensibility of Judaism. Thus, for example, a legend about the rabbi Moshe Leib of Sasov recounts how the faithful had to wait for him in the synagogue during the Kol Nidre (the solemn prayer spoken on the eve of the Day of Atonement) while he went home to feed his children and water his horses and cows. Another rabbi, Gershon from Kuty, set himself the task of freeing captured birds: he would buy them as long as he could afford it, and if he had no money, he would simply open the cages and set the birds free. They say that many a time he got a drubbing for his efforts. But that closeness to nature all but disappeared once the Hasidim began to leave the countryside and became city dwellers.

Another marked tendency within the Hasidic movement should be mentioned here. The Hasidim's decision to keep their distance from educated people and education in general inevitably brought them close to the local population, who spoke Polish or Ukrainian. The Hasidim Jews spoke, wrote, and prayed in Yiddish, but as their links with the peasants became stronger, they adopted elements of the local language. They attributed religious significance to Polish and Ukrainian folk songs, just as they did to the Song of Songs. In this way the simple content of these folk songs took on a deeper, symbolic value: a rose from a shepherd's love song became a symbol of the Kingdom of Heaven, and the impenetrable forest separating us from the rose was an emblem of our exile, during which we are to achieve salvation through love. It is in these poetic expressions that the depth of Hasidic religious longing is conveyed. A study of such songs and their reinterpretation in symbols constantly sought and found anew would in all its variety give living proof of the powerful religious imagination of the Hasidim. Undoubtedly the Hasidim are indebted to the Cabala for their number magic and for their number mysticism, but their heritage of song was an authentic, naturally cultivated folk poetry drawn from the treasury of long experience of life and suffering, which connected them in the most direct way with their non-Jewish surroundings.

The march of progress left its mark on the life of the Hasidim; the growing gap between rich and poor Jews, between merchants and artisans led, willy-nilly, to solidarity between poor Jews and Christians. But their religious life was subject to constant change as well, so that in the course of time there emerged two extremes: the Hasid and the Zaddik. Both words come from the Bible and the Talmud. In the Bible God appears as a Hasid: "I am a Hasid, says the Lord, I shall not be angry forever." In one of the commentaries God is referred to in these terms: "In the beginning God is a Zaddik and rules by the true Law. Then He becomes a Hasid, abandoning the Law and dispensing Grace." Thus in the Bible the Hasid occupies a higher rank than the Zaddik. In the later history of the Jews, especially during the diaspora, the Zaddik became a "mediator and holy man." The Zaddikim gained prominence as a result of the spread of Hasidism. The Zaddik is called upon to speak with God, and what is more, he can even judge God. The Zaddikim are the central figures of humanity, the world exists because of them, and their power is unlimited. According to a saying attributed to the followers of Rabbi Nachman of Braclav: "The Zaddik is Moses and the Messiah in one person."

This transformation of Hasidism led to the gradual drying up of a childlike faith in God and the spontaneity of feeling associated with it. Experts on Hasidism maintain that the degeneration of the Hasidic faith can be traced to the abuses of "Zaddikism," that is, exaggerated faith in their power and a belief in miracles. One of the legends that deals with the evil Samael, or Satan (it is difficult to ascertain whether the legend is of Hasidic or rabbinical origin), ironically credits him with the decline of Hasidism, but on closer scrutiny we realize that overzealousness in acquiring as great a number of followers as possible resulted in such a fatal development. Satan gave the order for this summons to resound throughout all possible worlds: "Let all become Hasidim!" And so it came to pass.

Undoubtedly the great religious power of Hasidism lay in prayer, in "duty to the heart," as the Talmud says. In conclusion, then, I take the liberty of recalling the image of Hasidic prayer as I experienced it in my childhood on the upper Czeremosz, the native realm of the Hasidim.

One day we saw Eisik walking slowly and with much dignity to the synagogue (shul). He was, it seemed to us, strangely dressed: he wore a dark-colored silk coat, a beautiful fox fur hat, white stockings, and patent-leather shoes and carried a prayer book wrapped in a silk scarf in his hand. Eisik's outfit reminded us of the chasuble worn by Ukrainian Catholic priests for the funeral mass, but even more of the costume of a certain Spaniard whose portrait hung in our grandmother's drawing room. We hastened to ask Grandmother why he had got himself up so, and we were given a terse answer that electrified me, probably because of the sound of the unknown word: "Eisik is a Hasid." This mysterious word sent shivers down my spine and caused me to do something I had never done before: one evening during the Jewish holidays on the way back from a stroll to a place called the Jewish Rock with my younger sister and our nanny, I went off and approached the brightly lit windows over the Varatyn. I stood there for a long time looking into the large room in which the Jews were praying. What I saw transported me into a totally alien world. Even now it seems to me as though back then I looked through mysterious cracks beyond the walls of the ordinary, everyday world.

All those present were part of a strange world of enchantment. One of the young Jews, lanky and tall, his head covered, stood motionless, leaning against the wall. From time to time he whispered something, then shuddered all over, seemed to burst into sobs, then scream. A moment later he was as immobile as before. It was terrifying. Someone in his family must have died, I thought, and he is grieving so. Or perhaps he is confessing? Perhaps he knows some terrible secret, and God's ear somewhere there in the wall is listening?

The master of prayer, a tall old man with a dry ascetic face, as though sculpted in yellow bone, and a long gray beard, rocked to and fro violently without stop in front of something that I said to myself must be an altar. He kept exclaiming something, chanted in long drawn-out tones, and wept openly. His voice faltered as he was sobbing, and he himself—and this I remember vividly—seemed to break down completely, only to resume his plaintive supplication the next moment. A dark-complexioned Jew I did not know, who seemed to be a stranger, his frantic black eyes flashing on all sides, violently shook the book he was holding in his hand. I looked at him in terror, he seemed to me to be almost mad, so feverish were his gestures. After each of the aged master's long orations, the participants, who each in his own fashion sat, stood, or paced back and forth, would proclaim something and wail in chorus.

Old Eisik, solemn and dignified, his gray beard disheveled, sat to one side. Tears streamed down his radiant, smiling face. Now and then he would lift the fingers of his left hand to his head and then move them away, as though he were pondering every word of the prayer and, as it were, sucking the nectar of sublimity out of them. After so many images that were a bit too serious, overly strange and forlorn, Eisik's well-known face, full of trustfulness, somehow had a soothing effect on me. The candles were burning brightly, the candelabra radiated light. The Czeremosz murmured somewhere off in the distance.

At this point the nanny came running up, grabbed me roughly by the arm, and pulled me away from the window. "I'll tell your grandma," she said threateningly and dragged me all the way home. But I was still completely dazed by what I had just experienced. Much later I learned that it was the Day of Atonement, a feast celebrated by the Hasidim in a particularly solemn manner. From that day on my ear has become very sensitive to the tales of the Hasidim.

How safe a child must feel growing up in a land protected year after year by such fervent prayers, even if they are the prayers of another religion. For centuries the rustle of those prayers has risen to the heavens, and now it is no more. Will it someday resound once again? And what was it that could be heard in it—was it an alien hope, or was it our own?

(1936)

TRANSLATED BY JADWIGA KOSICKA

Józef Czapski

Paradise Lost

For Ludwik Herling

Pierre Bonnard is dead.

On the day the news of his death was announced, the Parisian papers provided the date of his birth and a few trite phrases to the effect that he was a "painter of light" and did illustrations for works by Verlaine, Mirbeau, and Gide. On the day of his funeral I found only one or two microscopic notices in the press. That was all. More important things had been happening on that particular day: first of all, there was the problem of *ravitaillement*—the question of meat that wasn't reaching Paris in sufficient quantities—and also the exchange of telegrams and letters between Stalin and Bevin, and so many other current issues.

Could it be, I thought, that the French do not understand what they have lost? In fact, Bonnard is "out of date." He represents the past, without any doubt, and is for the French a "paradise lost."

But the foolish and trite initial notices in the daily press were followed by an avalanche of articles and reminiscences about Bonnard in the weeklies. A short interview with Georges Braque included a sentence that touches upon what I have wanted to discuss in connection with Bonnard: "Sa joie de vivre était le signe de son époque. Ce n'est peut-être pas celui de la nôtre" (His joy of life was the sign of his time, and perhaps is no longer the sign of our time).

I cannot think of any other modern French painter who called forth such a lively response among so many Polish painters as Bonnard did. I would say that the reaction was one not simply of admiration but also of a certain heartfelt tenderness. Many things contributed to Bonnard's fanatical following in Poland. His name became known in Poland somewhat earlier and by a more direct route than in other countries, thanks to his friendship of many years with Józef Pankiewicz, undoubtedly the most distinguished Polish teacher of painting. Owing to Pankiewicz, several generations of Polish painters "discovered" Bonnard, and thanks to Bonnard, many of us were able to get free of Pankiewicz's influence on our own painting. Their friendship and the divergent paths along which their painting developed shed some light on a number of central questions connected with Bonnard's art.

In an interview for the *Nouvelles littéraires* (23 July 1933) Bonnard said that for him it was not impressionism that was the first revelation of modern painting, but rather it was the work of Gauguin, which he saw in 1888. Now every child knows that the development of nineteenth-century painting went from impressionism through Cézanne, Seurat, van Gogh, and Gauguin and that it passed through a period of stylization and Gauguin's "flat" deformation on its way to cubism. (Fauvism was a movement more indebted to van Gogh.) Impressionism, as a pictorial form of naturalism, had preceded Gauguin's arabesque, his violent reaction against naturalism, and his *ligne abstraite,* which are genealogically linked with Degas and Ingres rather than with impressionism and Delacroix.

The history of art, conceived "academically," is misleading if it fails to stress that artistic trends and influences often spread very rapidly one after the other, that they intermingle, intersect, and almost completely overlap in time, although in our imagination they seem to be separated by many decades. In establishing the sequence of movements historians often make artificial schematizations for the sake of greater clarity.

When the young Bonnard began his studies in 1888 at the Académie Julien, along with such classmates as Ker-Xavier Roussel (1867–1944), Edouard Vuillard (1868–1940), and Maurice Denis (1870–1943), he had no acquaintance with impressionism, and his first revelation of modern art came to him in the form of a small canvas, or rather a board (brought to the studio by Denis), representing a highly stylized tree painted in violent colors.

That was Bonnard's first discovery of modernity. It was at a later point that the student at the Académie Julien became acquainted with impressionism. By his own account, contact with impressionism brought about his liberation. Why do I put so much stress on this sequence of events? Because in the entire early phase of Bonnard's work both influences are clearly discernible, but Gauguin's *ligne abstraite,* the Japanese woodcut, and a feeling for the arabesque appear prior to the discovery of the impressionist color revolution. The best evidence for this view can be found in his posters and illustrations from before 1900. His entering into nature through the discovery of impressionism moves Bonnard's painting into the world of impressionistic visual perception, which is more naturalistic and more analytically receptive to nature. But that phase of impressionism had already gone beyond a sensitive and conscious feeling for composition. Bonnard has Gauguin to thank for the fact that his paintings are so rarely impressionism pure and simple.

Bonnard met Pankiewicz in 1908. The two painters soon became friends; in 1909 they rented a villa together in St. Tropez next to Paul Signac's and spent the entire summer there painting side by side. From then until 1914 they spent many a summer together or close to one another, either on the Mediterranean or in Normandy. For all the respect and love I feel for Pankiewicz, and my recognition of his immense role in the history of Polish painting, I should like to avoid any ambiguity: as painters the two are not in the same class. For that matter I do not know who among Bonnard's contemporaries could be put in the same class with him except Matisse and possibly Picasso. However that may be, Bonnard and Pankiewicz met at a point when their paths crossed and undoubtedly they had a mutual influence on one another at a certain period of time. I remember seeing at Bernheim-Jeune's a sketch by Bonnard of a southern bay from before 1914 so like the Polish artist's work that I thought it actually was a painting by Pankiewicz. We all know Pankiewicz's painting *Stone-pines by the Sea,* in which many traces of Bonnard's direct influence can be detected.

For Pankiewicz, Aleksander Gierymski provided the first shock in his experience of painting (as Gauguin did for Bonnard), and it was Gierymski in his pre-impressionist phase, represented by such paintings as *Solec Street* and *A Jewish Girl with Oranges.* This contact imbued Pankiewicz with a life-long passion for *qualité* in works of art and sent him fleeing from Wojciech Gerson's academicism to embrace the masters so revered by Gierymski: Vermeer and the Venetian school. Impressionism was for Pankiewicz a transient phase which came *after* he had absorbed Gierymski, just as happened with Bonnard *after* he had absorbed Gauguin. In the last twenty years of his life, Pankiewicz returned more and more often to his earliest experiences, to Gierymski's realism, and then to the increasingly exclusive cult of the classics, which resulted in the uniquely personal neoclassicism found in some of his paintings.

The years between 1907 and 1918 were Pankiewicz's Sturm und Drang period. What can't we find in his paintings! Almost Matisse-like still lifes in brutal, vivid colors; Spanish landscapes and cubist Madrid streets, in which it is clear that he has been looking at Delaunay, with whom he once shared a studio (in Madrid); *pointes sèches* with a highly stylized line (perhaps the weakest graphics in his entire output); and finally flowers as Bonnardesque as those I included in color reproduction in the introduction to my book on Pankiewicz.

Around 1918, upon his return to France from Spain, Pankiewicz met Bonnard again, who, as he told me himself, "infected" him with "purer" and more autonomous arrangements of colored patches and colored arabesques. Bonnard in turn gets Pankiewicz away from a certain schematism of line passed on to him by cubism. They both "work through"—each in his own way—the years 1905–14, a period of artistic revolutions and upheavals, which were to have lasting effects (fauvism, cubism, futurism).

Only after 1918 does Pankiewicz gradually start to return to a more subdued style of painting. Of contemporary painters Renoir is the master closest to him. Even his application of paint so it appears as porcelain is reminiscent of Renoir. Yet at about the same time he paints a very Bonnardesque *intérieur* of the Laurysiewicz family. (This painting was part of a collection of Pankiewicz's work, unique in its high quality and rich diversity, that belonged to the Laurysiewicz family and was destroyed during World War II.)

With the passing years Pankiewicz consistently distances himself from modern painting and goes back to the great nineteenth-century realists—Courbet, Gierymski—and, beyond them, to the masters of the Renaissance. At that point he was found of repeating over and over again that Vasari was right in using *come vivo* as the highest praise for a painting. He becomes more and more of a classicist in his ideas and accuses the nineteenth century of destroying the unity of painting by "breaking down" the pictorial elements, reversing their classical hierarchy (line, value, color), and as a result ruling out drawing in the classic sculptural, rather than the painterly, sense of the word and eliminating naturalistic value, chiaroscuro, local color, in favor of an increasingly arbitrary transposition of tones.

In contrast, Bonnard, in connection with Corot's *Colosseum* at the Louvre, talked enthusiastically about the artist's "Vermeer-like striving for absolute objectivity" and "synthetic spot of color simultaneously expressing both the light and the object." From 1922 on Pankiewicz takes a direction diametrically opposed to Bonnard's line of development.

In his studio in Paris right up to his death Pankiewicz kept hanging on the wall a small study, or rather a sketch, of a female nude by Bonnard. The color of the body was in lemon-yellow tones and Naples yellow with delicate gray shadows and several green patches in the background. Those various patches, which had nothing in common with faithfulness to local color, were the very essence of Bonnard's canvases, which consisted of an unexpected, revealing, and always unique color harmony. In a similar fashion, the drawing of the nude, childish and clumsy to the uninitiated eye, was the epitome of a refined and radiant sensibility.

In Bonnard's work, in contrast to Pankiewicz's, the abstract element becomes more prominent with the passage of time. His work grows not alongside, not against impressionism (as did cubism), but out of the core of many years of work according to the basic assumptions of impressionism, using an almost impressionistic palette but infinitely richer (cubism in rejecting impressionism impoverished the palette quite drastically), employing the methods of divisionism and an increasingly free treatment of local color. In Bonnard's canvases the arrangements of "pure" colors start to become richer and the transpositions still bolder: it is a world of pure play with colors, a world of the colored arabesque. But this development in Bonnard's case does not take place at all rapidly. There is nothing about it of a conversion to or a repudiation of anything. It is simply a brilliant assimilation of ever new elements and a constant enlargement of his own vision.

Here I am going to call upon my own memories. I should like to set the scene in which I watched Bonnard's fame slowly gaining ground.

In 1924, the year of my arrival in Paris with a group of Polish painters known as the Kapists, cubism was fashionable enough in the circles frequenting the "progressive cafés"* and its pronouncements sufficiently obligatory that to call a young painter an impressionist bordered on insulting him, or so that when Picasso in a conversation allegedly said of van Gogh, "C'est un voyou sentimental" (He is a sentimental rascal), an eager German art critic immediately quoted it like scripture in one of those cheap editions devoted to modern art which are distributed throughout the world. In 1924 or 1925 one of the then most influential Parisian critics reviewing an exhibit of Picasso, Léger, and Bonnard held at the Bernheim-Jeune gallery wrote, "Picasso and Léger in magnificent Rolls-Royces and Bugattis lead the race while Monsieur Bonnard on his old-fashioned tricycle vainly tries to catch up with them."

Had it been someone else in Bonnard's place at that particular time, a person and a painter less talented and less keenly attuned to his own inner music, less sensitive to what he saw and experienced, less authentic and unselfish as a poet, he would undoubtedly have tried to "catch up" with what was then regarded as fashionable, modern, and "revolutionary." But when asked about his relation to modern art, Bonnard always answered modestly, or perhaps coquettishly, shunning photographers, interviewers, any form of publicity whatsoever: "Je ne suis qu'un pauvre impressioniste!" (I am only a poor impressionist!)

Yet in a conversation with Pankiewicz (I am unable to establish the date of that conversation, which the Polish painter mentioned to me in 1935; I assume it must have been in the later years), Bonnard suddenly asserted, "C'est la peinture abstraite qui sauvera la peinture" (It is abstract painting that will save the art of painting), which aroused a vigorous protest from Pankiewicz.

---

*I refer to café trendsetting without any irony. The Dôme, Rotonde, or Deux Magots were as instrumental then in shaping public opinion as the eighteenth-century salons had been in their day. The cafés were responsible for discovering "geniuses," spreading snobbery and "obligatory" slogans among the thousands of painters for whom France was the country of Cézanne, of Poussin, of van Gogh and Picasso. Cafés have been and still are the meeting place for people from all parts of world who keep coming to Paris for the sake of painting, and they are instrumental in creating ferment.

Year by year Bonnard's palette grows richer, the combinations of color more and more elaborate. Three-dimensionality becomes more and more unexpectedly transposed into color alone, requiring of the viewer a deep familiarity with the canvas if it is to be perceived at all, since the presented objects are often dematerialized and completely obliterated during the process of transposition.

First contact with Bonnard's work fills one primarily with admiration for the combination of color; only at some later point does one stop to think: Is that blue plane representing a woman's dress? Or is it a mountain? Is that form lying on a white and red checkered tablecloth a woman's hand or perhaps a cat? Only at a closer scrutiny does everything on the canvas become clear, intense, and intelligent both in color and in form.

In the last phase of Bonnard's work, local color undergoes constant changes, constant transitions into ever new units dependent on the systematic division of often noncomplementary tonalities.

"Donnez-moi de la boue, j'en ferai un corps de Venus" (Give me some mud and I'll make the body of a Venus out of it), Delacroix allegedly said at some point. Consider the dark browns, the yellow, violet, and pink tones that Bonnard uses for his Venuses in bathtubs!

Achieving effects through color becomes for Bonnard something as consistent and infallible as mathematics. He consciously puts aside values, consciously destroys all feeling for matter in order to discover more and more new color combinations. Perhaps no other painter in the world has ever created such a palette of violets, ranging from almost purple to almost vermillion and red. Yet despite all the "abstractionism" in the logic of the color range, these color combinations are always deeply rooted in the feeling of rapture that he experienced in contact with nature all around him. The colors are never separated from that experience. For that reason his pictures never produce the impression of a cold, cerebral combination (so often present in the cubists) but always of full emotion. As could be expected of such an extraordinarily sensitive man, everything in Bonnard has its immediate effect, setting him completely apart from the accepted classical principles of pictorial composition. Rapid movements of human figures, detached bits of faces and bodies or landscapes like those seen from a fast moving train or automobile, unexpected compositions that suddenly piece themselves together from cut-off fragments of a face on a movie screen—everything of that sort was utilized in Bonnard's compositions, just as the discovery of snapshot photography was utilized by Degas in his pictures of horses and racing scenes.

One day I was walking with Pankiewicz on La Boétie, the street where the *marchands* of art displayed their wares. In one window there was hanging a large canvas by Bonnard. One of its compositional elements was a human face and a torso cut in the middle seen against the frame of an open door. Pankiewicz shrugged his shoulders contemptuously as I pointed the canvas out to him, voicing my admiration. He considered it a bad joke, this massacring of forms, this building of the image, in which a piece of the human body has become a colored arabesque within the whole. He could not tolerate the obliteration of the object's materiality. But in Bonnard's case this was his special vision and his uniquely personal surprise, which in many respects was not unrelated to Degas's explorations in the same direction.

How Bonnard painted was completely of his own devising (I would never advise anyone to paint that way, God forbid). From what I have been told, he seems never to have cleaned his palette, which with time became heavy and very thick from all the successive layers of dessicated paints. Drying out, getting mixed accidentally, often changing color in the process of hardening, these paints on the palette were for Bonnard a source of inexhaustibly new ideas in the combination of colors. When he discovered a new admixture, he would very carefully transfer it to the canvas with a knife and out of this new patch often draw a new chromatic scale of colors that subverted the previous one. He couldn't stand clean brushes, he never cleaned his old ones, and when he bought a new one, it would so irritate him that he would soak it in oil paint and then roll it in the sand. I was told that there was nothing as amusing as Bonnard before each of his exhibitions. He never considered his pictures fully finished, and minutes before the opening he would appear at the exhibition, his pockets full of tubes of paints. He would systematically pull out the tubes one after the other, squeeze a little paint on his finger, and smear it on the canvas. Bonnard never bothered to mount on stretchers the canvases that he was working on in his studio; he would paint several pictures on a large piece of canvas, separating them by lines of white paint, and then roll it up. He would occasionally pull a roll out of many, fix it to the wall with drawing pins, and resume work on an already-existing picture, enriching and adding new elements to it.

One day in the Musée du Luxembourg Bonnard was almost arrested. A guard caught sight of a gentleman, surely a madman, who, to the guard's dismay, kept pulling mysterious tubes out of his pocket one after the other as he moved back and forth in front of a canvas and started smearing something on it. That was Bonnard touching up a picture of his that he had done some twenty years before. I was also told how the series of his paintings of women in the bathtub came into being. Bonnard's wife could never be sure that he wouldn't suddenly burst in on her and make a quick sketch, which would become the basis of one of those wonderful pictures, which he would work on for years.

An art critic told me how when he was visiting Bonnard's studio and looking at one of his female nudes, he covered a part of the picture with his hand.

"Oh, you're undoubtedly covering that particular hip," exclaimed Bonnard. "For the past two years I've been looking for the right color for that hip!"

For us, disciples of Pankiewicz newly arrived in Paris, Bonnard's art provided the same feeling of liberation that impressionism had once offered him; it helped to release limitless creative potential for the painter and offered the possibilities that result from a very careful observation and experiencing of nature and color. For that reason we were more responsive to Bonnard than to Pankiewicz, who was then in the classicist phase of his creativity and increasingly pessimistic in his theories, which reminded one of Chenavard's pessimism.* Chenavard saw in nineteenth-century painting only regression and disintegration, although he admired and recognized many great talents representing it, as did Pankiewicz in his assessments of twentieth-century art.

Along with Cézanne, Bonnard was for us the point of departure in our rebellion against the followers of cubism, who at that time started to swamp the exhibitions with schematic mandolins, perpetually using the same schematic forms and arrangements of the few colors of their impoverished palette. *Des poux sur ma tête—*

*Joseph Chevanard (1808–95) was a disciple of Ingres and a friend of Delacroix, Cornelius, and Overbeck.

lice on my head—Picasso maliciously characterized them. But it was Bonnard's world that opened new paths for us, which seemed more multifaceted because faithful to the Cézanne tradition, which had us all under its spell. Bonnard did not impoverish either color or form but rather enriched them both and created a difficult synthesis of the legacy of impressionism with abstract painting.

Nowadays painters have no idea to what extent studying nature was "frowned upon" in Paris during the years 1924–28. Modern young men and ladies from such places as Krakow and Chicago, with three months study at Lothe's Academy behind them, had already mastered the recipe for half-abstract still lifes and as a rule would show their pictures at the next Salon d'Automne a few months later. A painter who showed an interest in nature and shunned abstract schematism was considered a reactionary.

Bonnard, like Antaeus, always went back to nature, drawing from it the richness of its forms and of its palette.

In the winter of 1925 or 1926 I witnessed a little scene that demonstrated how the disparaging remark by the critic about Bonnard on a tricycle was not an isolated opinion, and to what extent Picasso was "outshining" Bonnard at the time.

I had met Bonnard for the first time a few days before the Kapists' ball, which we organized to take place in the largest available ballroom on the Left Bank of the Seine. I went to Bonnard to sell him tickets. An older man wearing a white apron and wire-framed glasses was standing by the window and poking at something on his palette. The first and almost only impression I had of him was of his naturalness, youthful spontaneity, and unassuming, friendly attitude. He not only bought the tickets then and there but actually came to our ball. Bonnard knew that we were Pankiewicz's disciples and probably did it for his sake. The entire ball was organized in the hope of raising some money to help us to survive in Paris. As a fund-raising venture it was a total fiasco. (I still remember the penny whistles that Józef Jarema, at present the *spiritus movens* of the Polish Art-Club in Rome, had purchased at the last moment with our last 500 francs in order to enliven the proceedings, and Hanka Rudzka-Cybisowa, now a professor at the Krakow Academy of Fine Arts, counting the silverware at noon the next day and weeping bitterly as our "bankruptcy" became evident.) All the walls had been painted for the occasion by

Władysław Waliszewski, Jarema, Jan Cybis, and others. Piotr Potworowski had constructed fanciful ships, and angels fashioned out of sacks filled with sand which we hung from the ceiling. Almost half of Paris attended the ball: Picasso and other celebrated painters, philanthropic countesses with the Polish Embassy in the lead, and fashion models wearing little more than Eve.

I remember Bonnard in a rather wrinkled, old tuxedo. He carefully examined our decorations in the as yet only half-filled rooms, and I still recall with pride his commenting, "Mais c'est très bien, c'est mieux que partout" (It's very nice, better than anywhere). That remark was a sign of spontaneous interest, and sympathy for young people as well, without a trace of temperament or self-importance. At that time he had an exhibition at the Bernheim-Jeune. I still vaguely recall the oranges and violets of the huge still lifes and the shattering effect of the bold and splendid juxtaposition of colors.

It was at our ball that Picasso went over to Bonnard and publicly congratulated him: "What you've shown at your exhibit is better than anything you've done so far." This remark was a magnanimous gesture on the part of the then uncrowned king of painting toward a painter "on a tricycle." And it was understood as such by all the friends of the two painters who were present. I can still see Bonnard's whole face breaking into a joyous, almost childlike smile. Obviously the compliment pleased him enormously. A mutual friend of both painters, Misia Godebska-Sert, who happened to be standing nearby, observed, "What a rascal that Picasso is; he would never pay another painter a compliment that wasn't ambiguous."

One of Bonnard's most characteristic traits was his modesty, which found expression in the childlike purity of his reaction.

It was only in the period 1925–30 that Bonnard's fame in the eyes of the world began to grow year by year, but the growing recognition that was accorded his work was totally free of the tricks, the cunning, and the opportunism so typical of the acclaim given Picasso or even Matisse. What we have here is simply the steadily widening impact of a modest, quiet life lived by a man devoted to painting, and of his unflagging inward joy of life and bedazzlement by nature. Bonnard gives us an entire world of coloristic surprises and plays of tonalities in rubies, amethyst violets, pearl grays, vivid greens, blacks, yellows, blues, and browns.

Whether it be ships in the harbor at Toulon; a nude in a bathtub; a radiator by the window; a table piled with papers; a cat
sitting near a table covered with a tablecloth, bananas, and apples;
or flowers in a room where members of the household are sitting or
have just gone out—each of these pictures leaves in the viewer's
memory a whole gamut of colors which stays with him for years
despite its richness and sophistication.

"Il ne voyait dans l'art que problèmes d'une certaine mathéma-
tique plus subtile que l'autre, que nul n'a su rendre explicite et dont
fort peu de gens peuvent soupçonner l'existence" (Art for him was
simply a series of problems in a kind of mathematics more subtle
than the real one which no one has been able to make explicit and
whose existence few people even suspect). If we omit the word *que*
(simply) from this opinion of Valéry about Degas, it can be fully
applied to Bonnard, but his "mathematics" was inseparably linked
not only to a love of life but also to a rendering of those everyday
happenings of a modest, domestic life which the artist extols amid
all the successes and failures and even his own personal misfortunes. (How much more abstract and less evocative are Cézanne's
"stills" and landscapes.)

Bonnard's wife was afflicted with a serious nervous disorder for
many years. She suffered from frequent fits of madness or persecution mania and allowed almost no one to come near her, forcing
Bonnard to break off relations with many of his friends whom she
did not want to see. Bonnard nursed her himself, never left her side
even in her worst moments, refused to let the doctors put her in a
clinic or an insane asylum, and after her death never allowed anyone to enter the room in which she had died. In an article published
in *Carrefour* (January 1947) Thadée Natanson, one of Bonnard's
lifelong friends, remembers him the way only a dearly loved friend
can be remembered. Natanson reverentially recalls the last summer
they spent together in the south of France by the sea and the joyous
atmosphere of those sunny days they would idle away, sitting in a
café looking at the sea and watching the illuminated bodies of the
bathers. He writes about the extreme emotional reticence of his
friend, who hated to have what was dearest to him even mentioned
in his presence. That is why, after Vuillard's death, even seeing a
picture of his would make Bonnard look away; he could not stand
to look at or talk about the art of a man who had been his colleague

and friend. Likewise, after the death of Ker-Xavier Roussel, one of his closest associates from that splendid *pléiade* of painters of which Bonnard was eventually the only living member, he would not let anyone even tell him the circumstances in which his friend died.

Bonnard's own death (at the age of seventy-nine) was as simple as his life. He died of tuberculosis. In the last days of his life, knowing that death was near, he refused to eat, turned his face to the wall, and said, "Laissez-moi, je ne serai bien que sous les choux" (Let me alone, I won't be happy until I'm in the cabbage patch).

The fact that after Pankiewicz the Kapists were the chief propagators of Bonnard's art in Poland during the 1930s by no means implies that they from the start unreservedly assimilated his style of painting. At first, even for us, directly after our arrival in Paris, Bonnard was clearly overshadowed first of all by the Louvre, and also by Picasso, the Douanier Rousseau, Utrillo, and many others. Waliszewski was one of the first to appreciate Bonnard. (Jan Cybis, another wise and enthusiastic disciple of Bonnard, was more than indifferent to his art for a long time.) A number of Waliszewski's canvases, including both his landscapes and still lifes, have something of Bonnard in them. And yet even Waliszewski's attitude toward Bonnard was subject to many ups and downs. Which brings me to the last conversation I had with Waliszewski, a few days before his death.

The conversation took place in 1936 in Waliszewski's small Krakow studio overlooking the Błonie. We had not seen each other for a long time. That summer Waliszewski had not left Krakow; he was painting a view from his window, a landscape with pinkish clouds and a grayish-green stretch of grass. Both his legs had been amputated many years before. For this man, who now could absorb the world and seek inspiration for his art only through his eyes, being deprived of free movement and the company of others must have been very hard.

On that particular day as we drank a bottle of white wine (I had brought the wine to commemorate the years we had spent together in France), Waliszewski talked passionately about painting and only about painting, moving animatedly in his wheelchair. He complained that he never saw his colleagues' work any more. He assured me that everything that he had done up till then did not "count" and that he was about to begin a new chapter. Perhaps as a reaction against Bonnard, whom he admired so greatly, Waliszewski had started to dream again of form and value. On the easel there was a portrait of a young girl in dark tones that he had just begun to paint and would never finish.

And then, all of a sudden he "jumped on" Bonnard. "Just think about Bonnard," he argued excitedly. "He is wonderful, but his influence in Poland is harmful because his art is too refined, too subtle for our painters. They imitate him, producing 'quaint' oddities, but all of that is alien to us."

Often in the years that followed I thought about Waliszewski's attack against Bonnard, which took on special meaning for me because it was our last conversation. Today I am certain that he was wrong, and that his words were the expression of the normal ebb and flow of sensibility on the part of an artist who now rejects, now embraces the values that he most needs at a particular moment.

Up to 1939 Bonnard's impact on Polish painting was considerable. He enriched us by his example and alerted us to a whole new world of problems by showing us how much can be discovered by looking carefully at nature and how limitless are the possibilities of invention offered by color. If some Polish artists have gone astray in confronting these issues and reacted to Bonnard falsely or superficially, this was an unavoidable "by-product" of his influence. And if I have cited that conversation, one of the many I have had about Bonnard, I did so because it illustrates through Waliszewski's example what a touchy subject the relation of Polish painting to Bonnard was at that time.

Only last month I saw a UNESCO-sponsored exhibition of painting at the Palais Chaillot in Paris. One of the rooms was devoted to modern Polish painting. When the exhibit opened, Bonnard was still alive. I was struck by the truly overwhelming influence of Bonnard, which could be seen and felt in this first postwar presentation of Polish painting abroad. Except for Tadeusz Kantor, who was represented by an interesting canvas depicting human figures against a brutal lemon-yellow background and who clearly has ties to Picasso, almost the entire room was postimpressionist. The green outline of a church tower seen from the window of a Krakow studio depicted on a harmonious canvas by Rudzka-Cybisowa would probably have been inconceivable had it not been for her long familiarity with the work of the impressionists and of

Bonnard. Although a rather unfortunate choice, the still life by Cybis, perhaps the outstanding Polish painter today, showed in its method of execution affinities with both Cézanne and Bonnard. Almost every painting in the exhibition could be connected either directly or indirectly to Bonnard.

Why looking at those pictures did I feel no joy at all?—even though I was convinced that the level of the works presented at the exhibition was in general higher than the level of those shown abroad by Poland twenty years ago, and even though I could see in this fact the result of our pre-1939 "bloody battles" fought over the future of painting, the achievement of the painters once grouped around the journal *Głos plastyków* (Painters' voice).

What I felt was an awareness of the chasm that lies between this painting of nature, joy, and pure color speculation and our reality today. It all reminded me of the "paradise lost" that was the world of our hopes and our painterly reality before the catastrophe. And now, after all we have had to live through, everything I saw at the exhibition seemed to be nothing more than closing one's eyes and stopping one's ears to reality, a kind of "this is my home in my country."

Love and the joy of life were for Bonnard the perennial themes. In his veins flowed the blood of a man who belonged to the French nineteenth century, and who, despite all blows and misfortunes, could love art and live in the world of art, who could exist surrounded by a whole world of the small joys that a reasonably normal life devoid of elemental disasters can provide. We who in newly independent Poland were fighting for an independent art of painting did not believe in the approaching disasters, in genocide, in the forced displacement of millions, in totalitarianism—these problems were still far away and had not as yet invaded our painterly world. We have all paid for our detachment with a sudden awakening. None of us has been spared heavy blows; we have all emerged naked from a burned-out world. Today even the most detached or the most opportunistic of Polish painters cannot blind themselves to the fact that either they are living in their own, occupied, country or else they have been scattered throughout foreign lands.

Looking at the pictures of the UNESCO exhibition I remembered the following passage from Stanisław Brzozowski's diary:

"I do not know what happens in painting, music, and other fields of creativity, but I do know what happens in literature, that is, all forms that are based on the word. In literature dependence on and linkage to an epoch are frightfully subtle, entering into the most fragile connections, in a net of the minutest veins and tissues. . . . Just try to write a comedy à la Ben Jonson, a drama à la Massinger or à la Racine, and if you are a human being capable of feeling deeply and truly, you won't be able to create even a passable illusion. Life would be an easy thing indeed if we could feel *vogelfrei* [free as a bird] to such an extent."

Let us replace "literature" with "painting" and "word" with "color" and the above passage could be applied to painting as well. Here I touch upon the most intricate of intricate themes, that of those "frightfully subtle" connections between painting and its epoch. I want to be properly understood. I don't in the least have in mind what is known as "controlled art," which ruined all of German painting during the Nazi period and all of painting in Bolshevik Russia. Art cannot be controlled or it ceases to be art; it cannot be compelled either by the Nazi whip or the Soviet knout, or even by too rigid demands on the part of the critics. It is entirely a matter for the artists themselves to decide; it depends on their deep instinct and their *unconditional inner freedom.*

When reality undergoes a total change, isn't our perception of it altered to some degree? Is a painter really totally free of those "frightfully subtle" connections with the epoch in which he lives? And if a man's perception is not affected by any such upheavals, is it proof that this vision of his is even stronger than death, or perhaps, simply put, that it is not a vision, but rather the repetition of something that already belongs to the past?

Perhaps the only salvation for humanity is allegiance to a certain vision in spite of reality, so that a person who has been subjected to humiliation and abuse would have a country to which he could return, a country of the "pure" joys that science and art give. If so, then Bonnard's disciples should live as he did in a world of their art and transform every experience and every blow into art so that the viewer gets only the pure elixir of joy. But perhaps not every person is capable of being as loyal or as indifferent. Perhaps among painters, too, an artist will be found who in his art will go

beyond that "paradise," a painter in whom present-day humanity
will find not merely consolations that are

> for truths what curtains are for windows
> on which rest beams of light
> illuminating the linen painted
> with verdant malachite landscapes,
> amethystine streams,
> gauze-robed shepherdesses,
> on earth that has never touched earth!
> They dream the window is a marble flooring!
> They intone: step up unsupported
> into the embrace of mincing fantasy.
> . . . . baubles . . . . baubles!

Was Norwid really "aimless and ailing" when he wrote this
splendid poem filled with bitter irony? In the previous stanza he
wrote,

> I thought we had as many seers
> as painful wounds, which
> by enchanting spell of forms and opportune moment
> dress themselves and heal in time.
> Oh, I've been aimless and ailing myself.

I am besieged by doubts as I write this. Perhaps I too am "aimless and ailing"? In independent Poland we fought for years for the
artists' right to live for art alone, assuming that no great art can ever
be created if it is to be, as Władysław Matejko wanted, a servant to
"more important things." But what can we do if those things—the
more important things as Matejko understood them—by covering
the entire world are so stifling that Bonnard's magnificent still life
strikes us as the manifestation of a "paradise lost," a world that *has
been*.

When for the first time I found myself in London, on my way
back from Russia and the Near East, I was asked to deliver a lecture
to a group of painters from Poland. I was to tell them what had
happened to those who spent the war in Russia or the Near East
and whether and in what circumstances we were able to carry on
our work. Everything I told the audience about our painters deported to Siberia or to Kazakhstan, about the exhibitions we orga-

nized in Baghdad, Jerusalem, or Cairo, was received with interest and friendliness until I began to talk—or rather to think aloud— about the terrible chasm that separated our art from the present-day reality of a Pole, and when I pointed out that unlike some poets who have already given expression to what we Poles have experienced, we painters have as yet failed to find any means by which we could assimilate those experiences into our art and give them plastic expression—perhaps the most transposed in all the arts, but nonetheless an expression of our experiences. Then I noticed ironic smiles and critical glances being exchanged among those present. Several young ladies with impeccable hairdos, who had come to London to paint their "stills" on scholarships provided by the Ministry of Education, looked at me with cool contempt, as though I were a traitor to "pure" art.

It is a sad business if art locks itself in a narrow circle, if it contemptuously rejects vast spheres of life as not belonging to it.

Bonnard, as no painter before or since, expressed the world of happy experiences and enchantments. Along that path he went further than anyone else in the field of the "mathematics of color," and he was firmly rooted in the second half of the nineteenth century, so favorable to the French. What are today's painters who wish to be faithful to Bonnard's memory supposed to do? To paint what he painted and paint as he did?

In one of his chronicles Proust cites the praise that a certain critic gave a contemporary writer: "He writes as well as Voltaire." "It is not true, in order to write as well as Voltaire," Proust says, "one has to write differently to begin with."

These reflections brought about by the death of the greatest of living painters are meant to alert all practicing painters to a problem that no artist responsive to human reality should ever dismiss too lightly or with nonchalance. There is a vast chasm between the world of Bonnard, who has enriched our vision and infected us with a wise love of life and art, between such a Bonnard and present-day reality, a chasm that only an ostrich can pretend not to see. Quite a few Polish painters have already been lost in that chasm.

(July 1947)

TRANSLATED BY JADWIGA KOSICKA

Jarosław Iwaszkiewicz

Dostoevsky

The writers cemetery in Leningrad or, to be more precise, the section of the cemetery called "Literatskiye Mostki," is the cemetery of the former village of Volkova. Here Radishchev—whose grave did not last to our times—was buried. Here lie the great critics: Belinsky, Pisarev, Dobroliubov; here Turgenev, Garshin, Saltykov-Shchedrin, Leskov, and many others are buried as well.

Dostoevsky came to rest in another cemetery, near Aleksandro-Nevskaia Lavra. He has somewhat humbler neighbors here: Krylov, Karamzin, Zhukovsky. His tomb is placed not far from the "musical" corner of the cemetery. Here one's breath is taken away as one reads: Dargomyzski, Mussorgsky, Balakirev, Borodin, Rimsky-Korsakov, Rubinstein, Tchaikovsky. Nearby is the stele of Teodor Stravinsky, father of Igor. As I walk among the graves, the lovely summer's day seems to play the most beautiful music.

It is summer, but here it is still spring; lilacs and lilies of the valley are in bloom. Leningrad lilacs, with branches stiffer than ours, create bouquets with their own peculiar contours. They smell the same, perhaps stronger. "Coin d'un cimetière au printemps"—I recall the sad and monotonous melody of Theodat de Severac.

I also remember a page from a book of French memoirs. "Renan," writes the author,

> said once about Turgenev: "There is no other man who embodies an entire race so perfectly. The whole world lived in him and spoke with his lips; generations of forebears, wordless, lost in the sleep of centuries, came alive through him and through him

spoke . . . ." And isn't this even more true in regard to Mussorgski, Rimsky-Korsakov, Tchaikovsky, Glazunov, Balakirev, Ladov? Songs, operas, ballets, symphonies, works for orchestra and piano, each of these works carries the mark of the land and the nation. In them one rediscovers, beneath their seductive, most enchanting, most eloquent forms, the entire temperament and entire character of the Russian people: their eternal uneasiness, their compelling drives, their indistinct and painful aspirations, their inclination to melancholy, their absorption in death and mystery, their facility for extreme emotions, their passionate instincts, capable of every subtlety and all enthusiasms, their tolerance for suffering and resignation as well as revolt and recklessness, their sensitivity to beauty in nature, its diffuse voices, its soporific or terrifying charm, their unclear premonition of everything that hangs—fatal and dark, tragic and disproportionate—over the Russian landscape, Russian history, and the Russian soul.

These rather dull words in the style of a bygone century, after being filtered through today's literary and philosophical concepts, could be applied instead to someone else: to the writer whose ashes lie not far from the ashes of those great composers. It was not they who captured the greatness of their homeland and the image of their city into a work of imperishable value; it was a writer who elevated this work *aere perennius*.

The tomb of Dostoevsky—a gray granite monument with a fine bust of the writer—lies a little to the side; when we walk up to it, a young worker is restoring the inscription on the stone:

> Verily, verily, I say unto you,
> Except a corn of wheat fall into the ground and die,
> it abideth alone; but if it die, it bringeth forth
> much fruit.
>
> ——John 12.24

The summery, sunny, cheerful Leningrad that surrounds us at this very moment does not correspond to the concept of Petersburg to which Dostoevsky's work is so closely bound. The entire personality of the writer seemed to result from the foggy lanes of the city, born of the white nights on the banks of the canals, coming always from Sienny Targ, like that young man Raskolnikov ("very handsome with beautiful dark eyes, dark blond, with more than average height, slim and graceful"), unable to become concrete in the summery, sumptuous light of day.

(I would like to complain a bit about the extreme changes in the street and square names, in Poland as well as in Leningrad. The old-fashioned Siennaia Ploshchad' corresponds exactly to the name Sienny Targ. Helena Szymanowska, older sister of Celina, notes in her diary that she used to go there at six in the morning with Adam Mickiewicz to buy potatoes. Now this square is called Peace Square, almost like the Place de la Concorde; how inappropriate a name for a square that is no less historical. The same goes for the street Millionnaia—which sounded so inviting to the ear of Balzac and Madame Hańska, who lived there—now changed to Khalturin Street.)

Petersburg never ceased to fascinate Dostoevsky. The writer offers no detailed description of the city as Balzac would have done, but this city, probably the strangest, most peculiar, and most fascinating European city, is present in his stories and novels. I would say that Petersburg and Raskolnikov are the chief protagonists of *Crime and Punishment*.

Yet this Petersburg is strange.

The author of a book on Dostoevsky's poetics writes about *Crime and Punishment:* "It is characteristic that the very setting for the action of the novel—*Petersburg* (its role in the novel is enormous)—is on the borderline between existence and non-existence, reality and fantasmagoria, always on the verge of dissipating like the fog and vanishing. Petersburg too is devoid, as it were, of any internal grounds for justifiable stabilization; it too is on the threshold."*

The city-phantasmagoria appears in literature later as well. Andrei Bely tries to re-create the fantastical aspect of the city in his novel *Petersburg*. But he does this in a childishly naive way—like with the car with the yellow Mongols that circles the city.

Of course for us this other—Dostoevsky's—city has fantastical characteristics simply because of the different historical context in

---

*Mikhail Bakhtin, *Problems of Dostoevsky's Poetics*, ed. and trans. Caryl Emerson (Minneapolis: University of Minnesota Press, 1984), p. 167.—TRANS.

which we examine it. Dostoevsky's Petersburg was a city of a different reality.

Raskolnikov "wandered along the bank of the Ekaterinsky Canal [today Griboyedov's Canal] for half an hour or more and looked several times at the steps running down to the water, but he could not think of carrying out his plan; either rafts stood at the steps' edge, and women were washing clothes on them, or boats were moored there, and people were swarming everywhere. Moreover he could be seen and noticed from the banks on all sides."*

Today Griboyedov's Canal belongs more to phantasmagoria than it did then, with its rafts and washerwomen. Nor do the saloons, ale houses, and stalls surrounding Sienny Targ exist, except for the entrance nooks, basement windows, and doors with bells that probably sound the same as they did at the old pawnbroker's.

Yet Dostoevsky's fascination with Petersburg was something quite exceptional. "In 'Petersburg Vision in Verse and Prose' (1861), Dostoevsky recalls the unique and vivid carnival sense of life experienced by him at the very beginning of his career as a writer. This was above all a special sense of Petersburg, with all its sharp social contrasts, as a 'fantastic magical daydream,' as 'dream,' as something standing on the boundary between reality and fantastic invention."†

Bakhtin compares Dostoevsky's sense of Petersburg with the significance of Paris for Balzac. Of course, he claimed that the Russian poet's sense of the city was more profound, but all comparisons are off the mark. Paris for Balzac was something different than what Petersburg was for Dostoevsky. Rastignac's challenge to Paris from the slopes of Père Lachaise—"Maintenant à nous deux"—is in no way similar to Raskolnikov's. Raskolnikov's chimerical challenge thrown to Petersburg is the challenge of a weak neurasthenic who does not believe in his own strength and must murder to believe in his own "might." Dostoevsky's commentators interpret this matter in all possible ways.

"I term my experience on the shores of the Neva a vision," remarks Dostoevsky. And it is not the dreams—Raskolnikov's

*Crime and Punishment, trans. Constance Garnett (New York: Bantam Books, 1958), p. 96.—TRANS.
†Bakhtin, Dostoevsky's Poetics, p. 161.

dreams are too realistic—that are the "vision": both the one in the bushes on Krestovsky Island about the killing of the horse and the one about the repeated murder of the old pawnbroker. But the "realistic" image of Svidrigailov's wanderings through nocturnal Petersburg, through rain and mud, the description of the squalid little hotel that is the last shelter of the nocturnal nobleman, and even the sums of money Svidrigailov carries are a complete phantasmagoria and belong rather to the area of dreams, far from an accountant's realism.

Bakhtin emphasizes Dostoevsky's sensitivity to social contrast; but it is worth noting that next to Petersburg's basement tenements and cheap inns, suspect hotels and miserable student quarters, the Petersburg of palaces and residences, fine equipage, and elegant ladies like Anna Karenina does not exist.

This is a Petersburg of nightmares, reminiscent of Goya's apparitions (let us compare, for example, the description of the pawnbroker Alona and her sister with Goya's portrait of two old women in the Lille Civic Museum), a Petersburg of terrifying people. And when the author writes that Raskolnikov and Dunia were beautiful, one has a hard time believing it.

Svidrigailov's last bit of meandering through Petersburg shows us the whole city as it was then—from its northern to eastern neighborhoods, from its canals to its ruins, to the Moyka, to Fontanka—and all in a dismal autumnal downpour, submerged in an unending night. For Petersburg is not only white nights but black days.

(I don't know if in studies of Dostoevsky—I have read too few of them—someone has attempted a detailed analysis of the names he has given his characters. What "rudiments" do they conceal? Why, for instance, Raskolnikov—from the heretical but fascinating Old Believers? Why Svidrigailov? Just one more trace of the Lithuanian-Polish phobia of this half-squire, half-Orthodox who will not forgive a Pole; he even gave poor Aglaia Epanchina a Polish swindler of a husband at the conclusion of *The Idiot*. Isn't this Svidrigailov some remnant of Lithuanian forebears, fictional to be sure, but so often encountered ["my *babushka* was Polish"]. Perhaps this is one of those false Poles swarming around Petersburg, like the Korwin-Krukowski sisters, like Kublicki-Piotuch, the future stepfather of Blok.)

Dostoevsky never reaches for the aristocracy. The hero of another "Petersburg tale," Prince Myshkin, is an underdeveloped scrawny creature who in no way, despite his title, belongs to "society." Dostoevsky, in seeing the marketplaces, stores, workshops, inns, Orthodox churches (let us note that he does not depict and never *describes* normal interiors), does not see what we see every step of the way in Leningrad: he does not see its beautiful palaces.

There is, however, a certain merchant's house with which Dostoevsky has very strong associations. The moment we see this building we get a cold chill down our backs. Its description makes it a most vivid apparition. The house is also a vision of Petersburg, more spectacular in *The Idiot* than in *Crime and Punishment.*

> As he approached the point where the two streets intersect, he was surprised himself at his extraordinary emotion; he had not expected his heart to throb so painfully. One house attracted his attention in the distance, no doubt from its peculiar appearance, and Myshkin afterwards remembered saying to himself, "That must be the very house!" With great curiosity he walked towards it to verify his conjecture; he felt that he would for some reason particularly dislike to have guessed right. It was a large gloomy house of three stories, of a dirty green color and no pretensions to architecture. A few houses of this kind, built at the end of the last century, are still standing almost unchanged in those streets of Petersburg (where everything changes so quickly). They are build solidly with thick walls and a very few windows, often with gratings on the ground-floor windows. . . . Without and within, the house is somehow inhospitable and frigid; it seems to be keeping something dark and hidden; and why it seems so from the mere look of the house it would be hard to explain. Architectural lines have, of course, a secret of their own.*

One can imagine what Dostoevsky would say today if in 1868, the year of writing *The Idiot,* he wrote that everything was changing so rapidly in Petersburg. Today these changes are happening at a gallop. But Leningrad has maintained its hallucinatory aspect to the present. Maybe there is a concrete reason for this—the configuration of the terrain: the completely level area on which the city is built where everything seems flattened and the visible propensity

---

The Idiot, trans. Constance Garnett (New York: Bantam Books, 1958), p. 197.—TRANS.

for vertical lines; the needles of the Admiralty, the Peter and Paul fortress, even more emphasized by the columns in front of the Winter Palace. The great palaces opening up in river perspectives seem very low, they are fixed to the ground by expanses of blue or green color and the powerful triumphant current of the Neva, which is unlike any other river in the world. The dense, leaden, undulating water renders the proportions of the buildings insignificant.

Dostoevsky does not notice the Petersburg palaces. But this simple, grim, gray-green building fascinates both him and us.

It is Rogozhin's house. The interior of this house is the setting for *The Idiot* and the only scene like it in nineteenth-century literature. Having, "of course, a secret of its own" but one difficult to explain. This great devastating scene, which one reads with an awful shudder, has something of an operatic finale to it, something of a tragic drama. Nastasya Filipovna's corpse is screened from the audience with a curtain, her friends sit on a pile of cushions in front of the curtain, reconciled at last and finding some sort of unearthly tranquillity . . . in the crime.

Dostoevsky does not prepare us for this. He merely draws our attention to it. On the first floor the uncurtained windows of the apartment of Rogozhin's mother. On the left the drawn curtains. One of them is raised on a memorable scene. An enormous, empty apartment, in it an old woman on the right, the corpse of Nastasya Filipovna on the left—and those two alone for the whole night. And also the mysterious picture, *The Deposition*. Astounding.

Apparently Dostoevsky began writing the whole novel by first creating this final scene. The whole novel, like a river, like the Neva, plunges toward this scene, everything is subordinated to this scene—it is the culminating moment. And this "dirty green" house in Petersburg is the omen of that extraordinary deed. The omen of a terrible happiness.

The dominating motifs of green flicker across the entire composition of *The Idiot*, just like the little green bench in Pavlovski Park upon which Aglaia conducts her young ladies conferences. And in general it is the motif of Pavlovsk as a park, as greenery—its motif of garden music, everything that is happening in Pavlovsk, exactly these caprices of Aglaia, the meeting on the terrace at Prince Myshkin's, Hippolit's confessions, the marriage *manqué* of Nastasya Filipovna; and the whole role of Nastasya Filipovna in Pavlovsk, where she acts as if she were in a forest, has a romp in the carriage, and bothers people gathered at the "station" or in the *kurzal**—that penetrates the whole novel. And those tall, green trees, which play such a great role in the last weeks of Hippolit's life, which are at the same time the last conscious weeks of Prince Myshkin's life.

"I am glad that all this happened in Pavlovsk," says Hippolit, one of the most mysterious characters ever created by Dostoevsky. "At least one can look at the leaves on the trees."

Everyone to Pavlovsk! "It is beautiful and heavenly and green and cheap and musical, that is why everyone goes to Pavlovsk."

All that seaside greenery, fresh, as one sees in Pavlovsk, suddenly illuminates half of Dostoevsky's novel. When we stand there on the hill over the exquisitely planned park, when we look at the old trees, when we recall that here every summer Fitelberg directed his orchestra, Paweł Kochański played on his violin, Russian and Polish *symfoniki* were played, all those splendid composers I mentioned in the beginning, I begin to understand Dostoevsky's words differently: "And green, and cheap, and heavenly, and musical. . . ."

In Pavlovsk, Mickiewicz visited Zhukovsky. We know nothing more about the visit except that it happened. The writers accompanying me point out a villa where Leningrad writers live from June to September. The old traditions have survived the war, the revolution, and the monstrous blockade. In the summer one goes to Pavlovsk because it is heavenly and cheap. The music, unfortunately, has been neglected at Pavlovsk. But the other, green, tradition lives on.

It seems to me that there exists a mysterious bond between the city, its environs, and the world Dostoevsky creates. This world is justifiably called a "vision." But it is sometimes imposingly real, like in a dream (let us take Hippolit's dream—less realistic than Raskolnikov's dreams and yet so revoltingly real when the bitch Norma bites the repulsive centipede to pieces), as if in a dream we were seeing stores, tiny, piled with cheap merchandise, stores where Prince Myshkin sees a certain object in the window; we do

*From German *Kursaal* (waiting room).

not yet know what the object is and already we are filled with dread. Then we find out that this thing costs sixty-five kopeks. We may have an idea of what it is but we banish the thought. And it is only later, somewhat reluctantly, that the author tells us that this object is a knife. A knife like the one that Myshkin plays with in Rogozhin's room, taking it from the desk of his friend and asking him if he uses it to cut pages. This is how we become acquainted with the knife Rogozhin uses to murder Nastasya Filipovna. We do not know exactly why he murders her. Jealousy does not suffice. "Why, we always kill the person we love. . . ."

> When at last they turned on opposite sides of the road into Gorohovy and began to approach Rogozhin's house, Myshkin's legs began to give way under him again, so that it was almost difficult for him to walk. It was about ten o'clock in the evening. The windows in the old lady's part of the house were still open as before; in Rogozhin's they were all closed, and in the twilight the white curtains over them seemed still more conspicuous.*

This image of the streets of Petersburg—having nothing of a carnival atmosphere about them—haunt us without respite. Great art can sometimes become a burden impossible to bear.

(1976)

TRANSLATED BY LILLIAN VALLEE

*The Idiot, p. 587.

Józef Wittlin

Sorrow and Grandeur of Exile

The remarks I now take the liberty of presenting to you constitute an introduction to an essay on which I have been working, unfortunately with great interruptions, since the end of the war. This essay should be a kind of outline of a physiology of émigré literature.

When I say *essay,* I deliberately employ that word in its literal meaning, for we are used to define by that term any study of literary or artistic criticism, and the very name of this club of which I am privileged to be a member and under whose auspices I am speaking here contains the word essayist. P.E.N.—playwrights, poets, essayists, novelists. However, in the strict sense of the word an essay is nothing but an attempt, and an essayist is a writer who only *tries to do* something. He tries to find a formula, a meaning of a certain phenomenon. And we know that the distance from the attempt to the final execution of an idea is very long. Even the work of Montaigne, which is something much greater than its title indicates, or John Locke's memorable *Essay Concerning Toleration* or his *Essay Concerning Human Understanding* does not absolve us from the obligation of modesty and from the duty of restoring to the word essay its original sense.

Thus in the essay to which the present talk is the introduction I am trying only to establish certain principles or laws governing the life and death of literary creativity in exile.

Ours is not a voluntary emigration, not one of free choice, but one to which writers are forced by bitter necessity, by a catastrophe, by the ruin of their nations. Or by opposition, that is, the need of actively resisting the calamity, and the hope of victory accompanying that need. In any event it is a condition of peril, of danger, if not to the writer's physical person, then to his literary personality and to his creative work, that was the cause of his staying away from his native country. But exile is not always associated with gloomy images of people driven out by the whip of other people, for among writers there are many exiles whom no one has driven out. They left their native country themselves, refusing to submit to conditions they would have been unable to bear.

I have also used the term *physiology of literature*. This term is not my invention. I owe it to the eminent French critic Albert Thibaudet, who died twenty-one years ago and to whom in addition I owe many other things. As far as I remember Thibaudet was the first to use the expression physiology in connection with literature.

However, before discussing literary creativity in exile, before considering the specific laws governing that creativity and causing émigré literature to be different from the literature developing in the exiles' countries of origin, let us ponder the meaning of the word *exile* itself.

At the close of the last war, that is, in the spring of 1945, Thomas Mann was celebrating his seventieth birthday in New York. During the observance in his honor he delivered an address in which among other things he explained the common origin of the English word *alien* (which derives from the Latin *alienus*) and of the German *Elend*. *Elend* once meant the same as alien land. Today it exclusively means misery, poverty. And yet to be an alien is not always unpleasant and not every alien feels a pauper either in the material or in the moral sense of that sad word. The fact of staying in a foreign country thanks to a regular visa in one's passport or without a visa (which is the privilege of American citizens in almost all European countries) not only is not regrettable, but on the contrary often causes the envy of many people residing in their own country but unable to afford traveling in foreign countries. Aga Khan, for instance, is an alien in France, where he has been residing for many years, but it is hard to imagine him as a pauper. It is true that today this old man arouses our sympathy, for he is paralyzed. Recently we have seen his picture in the magazines: Aga sits in a wheelchair, and next to him stands a young lady of exquisite beauty, his companion and nurse. But as a paralyzed person, Aga Khan would arouse pity even in his home country and not only on the French Riviera. If, however, thanks to the common etymology of the words alien and *Elend,* even Aga Khan has something to do with misery, what could be said of the real exile?

In the beautiful antiphon Salve Regina sung in Catholic churches, we twice find the word exile. The author of the antiphon first calls all of mankind "exsules filii Haevae" and then he qualifies our earthly life as "exilium." From where have we been exiled? Since early childhood I have been haunted, or rather followed, by the image of an angel with a fiery sword. This was a reproduction of some baroque or rococo engraving on copper or steel, I don't remember which. Obviously this is the angel that expels Adam and Eve from Paradise, and the devout author of the antiphon Salve Regina had in mind just that kind of exile.

Consequently, if we assume this view, we owe it to our first parents that our stay on this earth, regardless of where it is and regardless of whether we are happy or unhappy, is exile. Exile from a country in which we have never been ourselves. The same doctrine that makes us believe that our earthly stay is exile nevertheless gives us the hope that when this exile will pass and we shall have fulfilled some difficult but indispensable requirements, we will be permitted to return to the place from which our first parents were exiled.

In our, and not only in our, time there are plenty of people who do not want to consider temporal life as exile, either from Paradise or from anywhere else, although not for everybody is that life full of charm and sweetness. On the contrary, precisely those whom temporal life does not spare disappointments and sufferings, those who should hate that life, are most strongly attached to it. Many people also do not derive any encouragement from their consciousness that some time after this exile—*post hoc exilium,* to use the words of the author of Salve Regina—they will be able to stay in their true country, not only temporarily but forever. It would be hard to demand from such people that they should long for Paradise, that is, for something they do not know. They regard only their stay on earth as real; here and only here is their home, no matter what kind, a splendid palace or a ramshackle hut. Only here on earth does their life go on, no matter what kind, good or bad.

And often they sacrifice this life in order to renovate their home, if not for themselves, then for their descendants. And even if they do not succeed in this, even if their whole existence is only a series of disappointments and failures, they have no intention of giving up their earthly citizenship. They do not try at all to obtain their first citizenship papers for eternity. Such people know well, and if they do not know, they feel, that their stay on earth is not durable. In spite of this, they behave in such a way as if it were to last forever, as if the purpose of their life were life itself. Consciously or unconsciously, these people are existentialists of various nonreligious shades. But let us assume that these people are greatly mistaken, and the author of the antiphon Salve Regina, as well as numerous authors of other texts, in verse and prose, expressing a kindred view of the world and of the beyond, is right. If it is true that our entire life is exile, we, the members of the International P.E.N. Club in Exile, are double exiles, and who knows whether the nucleus of the grandeur of our situation does not lie in that consciousness. But let us not hurry.

The view has been often voiced, and not only by political émigrés, that any major artist and truly creative mind is a foreigner in his own country. The very fact of his distinctiveness or nonsolidarity with common sense, the fact that everything that the artist brings with himself is unusual, sometimes odd, and mostly foreign to his closest environment, makes him an exile. He is an exile even if he lives in the same, his own, home from birth to death. We will not give here the long list of names of those heroic or tragic solitary minds who only after their departure from this world have become close and dear to that world and who only *post hoc exilium* have ceased to be exiles in their own society. Almost every nation takes pride in its *poètes maudits*, its Edgar Allan Poe, Baudelaire, Rimbaud, Hart Crane. Every nation has its van Gogh or Cézanne. You see, I could not refrain from quoting names. Since, therefore, every man as long as he lives is an exile, and almost every artist, poet, or writer is an exile because he sees and expresses the world in his own way, we, the members of the International P.E.N. Club in Exile, American Branch, are three-fold exiles. In my estimation, this is not only a misfortune but also a privilege, which we are going to discuss later on. But certainly no one will deny that artists are able to throw proper light on many matters of our earthly life, that only poets are able to look at *la condition humaine* from a proper distance. A perfect distance or perspective is created for them by their lost country. I say "country" in order not to abuse the title of Milton's masterpiece.

But let us go down to earth, where political emigration, that is, exile, is above all a misfortune. He who makes out of that misfortune a religion for himself will not be saved. Far removed from glory is he who is unable to overcome that misfortune but considers exile a normal form of existence beyond which there is only nothingness.

An outstanding contemporary writer, E. M. Cioran, a Rumanian exile living in Paris and writing in French, the author of the fascinating books *Précis de décomposition* and *Syllogisme de l'amertume,* winner of the Prix Rivarol, a prize for foreigners writing in French, has devoted extremely acute observations to our problem. Among other things, Cioran considers the fate of the poet in exile, and fears that that fate may bring the poet to like his exile. "No one is able to conserve the youth of his sorrows," says Cioran. "Sadness wears off. So it is also with longing for one's country, with nostalgia. Inspiration dries out in the poet as a result of lack of variety in his experiences, and lack of authenticity of his anxieties." Obviously, exile in the purely lay and brutal meaning of the word is not exclusively a matter of the writer, who, as we know, is already an exile because of his vocation. Not only writers feel the sorrow and grandeur of exile.

Recently I had the opportunity of seeing Shakespeare's *Richard II* played by the Old Vic Company. (I am a little afraid to speak about Shakespeare in the presence of such an authority on Shakespeare as Miss Marchette Chute, the president of the American P.E.N. Club, who has written several outstanding works about Elizabethan literature.) In the third scene of act I, King Richard II condemns the Duke of Norfolk to lifelong exile. As far as we know, the Duke of Norfolk was not a literary man, and yet after hearing the royal verdict he bursts forth with the following lament:

> The language I have learn'd these forty years,
> My native English, now I must forego:
> And now my tongue's use is to me no more
> Than an unstring'd viol or a harp,

Or like a cunning instrument cas'd up,
Or, being open, put into his hands
That knows no touch to tune the harmony:
Within my mouth you have engaol'd my tongue,
Doubly portcullis'd with my teeth and lips;
And dull, unfeeling, barren ignorance
Is made my gaoler to attend on me.
I am too old to fawn upon a nurse.
Too far in years to be a pupil now:
What is thy sentence, then, but speechless death,
Which robs my tongue from breathing native breath?

If the Duke of Norfolk so much regrets the loss of his native language that threatens him in exile, how painful is it for the writer? Even writers staying in exile in countries where the common language is their own do not feel quite at home there—for instance, Spanish writers in the countries of Latin America. Unfortunately we no longer live in a world in which Greek or Latin is the common instrument of poetry and prose among the enlightened elite of various nations, regardless of whether they are large or small. Today we live in a world in which even the Icelandic language makes the same demands on the contemporary writer in Iceland and produces among his fellow citizens the same response as the English language does in Great Britain or in the United States. And yet the Icelandic language is used only by a hundred thousand people.

To uproot a writer from the soil on which he lived for a longer or shorter period of time in a symbiosis with the language of that soil can be a cruel act of violence. To be cut off from one's native stem is painfully felt even by writers who are staying outside their country temporarily and voluntarily. For instance, Dostoevsky wrote from Vevey in Switzerland to Nikolai Nikolayevich Strakhov: "With regard to my work here, I obviously will lag behind as far as the knowledge of what is happening at home is concerned (although I know about this better than you because every day I read three Russian newspapers from cover to cover and I get two periodicals), but I will get away from the living current of existence, and this is bound to affect my literary work!"

Dostoevsky is not a typical example of a writer who finds it difficult to live uprooted from his native soil. He did not write the words quoted above as an exile but as a traveler in Western Europe, which he disliked. He spent four years in it, but not much of that West found its way into his work. Dostoevsky walked the streets of Berlin and Dresden as if he were wearing blinkers. He could not stand the Germans nor did he show any desire to become more intimately acquainted with their life, civilization, and culture. His rather unfavorable opinion of the culture of Western Europe had been formed before he set out for the West. It is true that in Dresden he visited museums and art galleries. But more than by museums he felt attracted by gambling casinos. Purportedly to improve his health, the author of *The Gambler* went to Wiesbaden and to the Swiss spa of Saxon-les-Bains, where there were not only therapeutic waters but also a famous casino. Besides roulette and silhouettes of gamblers, the most important "echo" in the great novels of Dostoevsky's stay in Western Europe are the guillotine in Lyons and the last moments of a condemned man. We hear about this from Prince Myshkin in *The Idiot*. Obviously, Dostoevsky was more interested in what a man thinks a few minutes before his head is cut off than in the people surrounding the guillotine, than in the city of Lyons and France in general. The four years of his stay in the West flowed off Dostoevsky like brackish and impure water. However, perhaps without these four years we would have had neither Ivan Karamazov nor "The Story of the Grand Inquisitor," even though Dostoevsky had brought his dislike for the West and for Catholicism from Russia.

If, therefore, during those four years outside Russia his imagination drew some sustenance from what was going on around it, this sustenance was, if one may say so, full of "negative vitamins." Because even in the West, Dostoevsky lived by Russia and in the Russian manner probed the depths of Russian souls. The fact that the scene of the criminal's execution—which, like Myshkin, the hero of the *The Idiot*, Dostoevsky saw in Basel in some illustrated magazine—made such a shocking impression on him is not exclusively a memory of his trip to Western Europe. The author of the *The Idiot* had himself once stood on the scaffold as a convict, not in Lyons but in Russia, and he was not to be guillotined but shot. Thus from the West Dostoevsky brought to his work what had long suited it. Consequently he was not threatened with the barrenness of which he had such nervous fear at Vevey when writing that letter to Strakhov. Uprooting or barrenness threatens rather the artist who easily and willingly yields to the fascination of a foreign world but is unable to assimilate it in such a way that the foreign environment becomes consummate material for him. Some artists even make an effort that their works should have the fewest possible elements of the life of their country. They roam the world in search of exoticism, foreign color, and foreign *condition humaine*. We do not speak here of those who professionally engage in travelogues. Let us look, for example at Hemingway's work. In his major books the characters operate mostly in non-American lands, if they are Americans at all. We see them in Italy, Spain, France, Africa, Cuba. Hemingway himself has probably spent a major portion of his exuberant life outside the United States. For many years he has been residing in Cuba, whence he sets out to various parts of the globe in search of unusual impressions. He doubtless finds it useful to remain outside his native land, from which, as far as we know, no one has expelled him.

The Pole Witold Gombrowicz has been living for the past eighteen years in Argentina, but there he does not stop thinking in his own, very specific manner about Poland and the Poles. In an interesting polemic with the previously mentioned Rumanian émigré Cioran, Gombrowicz rightly says that "it makes no difference in which spot of the world writers toil," because "every prominent writer as a result of his prominence was a foreigner even in his home country." The bitter taste of this truth is familiar to all true creators of new values in art, even if they are members of Academies or Nobel Prize winners.

In Spanish, there exists for describing an exile the word *destierro,* a man deprived of his land. I take the liberty to forge another term, *destiempo,* a man deprived of his time. That means, deprived of the time that now passes in his country. The time of the exile is different. Or rather the exile lives in two different times simultaneously, in the present and in the past. This life in the past is sometimes more intense than his life in the present and tyrannizes his entire psychology. This has its good and bad aspects. An exile living in the past is threatened by many dangers. For instance, by the danger of pining for trifling things whose real or alleged charm has gone forever. He is threatened by the danger of pining even for the stage properties employed by older, today no longer living, worlds. In the normal, pre-exile world, these stage properties were not worthy of any attention. I am going to give you an example from my own experience. In 1950 in New York I often stopped before the window of a certain antique shop on Lexington Avenue. There were ancient armor, weapons, helmets and shakos there. My attention was particularly attracted by the shako of an officer of the Imperial and Royal Austro-Hungarian Fourth Regiment of Uhlans. Before World War I that regiment was stationed in my home town. However, please do not think that I served in that regiment. I was only a simple infantry man. In a normal existence, daydreaming at the sight of such a shako would be dangerous infantilism. But in 1950 in New York, after World War II and during the Korean War, I confess it without false shame, that Uhlan's shako produced nostalgia. Nostalgia for what? For the Austro-Hungarian cavalry? For the army in general? Nothing of the kind. Only nostalgia for the past. For a world that ceased to exist in 1914, and which might have been better than the present one. But perhaps it was only better in our imagination or illusion. That shako aroused nostalgia for the old Europe, for the colorfulness of its life, for the sense of security, false as it might have been, and last but not least, for our own youth. Such fixation on a stage property that is useless today is one of the dangers lurking for a writer in exile. Each of us is threatened by some shako or other, and together with that shako we are threatened by a false evaluation of bygone events and forgotten people. The writer in exile is also threatened by the disappearance of his ability to select reminiscences as material suitable for literary adaptation.

The life of the exile, like the life of any other person, speeds onward to its end, but an exile professionally as it were, moves backward. Hence, serious and even tragic conflicts often arise. It happens that the émigré lives in a complete vacuum, which his imagination fills exclusively with phantoms of a dead world. Not every writer in exile is a Proust or a Joyce or a Polish Mickiewicz. They bravely engaged in *la recherche du temps perdu*, not in order to glorify the past, but in order to unmask it mercilessly, or, like Mickiewicz, to play with it forbearingly. Let us therefore call this segment of our research in the physiology of literature in emigration "the boon and the curse of retrospection."

The boon is as great as the curse. In his book on James Joyce, Professor Harry Levin rightly says: "The first principle of artistic economy was isolation. Joyce had detached himself from his nationality and his religion, but he found his medium, his language, pointing back to them." Joyce was a voluntary émigré, a so-called expatriate, and who knows whether it was not precisely because he spent the greater part of his life in Paris, Trieste, and Zurich, and not in his native Dublin, that he created an authentic great style and original language of his own.

On the other hand, cases are known in which a writer cut off from his people and staying for a long time far from his country suffers serious losses because of this. For instance, Turgenev. His two novels *Smoke* and *Virgin Soil* in which, during his long stay in Paris, he tries to depict the current life of Russia "only show the depth of his bitterness and his complete loss of touch with contemporary Russia," according to the *Encyclopaedia Britannica*.

An exiled writer lives in a restricted society in which it is not easy to create, and especially to publish, revolutionizing works. Such a restricted society most gladly listens to that which it already knows, and it demands from the artist primarily a confirmation of its own views. Therefore, it is difficult for an émigré writer to impose his own taste on the émigré society. Woe to him if he yields! He will do best if he isolates himself from his fellow émigrés and renounces popularity among them. Because if in a normal society each artist is threatened by the danger whose name is "desire to please," that danger is a hundred times greater in a restricted, ghettolike society, condemned to rely on its own strength and resources. In the emigration there almost always occurs a confusion of concepts and criteria. There are no real yardsticks for measuring the true value of a writer's work. That value is determined mostly by sentimental considerations. As the duration of exile becomes extended, and as literature moves further away from the life of its nation, even comparatively young writers, who have not broken with the language of their fathers, change into chatterers. Separation from the problems of his time may nevertheless be salutary for a writer, even for one who lives in his own country. Because everyone who is too passionately rooted in his time may become its slave, may become a prisoner of his time. Woe to the writer sentenced to life imprisonment in his time. Only a *destiempo* can be really free. He has received the treasure of freedom automatically, without a special effort on his part. Every prominent writer, even one whose ambition is to reflect his time, strives to jump over that time, stating that he wishes to produce values not conditioned by time: the so-called eternal values. A *destierro-destiempo* writer should start his real career with this.

The question of language. If we assume that the language of a people undergoes changes depending on the life of that people, in exile we have at our disposal only such elements of that language (*a*) which we have brought from home, (*b*) which have been produced abroad by former émigrés, and (*c*) which we ourselves create in exile. Therefore, our language no longer comprises the elements that have arisen at home during our absence, even though we diligently follow what is written there. We know the living speech of our country at second hand from reading.

In exile, we may also observe an interesting phenomenon that I would call the return of words. Words forgotten, no longer used in present life, return themselves to our present consciousness. They return as memories. Only their purely sonorous content, from which life has evaporated, remains. Such a word is no longer the voice of life, but its echo. It is an empty shell in which, however, one may hear the hum of the sea, the hum of life. If we put it to our ears, it still rings, sometimes even more beautifully than before, when it was filled with a living organism. Such a word also often means something else than it used to mean in one's native land. Thus the imagination of the exile is filled not only with memories of places and people left behind, memories of events, but also with memories of words heard only before his exile. Such words haunt a writer like shadows, like phantoms. After some time these shadows begin to live a life of their own and become myths. Every writer in exile possesses a whole store of such verbal myths. There also begins to operate in a writer, and especially in a poet, a peculiar magic of words that in everyday life mean nothing, or almost nothing. It is up to us to use this magic. And again, please think of Joyce, who, far from his Ireland, and far from England, created whole cosmoses from words invented or transformed by himself.

The Rumanian thinker Cioran considers the fate of a writer who in exile works in a foreign language. He himself writes, as you know, not in Rumanian but in French. He reaches the following conclusion: "He who abandons his language for another changes his personality, commits heroic treason, breaking with his past,

and to a certain extent, with himself." Cioran sees only two forms
of release for a poet in exile. In his opinion, these forms are radically contradictory; they are humor and faith. "Depending on this
temperament," says Cioran, "the poet devotes himself to piety or
sarcasm." I do not understand why humor cannot be reconciled
with faith. Léon Bloy, for instance, was a man of profound faith,
and yet in his works there is no lack of bitter sarcasm. Nor do I see
why we should leave humor exclusively to the Devil. It is one of the
false legends of the end of the nineteenth century that Heaven is
hopelessly boring, while Hell is an extremely interesting intellectual club, something like a super P.E.N. club. The spread of that
legend was considerably helped by G. B. Shaw's splendid play *Man
and Superman.* For me boredom itself is Hell.

Nor can I share Cioran's view that exile is a school of folly. To
be sure, all of us émigrés are slightly crazy, but many an émigré
writer has found himself, his mission, his proper role, and has
created truly outstanding works precisely in exile. It suffices to
recall here the great achievements of the German émigrés from the
period of 1933 to 1945. Exile is not always a school of folly. On the
contrary, it can be a school of reason, of a clear and penetrating
view of the world. In his own country, at home, in the hubbub of
public life, the writer encounters insuperable obstacles on the way
to a clear evaluation of the phenomena of that life, and he is often
unable to perceive its inner truth. Only in exile does he recognize
them. Thus, often a person acquires only in prison the treasure of
inner freedom, the ability of detachment. As did Guillaume Apol-
linaire, who felt truly free in the solitary cell of the Paris Santé
prison and exclaimed in his poem *A la Santé (VI):*

> Nous sommes seuls dans ma cellule
> Belle clarté Chère raison.

Even Sartre, when he was still seeking *Les chemins de la liberté,*
the roads of freedom, in the second volume of his cycle in the novel
Le sursis, had one of his heroes exclaim, "La liberté c'est l'exile et je
suis condamné à être libre." All of us in exile can repeat after
Matthieu Delarue, that hero of Sartre's novel, "I am condemned to
be free." Indeed—an émigré writer, if he wishes to, may have unlimited freedom. His isolation, often intolerable, nevertheless also
contains elements indispensable for truly free creative work. Soli-

tude cools our passions but also sharpens our perspicacity. It is an invaluable treasure, and even a writer who regards himself as a leader of people, a prophet, only in solitude finds that message which he later carries to the people from his desert hermitage. Solitude is a miraculous soil in which the ability of an objective view of human affairs is born. However even a writer is not free from ambition or vanity. In exile he should persuade himself that one may be a star only in an authentic and not an artifical firmament. And exile permits him to shine only in an imagined sky, or rather in a decoration representing the sky.

How do you spell your name? A foreigner is constantly confronted with such a question. A writer usually likes his name, values it, and considers that his name at least should be known if it is not popular or appreciated. The question "how do you spell your name?" does not cause him pleasure. Some even consider it an insult. It is true that we know émigré writers whose names have won fame only in exile. For instance, Arthur Koestler owes his fame to the very fact of exile. But as a rule, the majority of writers in exile have anonymous status, and most of them feel it as sorrow. We are not going to analyze this fact. Let us rather turn our attention to the favorable aspects of a writer's anonymity. Exile, where he is unknown, may offer him an excellent opportunity of confronting his own opinion of himself with what he really represents. He can compare his works with those of his indigenous colleagues. Such a confrontation often leads him to lethal megalomania, or produces in him an equally lethal inferiority complex. According to psychoanalysts that complex is allegedly also a child of megalomania.

Let us, however, think of the virtues of those great artists who centuries ago decorated the Byzantine basilicas with mosaics, built Romanesque and Gothic cathedrals, and in these cathedrals put stained glass windows and outsized images of saints and martyrs. Not only do we not know the names of those great and inspired artists, but they themselves did not care about their names and did not count on posterity to discover them. They worked for the very beauty of their work, for the very—please excuse me—holiness of their work.

Anonymity gives an artist great advantages and can even have a charm. However, often, perhaps too often, writers and artists adapt their work, and even ideas, to their names, that is, to their reputation, which they have won in the world thanks to their preceding works. This can have a very bad effect on their new works. Such an artist becomes a slave of his own name. On the other hand, when working on the basis of anonymity, an artist may not look back at his older works. With each new work he begins a new life, as if in a state of virginity.

"To forget its creator is one of the functions of the creations," writes E. M. Forster in his beautiful essay "Anonymity," "because the poet wrote the poem no doubt, but he forgot himself while he wrote it, and we forget him while we read." "It was not the speaker who was in the beginning, but the word."

When speaking about the advantages, virtues, and attractions of anonymous creation, I do not recommend to any of my colleagues writing in exile to publish their books anonymously. God forbid. But I wish for all my colleagues and myself too that our works might be so well known as *Lorelei*, although the name of the author of that lyrical work was for twelve years taboo in his own country.

The fact that not only our ambition but our creativity itself has in exile no wide field of radiation and must give up the aura in the past surrounding our names may be favorable for our work, but more often it hampers it. It is difficult to feel useful where no one needs us. The creators of the cathedrals and stained glass windows knew that crowds would worship in those cathedrals. It is hard to be even a shoemaker where people prefer to walk barefoot. And a shoemaker who makes shoes for imaginary feet may in time lose his interest in making shoes and take up another trade. Every one of the émigré writers has often found himself in a similar situation. However, not everyone abandoned his shoemaking. Apparently, some hope, or illusion, won out. Every writer creating temporarily without response writes in the hope that in the future his books will be on the best-seller lists. It was so with Stendhal, who also to a certain extent was in exile in Civitavecchia. He consciously dedicated his *Charterhouse of Parma* "to the happy few" and precisely predicted the years when he would be discovered by the reading public and properly understood and appreciated. Every other novelist without a following, either in his own country or in exile, hopes that he will become a new Stendhal. Such a maximalistic attitude to one's own hope also imposes maximalistic duties. Who wishes to be read in fifty or in a hundred years must write differently from an author complying with present-day tastes. We do not know how the readers will look in fifty or a hundred years, if there will be readers at all; however, we count on the existence at that time of some people sensitive to certain moral, aesthetic, and perhaps also religious values, just as we are today sensitive to the universal and timeless elements handed down to us by the ancient literatures or by writings of the fifteenth, sixteenth, or seventeenth centuries.

In the twenty-second century, people will perhaps no longer play football, and the tragedy of the football player will then be interesting for the reader only when he finds in it motifs independent of football. No general today conquers besieged cities with the help of a wooden horse within which are hidden armed doughboys. And yet even in the atomic-hydrogen era, people are interested in the history of that siege. This is an alluring temptation for a writer in exile. This is the grandeur of the solitary exile. We can make shoes for feet that will tread this earth only a hundred years from now, of course, if the earth still exists.

But it is time to conclude. I tried to point out some of the contradictions in the life and work of an exiled writer. Let us return to the beginning of our discussion. If, as the author of Salve Regina wants us to believe, it is true that our life is exile, we are bound to bring to this exile some hazy memory of Paradise, lost thanks to our sinful first parents.

Amid the horror of life, amid Hell on earth, time and again there suddenly awakens in us an unconscious nostalgia for something that is not Hell or horror and exile or even our native soil, and who knows whether it is not the mission of writers and artists to grasp and express these very longings and presentiments of man. I believe that working in exile, under conditions of more or less forced anonymity, we may come near those artists who in the Middle Ages were preparing the soul of man for another, no longer an exile's, existence, where no one asks the question "how do you spell your name?"

(1957)

TRANSLATED BY LUDWIK KRZYŻANOWSKI AND THE AUTHOR

P · A · R · T   T · W · O

Stanisław Ignacy Witkiewicz

On a New Type of Play

Theater, like poetry, is a *composite art,* but it is made up of even more elements not intrinsic to it; therefore, it is much more difficult to imagine Pure Form on the stage, essentially independent, in its final result, of the content of human action.

Yet it is not perhaps entirely impossible.

Just as there was an epoch in sculpture and painting when Pure Form was identical with metaphysical content derived from religious concepts, so there was an epoch when performance on stage was identical with myth. Nowadays form alone is the only content of our painting and sculpture; and subject matter, whether concerned with the real world or the fantastic, is only the necessary pretext for the creation of form and has no direct connection with it, except as the "stimulus" for the whole artistic machine, driving it on to creative intensity. Similarly, we maintain that it is possible to write a play in which the performance itself, existing independently in its own right and not as a heightened picture of life, would be able to put the spectator in a position to experience metaphysical feeling, regardless of whether the *fond* of the play is realistic or fantastic, or whether it is a synthesis of both, combining each of their individual parts, provided of course that the play as a *whole* results from a sincere need on the part of the author *to create a theatrical idiom capable of expressing* metaphysical feelings within purely formal dimensions. What is essential is only that the meaning of the play should not necessarily be limited by its realistic or fantastic content, as far as the totality of the work is concerned, but simply that the realistic element should exist for the sake of the purely formal goals—that is, for the sake of a synthesis of all the elements of the theater: sound, decor, movement on the stage, dialogue, in sum, performance through time, as an uninterrupted whole—so transformed, when viewed realistically, that the performance seems utter nonsense. The idea is to make it possible *to deform either life or the world of fantasy with complete freedom so as to create a whole whose meaning would be defined only by its purely scenic internal construction, and not by the demands of consistent psychology and action according to assumptions from real life. Such assumptions can be applied as criteria only to plays that are heightened reproductions of life.* Our contention is not that a play should necessarily be nonsensical, but only that from now on the drama should no longer be tied down to preexisting patterns based solely on life's meaning or on fantastic assumptions. The actor, in his own right, should not exist; he should be the same kind of part within a whole as the color red in a particular painting or the note C-sharp in a particular musical composition. The kind of play under discussion may well be characterized by absolute freedom in the handling of reality, but what is essential is that this freedom, like "nonsensicality" in painting, should be adequately justified and should become valid for the new dimension of thought and feeling into which such a play transports the spectator. At present we are not in a position to give an example of such a play, we are only pointing out that it is possible if only foolish prejudices can be overcome. But let us assume that someone writes such a play: the public will have to get used to it, as well as to that deformed leg in the painting by Picasso. Although we can imagine a painting composed of entirely abstract forms which will not evoke any associations with the objects of the external world unless such associations are self-induced, yet it is not even possible for us to imagine such a play, because pure performance in time is possible only in the world of sounds, and a theater without characters who act, no matter how outrageously and improbably, is inconceivable; simply because theater is a composite art and does not have its own intrinsic, *homogeneous* elements, like the pure arts: painting and music.

The theater of today impresses us as being something hopelessly bottled up which can be released only by introducing what we have called *fantastic psychology and action.* The psychology of the characters and their actions have to be a pretext for a clear succession of events: therefore, what is essential is that the need for a psychology of the characters and their actions to be consistent and lifelike should not become a bugbear imposing its particular construction on the play. We have had enough wretched logic about characters and enough psychological "truth"—it already seems to be coming out of our ears. Who cares what goes on at 38 Wspólna Street, apartment 10, or in the castle in the fairy tale, or in past times? In the theater we want to be in an entirely new world in which the fantastic psychology of characters who are completely implausible in real life, not only in their positive actions but also *in their errors*, and who are perhaps completely unlike people in real life, produces events which by their bizarre interrelationships create a performance in time not limited by any logic except the logic of the form itself of that performance. What is required is that we accept as inevitable a particular movement of a character, a particular phrase having a realistic or only a formal meaning, a particular change of lighting or decor, a particular musical accompaniment, just as we accept as inevitable a particular part of a composition on a canvas or a sequence of chords in a musical work. We must also take into account the fact that such characters' thoughts and feelings are completely unfettered and that they react with complete freedom to any and all events, even though there is no justification for any of this. Still, these elements would have to be suggested on the same level of formal necessity as all the other elements of performance on the stage mentioned above. Of course, the public would have to be won over to this fantastic psychology, as with the square leg in the painting by Picasso. The public has already laughed at the deformed shapes on the canvases of contemporary masters; now they will also have to laugh at the thoughts and actions of characters on the stage, since for the time being these cannot be completely explained. We believe that this problem can be resolved in exactly the same way as it has been in contemporary painting and music: by understanding the essence of art in general and by growing accustomed to it. Just as those who have finally understood Pure Form in painting can no longer even look at other kinds of painting and cannot help but understand correctly paintings that they laughed at before as incomprehensible, so those who become used to the theater we are proposing will not be able to stand any of the productions of today, whether realistic or heavily symbolic. As far as painting is concerned, we have tested this matter more than once on people who were apparently incapable of understanding Pure Form at the beginning, but who after receiving systematic "injections" over a certain period of time reached a remarkably high level of perfection in making truly expert judgments. There may be a certain amount of perversity in all this, but why should we be afraid of purely artistic perversity? Of course, perverseness in life is often a sad affair, but why should we apply judgments that are reasonable in real life to the realm of art, with which life has essentially so little in common? Artistic perversity (for example, unbalanced masses in a pictorial composition, perversely tense movements or clashing colors in a painting) is only a means and not an end; therefore, it cannot be immoral, because the goal it enables us to attain—unity within diversity in Pure Form—cannot be subjected to the criteria of good and evil. It is somewhat different with the theater, because its elements are beings who act; but we believe that in those new dimensions which we are discussing even the most monstrous situations will be no less moral than what is seen in the theater today.

Of course, assuming that a certain segment of the public interested in serious artistic experiences will come to demand plays written in the style described above, such plays would still have to result from a *genuine creative necessity* felt by an author writing for the stage. If such a work were only a *schematic nonsense,* derived in cold blood, artificially, without real need, it would probably arouse nothing but laughter, like those paintings with a bizarre form of subject matter which are created by those who do not suffer from a real "insatiable pursuit of new forms," but who manufacture them for commercial reasons or *pour épater les bourgeois.* Just as the birth of a new form, pure and abstract, without a direct religious basis, took place only through deforming our vision of the external world, so the birth of Pure Form in the theater is also possible only through deforming human psychology and action.

We can imagine such a play as having complete freedom with respect to absolutely everything from the point of view of real life, and yet being extraordinarily closely knit and highly wrought in the way the action is tied together. The task would be to fill several hours on the stage with a performance possessing its own internal, formal logic, independent of anything in "real life." An invented, *not creat-*

ed, example of such a work can only make our theory appear ridiculous, and, from a certain point of view, even absurd (for some, even infuriating, or to put it bluntly, *idiotic*), but let us try.

Three characters dressed in red come on stage and bow to no one in particular. One of them recites a poem (it should create a feeling of urgent necessity at this very moment). A kindly old man enters leading a cat on a string. So far everything has taken place against a background of a black screen. The screen draws apart and an Italian landscape becomes visible. Organ music is heard. The old man talks with the other characters, and what they say should be in keeping with what has gone before. A glass falls off the table. All of them fall on their knees and weep. The old man changes from a kindly man into a raging "scoundrel" and murders a little girl who has just crawled in from the left. At this very moment a handsome young man runs in and thanks the old man for murdering the girl, at which point the characters in red sing and dance. Then the young man weeps over the body of the little girl and says very amusing things, whereupon the old man becomes once again kindly and good-natured and laughs to himself in a corner, uttering sublime and limpid phrases. The choice of costumes is completely open: period or fantastic—there may be music during some parts of the performance. In other words, an insane asylum? Or rather a madman's brain on the stage? Perhaps so, but we maintain that, *if the play is seriously written and appropriately produced,* this method can *create works of previously unsuspected beauty;* whether it be drama, tragedy, farce, or the grotesque, all in a uniform style and unlike anything that previously existed.

On leaving the theater, the spectator ought to have the feeling that he has just awakened from some strange dream in which even the most ordinary things had a strange, unfathomable charm, characteristic of dream reveries and unlike anything else in the world. Nowadays the spectator leaves the theater with a bad taste in his mouth, or he is shaken by the purely biological horror or sublimity of life, or he is furious that he has been fooled by a whole series of tricks. For all its variety, the contemporary theater almost never gives us the other world, other not in the sense of being fantastic, but truly that other world which brings to us an understanding of purely formal beauty. Occasionally something similar occurs in the plays of writers of previous ages, plays which after all have their significance and greatness that we certainly do not want to deny them with any fanatical fury. This element we are discussing can be found in some of the plays of Shakespeare and Słowacki, for example, but never in its purest form, and therefore, despite their greatness, these plays do not create the desired effect.

The climax and the conclusion of the kind of play we are proposing may be created in a complete abstraction from what might be called that debasing feeling of pure curiosity about real life, that tension in the pit of the stomach with which we watch a drama of real life and which constitutes precisely the one and only appeal of plays today. Of course we would have to break this bad habit, so that *in a world with which, on the realistic level, we have no contact* we could experience a metaphysical drama similar to the one that takes place among the notes of a symphony or sonata and only among them, so that the dénouement would not be an event of concern to us as part of real life, but only as something comprehensible *as the inevitable conclusion of the purely formal complications of sound patterns, decorative or psychological, free from the causality found in real life.*

The criticism of absolute freedom made against contemporary artists and their works by people who do not understand art can also be applied here. For example, why three characters, not five? Why dressed in red, not green? Of course, we cannot *prove* the necessity for that number and color, but it should appear inevitable insofar as each element is a necessary part of the work of art once it has been created; while we are watching the play unfold, we ought not to be able to think of any other possible internal interrelationships. And we maintain that if the work is to be created with complete artistic sincerity, it will have to compel the spectators to accept it as inevitable. It is certainly much more difficult with the theater than with other arts, because, as a certain expert on the theater has asserted, the crowd as it watches and listens is an essential part of the performance itself, and moreover the play has to be a box office success. But we believe that sooner or later the theater must embark upon the "insatiable pursuit of new forms," which it has avoided up until now, and it is to be hoped that extraordinary works, within the dimensions of Pure Form, still remain to be created, and that there will not simply be more "renaissance" and "purification" or repetition ad nauseam of the old repertoire, which really has nothing at all to say to anybody.

We must unleash the slumbering Beast and see what it can do. And if it runs mad, there will always be time enough to shoot it before it's too late.

(1920)

TRANSLATED BY C. S. DURER AND DANIEL C. GEROULD

Bruno Schulz

An Essay for S. I. Witkiewicz

The beginnings of my graphic work are lost in mythological twilight. Before I could even talk, I was already covering every scrap of paper and the margins of newspapers with scribbles that attracted the attention of those around me. At first they were all horses and wagons. The action of riding in a wagon seemed to me full of weight and arcane symbolism. From age six or seven there appeared and reappeared in my drawings the image of a cab, with a hood on top and lanterns blazing, emerging from a nocturnal forest. That image belongs to the basic material of my imagination; it is a kind of node to many receding series. To this day I have not exhausted its metaphysical content. To this day the sight of a carriage horse has lost none of its fascination and troubling power. Its schizoid anatomy, sprouting antlers, whorls, knotholes, outcroppings at every extremity, was arrested in its development, as it were, at a time when it still wanted to reproduce and branch into other forms. And the wagon is a schizoid structure, too, derived from the same anatomical principle—multiarticulated, fantastic, made up of sheet metal warped into flipper shapes, of horse hides and huge clattering wheels.

I don't know how we manage to acquire certain images in childhood that carry decisive meanings for us. They function like those threads in the solution around which the significance of the world crystallizes for us. Another of those images for me is that of a child carried by its father through the spaces of an overwhelming night, conducting a conversation with the darkness. The father caresses the child, folds him in his arms, shields him from the natural element that chatters on and on, but to the child these arms are transparent; the night cuts straight through them, and over the father's soothing words he hears its sinister blandishments without interruption. And oppressed, full of fatalism, he answers the night's importunities with tragic readiness, wholly surrendered to the mighty element from which there is no escape.

There are texts that are marked out, made ready for us somehow, lying in wait for us at the very entrance to life. This is how I absorbed Goethe's ballad, with all its metaphysics, at age eight. Through the half-understood German I caught, or divined, the meaning, and cried, shaken to the bottom of my soul, when my mother read it to me.

Such images amount to an agenda, establish an iron capital of the spirit, proffered to us very early in the form of forebodings and half-conscious experiences. It seems to me that all the rest of one's life is spent interpreting these insights, breaking them down to the last fragment of meaning we can master, testing them against the broadest intellectual spectrum we can manage. These early images mark out to artists the boundaries of their creative powers. The works they create represent drafts on existing balances. They do not discover anything new after that, they only learn how to understand better and better the secret entrusted to them at the outset; their creative effort goes into an unending exegesis, a commentary on that one couplet of poetry assigned to them. Art, for that matter, does not resolve that secret completely. The secret stays in a tangle. The knot the soul got itself tied up in is not a false one that comes undone when you pull the ends. On the contrary, it draws tighter. We handle it, trace the path of the separate threads, look for the end of the string, and out of these manipulations comes art.

If I were asked whether the same thread recurs in my drawings as in my prose, I would answer in the affirmative. The reality is the same; only the frames are different. Here material and technique operate as the criteria of selection. A drawing sets narrower limits by its material than prose does. That is why I feel I have expressed myself more fully in my writing.

The question of whether I'd be able to interpret the reality of *Cinnamon Shops* in philosophical terms is one I would much rather avoid. It is my opinion that rationalizing one's awareness of what inheres in a work of art is like unmasking actors; it means the end of enjoyment and impoverishes the problems inherent in the work. The reason is not that art is a crossword puzzle with the key hidden, and philosophy the same crossword puzzle solved. The difference lies deeper than that. In a work of art the umbilical cord linking it with the totality of our concerns has not yet been severed, the blood of the mystery still circulates; the ends of the blood vessels vanish into the surrounding night and return from it full of dark fluid. A philosophical interpretation gives us only an anatomical sample dissected from the total body of the problems involved in the work. Just the same, I am curious how the philosophical credo of *Cinnamon Shops* would sound in the form of discourse. It would have to be an attempt to describe the reality given there rather than a justification of it.

    Cinnamon Shops offers a certain recipe for reality, posits a certain special kind of substance. The substance of that reality exists in a state of constant fermentation, germination, hidden life. It contains no dead, hard, limited objects. Everything diffuses beyond its borders, remains in a given shape only momentarily, leaving this shape behind at the first opportunity. A principle of sorts appears in the habits, the modes of existence of this reality: universal masquerade. Reality takes on certain shapes merely for the sake of appearance, as a joke or form of play. One person is a human, another is a cockroach, but shape does not penetrate essence; it is only a role adopted for the moment, an outer skin soon to be shed. A certain extreme monism of the life substance is assumed here, for which specific objects are nothing more than masks. The life of the substance consists in the assuming and consuming of numberless masks. This migration of forms is the essence of life. Thus an all-pervading aura of irony emanates from this substance. There is an ever-present atmosphere of the stage, of sets viewed from behind, where the actors make fun of the pathos of their parts after stripping off their costumes. The bare fact of separate individual existence holds an irony, a hoax, a clown's stuck-out tongue. (Here, it seems to me, we have a point of contact between *Cinnamon Shops* and the world of your paintings and plays.)

    What the meaning of this universal disillusioning reality is I am not able to say. I maintain only that it would be unbearable unless it were compensated for in some other dimension. In some sense we derive a profound satisfaction from the loosening of the web of reality; we feel an interest in witnessing the bankruptcy of reality.

There has been talk about the book's destructive tendency. From the viewpoint of certain established values, this may be true. But the work operates at a pre-moral depth, at a point where value is still *in statu nascendi*.

As a spontaneous utterance of life, a work of art poses tasks for ethics, not the reverse. If art were merely to confirm what has already been established elsewhere, it would be superfluous. The role of art is to be a probe sunk into the nameless. The artist is an apparatus for registering processes in that deep stratum where value is formed. Destructive? But the fact that these contents express themselves as a work of art means that we affirm them, that our deep perception has spontaneously declared in their favor.

To what genre does *Cinnamon Shops* belong? How should it be classified? I think of it as an autobiographical narrative. Not only because it is written in the first person and because certain events and experiences from the author's childhood can be discerned in it. The work is an autobiography, or rather a spiritual genealogy, a genealogy par excellence in that it follows the spiritual family tree down to those depths where it merges into mythology, to be lost in the mutterings of mythological delirium. I have always felt that the roots of the individual spirit, traced far enough down, would be lost in some matrix of myth. This is the ultimate depth; it is impossible to reach farther down.

I later found an imposing artistic realization of this idea in Thoman Mann's *Joseph and His Brothers*, where it is carried out on a monumental scale. Mann shows that beneath all human events, when the chaff of time and individual variation is blown away, certain primeval patterns, "stories," are found by which these events form and re-form in great repeating pulses. For Mann, these are the biblical tales, the timeless myths of Babylon and Egypt. On my more modest scale I have attempted to uncover my own private mythology, my own "stories," my own mythic family tree. Just as the ancients traced their ancestry from mythical unions with gods, so I undertook to establish for myself some mythical generation of forebears, a fictitious family from which I trace my true descent.

In a way these "stories" are real, they represent my way of living, my personal fate. The overriding motif of this fate is profound loneliness, isolation from the stuff of daily life.

Loneliness is the catalyst that makes reality ferment, that precipitates its surface layer of figures and colors.

(1935)

TRANSLATED BY WALTER ARNDT

Bruno Schulz

Afterword to Kafka's *The Trial*

Only a few of his minor stories saw the light of day during Kafka's lifetime. The unimaginable sense of responsibility, the quasi-religious rigor of judgment he applied to his work, allowed him to rest content with no single achievement and compelled him to cast away fruit after fruit of his inspired and happy talent. At that time only a small coterie of friends was even aware that here was creative genius on a grand scale, reaching its maturity before their eyes, grasping for ultimate goals, struggling to solve life's deepest problems. For him, writing was not an end in itself but a means of attaining a higher truth, of finding the proper way to live. It is its tragic destiny that the life rushing with desperate urgency to the light of faith does not find it and goes off into darkness after all. This explains the last will of a writer who, dying before his time, consigned his entire literary oeuvre to destruction. Max Brod, appointed executor by Kafka, resolved to defy his wish and publish the surviving remnants of Kafka's literary estate in a series of volumes that established Kafka's position among the spirits that represent his generation.

All that rich, dense body of work, ripe and realized from its inception, was even at its earliest an inspired account and testimony from the universe of deep religious experience. Once and always under the spell of an otherworldly, religious sense of reality, Kafka's unwavering gaze penetrates the structure, organization, and underlying order of this hidden reality and sets its boundaries where human life impinges on the nature of God. He is a bard and worshiper of the divine order; a bard of a strange stripe, to be sure.

The most poisonous and scornful slanderer could not depict this world with more twisted caricature, through figures so overtly compromising and absurd. The sublime nature of the divine order, according to Kafka, can be rendered only by the power of human negation. This order is so far beyond the human range, it so greatly transcends all human categories, that its sublimity is measured by the force of the disapproval, resistance, and elemental rebuke that man marshals against those high authorities. How else, after all, could the human condition react to the usurpation of those powers except by protest, sheer lack of comprehension, shattering bursts of outrage?

The hero of *The Trial* subjects the entire hierarchy of the "judiciary" to just such bursts of outrage during the first court hearing. He attacks it passionately, threatens it with his apparent success, turns from accused into accuser. The seeming consternation of the Court, its withdrawal and perplexity, which symbolizes the fundamental incommensurateness of its majesty with human categories, excites the hero's audacity and reforming zeal. This is the way the blinded nature of humans reacts to the incursion of those powers, to a confrontation with them: by exaggerated self-assertion, that hubris of the ancients which is not the cause but a by-product of divine wrath. Jozef K feels a hundred times superior to the Court; its alleged trickeries and deceits fill him with disgust and contempt. To these traits he opposes human *raison d'état*, civilization, work. Comical disillusion follows. All his superiority and reason do not shield him from the inexorable progress of the prosecution, which barges straight into his life as if all this were utterly beside the point. Feeling its ring drawing tighter and tighter around him, Jozef K dreams endlessly of the possibility of eluding it after all, of living outside its realm; he deludes himself that it might be possible to cadge something out of the Court by backstairs maneuvers involving women, who are, according to Kafka, intermediaries between the human and the divine; or by means of a beggarly painter who is rumored to have "connections" with the Court. In this way Kafka brands, holds up to unremitting ridicule, the dubious and hopeless nature of human endeavor in relation to the divine order.

Jozef K's mistake lies in clinging to his human reason instead of surrendering unconditionally. He persists in his stubbornness, submits endless petitions in which he attempts to present, day after day, his airtight human alibi. All these efforts and "legal recourses" drop into a mysterious void, never reaching the exalted authorities they orbit around. Human traffic, with this violently centripetal universe it is forever bumping up against, must always take the form of misunderstanding, failure to coincide, random shots that never find their target.

In the next to last chapter, which may be regarded as the key to the whole work, yet another aspect of the matter is developed in the prison chaplain's parable: it is not the law that pursues the guilty person, but rather he or she engages in a lifelong search for "entry into the law." It looks as if the law were hiding from man, wrapping itself up tight in its inaccessibility and holiness, but counting at the same time, surreptitiously as it were, on the sacrilegious invasion, the intrusion of man. The defense of the law that the chaplain undertakes in the astounding exegesis of this parable picks its way along the very edge of sophistry, borders on falsehood and cynicism—the hardest test to which devotion to the law may be put, the peak of self-denial to which it may rise.

In this work Kafka depicted the intrusion of the law into man's life, presenting it in a somewhat abstract manner. He did not demonstrate it concretely in a "real" individual fate. Right down to the end we never find out what Jozef K's guilt consisted in, we never come to know the form of law his life was to have fulfilled. Kafka only renders the atmosphere—the climate and aura—of a human life's involvement with the suprahuman, with supreme truth. The feat of artistic genius performed in this narrative lies in the fact that for these matters, which possess neither shape nor expression in human language, Kafka has found an adequate corporality as it were, a substitute material in which to build their structure and fashion it down to the smallest detail.

The perceptions and insights Kafka means to give expression to here are not his exclusive property. They are the common heritage of the mysticism of all times and nations, which has, however, always been couched in a language that was subjective and extraneous, the adopted language of certain esoteric communities and schools. Here for the first time the magic of poetry has created a species of parallel reality, a fictional body upon which mystical experience can be demonstrated; not substantively, to be sure, but in such a way that even the uninitiated may feel the chill breath of its distant majesty and realize that they are being offered a poetic equivalent of the actual experience.

In this sense Kafka's procedure, the creation of a doppelgänger or substitute reality, stands virtually without precedent. The dual nature of his reality is achieved with the help of a kind of pseudorealism that merits special attention. Kafka sees the realistic surface of existence with unusual precision, he knows by heart, as it were, its code of gestures, all the external mechanics of events and situations, how they dovetail and interlace, but these to him are but a loose epidermis without roots, which he lifts off like a delicate membrane and fits onto his transcendental world, grafts onto his reality. His attitude to reality is radically ironic, treacherous, profoundly ill-intentioned—the relationship of the prestidigitator to his raw material. He only simulates the attention to detail, the seriousness, and the elaborate precision of this reality in order to compromise it all the more thoroughly.

Kafka's books present neither allegory, nor analysis, nor exegesis of a doctrine; his fiction shapes a poetic reality in its own right, rounded, hermetically sealed on all sides, self-justified and self-supporting. Aside from its mystical allusions and religious intuitions, the work lives its own poetic life—polysemantic, unfathomable, not exhausted by any interpretation.

The present narrative, which Max Brod received in manuscript from the author in 1920, is incomplete. A number of chapter fragments that were to find their places somewhere before the last chapter were omitted from the book by Brod, who acted upon Kafka's statement that the trial, ideally speaking, had no end, and that further elaboration would add nothing of substance to the meaning of this fiction.

(1936)

TRANSLATED BY WALTER ARNDT

K. A. Jeleński

Avant-garde and Revolution

A major exhibit of modern Soviet painting will open in Paris this May. Ironically, the exhibit will take place in the halls of the Musée d'Art Moderne. It is not my intention, of course, to reiterate here the familiar banalities about the value of socialist realism in painting. Rather, I prefer to point out a certain paradox: the modern and abstract West forgets all too easily that its recognition of nonrepresentational painting was relatively belated. Abstraction was already an official school in the Soviet Union at the time when Mondrian was derided as a pitiful madman in Paris. And in the United States, nonrepresentational art was but an exotic import up to the last world war. Why was the symbiosis between the avant-garde and the Revolution so short-lived? It seemed like a perfect match. . . .

The terrain had been prepared. In 1913 the art critic Sergei Diaghilev thus described the artistic life of Moscow:

> Twenty new schools are born each month: futurism, cubism— they're already prehistoric. Three days pass, and you look like a conservative. Mototism overcomes automatism, which yields to trepidism and vibrism, which are then overturned by planeism, sereneism, omnism, and neoism.
>
> Exhibitions are shown in palaces and attics lit up by three candles where princesses admire the paintings of neo-verist masters. Big landowners are privately tutored in metachronism.

Five years later, Alexander's Column in Petrograd will be covered with enormous colorful posters of stripes and squares, and cubism's symbiosis with fauvism will rule the city. Every chimney becomes a flute, an oboe, or a clarinet, and factories perform the famous "siren symphony" off in the distance. Mayakovsky proudly proclaims, "The streets are our brushes! The squares are our palettes!" It was more than just princesses, "big landowners," or the general enthusiasm of society that made the leap from feudalism to cosmopolitanism within a generation. It was a full-scale identification of the avant-garde with the Revolution.

So it is with some difficulty that the twelfth volume of *The History of Russian Art,* published in Moscow in 1955, comes to terms with this period. The years from 1917 to 1924 are condensed into about twenty pages. Prophetically, the dark designs of the "left" are detected at their inception: after all, it is hardly implausible to suppose that "objective reaction" conspired to squelch Soviet art, given that Trotsky, Bukharin, and some others almost toppled the Soviet state.

The fate of Soviet art deserves a more thorough examination. Why did a state founded upon a utopian ideology disavow the art that was created in its own image? If obvious considerations played a part—that is, as hopes for a swift transformation of human nature vanished, art had to be brought down to society's level—why was the Soviet Union unable to revive classicism on its own scale? Why did it fail to produce its own David, or even its own Praxiteles?

Let us start with an anecdote. Shortly after the October Revolution, the commissar for education, Anatolii Lunacharsky, bivouacked in the barren halls of the Winter Palace. The young painter Pavel Mansurov called on him to propose an alliance between Revolution and Art. This episode, described with relish in the voluminous *History of the Revolution,* is a colorful index of a deeper current. The Russian avant-garde's identification with the Revolution must have occurred on several levels. Recently, Yurii Anenkov suggested to me the most skeptical interpretation: "We were revolutionaries in art who were repudiated by official critics and a bourgeois public. When the revolution came, we naturally expected it to open all doors for us." Shaking his head, he added: "But this was a misunderstanding. The term 'revolution' confused us. We were revolutionaries in art but only in art."

In my view, however, the affiliation between the October Revolution and the art of the avant-garde has deeper roots. The Communist vision of the world is teleological. Its goal is the end of history, making way for a golden age that will transform the relations between people. A Soviet poet exclaims:

> If you could only see the other world,
> What words and colors has our story woven!
> There, every whore is but a virgin;
> The hangman as tender as a mother!

It is worth noting that the two major branches of the Soviet avant-garde that are associated with the Revolution, suprematism and constructivism, both stem from geometric abstraction. All of man's utopian visions, the yearning for a golden age and the arrival of God's kingdom on earth, which were supposed to have been the fulfillment of communism, have in common an aversion not only to "figurative art," as Plato would have expected, but to everything that connects art to organic life. Dante's paradise is a mechanism of spheres lacerated with rays of pure color. In his republic, Plato would allow only those "figures" to blossom whose beauty he extols in the dialogues: "The straight line, the circle, and those figures drawn on a line and in a circle by means of a compass." Idealists, knee-jerk Platonists, vertically religious and puritanical souls feel drawn to geometric abstraction. It is remarkable how frequently the word *mystical* is invoked in monographs on Mondrian and Malevich. From other accounts, we know how susceptible these types are to communism and how they tend to displace religious instincts onto the social plane.

"The world we envision," writes the Soviet author Leonid Leonov, "is both more material and more responsive to human needs than the Christian paradise." But we sense "paradise" carries more weight in this sentence than "material." Rectangles, triangles, rays, obelisks, pyramids: what could be more appropriate for a world finally reclaimed, an earthly kingdom of God where God is absent but his laws are not. This has been sensed by all writers who project communism (or modern collectivism) and thus a utopian, nightmarish future. The novels of Aldous Huxley, George Orwell, and Yevgeny Zamyatin all take place against a backdrop of frigid, geometric abstraction.

I can perhaps make myself clearer by juxtaposing the geometric avant-garde with another important movement, superrealism, which for various reasons became identified with the Revolution fifteen years later. The superrealists' protests against a rampart of values circumscribing man's freedom led them to join hands with the Communists. They appealed to Marx, who destroyed the world of value, as well as to Freud, who erased man's conventional understanding of himself. In their mythology, the dark shadow of the Marquis de Sade is cast upon Lenin's fatherly smile. Superrealism is the only intellectual movement to take the Revolution seriously while harboring no illusions about human nature. For superrealists, the slogan "freedom" truly meant freedom, and not merely another form of order. It is therefore not surprising that the rebellious superrealist art, which went to the core of man's innermost inhibitions, was unacceptable to Communists. The later, always lyrical and organic, abstract superrealist canvases were equally unacceptable.

At first glance, however, no style would seem closer to idealist and mechanistic conceptions of man than geometrical abstraction: a labyrinth, devoid of the mystery of organic life, in which man may seek to discover himself. No style is closer to the communism of Lenin's formula: "Soviets plus electrification." The reasons for the failure of the symbiosis are complex; the very conception of art was at stake. Although the rivalry between Malevich and Tatlin during the years after the Revolution is well known, the fundamental contradictions between Malevich's suprematism and Tatlin's constructivism have never been scrutinized. In 1915 Malevich expounded his theories in *Die gegenstandlose Welt,* a book that at once makes clear what would bring him closer to the Revolution two years later: "Values have become a yoke fit only for display in a museum, a necklace around the corpse's neck." In 1919 this would lead him to say that cubism, futurism, and suprematism "were revolutionary art forms that presaged the political and economic revolution of 1917." But we also see in Malevich's *Welt* what will distance him from the Revolution:

> Suprematism in painting as well as in architecture is devoid of any social or material aims. Every social idea, no matter how great and profound, is a daughter of hunger and need; every work of art, however mediocre or shallow, is the product of a visual sensibility. It is high time to recognize that the problems of art and the problems of the stomach are indeed far removed from each other.

Suprematism apparently attests to the eternal nature of art. Constructivism, however, seems to deny it. Antoine Pevsner and Naum Gabo proclaimed in their *Realistic Manifesto* (Moscow, 1920): "Life does not offer the beautiful as an aesthetic measure of things: the real is what is ultimately beautiful." For Communists, this problem is not without significance. If art belongs to the superstructure, whose interests will it express in a world free of conflict? If, however, art is merely a crutch for the alienated man, will the nonalienated man still need it? To express the splendors of the Communist world, Lenin joked about "toilets made of real gold," absurdly limiting himself to ennobling the utilitarian realm. Anenkov recounts that when Lenin posed for his portrait, he would compare art to an incidental wart that would fall away with the arrival of communism. But one should not assume that some barbaric design lies behind such distrust or distaste toward art. How was one to predict the rhythm of life in the transformed world, the arrival of which was an article of faith? Was it not plausible to suppose that this very rhythm would acquire the qualities of art?

Of course, both suprematism and constructivism spring from the same sources. Marinetti's cry, "Eviva Futurista! . . . A speeding automobile is more beautiful than the Victory of Samothrace!" resounded as powerfully in Moscow as it did in Milan. For Malevich, as well as for Tatlin, the Communist Revolution held the promise of a world re-created in the image of a perfect machine. Arguing that art constitutes an autonomous and eternal sphere of human expression, Malevich nevertheless hoped to entrust to art the task of transforming the world: "According to the aestheticians of yesteryear," he wrote in 1919, "art has no role to play in the construction of the modern world. . . . But art must develop along with the organism, giving it shape and participating in its movement. . . . We want to rule the world, to tear it out of nature's hands and build a new world that will belong to us at last!"

There are clear Marxist echoes in this text, but Malevich wished to assign a role to artists similar to the one reserved for philosophers in Plato's *Republic*: "Everything should assume a suprematist shape: fabrics, carpets, household utensils, furniture, and road signs. Everything should be produced in accordance with the new forms of harmony." Malevich actually attempted to realize some of his projects. One of his objects, a teacup that was exhibited last year at an enormous retrospective of his work in London's Whitechapel Gallery, represents "a suprematist notion of cup," but hardly a functional or a practical shape. This is not very surprising. For the suprematists, an object of everyday use was designed to reflect their Platonic dream about squares and vectors. The light of grace was finally to fall upon the world from a painting, a work of art. The constructivists' position (the etymology itself seems to confirm my hypothesis in both cases) was the opposite. Tatlin's *Mobile* appeared in capricious, mysterious motion twenty years ahead of Calder. For Konstantin Umanski, a contemporary critic, it represented "Planes? Dynamo machines? Dreadnoughts? . . . These semimechanical, semidecorative constructions delve into the mystery of the modern machine." At this time, Pevsner's and Gabo's sculptures resembled turbines, electrical coils, and collectors. Clearly, constructivists "construct" works of art, starting with the machine. It is no wonder that leading constructivists, Tatlin, Popov, Rodchenko, and Stepanov, declared that their artistic work was "senseless" and in 1921 left the Moscow Institute for the Arts to devote themselves to perfecting the design of objects, which for them meant increasing their functional value. Paradoxically, this field continued to be known as "applied art."

I think it is very important that the revolutionary avant-garde was not content to dream about the world in the image and likeness of its utopian art. Some of its exponents accepted the most extreme implications of Communist ideology, which allowed no place or justification for "pure art" in a world transformed and reconciled with itself.

Unfortunately, the causes of the crisis of abstract and "formalist" art in the USSR are not to be found at this level. From 1917 to 1922 suprematists, constructivists, and futurists, which is how the Soviet audience referred to the avant-garde, were the official artists of the young state. Realistic painters who were more or less linked to official institutions of czarist Russia were stigmatized as "reactionaries." The identification of communism with the avant-garde went so far that the International Arts Bureau, an artistic comintern of sorts, was founded immediately after the Revolution. Under its aegis, Malevich, Kandinsky, and Tatlin worked together with Lunacharsky to prepare the First International Congress of the

Arts, which, however, would never take place. The Committee for Fine Arts at the Commissariat of Culture was composed of Kandinsky, Brik, and Sterenberg. Kandinsky was also involved in organizing the Soviet Academy of Arts and Sciences, and, along with the Polish painter Władysław Strzemiński, joined the Exhibit Bureau of the Soviet Union. *Vkhutemas,* new schools of artistic technique that sought to affiliate themselves with factories, replaced traditional academies. Tatlin and Mansurov established a production lab in a Petrograd metallurgical factory called New Lesner. Anenkov, a set designer and a colleague of Tatlin's, actually manufactured parts of his constructivist stage sets in factories. The other great names of the Soviet avant-garde may be found on the faculty rosters at the Academy's Institute of Fine Arts: Popov, Punin, El Lissitzky, Matyushin, Yakulov. Between 1918 and 1921 thirty museums devoted to modern art were established in the Soviet Union, which became the first nation to consecrate abstract painting on such a wide scale. In 1918 David Sterenberg, who was appointed chairman of the artists' *Kollegium* by Lunacharsky, chief of the Commissariat of Education (*Narkompros*), declared that "only the art of the future, the ideas of collectivism and revolutionary nonrepresentational art" have the right to exist in the USSR. Nikolay Punin, Brik, and Altman edited the official art bulletin, the monthly *Iskusstvo komuny.* In the first issue, Punin wrote: "Explode, destroy, eradicate from the face of the earth all old artistic forms! You must have this dream if you are a young artist, a new artist, a proletarian artist, and a new man." In the second issue, Altman proclaimed, "Today futurism is the only true art of the proletariat!"

In the new *History of Russian Art* the interpretation of this period wavers between post-Stalinist indulgence ("Some of these artists were subjectively convinced that their art was revolutionary") and the more familiar argument that the abstractionists "could not paint" ("Frequently the untalented used these slogans to conceal their inability to meet the Revolution's challenge to art"). In fact, the main obstacle was apparent to the "leftist" artists. In the introduction to their tenth group exhibit in Moscow in 1919, they conceded, "The Soviet viewer is not yet sufficiently mature to understand nonrepresentational art." *The History of Russian Art,* while citing no sources, describes these artists as scheming "to use state apparatus to achieve their artistic goals." More convincing, however, are the comments Pevsner would make thirty years later in Paris in an interview about the *Realistic Manifesto,* the tract he had coauthored with Gabo. "We were young, revolutionary Communists," he said. "Some of the points are utopian. When we wrote it, Lenin and Trotsky were still around; I was a professor at the Moscow Academy. . . . It was not the age of Stalin."

The first warning signs would soon appear. Lunacharsky, despite his role as the guardian of the "leftists," wrote in *Iskusstvo komuny* in 1920, "Two phenomena are dangerous in this journal: the tendency to negate the past totally and the tendency to speak in the name of the authorities when speaking for a particular group." But this was only to be expected. Lunacharsky was often summoned by Lenin, who was interested in art, but solely for its potential utility as an instrument of propaganda. Lenin's observations about art, which were industriously collected by Klara Zetkin, display a "common sense" typical of the intelligentsia at the time: "I'm totally incapable of regarding the products of expressionism, futurism, cubism, and other "isms" as expressions of a superior artistic genius. I don't understand it or derive any joy from it."

Nevertheless, Lenin's conception of monumental art in service to an idea is more interesting than Stalin's. He would read aloud to Lunacharsky passages from Tommaso Campanella's utopian work, *The City of the Sun,* and he yearned to apply this Renaissance Italian's idea of enormous didactic frescoes in his own realm. Lenin's "Monumental Propaganda Plan" called for huge signs on office building facades as well as for monuments of revolutionary heroes. Were it not for the lack of raw materials, this peculiar style, also created in part by avant-garde artists, would have left its mark on the Soviet Union during this period. As it happened, communism's most interesting collective style left its imprint only on cardboard and plaster. Regrettably, tsarist semiprecious stones were not used again in Russia until the Stalinist subway was built.

But the avant-garde did not cease to flourish because of the public's incomprehension or bureaucratic mistrust. The implementation of the New Economic Policy and the growing influence of the Red Army were the more immediate causes of its decline. The policy's main feature, partial reestablishment of a free market, took patronage out of the state's control and gave it to the new bourgeoisie, a group far less sophisticated than its prerevolutionary counterpart.

As a result, *Peredvizhniki*, a "people's" movement created in 1870 to "bring art to the masses" through anecdotal and edifying paintings, gained new momentum. This art was more accessible to the petit bourgeois public than the prerevolutionary figurative paintings by such groups as the aestheticist Mir Iskusstva or the Cézanne-influenced "Jack of Diamonds." They were also the only group, apart from the abstractionists, which collaborated, if not with communism, then certainly with the progressive movement, already at this point known to be an arm of the revolutionary movement. Their leader, Ilya Riepin, severely condemned the principle of "art for art's sake," which was so dear to the "modernists." "There is only one principle," he wrote, "art for life's sake. Everything must serve life, and life must be served by every work of art." The effect of Riepin and the *Peredvizhniki* on the history of Russian art appears to have been similar to Gorky's effect on literature. Although it is the great inventors of abstraction who are now associated with the heroic epoch of the Revolution, and not Riepin and his followers (as Mayakovsky represents revolutionary literature for us, and not Gorky), the heyday of the *Peredvizhniki* would prove no less fateful for Soviet art than Gorky's preeminence proved to be for literature.

Organized in 1922 in Moscow, the forty-seventh exhibit celebrating the New Economic Policy still did not mean victory for the *Peredvizhniki*. But it was the first manifestation by exponents of "realism" or the artistic "right" since the Revolution. Accused of being "reactionary" and "backward" in newspaper articles that appeared after the exhibit opened, the shrewder "realists" took their cue from the charges leveled against them. They established the Revolutionary Russia's Painters Union (AKhRR).* For the first time, realistic painters as a group came out in support of the Soviet state, thus breaking the avant-garde's monopoly. Their crude program offered a preview of "socialist realism": "We mirror daily life: the life of the Red Army, workers, peasants, servants of the Revolution and heroes of labor. Our style is heroic realism in monumental form." One does not need to wonder why an artistic movement supported by political officers in a country dominated

*AKhRR stands for Assotsiatsiya Khudoznikov Revolyutsiyonnoi Rosii (lit., association of artists of revolutionary Russia).

by the military would grant first place in its program to the Red Army. Not surprisingly, the Red Army's Fifth Anniversary Exhibit was a triumph for the AKhRR. The exhibit would serve as the nucleus for the famous Museum of the Revolution, which would be deluged with "generic" paintings by new "revolutionary" realists in the years to come.

The "left" did not succumb without a struggle. In 1923 its journal *Lef* proclaimed that the realistic "right" always served up the same "cold, putrid fish." At a public discussion Mayakovsky declared: "I haven't seen this year's Revolutionary Russian Painters Union Exhibit. But one might very well ask if this can be called culture at all! I've my own views on the subject. Take Brodsky's well-known *Comintern Meeting,* which so much has been written about, and you will see to what depths of banality and hideousness a Communist painter can sink. . . . Forgive me, comrades, but I can see no difference in the way the State Council [An allusion to a 1901 Riepin painting—K.A.J.] and our Comintern delegates have been painted." Mayakovsky ended his speech with a call to replace painting with photography.

In 1924 a joint exhibit of the "left" and "right" entitled "Debate Exhibit" juxataposed constructivist and realist works for the first time. Constructivists had never addressed the ideal aims of communism more directly: their installations in this exhibit were a genuine blueprint for a "transformed world," with transparent factories, the first industrial designs, and works of graphic imagination, including El Lissitzky's charming abstract fairy tale for children, *A Suprematist Tale of Two Squares.*

Is this why the exhibition marks the twilight of the avant-garde? Although *aparatchiks* continued to refer to the "Great Aim" in their ideological rationalizations, any practical attempt at its realization made them jittery. Artists considered "proletarian" became "utopian" overnight. AKhRR's "Heroic Realism" was more flattering to the bureaucracy, which preferred the golden legend of the Revolution to revolutionary art. In spite of the change of climate, the Party's first cultural policy statement, edited by Bukharin and issued in 1925, declared that the Party was not yet ready to determine which artistic group truly represented the proletariat. Nevertheless, abstractionist exhibits began to face increasing opposition, a change that, along with a decrease in state-sponsored commissions, convinced Pevsner, Gabo, Chagall, Kandinsky, Anenkov, and Mansurov to emigrate. It is worth noting that avant-garde artists were still allowed to travel freely and to show their work abroad during this period. Lissitzky left Russia in 1920, playing a significant role in Germany's artistic life until his return to Moscow eight years later. When Malevich arrived in Warsaw in 1927, he received a triumphant welcome from the Polish avant-garde (who saw him as a fellow countryman), and in Berlin at the Grosse Berliner Kunstausstellung, an entire hall was dedicated to his work. His suprematist paintings would be shown in Moscow even as late as 1939.

We often forget that Stalinism did not start out as the perfectly hermetic construction it became in its final years. At the beginning of his reign, Stalin was more restrained than Lenin in his literary and artistic judgments. Gorky's return to Russia and his idyllic conversations with Stalin on a garden bench strengthened, it has been suggested, the dictator's confidence in his views on art, since his own proclivities were shared by "the greatest Russian genius." Whether this was the case is an open question. Yurii Anenkov, for instance, has tried to persuade me that Gorky favored the use of abstraction for book illustrations. People close to Gorky confirm his antipathy toward Kandinsky, which is understandable given Gorky's aversion to Maeterlinck and Stefan George, writers whom Kandinsky saw (and this shameful secret is well guarded by contemporary critics) as his counterparts in literature. Gorky felt nothing but contempt for Tatlin, who married Gorky's jilted mistress: "a ne'er-do-well idler and a fraud" whose proposed statue of the Third International was "trash." Gorky's predilections are well known. He is effusive about Shadra, a banal academic sculptor: "The Zagier power station with its sculpture of Lenin in the middle of the Kura River is wonderful. Here we have the first truly monumental work showing a man in a jacket. The artist deftly captured Ilyich's gesture, pointing his finger at the river's furious current."

One of the best analyses of Stalinist aesthetics is an essay entitled "What Is Socialist Realism?" by an anonymous Soviet writer that appeared in *Kultura*.* "Does this irrational conception exist at all?" he wonders. "Perhaps it's only a dream visited upon the mind

*A Polish émigré monthly published in Paris.

of a terrified clerk during the dark, bewitching night of Stalinist dictatorship? Is it Zhdanov's vulgar demagogy or Gorky's doddering outlandishness?"

Socialist realism, which has never been precisely defined, was imposed gradually upon Soviet artistic life before hardening into indisputable dogma. "The Five-Year Plan for Cultural Affairs" drafted in 1930 was used to promulgate the regime's official philosophy of art. While suprematists and constructivists had already lost all influence, various new groups began to thrive during the "liberalization" in the years 1922–28. "Ost" was comprised of easel painters educated in the new schools, the *Vkhutemas*. Under the influence of German expressionism and photomontage techniques, these students of the constructivists turned to figurative art. Of course, their work was more interesting than AKhRR's. These epigones of "Jack of Diamonds" fell into two groups: "Objective Reality" and "Poppyseed Cake."

"Absorbed by the beauty of things," according to a contemporary critic, "the Moscow painters apply wild colors and subscribe to no philosophy."

In 1930 the artistic section of *Narkompros* decided to unite all "permissible" groups into a single Fine Arts Workmen Union, in which AKhRR and a few kindred factions gained the upper hand. Finally, the Party resolved in 1932 "to unite all existing literary and artistic groups into the Soviet Artists Union," with the goal of "uniting all those who support the Soviet system and actively participate in the construction of socialism."

The hazy and ambiguous theory of "socialist realism" as it applies to literature is reduced in painting to two principles: 1. "Composition in painting is a concern unworthy of a thinking person," and 2. "Subject matter will create its own style." In the meantime, however, not only was the subject matter imposed on Soviet painting, but above all so was the style—nineteenth-century Russian realism of Riepin and the *Peredvizhniki*.

Surely, this is the reason that the Soviet system never produced an authentic form of artistic expression. It is also why, after the loss of abstraction, which was uncomfortably linked to the utopian ideal, the Soviet Union was incapable even of reflecting its own inhuman magnitude in a classical mirror. As the anonymous author of "What Is Socialist Realism" points out, social oppression alone cannot destroy art:

> Art does not fear dictatorship, nor severity, nor repression, nor even conservatism and clichés. If necessary, art can be narrowly religious, openly servile, rather than individualistic, and still be great. We admire the commonplaces of ancient Egyptian art, Russian iconography, and folk art. Art is malleable enough to fit into every procrustean bed history offers. What it cannot tolerate is eclecticism.

Stalinist Russia borrowed its visual commonplaces from an epoch that was itself already eclectic: nineteenth-century academicism. The state enforced this rhetoric by edict, destroying what was vital and in a sense authentic in the naive idiom of Riepin, Matejko, and Meissonier. Socialist realism, which never existed as a theory, portrayed with some accuracy a society that sought to realize petit-bourgeois norms through purges, five-year plans, and labor camps. This aim seems paradoxical, given the sheer magnitude and hideousness of the means. In Russian novels from the Stalinist era, we find numerous analogues to paintings of that period:

> A sparkling, intricately cut chandelier with its transparent and slightly colored tassels dangling like icicles hung from a white ceiling. . . . High silver columns supported the dazzlingly white dome strung with a necklace of light bulbs. . . . Raitkin stood on stage next to a glittering piano. His tie flowed in a stream of blue down his chest, which was girded by a pale grey suit.

Here we see a party functionary pontificating in an auditorium around 1950. "Socialist realism" is no more than a reflection of this banality, *savoir-vivre*, and comme il faut as expressed by a compulsory *kulturnost*.

The post-Stalinist system faces a dilemma as it chooses to embark on a pragmatic path, for its legitimacy depends upon ideological continuity. Artistic problems presented no difficulty for Khrushchev: "The question of freedom in artistic endeavor never arises for the artist who faithfully serves his country. This artist knows how to approach reality, and he does not need to 'conform' or to discipline himself. His soul demands that he faithfully depict reality in a manner consistent with his Communist convictions. He stands tall, affirming his position through his work." Despite such confidence, the Union of Soviet Artists felt compelled to organize a conference entitled "Revisionism in Soviet Art Criticism" in Moscow last October. Heresies that had been silenced in Russia for thirty years were cited, among them those committed by art critics and journals that had defended young "formalist" and "even abstract" painters. Today we know about young abstract painters in Soviet Russia, and we hear of older painters whose oeuvre is divided into "official" and "private" spheres, with the private sphere open to all forms of experimentation. It is less well known that this "semiunderground" art has its audience, its fans, and even its patrons, including (nuclear affinities or the privilege of the irreplaceable?) several nuclear physicists. Although abstract painters were not allowed to show their work, the Fifth Exhibit of Young Moscow Painters shown last June incurred the wrath of the old academicists because of its "formalist" tendencies.

"Deeply upset by the disturbing paintings shown in the exhibit," Yoganson, the chairman of the USSR Fine Arts Academy, wrote an article, "In Defense of Realism in Painting," which appeared in *Soviet Culture*. In Stalin's time, an article by Yoganson or Gerasimov would have had the authority of an edict. In this case, however, *Literaturnaia gazeta* published a rebuttal of the chairman's arguments, turning the tables on him and charging him with "formalism" evident in his attachment to the nineteenth-century style of painting.

We should now watch developments in the Soviet Union ever more closely and with greater hope, particularly as Western experts on contemporary Soviet art agree that a renewal is underway in the Soviet Union itself. Camilla Grey says that the appearance of a new decorative element, a recurrent feature in Russian art, is a sign of a revival. And E. Steneberg, curator of the excellent "Russia's Contribution to Modern Art" exhibit in Frankfurt in 1959, writes in *Das Kunstwerk:* "The direction that art will take in Russia today is an open question. While I was there, I saw abstract canvases being painted; I spoke with young painters who were deeply affected by the newest trends. Is there another restless generation coming of age in Russia?"

The problem of the renewal of art in Russia is no longer linked to the idea of revolution. But if the new Soviet avant-garde can no longer draw its strength from communism's utopian theology, perhaps it can now draw it from its desacralization.

"Before anything happens," writes the anonymous Russian essayist, "our art will stand still, wavering between unfulfilled realism and unrealized classicism." But it is hard not to share his hope for a revival of Russian art, which could acquire universal significance once again. "We don't know where we are going, but having recognized that we have no choice, we reflect, follow hunches, and make hypotheses. Perhaps we will invent something amazing. But this *something* is not going to be socialist realism."

(1960)

TRANSLATED BY MICHAEL KOTT WITH TARA MCKELVEY

Zbigniew Herbert

Defense of the Templars

HIGH JURY,

The role of the defense in this trial, lasting six and a half centuries, is not an easy one. We cannot summon the prosecutors, witnesses, or defendants, whose bodies were consumed by fire, their ashes scattered by the wind. Apparently everything speaks against them. The prosecutor has thrown down upon the table a pile of documents, from which an unbiased reader can reconstruct a somber picture of the crimes and misdeeds of the accused and find convincing proof of guilt. Convincing, since the accused level the most severe accusations at themselves. We shall make it our task to call the reliability of these documents into question and to encourage you, High Jury, to read between the lines, to make you understand the background and mechanism as well as the methods of the investigation. Thus we must return to events preceding this cool evening when the stake was set alight. The leaders of the Templars, Jacques de Molay and Geoffroi de Charney, died in its flames. The time and place of the execution: 18 March 1314, a small island in the Seine within the borders of Paris. The sole mercy granted to the executed was to die facing the white towers of Notre-Dame. The last words: "The bodies belong to the King of France, but the souls belong to God."

Experts usually treat these final words with skepticism. Historians question their authenticity. But their value consists in the fact that they are the creation of collective consciousness, an at-

tempt at synthesis, a definition of fate. Please accept them, High
Jury, as yet another uncertain testimony.

And now let us try to reconstruct briefly the history of the
Templar order.

* * *

Among the Crusaders setting off to the Holy Land in 1095 was
an elderly nobleman from Champagne. As we know, this expedition resulted in the conquest of Jerusalem in 1099 and the creation
of the kingdom. But only a small number of Western knights remained in Palestine. The vast majority, exhausted by bickering and
the toils of war, returned home. The fate of the young kingdom of
Jerusalem, surrounded by a sea of infidels, was far from secure. In
order to keep this island, not only were stronger walls needed but
also a new society. The old method of Greek and Roman colonists
had its advocate in the chaplain of Baldwin I, Foucher de Chartres.
"We, who were people of the West," he wrote, "have become
people of the East. We, who were dwellers in Reims or Chartres,
have become citizens of Tyre and Antioch; we have already forgotten the place of our birth, and many do not know it at all. Some of
us have houses and servants in this country, which we will give to
our descendants as their heritage. Others have married women who
are not their countrywomen but are natives of Syria, Armenia, or
are even Saracens, but who have received the grace of baptism.
Some tend to their vineyards, others to their fields; they still speak
in different tongues, but already they begin to understand each
other; those who were poor in their country, God made rich; those
who did not even have a manor, now rule over cities. Why should
they return to the West, if they do so well in the East?" It is a
noteworthy text, even if we reject the element of obvious official
propaganda.

The new monarchy was more democratic, so to speak, and
more republican than many monarchies in the West. Royal authority was limited by a parliament of both barons and burghers. And
its voice was decisive in important matters, such as taxes. The peasants were free. Religious freedom was respected. In many temples
there was the practice of *simultaneum*—religious celebration according to various rites and creeds. The Torah, Koran, and the

Bible, on which one swore oaths in front of tribunals, coexisted peacefully—probably for the first time in history, and not only in courtrooms. Of course the real picture changed according to events, social tensions, and was far from ideal. However, one should be aware of this effort to create a multiracial, multireligious society.

Let us return now to our knight from Champagne. His name was Hugues de Payns, and he was, as noted, of advanced age but brave and vigorous. He has exchanged the green hills of his native country for the parched land of Palestine, but not for the material profit advertised so convincingly by Chaplain Foucher. With a handful of companions he has founded an order whose task is to defend pilgrims from bandits and Saracens and to protect wells. It is, in short, a kind of roadside militia. King Baldwin gave them a dwelling situated on the site of the Temple of Solomon, hence their name: the Templars. They took vows of purity and poverty. An ancient seal provides evidence, depicting two knights riding on one horse. If we can anticipate future events, High Jury, this second knight was interpreted during the investigation as Satan, the evil instigator. The inventiveness and imagination of slanderers, High Jury, know no bounds. Hugues de Payns travels to France and England, where the new order is enthusiastically received in both lay and clerical circles. There is a flow of benefices and donations. The order is joined by princes and barons. The ecumenical council in Troyes establishes its rule in 1128, and the highest moral authority in Europe, Saint Bernard, becomes its spiritual sponsor. In his well-known *Liber ad milites templi de laude novae militiae*, he contrasts the austere, virtuous knights of the temple with the newly enriched, vain knights of the West.

"They dislike all excess in food and clothing, and they strive only for what is necessary. They live together, without women and children . . . offensive words, superfluous acts, unmitigated laughter, complaining and grumbling, if noticed, do not pass among them unpunished. They abhor chess and dice; they are repulsed by hunting. They find no pleasure in the mindless chase of fowl; they are revolted by and avoid mimes, magicians, jugglers, light songs, and jokes. They cut their hair short, and they know from the Apostles that care for hair humiliates a man. No one ever saw them use a comb; they wash rarely, their beards are rough, full of dust, stained by heat and toil."

In Jerusalem the Templars soon took over two mosques, under which there were huge vaults designed as stables. In fact the fortified templum was a city within a city. Life was isolated, austere, and simple. Meals were served in a vast refectory with unadorned walls. The knights ate in silence and left a portion of their food for the poor. When one of the brothers died, his ration was given to a beggar for fourteen days. Three days a week no meat was served; twice a year there was a total fast. The day began with a mass celebrated two hours before sunrise. Then each knight visited the stables, groomed his horse, and inspected his weapons. At sunrise there was another mass, and during the day there were scores of obligatory prayers. Lunch, then roll call supervised by the master. Vespers, prayers, and silence until the end of the day. The rule also contained a penal code. Ten offences were punishable with exclusion from the order, or even life imprisonment. These were simony to gain admittance to the order, repetition of conversations heard in the chapter, stealth, desertion from the battlefield, robbery, murder of a Christian, sodomy, heresy (this offence, High Jury, should be kept in mind), lying, and abandoning the order.

Laudatory remarks by Saint Bernard of Clairvaux (O paradox of history) made the Templars powerful bankers in the Middle Ages. During the Second Crusade, the order had properties throughout Europe. Pilgrims traveling to the Holy Land, in order to avoid risk, would deposit money in one of their houses and receive the equivalent in Jerusalem. That they soon became lenders not only to the king of Jerusalem but also to sovereigns of England and France is evidence of their financial power. This very fact, High Jury, as we shall try to demonstrate, became the source of their downfall. The order's profits did not enrich its members. There was a strict rule that if a dying brother was found carrying money, he had to be buried in unconsecrated ground.

The Templars, who from a handful of monk-knights became an army of many thousands, were known as outstanding warriors. Let us call on the evidence of Louis VII, who wrote to Abbot Suger: "I cannot imagine how we would be able to hold our ground in this country [the Holy Land] without their assistance and presence. We ask you, therefore, that you double your kindness to them, so that they feel our intercession." There is reference further on to the large sum of two thousand marks lent to the sovereign, and a request that the regent-abbot return it to the order in France. Until the middle of the twelfth centry we cannot find a single document mentioning the Templars which does not extol their knightly virtues and loyalty.

And then? It is obvious, High Jury, that every social organism has its bright and dark moments. But the prosecutor has omitted all those facts which could speak for the defendants. He has ignored the heroic period of the order, underscoring only those moments that show its decadence and secularization, its abandonment of its ideals, its vanity and intrigues. The defense is far from blindly glorifying the Templars: we shall not challenge the prosecution where documents and sources testify against the order. We propose, however, that these facts should not be treated in isolation but be judged against the political and social background of their time.

The history of the kingdom of Jerusalem belongs to one of the most complicated and obscure chapters of history. While studying this period, we have the impression of looking into a simmering caldron of passions, intrigues, desire for fame and fortune, unnatural ambitions, complex political and dynastic machinations. The Templars, who had become a force of over ten thousand knights, could not stand aside and watch events on which rested not only their prestige and profit, as the prosecutor claims, but also their lives. They were forced to join in power politics. But let us add, High Jury, that they also participated in every great battle, sharing the Crusaders' miseries for two centuries: imprisonment, long sieges, marches through the desert, wounds, and death. The Crusaders came and went, and the miscalculations of their military raids fell on the heads of those who, like the Templars, decided to hold onto the patch of conquered land until the very end. This is, High Jury, indispensable to our understanding of the affairs and politics of the order.

In 1187 Saladin recaptures Jerusalem from the Crusaders. For a long time the kingdom is without a capital. Two years later the Third Crusade begins. Three great sovereigns could have changed the run of bad luck, yet it happened otherwise. Frederick Barbarossa was eliminated by an accident—death in the undertow of a river. Richard the Lion-Hearted was from the outset in rivalry with

Philip Augustus. Upon learning that the French monarch paid his followers three pieces of gold, Richard sold Cyprus to the Templars and announced that those who chose his banner would receive four gold pieces. As a result, Philip withdrew from the expedition. What is more, despite Saladin's intervention, in which the order served as an intermediary (later this fact will be used to prove that the Templars had good relations, or even plotted, with the Muslims), he murdered 2,700 captives, which provoked the massacre of French prisoners in retaliation. Nevertheless, the Templars were the vanguard of the ill-fated expedition, from which Richard withdrew upon learning that John Lackland had claimed his throne. He left Palestine on a Templar ship, dressed in a cassock of the order.

In the second decade of the thirteenth century, the already bad situation of the kingdom of Jerusalem was worsened by the Mongol invasion. Pope Honorius III persuaded the German emperor, Frederick II, to marry the heiress to the Jerusalem throne, Isabelle, the daughter of Jean de Brienne. The emperor reached hungrily for the fruit presented to him, forced the king to leave, and entertained an alliance with the sultan of Egypt, which brought about his excommunication.

Let us add that the policy of the Templars was based on just the opposite premise: they tried to maintain good relations with the sultan of Damascus, quite effectively, and relied on the old principle of exploiting differences in the opponent's camp. Through the emperor's alliances Jerusalem was reclaimed, and Frederick illegally proclaimed himself king. The capital was at last in Christian hands, which might seem to be a signal for pride and rejoicing. But it turned out that according to a secret agreement with the sultan, Jerusalem was not to be fortified or defended. The entire district belonging to the Templars, who from the beginning opposed the excommunication of the ruler, was given to the Muslims. The emperor also endowed them with property which was not his, namely, the fortresses of the order: Safet, Toron, Gaza, Darum, Krak, and Montréal. As if that were not enough, Frederick took over the order's castle, Château Pélerin.

One can hardly be suprised by the Templars' rage. They notified the emperor that if he did not leave Palestine, "they would lock him in a place from which he would never depart." Frightened by the uprising of the Guelfs, Frederick set out for Europe, leaving the power and care of the kingdom to the Teutonic Knights (well known to Poles and hostile toward the Templars). From a safe distance he initiated a campaign of slander against the order that dared to oppose his will. He repeated the old argument discrediting the Templars in the eyes of the Christian world: they plot with the infidels. He himself, with typical cynicism, assumed Eastern habits, maintaining good relations with the sultan of Damascus. At his court he was host to the ambassador of the sultan of Egypt. He even received the envoys of the Ismail sect of the Assassins, who, in all probability, killed at his instigation his opponent, Duke Louis of Bavaria.

Finally in 1248 there came the Crusade of Louis IX. One might expect that this time there would be harmonious cooperation between the Crusaders and the local knights. The disinterestedness of the leader of the expedition and his good relations with the Templars should have assured that much. Unfortunately, the plans of the expedition were prepared in Europe and completely overlooked local conditions. Against the advice of the Templars, the hopeless campaign against Egypt recommenced. Despite the order's opposition, its knights formed the vanguard of the army led by the king's brother, Robert, count of Artois. The Nile split the army into two parts. Against the arguments of the Templars, Robert decided not to wait for the rest of the forces and, after a short, victorious battle with the Turks, moved into the territory. Yet in the narrow streets of Mansûra the Crusaders were met by the Sultan Baybars and his Mamluks. From the roofs and barricades came a rain of missiles. Trapped, lacerated with arrows like hedgehogs, the Crusaders were smashed to pieces. The sultan's counterattacks resulted in a disastrous situation for the royal army: scurvy, hunger, and ditches filled with corpses forced Louis to surrender. There came captivity, from which the invalid king had to be ransomed for the staggering sum of £500,000.

Aware of the political misjudgments, in which they had no part, the Templars started negotiations with Damascus. Learning of this, Louis IX took strict disciplinary measures, including the dismissal of the grand master of the order and the exile of those who tried to make a treaty without his consent.

High Jury, these three selected episodes illustrate the permanently endangered state of the order, growing misunderstandings, numerous humiliations—the web of intrigues in which it was snared.

The sole consolation was the favor of the popes, who interceded effectively in a number of conflicts. In the end, even this support was lost.

The marshal of the Templars, Etienne de Sissey, was summoned to Rome in 1263 and stripped of his powers. If we are to believe the chronicler Gérard de Montréal, the reason was an amorous affair, a notorious and compromising rivalry for the favors of a certain beautiful lady from Acre.

The final act of the drama began on 5 April 1291 in this very town, Acre. The port city defended itself for two and a half months. The situation of the Crusaders was hopeless. Though they could have easily abandoned the fortress, a group of monk-knights together with the grand master, Guillaume de Beaujeu, defended it to the end. Acre was drowned in the onslaught. The kingdom of the Crusaders ceased to exist.

* * *

High Jury, after this extensive but necessary introduction, the defense will address itself to the central issue: that is, to the trial of the Templars (then led by the grand master Jacques de Molay) staged by the grandson of Louis IX, Philip the Fair, king of France. His hard rule was autocratic almost in the modern sense of the word, and he is justly considered a prototypical European dictator. His numerous wars exhausted the country's treasury. His rule was characterized by a series of great economic crises. Almost from the day he was enthroned, Philip was in conflict with the Holy See, which, as we know, led to the pope's captivity in Avignon. These political elements played a decisive role in the trial of the Templars.

The trial was initiated, High Jury, in order to eliminate power independent of the state. It was started—I shall not hesitate to claim—in order to appropriate the order's wealth. It was started in order to prevent the Templars, who were the third international power, from siding with the Vatican in the confrontation between king and pope. We shall attempt to demonstrate that the religious, moral, and ideological accusations voiced during the trial were but a smoke screen for the political motives of the entire operation.

Despite the loss of their properties in the kingdom of Jerusalem, the order was a force that every realistic sovereign had to take into account. Twenty thousand armed Templars could decide the fate of wars. They had properties and castles not only in France but also in Italy, Sicily, Portugal, Castile, Aragon, England, Germany, Bohemia, Hungary, and even Poland, where they kept two battalions and supported King Henry the Pious in the Battle of Legnica. Two centers, however, had special importance: Cyprus—the strategic center and base for expeditions to the East, and Paris—the political center.

In the French capital the walled Templars' quarter was a city within a city, with separate jurisdiction, separate administration, and the right of asylum. Philip the Fair's relations with the papacy were clear and unscrupulous. Bulls flying over "our dear son" and the persuasive *Ausculta fili* were viewed like exotic birds from a distant epoch. The ultimatum issued by the Council of Rome in 1302 had only one effect: the king established the Estates General, which accepted his politics "in the name of the nation." What are two theoretical swords for someone who trusts only the one in hand? The response to Boniface VIII's proposed excommunication of Philip was to send an envoy, Guillaume de Nogaret, to Italy to bring the pope by force to France.

What was the Templars' relation to Philip? The prosecutor has told us that according to numerous proofs, retired officers (that is how one could describe the order's situation after the fall of the kingdom of Jerusalem) like to plot. The facts, however, testify to their deep loyalty to the French sovereign, and at least their financial, but quite decisive, support of his actions. Nothing foreshadows the conflict, there are no warning signs, but in the inner circle of royal counselors a plan of attack ripens. In the same year that the king declares "our genuine and particular attachment to the order," an occasion arises to provide the necessary pretext for the affair. As the High Jury has probably guessed, we are talking about the secret denunciation.

At the beginning of 1305, a certain Noffo Dei, a Florentine and—let us add—a criminal, gives testimony from prison which indicts the Templars with apostasy and bad conduct. In addition, the king is feverishly collecting information from brothers expelled from the order. The castles and homes of the Templars are invaded by an army of spies.

At the same time, unconnected to the denunciations, the new pope, Clement V, proposes a merger of the Templar order with the Order of the Hospitalers. The purpose was to join forces before a new Crusade, which was not in fact launched. The grand master, Jacques de Molay, rejects this suggestion. One can guess that his motive was not just pride, but the difficulty of reconciling two rules. This move would prove tragic in its results.

When we reflect, High Jury, on the trial of the Templars, we should note that Philip the Fair was not acting solely on cold calculation. His attitude toward the order was marked by authentic passion. It is a psychological moment not without importance. We shall try to explain.

Toward the end of 1305, after the third currency devaluation, the *petit peuple* of Paris rebelled. The upheavals reached such a state that the king and his family were forced to escape to the Templars' fortress, the famous Tour du Temple, where he endured a humiliating siege by the "populace." Within a few days the leaders of the rebellion were hanged at the gates of Paris, but the taste of defeat was bitter. Nothing humiliates a monarch more than the feeling of gratitude, especially toward those whom one plans to pronounce criminals. In the same year Philip conducted a dress rehearsal for the trial of the Templars. The object of the maneuvres was a defenseless nation, the Jews, whose property was confiscated, they themselves being cruelly tortured and finally condemned to exile.

Philip the Fair knew that in a widespread action the political police should act swiftly to eliminate any danger of resistance. The thunderbolt must strike before the victim sees the lightning.

On Thursday 12 October 1307 Jacques de Molay walked beside the king during the funeral of the wife of Charles of Valois. On Friday morning all the Templars in France were arrested. We must bow, High Jury, in sad admiration to this unprecedented display of police precision.

The prosecutor has said that the imprisonment of the Templars surprised no one, that charges against them were voiced many times. He added that Philip the Fair conferred with Pope Clement V over this matter, but again he omitted the background of these talks. It is known that these negotiations concerned a new Crusade.

The pope wanted to send as its leader the dangerous kidnapper of popes de Nogaret, hoping to break his political career and return him to a virtuous path. The idea of a Crusade, however, was totally unwelcome to Philip. He presented its difficulties, claiming trouble in the Templar order, which, as usual, was to constitute the nucleus of the army. The prosecution has also ignored the fact that the order's master, Jacques de Molay himself, asked the pope for an investigation to clear the order of frequent yet vague accusations. Clement V in turn, unable to find reliable evidence against the Templars, in September 1307 asked Philip the Fair for the results of his investigation. It is obvious, High Jury, that the king could not compromise himself by providing testimonies of criminals or obviously bribed brothers who had been expelled from the order. One had to extract, by means of a hot iron, self-accusations from those who currently belonged to the order.

The warrant of arrest sent to barons, prelates, and royal officials in the provinces is a masterpiece of rhetoric: "It is a bitter thing, a lamentable matter, a matter truly horrible to contemplate, and terrible to hear about—an odious crime, an execrable evil, an appalling act, a detestable disgrace—truly inhuman deeds have reached our ears, causing our deep astonishment, and most shocked repulsion. . . ." High Jury, please count the adjectives. Abundance of adjectives is a sure sign not only of bad poetry but also of accusations weak in fact; further on, the text contains nothing but the gurgle of rage.

The investigation immediately followed the arrests and was conducted by lay authorities. Instructions for the commissioners recommend "thorough examinations, if necessary with the use of torture." The accused are faced with the alternative either confess and be pardoned or die at the stake.

Progress in our civilization, High Jury, consists mainly in the fact that simple tools for splitting heads have been replaced by hatchet words, which have the advantage of psychologically paralyzing an opponent. Such words are "mind-debaucher," "witch," and "heretic." The Templars were accused of heresy, chiefly to deprive the pope of the possibility of intervening on their behalf. Moreover, the battle was difficult from the start. Philip the Fair had power, the Holy See just diplomacy.

Now comes the moment most taxing for the defense, and it is hardly surprising that the prosecution placed its emphasis here. It is true that Jacques de Molay admitted publicly, in the presence of theologians and representatives of the church and the University of Paris, that there was a long-standing custom practiced during the admission of new brothers: they denounced Christ and spat on the cross. Another dignitary of the order, Geoffroi de Charney, gave similar testimony, making the exception, however, that he himself was never involved in such practices, as contrary to the principles of the Creed. One should add that both confessions were made just twelve days after the arrests, which may suggest that they were spontaneous. Let us remember, however, that for suspects under investigation time is not measured in days but in hours, and that conforming to royal instructions, the investigative apparatus worked "thoroughly."

It is quite probable that the grand master, who as the trial demonstrated was a very naive politician, was promised that public confession would save the order. Moreover, the very act of spitting on the cross does not indicate apostasy, but according to many experts is an element of initiation, dialectical in character. One might recall the well-known ritual of knighting, when a symbolic slap in the face is the only affront that a knight must endure without return. In addition, the testimonies of various Templars are contradictory. Some say that they were spitting not on the cross but to the side. Others deny the practice. Geoffroi de Gonneville explained that the custom was introduced by a bad master, who having been in Saracen captivity, regained his freedom by renouncing Christ, though the accused could not identify this master.

Brother Gérard de Pasagio declared: "A novice entering the order was presented with a wooden crucifix and asked if that was God. He answered that it was the image of the Crucified. A receiving brother told him: 'Do not believe this. That is but a piece of wood. Our Lord is in Heaven.' " This is evidence against idolatry, of which the Templars were accused, and a proof of the high spiritualization of their faith. In short, High Jury, the testimonies were contradictory as to the custom itself and as to its origin. More important, neither written records nor preserved rules contain such an ordinance.

The case of the idol which was supposed to be venerated by the Templars and over which a sea of ink was spilled, so that even if it were an angel it would have turned into a devil, is similar. The Grand Inquisitor, Guillaume de Paris, instructed the investigative organs to quiz the accused about the statue with a human head and a huge beard. Again the statements are contradictory and vague. For some it was a statue of wood, for others of silver and leather; feminine or masculine; bare-faced or bearded; resembling a cat or a pig; it had one head, or two, or even three. Despite the confiscation of all sacred objects, nothing resembling the descriptions could be found.

What we have here, High Jury, is a classic case of collective psychosis. And we—who know the logic of fear, the psychopathology of a hunted man, the theory of group behavior in the face of extermination—we should not believe it. Let us remember that the medieval imagination was haunted by the devil. Who could better explain to the tortured, to those imprisoned in dungeons, the sense of their fate?

What remains, High Jury, is the name of that demon. It has survived until our time, being the subject of numerous experts' consideration. Not the object but the word is the sole evidence in this trial. Let us utter this word at last: Baphomet.

A German expert, the orientalist Baron von Hammer-Purgstall, finds its origin in the word *Bahumid*, which was supposed to mean an ox. Hence the conclusion that it was a case of the cult of the Golden Calf, of which the Templars in fact were accused. This thesis did not hold water, and the author himself later changed it into an equally unconvincing one. A specialist in the history of the Templars and a prominent scholar, Emil Michelet, saw in it an acronym that according to the Cabala should be read backward: *TEMpli Omnium Hominum Pacis ABbas*. It was noted also that the name could originate from a port held by the Templars: Bapho, where in ancient times stood the temple of Astarte—Venus and Moon, Virgin and Mother—to whom children were sacrificed. This hypothesis was mentioned by the prosecutor, who followed a line of fantastic charges against the Templars, including cannibalism.

A rather more plausible explanation, at least from a philological point of view, was provided at the turn of the nineteenth century by an outstanding Arabist, Sylvestre de Sacy, who derived the name from the mispronounced name of Mahomet. This theory was supported by a poem composed by a Templar, Oliver, in the *langue d'oc*, "E Bafonet obra de son poder" (And Mahomet has flared with his might). It is by no means proof, as the prosecution would have it, of the infiltration of the Templars' esoteric doctrine by Islam. Though they were attracted to a certain extent to the religions of the East, no document indicates that they were a religious sect. In their minds the perspective on faith was certainly enlarged. What was an axiom for every French nobleman setting forth on a Crusade—that Christianity was the only religion worthy of the name—was unsettled by new contacts and experiences. The Koran, recognizing Christ as one of the Prophets, certainly facilitated that process.

Let us return from the East, which at the time of our story is just a fading echo, to France, where the life and honor of the order are at stake. As becomes a modern leader, Philip the Fair could use propaganda with outstanding skill. As the tortured moan in the dungeons throughout France, the king writes a letter to European sovereigns denouncing the "crimes" of the Templars. However, not all gave credence to the charges. The king of England, Edward II, saw them as calumnies and conveyed his favorable disposition toward the Templars to the kings of Portugal, Castile, Aragon, and Sicily, and to the pope. One can easily conclude that the allegedly bad reputation of the Templars was not as universal as the prosecution would have us believe.

After the initial self-accusation extracted from the grand master, the Templars had only one hope: that they would be entrusted to Church jurisdiction, or, more precisely, that they would be judged by the pope. And in fact at the end of 1307, the king agreed to send the prisoners to Clement V. Hearing this news, the Templars revoked their testimonies. According to tradition, Jacques de Molay did so in front of a crowd gathered in a church, showing them the marks of his torture.

Seeing the threads of the intrigue slipping through his fingers, Philip presses the pedal of propaganda—this time internal propaganda. Letters circulate in Paris accusing the pope of being bribed by the Templars. Nothing fosters emotion better than pecuniary arguments. Having excited the mob, the king turns toward parliament and the University of Paris for support of his antipapal politics, demanding a statement on the Templars. The university, however, responds that matters of heresy should be judged by an ecclesiastical tribunal, offering additional proof that not all public opinion turned against the order. The intellectuals, as usual, proved unreliable; but the parliament that assembled in May 1308 in Tours—admittedly incomplete, since many noblemen preferred to excuse their absence than to take part in the farce—after acquainting itself with the forced testimonies, declares that the Templars deserve death. Strengthened by public opinion, Philip travels to Poitiers to meet the pope.

Clement V confronted the king in a masterly way, by immediately turning the conversation to matters of the Crusade while keeping silent about the trial of the Templars. The king had no alternative but to use his faithful dignitaries of the Church, the archbishops of Narbonne and Bourges, who together with royal confidants violently attacked the order and the indifference of ecclesiastical power, sparing no offensive words against the pope himself. Clement V maintained his position. He even remarked that some of the Templars' testimonies seemed unconvincing and in order to gain time promised that the Council of Vienne, due to gather the next year, would address itself to the problem of the order. He also demanded to see the principal defendants.

The defendants were transported by armed convoy from Paris to Poitiers. The journey was suddenly interrupted in Chinon, on the pretext of the indisposition of the accused. Beyond any doubt, High Jury, it was a scheme prepared in advance. Chinon, whose somber walls have been preserved to this day, was a suitable place for that interlude, with its immense dungeons. When the pope's envoys reached the place of new torment, accompanied by the sworn enemies of the Templars, de Nogaret and de Plaisians, the accused kept silent or admitted their guilt. Returned to the dungeons, they could write their testament on the walls.

While examining the dossier of the case, we can easily note how often the interrogated retract their testimonies, only to return, after some days, to the most severe self-accusations. One cannot explain it except by the use of fire, cauldron, estrapade, iron boots, and hoop-iron. The defense takes the liberty of quoting fragments from some of the testimonies.

Ponsard de Gizy, 29 November 1309:

"Asked if he was subjected to torture, he answered that in the three months that elapsed before the confession made by him in the presence of the Lord Bishop of Paris, he was thrown into a pit with his hands tied so tightly that blood ran to his nails; he had said then that if they tormented him, he would recant previous testimonies and say everything they wanted. He was ready for anything, only to make his suffering short: a beheading, the stake, submersion in boiling water for the honor of the order, but could not bear the long torment he had to endure in prison for over two years."

Brother Bernard from Albi:

"I was tortured so much, so long was I interrogated and kept in the fire, that my feet were burned, and I felt my bones breaking inside me."

Brother Aimery de Villiers-le-Duc, 13 May 1310:

"The protocol says that the accused was pale and terrified. He had sworn with his hand on the altar that the crimes of which the order was accused were an invention. 'If I lie, let my body and soul be consumed by Hell right here in this place.' When his previous testimonies were read to him, he answered: 'Yes, I confessed many misdeeds, but that was because of the torment inflicted upon me by royal knights, Guillaume de Marcilly and Hugues de la Celle, during interrogation. Yesterday I saw fifty-four of my brothers taken on carts to be burned alive. . . . Ah, if I am going to die at the stake, I shall confess that I am very afraid of death, that I cannot endure it, I shall yield to terror. . . . I shall confess under oath, in front of you, in front of anyone, to any crime you charge the order with; I shall admit I have killed the Lord if they so demand.' "

I would like to stress, High Jury, the psychological side of death at the stake. The animal fear of fire rests on the knowledge that it will inflict the most acute pain. What spiritual strength is needed to keep faith, in order to carry at least the smallest part of ourselves through this destructive element. For medieval society the taste of ash was not, as for us, the taste of nothingness. Death at the stake was the vestibule of Hell, a never-ending stake where bodies suffer inextinguishable pain. The physical fire merged with the spiritual. Present suffering foreshadows eternal torment. Heaven—the domain of the chosen, the cool, silent masses of air— was in the eyes of the dying remote and inaccessible.

At the beginning of 1309 the investigation is renewed. This new phase is characterized by tightening of the screws of the machine for extracting testimonies (in Paris alone, thirty-six Templars died during interrogation). On the other hand, a seemingly inexplicable thing happens: the unprecedented resistance of the prisoners, who abandon all tricks and politics. Jacques de Molay states that he will defend the order, but only in front of the pope. Other brothers make similar declarations. By 2 May the number of Templars ready to defend the order has grown to five hundred and sixty-three. The answer to this mass resistance is a stake at which fifty-four Templars perish. The old Roman method of decimation triumphs.

In June 1311 the investigation is closed and the dossier sent to the pope. The Council of Vienne did not bring the expected relief for the order. These were the years of the Avignon captivity, and the pope considered the case as lost. The bull *Vox in excelso* of 22 March 1312 dissolved the order, yet it did not contain a condemnation of the Templars. By the bull *Ad providam* of 2 May, their property was to be handed over to the Hospitalers. The blood of the brothers of the Temple did not turn into Philip's gold. The prisons of France, however, were full; and something had to be done with the dignitaries of the order, who wanted to defend themselves, "since we do not even have four pennies to pay for a fresh defense." They constantly demand to be brought before a papal tribunal.

The investigation, however, was over and the envoys of Clement V assisted passively at the passing of the sentence. The leaders of the Templars faced life imprisonment. The sentence of Jacques de Molay and Geoffroi de Charney was read in Notre-Dame Cathedral. A great crowd listened in silence; but before the reading of the sentence could be completed, both men—perhaps the dignified Gothic of Notre-Dame exercised its influence—faced the people and shouted down the charges of crime and heresy leveled against the Templars, whose rule "was always sacred, right, and Catholic." A sentry's heavy hand fell on the mouth of the master to muffle the last words of the condemned. The cardinals handed over the recalcitrant to the court of Paris. Philip the Fair commanded burning at the stake on the same day. To appease his anger, he gave to the flames another thirty-six unrepentant brothers.

High Jury, that appears to be the end of the drama of the Templar order. Experts rummage the tombs for a clue to the mystery. Sometimes they come across the gifts of eternity, sometimes they are fascinated by the smile of the alleged Baphomet found on a portal. The defense set forth a more modest task: examination of the tools.

In history nothing remains closed. The methods used against the Templars enriched the repertoire of power. That is why we cannot leave this distant affair under the pale fingers of archivists.

(1962)

TRANSLATED BY JAROSLAW ANDERS AND MICHAEL MARCH

Bolesław Miciński

Portrait of Kant

Dedicated to Father Augustyn Jakubisiak, author of Essai sur les
limites de l'espace et du temps

> *Each night I see the black abyss*
> *Above us in the sky,*
> *The heavens vast, trembling with stars,*
> *A swirl of nebulae.*
>
> *Eternal valley, black ravine*
> *Of God that brings dismay,*
> *Streaming down whirlwinds of creation*
> *The milky, sun-drenched way.*
>
> *But greater dread begins to reign*
> *When in myself I look—*
> *The lawless orbits' flaming mane*
> *My ego swings along.*
>
> *There whirl no nebulae, no seeds*
> *Of rebirth dwell,*
> *Night unseeing, dark and endless—*
> *Immanuel!*
>
> —*Jarosław Iwaszkiewicz, "Immanuel Kant"*

*Time is the supreme illusion. It is only our inner prism by
means of which we decompose life and being, the mode
according to which we perceive what is simultaneous in the
idea. The eye does not see a sphere all at once, although the
sphere exists all at once; it is necessary for the sphere to turn*

before the eye that watches it, or for the eye to turn around
the sphere that is being contemplated. In the first case, it is
the world that unfolds or seems to unfold in time, in the
second case, it is our thought that analyzes and recomposes it
successively. For the supreme intelligence, time does not exist;
that which will be IS.

—*Henri Frédéric Amiel*

1

The division of the arts into "spatial" and "temporal" belongs to one of the most interesting chapters in the history of aesthetics. But it is already past history. The eighteenth-century charm of Abbé Dubos lives on fresh in our memory; memory likewise has preserved the cool pages of *Laocoon*, which resemble the steel plates on which Lessing's sharp etching needle drew with such precision those ancient lines. That is all that remains of this theory in the memory of the ordinary lover of art.

Essentially the matter is quite different from what Dubos and Lessing thought. The division of the arts into spatial and temporal is, if not altogether false, at least somewhat risky. A painting, no doubt, is spatial in a physical sense, but in our experience of it we "construe" a Rembrandt at a very slow pace; and as the years pass by, we seem to notice ever new shadows on Bathsheba's arm, just as with the passing of the years we notice ever new wrinkles spreading around the hollow of one's eyes, which catch in their net the dimming pupil and the slowly fading iris. Through time we grasp the space of the stony sky on which Michelangelo recorded the history of this world: its past and its future. And the present? There is no such thing as the present—there is only memory and expectation. That is precisely the crux of the so-called spatial arts.

In his letters Mozart writes that one day he heard a new composition "all at once" like a chord. He looked at the fully developed musical idea as at a picture or a piece of sculpture which can be taken in at one glance. Gluck likewise saw one of his compositions in spatial forms: in the rhythm of chairs placed upside down on the tables of a sleeping tavern. One of the best musical masters of the past, who wished to give an artistic rendition of Christ's Passion, while reading verse 34, chapter 19 of the Gospel according to John, *pierced* the lines of the score by writing the musical notes as though with a spear, imitating the soldier who ran through the side of our Redeemer.

There are no "spatial" or "temporal" arts—that is true enough. But the traditional division should not be thoughtlessly discarded out of sheer nonchalance. The matter is more complicated: in literature itself, for example, we can find both spatial and temporal forms. The psychological novel is entangled in time, just because every individual is entangled in "his own human" time. If understanding another person is based on understanding our own psychic processes, if a blind human monad—that "windowless" being—cannot transcend itself, then how can we, bounded by time, understand the adventures of Conrad's heroes otherwise than in time? Chained—as though to a single oar—side by side with the heroes of the psychological novel, we sail through the dim ocean of personality, and in their company we cross the shadow line under a black layer of clouds, under an overcast sky, above the trail that leads to the heart of darkness. Confined in the narrow frames of consciousness, the heroes of the psychological novel live in time— as do we.

However, there are literary forms that can be "reduced," so to speak, to *space*. These are forms that time does not "devour." The epic depicts man "from outside" in a painterly fashion. The epic writer, passing with a light step over the abyss of the personality, betrays a lack of awareness of the hidden forces at war within man, but in so doing he displays both contempt and tolerance for beings who "are as leaves are, and now flourish and grow warm with life . . . but then again fade away and are dead."*

The epic writer strips colors from the spring, summer, and October leaves—and out of their green, red, and gold he molds his world as *unchangeable* as the world of Plato's ideas. In that world the human faces are forever frozen in the same grimace. What gives motion to an epic structure is the ordinary sequence of events and the facts graspable from outside—like a painting taken in at one glance, or a fresco in which we do not seek for any other content beyond that provided by the arrangement of the shapes and colors.

---

*From Homer, *The Iliad*, trans. Richmond Lattimore (Chicago: University of Chicago Press, 1966). All subsequent quotations from *The Iliad* are from this edition.

An epic work is animated by motion only during the first reading. Our curiosity as to "what will happen next" animates the picture for a moment: Odysseus builds a flat-boat . . . it sails out into the open water . . . the ship ploughs through the waves of the sea . . . the waves drive at the sail . . . Leukhotea breaks the surface of the water like a diving bird. Our curiosity—what will happen next—puts the image into motion. But it is only apparent motion, similar to the motion of figures drawn on the margins of a book whose pages flash by rapidly under the thumb of a child who plays at moviemaking.

It is solely curiosity about the sequence of events that prevents us from looking at the epic whole as we would at a painting. It suffices to become acquainted with the plot once only—during the first reading—in order to render the whole construction motionless and to transform the literary work into a painting. In an epic work all things are given *together:* Hermes remains suspended in flight above the violet ocean, like a seagull that has perfectly matched the resistance of its wings with the force of the wind; Polyphemos standing on a hilltop has thrown his arms back—motionless as the rock he is clutching in his veiny hands, he becomes transformed into a stone, a piece of sculpture.

Everything is motionless in that world freed from the curiosity of the reader who already knows the course of Hermes' journey and who, with a precision almost in keeping with the laws of ballistics, can chart the flight of the rock now frozen in the giant's hands. "Nausicaa like a fresh palm"*resembles a tree that has not yet been touched by the wind. The smile on her face has become frozen. The trees on the island of the Pheiakians have become petrified, the waves of the sea have become petrified, and Odysseus too, standing up to his knees in the stony sea bath, has become petrified.

Once read, the epic becomes transformed into a folder of engravings which we can pick up separately and put together in such a way that Telemachus, greatly distressed about his father's fate, appears side by side with Odysseus, equally distressed about his son's fate. The work of the epic writer is like the shield of Achilles on which the divine smith forged an image of the world: "the sky, the earth upon it, the sea's water, the tireless sun, and the moon waxing

*From Homer, *The Odyssey,* trans. Robert Fitzgerald (New York: Doubleday Anchor, 1963). All subsequent quotations from *The Odyssey* are from this edition.

into her fulness, and all the constellations that festoon the heavens." On that shield are golden Pallas Athene and golden Ares, and thirsty creatures bending over the water, and flocks of animals forged in gold, and vineyards, and soft golden fields freshly plowed, and nine hunting dogs, herdsmen and fallow lions leaving their traces in the golden slime of the flood waters. Bordered by the Ocean River—like the image of the world drawn by the cartographers of antiquity—the shield of Achilles is the Genesis of the ancient world—it is the history of creation. In just such a fashion all things have dropped down from the Creator's hands: trees, birds, reptiles, horses, raging rivers, dark waters of the ocean, and history itself.

"He that liveth forever created all things together," says Ecclesiastes. *Qui vivit in aeternum, creavit omnia simul.* Like the shield forged by Hephaestus, the "ready-made" world has dropped down from the Creator's hands. For if we see the work of the lame smith as a sequence of ever new shapes spreading out over the surface of the shield, it is only thanks to the restless *eyes* of Thetis, who watched over this work. Narrow are the frames of our perception, and prescribed are the limits of our conscious attention. *Unable to grasp everything all at once in a comprehensive glance, we bestow sequence upon the facts:* thus, first there is spring, then summer, then autumn. But on the shield of Achilles spring blossoms side by side with the ripeness of summer, and autumn fruits fall straight into the cool hands of winter—and from her icy arms the smoky domes of chestnuts spread upwards—and autumnal figures scorched by the summer sun pluck coarse walnuts. Since the shield of Achilles is round, it is a *circulus vitiosus.* We *read* this Genesis entangled in time and day after day we study the history of creation, because we do not know how to *look* at the world that has dropped down from the Creator's hands like an unripe apple hurled down by the wind of sin. The shortcomings of our vision implant in our consciousness the notion of time and its divisions. For us, the light comes first, then the muddy waters, the earth, trees, and birds.

But he that liveth forever created all things together.

* * *

Under the meager circle of light provided by our consciousness, a black disk whirls like a phonograph record on which history has been transcribed once and for all—to the banging of kettle-drums, the clashing of cymbals, the wailing of a chorus. The black disk whirls like the enormous sky, or the stars by which we wish to read the future.

—Oh! If we only could know "what will happen next"! If we could set out the future lines of our paths through life with the same certainty with which we trace the trajectory of the rock held in the blind giant's hands; if we could sever the threads of curiosity and anxious expectation that make the incomprehensible puppets of history dance. If it were possible to know the "action" of history and to reduce the epic work to its actual dimensions. If it were possible to look at history as at the shield that was supposed to protect Achilles from death! If we could, like the visionary genius of Patmos, pull apart the threads of curiosity and take a look at history "all at once," and hear—as Mozart heard his quartet—and see—as Gluck saw his music. If we could deliver ourselves from our human time and expand into infinity the circle of our narrow consciousness and know: *what will happen next.*

If.

In that case we would not be carried along by the impetuous currents of restless time, and once we had reduced history to its actual spatial dimensions, we could walk alongside the immense fresco and study its ever new details. We could, like the visionary of Patmos, measure history by ells, measure the world by ells, and reduce our pride, conceit, and madness to decent proportions, since they too would be measurable by ells.

We would be able to "tour" the future the way one "tours" the Sistine Chapel, and without raising our eyes to the dome, we could bend over the mirror, following the practice of tourists, and see reflected in it the history of this world as recorded by Michelangelo on that stony sky above.

Like a bird blinded by a sudden flash in a looking glass, the world falls into hands that clutch the mirror by its handle. Clouds, glints of light, shadows sway in its congealed glassy stream. From that stony sky stream down the light of creation, the dust of history, the soot of ever-burning candles, and the warm blood like the fresh paint that dripped down into Michelangelo's eyes. It suffices to tilt the mirror slightly, and history will flow through our fingers in streams of faces, gestures, and contorted bodies. It suffices to turn the mirror in order to see . . .

. . . to see the narrow shoulders encased in brown woolen cloth, the fragile arms, the white wig tied with a black ribbon, and the face reflected in the mirror: the vaulted forehead, the eyes in a net of wrinkles, the sunken cheeks, and the withered lips—the face of Immanuel Kant.

The mirror in a mahogany frame hangs on the white wall of the modest living room. The metal spirals of a barometer glitter nearby. The face slowly floats out of the mirror, bends for a moment over the barometer, and fades in its transparent glass so that it is scarcely possible to make out the dark outlines of the eye sockets, the nose, and the lips.

The barometer indicates fog, and fog is drifting above Königsberg. The morning fog whirls through the windings of a narrow street, sticks to the branches of the trees, and clouds the window panes of the living room. In the hazy light outside the window loom unreal, almost two-dimensional trees resembling damp, brownish patches on a still-wet watercolor. The metal buttons on a servant's livery glitter in the back of the room—Martin Lampe wearing a white apron dusts the sofa and armchairs and with a cloth wipes a windowed cupboard filled with porcelain and silver. A small door leads from the living room to the study, where there are two tables, a sofa, a few chairs, a wooden armchair with a headrest, a picture of Rousseau in a gold frame, and a piece of green silk curtain hanging over the window.

At five o'clock in the morning Lampe knocked at the bedroom door: "It is time," he said, like the angel who wakes the shriveled bodies lying in their coffins awaiting the Last Judgment.

Now it is seven o'clock, and Kant has already smoked his pipe. Tremendous coils of smoke engulfed the delicate mist rising above his cup of tea and spread throughout the entire apartment like the fog over Königsberg. Kant walked across the living room, knocked on the barometer with his bony finger, and appeared at the doorway of his house. Now we see Kant as Borowski* described him: the three-cornered hat, the powdered wig, the black necktie, the

---

*L. E. Borowski, archbishop of the Evangelical church in Königsberg. Longtime friend and pupil of Kant's.

shirt with lace ruffles, the coat of brown woolen cloth, the gray stockings, the shoes with silver buckles, and the sword on his left side. He walks down the narrow alley lined with lime trees to the university to deliver his lecture.

Even with his weak voice, he knew how to command attention and how to dominate the lecture hall from his lectern. He used to fix his fading eyes on the face of the student sitting nearest to him. Rows of benches, foreheads, heads supported on elbows, slowly receded and became outlined on the white walls in a multitude of lines and geometrical planes as on an engraving. Kant intently watched the face he had chosen as though trying to infer from it the level of attention and understanding of the whole audience. The slightest change in appearance or clothing could throw him into a state of confusion. Once it happened that noticing a button missing on the coat of one of his students, he interrupted his lecture. Likewise, when the student sewed the button back on, Kant staggered, his thoughts utterly confused, and asked shyly, "Would you be so kind as to cut that button off, I am no longer accustomed to the sight of it."

After the lecture, he played a game of billiards at the café. The motion of the balls, as obedient as Galileo's spheres, did not disturb his sense of reality. In their movements there was the symmetry of trapezoids, triangles, and squares. The glints of the balls against the "Euclidean" green plane traced the lines of familiar geometrical figures and revolved like heavenly bodies entangled in immutable laws. On his way home, in the lime alley, there unfolds before his eyes a shifting panorama of tree trunks, blurred outlines of houses, faces of passersby deformed from out of the corner of his eye, bows and smiles barely recorded in his consciousness.

At noon the blue sky has swallowed up the fog. The shadows of the trees grow dark on the pavement, and the windowpanes are blinded by the sun over Königsberg.

At dinner, Kant shines, displaying the charm of an old-fashioned man of the world. We perceive him differently at noontime—there is less of the pedant in him, less of the eccentric with a shaky sense of reality, and more of the *charme* of an eighteenth-century intellectual. Here, at the modestly set table, over a bottle of wine, the conversation deals with "nonphilosophical" themes: politics and geography, Lampe and Napoleon, Frederick the Great and linguistics, phrenology and magnetism. How beautiful were those conversations with his friends, those unforgettable hours, which have been immortalized for us by Rink, Wasianski, Borowski, and Jachmann!*It was only in the last years of his life that Kant began to shun the company of people his own age and surrounded himself with young people. We can well imagine that the lack of a *convive* would have been no less upsetting than that missing button on the student's coat. . . . Those conversations were beautiful indeed! One day it even happened that Hippel† got up from the table only at eight in the evening.

But it happened only once.

After dinner is the time set aside for a walk—always alone. Dressed in a gray coat and carrying a Spanish reed, later replaced by a walking stick, Kant walks with a measured step down the alley lined with lime trees.

In July 1789 the French Revolution cut Kant's walk shorter than usual. Another time he stopped for a moment and with the sharp end of his ferruled cane turned over the dead bodies of some young fledgling swallows crushed on the sidewalk. It was in early spring and almost at the end of his life. "Once when a cold spring had killed even the insects," Kant later confessed, "I noticed quite a few young unfledged swallows lying dead on the ground. I raised my eyes up to the nests and immediately understood that it was the parent birds who had condemned a certain number of their young to death in order to sustain the rest in a state of adequate vigor. My imagination stood still, and there was nothing left but to fall down and worship instinct, so close is it to intelligence."

On the way back home, lost in thought, he tried to put together various scattered words: ". . . to organize a community of rational beings, even if they were demons . . . to organize them in such a way so that they would become a society. . . ."

He formulated this idea back in his study, in the shadow of Rousseau's portrait, at six in the evening. . . .

* * *

GLOUCESTER: When shall I come to th' top of that same hill?
EDGAR: You do climb up it now; look how we labour.

*All members of Königsberg's literary circle. Friends and students of Kant's.
†T. G. von Hippel, a literary man in Königsberg and an author of some repute.

. . . at six o'clock, with a scrap of paper in his hands, sunk in his armchair, which faces the window, Kant looks at the ruins of Königsberg castle. The blackened redness of its walls contrasts sharply with the pale sky across which helpless white clouds are drifting. The castle on the hill seems to look all the higher because the tops of the poplars growing outside the window reach the embankments and extend the lines of the towers.

The redness of the walls slowly fades out, and the castle dissolves like fog. The clouds become dispersed; the poplars grow more and more slender—and finally become invisible too. The green of the window curtains turns gray, and the contours of the furniture blur. The white walls of the study swallow up shades and shapes. But the portrait of Rousseau that hangs above the desk is still visible. Now even Rousseau sinks into the thickening nothingness. If Lampe had opened the door to the study at this moment, he would have gone mad: there were no ruins of the Königsberg castle, there were no trees outside the window, there was no green silk curtain, there was no desk, there were no thin hands resting on the wooden arm of the chair, in fact, there was no armchair at all, no time, no space—only the "impenetrable, bottomless dark night."

> . . .When shall I come to th' top of that same hill?
> You do climb up it now; look how we labour.
> . . .Come on, Sir, here's the place; stand still;
> How fearful,
> And dizzy 'tis to cast one's eyes so low!
> . . .I look no more,
> Lest my brain turn, and the deficient sight
> Topple down headlong.

Slowly the bony white hands reappear and locate once again the familiar polished arm of the armchair. Returned to reality, the contours of the chairs and tables regain their solidity, a circle of light gleams above the candlestick, and only the portrait of Rousseau hanging above the desk is scarcely visible because it is covered by a powerful profile—the shadow of Immanuel Kant's head. The glow of the candles strikes the frame of the portrait and scatters golden dust along the wall above the vaulted forehead.

The swaying shadow moves along the wall and dies out in the black rectangle of the window. High above, in the Kantian starry sky, the beads of distant worlds sparkle like silver for a moment until the silk curtain hides them from sight. The dark profile grows dim against the green cloth, withdraws, and a minute later is seen bending over a book.

Now it is time for reading.

The pages of the Dutch thinker rustle in hands white as parchment: "Insects dwelling in a beggar's hair were accustomed to call their residence a gigantic globe and themselves the masterpiece of creation. But once one of them—a sort of Fontenelle of the species—said to all free-thinkers of his district, pointing at the head of a certain nobleman: 'We are not unique in nature! The whole of nature seems to be inhabited by lice too.' " A faint smile of delight appeared on Kant's face, and he marked the margin of the book with his sharp, pale fingernail. "Most people miss the purpose of life," he noted down. "To digest . . . to multiply. Animals attain the same result at far less a price." What is the possible use of the crooked, tangled trunk of a tree? And after a moment he added, "Aus so krummen Holz, als voraus der Mensch gemacht ist, kann nichts gerades gezimmert werden" (From such a crooked stick as man, nothing exactly straight can be formed).

The evening fog drifts across the windowpanes, seeps into the crevices, and grows thick in the folds of the curtain. The shadows wander aimlessly along the walls, disperse for a moment, intersect, and grow dark. The shadows absorb the gold of the frame, the green of the curtain, and the cherry sheen of the desk. The shadows drift along the shiny parquet floor, glide over the sheets of paper, reach the hand, edge its dry fingers with a dark contour, outline the eye sockets, lie on the sunken cheeks, and circle in black the line of the lips.

At ten o'clock Kant enters the cold bedroom, whose windows are eternally covered by curtains. He undresses "according to the method," and "according to the method" carefully wraps himself up in a brown quilt like a silkworm in its cocoon. He will fall asleep in no time. And then an enormous moth will fly out of the cocoon and encircle his head in unsteady flight.

Next morning Kant will write down in his notebook: "Avoid bad dreams."

2

Few philosophers, it seems clear, have had as many biographers as Kant, and none certainly led such a dull and methodical life. Historians were undoubtedly attracted by the history of his thought, by the development of a conceptual construction that had been erected as it were ex nihilo, for it had no "model" or archetype in antiquity. Undoubtedly, but there must also have been something extraordinary in the life of the Königsberg philosopher, since among Kant's biographers we find the name of De Quincey, the author of the essay "Murder as One of the Fine Arts."

The life of Kant is *structure*, it seems to be a work of nature rather than of man. But if there is something in his life story that suggests the precision of a spider web or a crystal, such an association is based on a superficial analogy. His life lacks that asymmetry which we find in the lines of a maple leaf and in the lines of a human palm so similar to a maple leaf. It lacks that asymmetry which differentiates the left side of the face from the right—there is instead the horror and peacefulness of a death mask.

"Art," Kant wrote with the pedantry so characteristic of him,

> is distinguished from nature as making (*facere*) is from acting or operating in general (*agere*), and the product or the result of the former is distinguished from that of the latter as work (*opus*) from operation (*effectus*).
>
> By right it is only production through freedom, i.e. through an act of will that places reason at the basis of its action, that should be termed art. For, although we are pleased to call what bees produce (their regularly constructed cells) a work of art, we only do so on the strength of an analogy with art; that is to say, as soon as we call to mind that no rational deliberation forms the basis of their labor, we say at once that it is a product of their nature (of instinct). . . .*

Taking reason and will as the basis, Kant created his life as a work of art (opus).

Not without reason Kant was proud of his health. "I know from my own experience," he used to say, "that mental alertness is the best remedy for effectively fighting any bodily discomfort.

*From *The Critique of Judgement,* trans. James Creed Meredith (Oxford: Clarendon Press, 1964). All subsequent quotations from *The Critique of Judgement* are from this edition.

Though nature has given me a weak constitution, and I have a wretched inclination toward hypochondria, I have become the master of my mind and learned how to avert my thoughts from unpleasant sensations which have their source in my hollow chest cramping my lungs and heart."

Thin, almost lame, with a flat chest and misshapen arms, he accurately resembled a crooked stick from which "nothing exactly straight can be formed." *Aus so krummen Holz, als woraus der Mensch gemacht ist. . . .*

He seemed to be condemned to permanent feebleness, and yet he succeeded in maintaining a good state of health throughout his entire life, and he was able to provide his life with simple forms similar in shape to a plant stretched along a wall in the frames of a wooden trellis or a network of wires. Everything had been perfectly planned and measured down to the smallest details: rest and working hours, the quantity and quality of food, the cut and color of his clothes. Schubert asserts that he knew no woman who could talk on the subject of fabrics and laces with an expertise equal to Kant's. He was extremely hard to please in the matching of materials, and he used to combine yellow and brown, citing as his authority the order of nature, which joins these colors on a bear's ear. He wore only white or gray stockings, since the color black would make his already thin legs look even thinner, and he used an elaborate system of cords to take the place of garters, which obstructed the circulation of the blood. He always dined in company, for "a solitary meal is not healthy for a man of learning." The conversations were full of charm and fortified the health, since the number of his table companions had to fluctuate between the number of the Graces and Muses. Graver subjects were ruled out: philosophy and death were strictly forbidden as themes of conversation. "Let the dead bury their dead," Kant abruptly cut in, when Hippel's death was mentioned. "Now is the time for the metaphysics of life." And so saying, he bent his pale face over the goblet of red wine, and opened his mouth wide so as to absorb as much oxygen as possible along with the wine. Such a drink was supposed to increase one's strength and enliven the activity of the stomach. Even during working hours this ever-present anxiety about his health never left him; he would drape a white handkerchief on the chair in his study to remind himself to take short breaks for relaxation and physical movement. During his walks he breathed very slowly and through his nostrils in fear of gusts of fresh air. The invariable order of the day preserved his feeble strength and protected his fragile psychic structure against any unexpected visit, as dangerous for his inner calm as the fresh breeze and fog were for his lungs. Bound by a whole series of self-imposed restrictions, he vegetated like a plant in a network of wires; his emotional life was cramped the way his lungs and heart were crushed by his chest.

The stubbornness with which he stuck to the regimentation of his daily life betrayed an enfeebled sense of reality. The external world was distant, unreachable, alien. Enclosed in a circle of concepts, he lived on *memory* and *expectation*. The present, if he did not predict it in advance, was an intruder who suddenly appeared at the door of his study like an unexpected guest, or like the Angel of Death, who mocks at time. Kant lived on "inner" time, which poured forth from the dark sources of memory, indistinct and unstable as memory itself.

Like a roaring stream, time caught up scraps of remembrance, noisily flowed across the powerful spans of conceptual constructions, and in whirling eddies bore off the entire world: the branches of the poplar trees, the glints on the windowpanes, the red of the walls, the faded blue of the sky, the clouds, shadows, and faces. Like a gust of wind, time rustled through the pages of the wall calendar, carried off pieces of paper from the table, and stirred the green window curtain. The faces of the passersby from the lime-tree alley and the hands he had absentmindedly shaken flowed through his memory like leaves fluttering in the wind.

Reality seeped through his fingers like fog, and the raging stream of time foamed. Thus he lived like a clock, and to strengthen his shakened sense of reality, he imposed upon himself and his world the punctuality of dawn, midday, and twilight. He guarded the order of the day with stubbornness and despotism. He disliked unwelcome visits, bursts of laughter, tears, and music that "undesired visits its neighbors."

But music in fact visited him too often. He grew accustomed to the daily marching by of the Königsberg garrison, and with time he grew fond of the clamor of the military band. It even happened that—according to reports—the tears came down his face while he was listening to a nightingale's song. But he was irritated by the singing of the prisoners, who (unfortunately) were his neighbors. "Those who recommended the singing of spiritual songs as part of the religious service," Kant explained to the mayor of Königsberg, angrily pouting his lips, "do not consider that they inflict a great annoyance upon the public, since the neighborhood is obliged either to join in the singing or else to suspend all effort at thinking. . . ."

According to the philosopher's wish, the windows of the prison were kept closed during the religious service; the singing thus confined whirled through the damp cells and halls of the prison.

Kant—as Heine said—was like the clock on the Königsberg tower: dispassionate and methodical.

It must be noted, however, that some unexpected diversions took place in Kant's life: an invitation to a dinner party, a protracted game of whist, a carriage ride with the Baron M., or a visit by a famous foreigner. Sometimes, upon the completion of his daily stroll, Kant would visit Mr. Green, an English merchant. Since Kant's visit invariably occurred during his host's habitual afternoon nap, Kant would come in on tiptoe, sink into an armchair, and fall asleep too. Ruffman, the director of the Königsberg bank and a constant guest of the house, would fall asleep nearby a minute later. Pleasant dreams would fly out of Homer's underworld through the ivory gate and float under the half-closed eyelids of the sleeping friends.

> Such were the pleasures and the petty strife
> . . . When all the world in blood and tears was drowned
> And that man-god of war, his troop around
> Him like a cloud and armed with guns untold,
> Who yoked the silver eagles with the gold,
> From Lybian desert to the Alps was winning. . . .*

From time to time their sleep was disturbed by the sound of distant shots, and if the napping took place on Thursday . . .
. . . on Thursdays Councillor Otto Hoffmann used to visit his friends, and his young son, Ernst Theodor,† already bored by the monotony of life, would sneak out of the house. Wearing a judge's

---

*From Adam Mickiewicz, *Pan Tadeusz*, trans. Kenneth Mackenzie (New York: Dutton, 1966).
†This is E. T. A. Hoffmann, the well-known author of fantastic tales.

wig, in black ermine, and with a viola da gamba slung over his shoulder, he would run across the lawn in front of the house. Frail and sickly, he resembled a dwarf. The black wings of the ermine and the threads of the wig flapped in the breeze. Like a wounded bird, he fluttered above the lawn, scattering bright shadows about. If only they could reach the green groves; young Hippel was already hurrying along the fence with his flute. Werner, Matuszewski, and the others clutched their violins under their arms, each dressed in his father's wig and ermine. The sides of the formal uniforms fluttered in the green grove, the bows and cellos gleamed:

Ta ra ta ta ta ta—tam!
Ta ra ta ta ta ta—tam!

Hoffmann conducted, and with the end of his rhythmically vibrating bow, he would chop off the leaves of a lilac bush, which fell on the hands and faces of the musicians.

Ta ra ta ta ta ta—tam. *Eine kleine Nachtmusik!* They would attack it briskly from the very first beats: the white wigs slipped far back on their heads, disclosing the red stubble of their closely cropped hair, the youngsters' freckled hands glided over the strings, and their fingers, spotted with ink, thumped the black necks of their instruments. Smoothly, in a single breath, they made the transition to the andante, twanged a few subdued bars, the music seemed to moderate for a moment and then burst forth again in a joyous tumult:

Ta ra ta ta ta ta—tam!
Ta ra ta ta ta ta—tam!

"There is something actually indecent about music which arises from the very nature of the instruments," Kant explained to his friends. "Often music pays an undesired visit to its neighbors and disturbs the tranquillity of those who do not belong to the group of musicians. The arts which gladden the eye are free from this vice. . . . I would compare music to a scent. . . . He who draws a perfumed handkerchief from his pocket, treats all who are about him to an odor against their will, for if they breathe at all, they are obliged to inhale it. For this reason it has gone out of fashion. . . ."

The music burst forth from the green thicket, the lilac leaves shuddered, and the strings thundered in a harmonious tutti.

Ta ra ta ta ta ta—tam!
Tam—tarra—ta—tam!

3

. . . at six o'clock, with a sheet of paper in his hand, sunk in the
armchair facing the window . . .

Sublime is the name given to what is absolutely great [Kant
wrote]. But to be great and to be a *magnitude* are entirely different concepts (*magnitudo* and *quantitas*). In the same way to assert without qualification (*simpliciter*) that something is great, is
quite a different thing from saying that it is absolutely great (*absolute non comparative magnum*). The latter is what is beyond all
comparison great. . . . A tree judged by the height of man gives,
at all events, a standard for a mountain; and, supposing this is,
say, a mile high, it can serve as unit for the number expressing the
earth's diameter for the known planetary system; this again for
the system of the Milky Way; and the immeasurable host of such
systems, which go by the name of nebulae, and most likely in
turn themselves form such a system, *holds out no prospect of a
limit.* Now in the aesthetic estimate of such an immeasurable
whole, the sublime does not lie so much in the greatness of the
number, as in the fact in our onward advance we always arrive at
proportionately greater units. . . . For it represents all that is
great in nature as in turn becoming little; or, to be more exact, it
represents our *imagination* in all its boundlessness, and with it
nature as sinking into insignificance *before the ideas of reason,*
once their adequate presentation is attempted.
     . . . Bold, overhanging, and, as it were, threatening rocks,
thunder-clouds piled up the vault of heaven, borne along with
flashes and peals, volcanoes in all their violence of destruction,
hurricanes leaving desolation in their track, the boundless ocean
rising with rebellious force, the high waterfall of some mighty
river, and the like, make our power of resistance of trifling moment in comparison with their might. But, provided our own
position is secure, their aspect is all the more attractive for its
fearfulness; and we readily call those objects sublime, because
they raise the forces of the soul above the height of vulgar commonplace, and discover within us a power of resistance of quite
another kind, which gives us courage to be able to measure ourselves against the seeming omnipotence of nature . . . but with

this we also found in our rational faculty . . . a pre-eminence over nature. . . . From this it may be seen at once that we express ourselves on the whole inaccurately if we term any object of nature sublime . . . all that we can say is that the object lends itself to the presentation of a sublimity discoverable in the mind. For the sublime, in the strict sense of the word, cannot be contained in any sensuous form, but rather concerns ideas of reason. . . .

In the face of nature, boundless in its expanse and might, man recognizes his own insignificance, and at the same time discovers his superiority; he rises above the starry sky, above the mountain ranges along which creeps the gray, ragged fog. Man bears within himself notions of God, immortality, and the Last Judgment: ideas so brilliant that in comparison the stars pale, like blown-out candles, the constellations curl up like blades of grass cropped by flames—the sound of the sea is scarcely audible, the mountain ranges so small that they could be covered by a dry, bony hand. This conquered world, thrust down beneath man's feet, recalls the landscape in front of which Shakespeare placed a blind man.

Fields near Dover

GLOUCESTER: When shall I come to th' top of the same hill?
EDGAR: You do climb up it now; look how we labour.
GLOUCESTER: Methinks the ground is even.
EDGAR: Horrible steep.
            Hark, do you hear the sea?
GLOUCESTER: No, truly.
EDGAR: . . . Come on, Sir, here's the place; stand still.
            How fearfull,
            And dizzy 'tis to cast one's eyes so low!
            . . . The crows and choughs that wing the
                midway air
            Show scarce so gross as beetles. Half way down
            Hangs one that gathers samphire—dreadful
                trade!
            Methinks he seems no bigger than his head.
            The fishermen that walk upon the beach
            Appear like mice: and yond tall anchoring bark
            Diminished to their cock; her cock a buoy
            Almost too small for sight. The murmuring
                surge,

> That on th' unnumb'red idle pebbles chafes,
> Cannot be heard so high . . . I'll look no more,
> Lest my brain turn, and the deficient sight
> Topple headlong.

If Kant knew *King Lear,* in the last days of his life he undoubtedly would have bent over the unreal abyss that Gloucester saw with his blind eyes:

> Get thee glass eyes
> And, like a scurvy politician, seem
> To see the thing thou does not.

Sunk in the armchair facing the window, he had before his eyes the ruins of the Königsberg castle, the poplars, and the faded sky: *The limited picture of nature enclosed in the rectangle of the window like a painting in its frame. How could he possibly extend the boundaries of his imagination and free within himself the sublimity of the idea of reason?*

In vain he strained his memory and his meager imagination. They both were hopeless. His memory could furnish his imagination only as much as it had absorbed during his after-dinner strolls: the trunks of the lime alley trees, the blurred contours of the houses, and the faces of the passersby.

He squinted his glassy eyes, then under his eyelids the frames of the windows and the contours of the table and chairs came into view, and then spots resembling the shadows of fishes in the depths of the sea floated by against the background of his fleeting observations, upon the background of the green silk curtain as in green water. Etchings, illustrations, and pages of natural science atlases stubbornly emerged from his memory—diagrams of sea life, geometrical skeletons of fishes grew transformed in his half-closed eyes into the intersection of the window frame. And once again before his eyes there reappeared the scrap of the window curtain, the ruins of the Königsberg castle and the faded sky. He leafed through his memory as through a dictionary, and out of the well-known forms, as out of wooden blocks, he tried to reconstruct in his imagination those "bold, overhanging, . . . threatening rocks . . . volcanoes in all their violence of destruction, . . . the boundless ocean rising with rebellious force." The boundless ocean of his memory (*abso-*

lute non comparative magnum) threw on the shore of his consciousness the remnants of remembrances—*always the same ones.* Azure and gold rings kept growing under his half-closed eyelids. In these luminous circles, as though bathed in foam, there were swaying the branches of the lime alley trees, leaves, hands, faces. Walls of the Königsberg houses, roof tiles covered with soot, chimneys in coils of smoke, windows all floated by. The smoke slowly dispersed and the whitewashed walls regained their brightness—the windowpanes in the cracked plaster seemed to extend the reflections of the lights and the cracks into the rays of some gigantic spider web. The images like nebulae circled around the center of gravity; shadows gathered in the hollows of his eye sockets, in his sunken cheeks, and lay down in the narrow lines of his lips. From far-off shores, from "non-Euclidean" space, there were emerging the outline of the eyes in a net of wrinkles, the vaulted forehead, and the withered lips.

As though holding a seashell, he would hold up to his ear huge volumes *in octavo* and *in quarto* so as to hear from within them as from within a shell the thundering rush of distant waters, he would tightly close the shutters in his bedroom in order to avoid the sight of the sky, he would run his finger across the map along mountain ranges no bigger than a caterpillar. He carried within himself the idea of God—the sky over Königsberg paled in comparison with the brilliance of this notion. He carried the idea of immortality within himself and could cover the ocean with his palm. But he did not know God, as he did not know the sky, did not know immortality, as he did not know the ocean, and did not know the dread of the Last Judgment. Mountains crept off the map, and the sky outside the window and the sea, "that flowing mirror mounted in the sky," faded out. He knew only the postulates of morality: God was a postulate, immortality was a postulate, and the drama of justice in the valley of Jehoshaphat was a postulate. He was alone, and "there is little good in man . . . *homo homini non Deus sed diabolus.*" Thus, as Gloucester says, bent over a nonexistent abyss:

O, you mighty gods!
This world I do renounce, and in your sights
Shake patiently my great affliction off.
If I could bear it longer, and not fall

To quarrel with your great opposeless wills,
My snuff and loathed part of nature should
Burn itself out.

He was alone with death, which had him cornered: "Life is a burden to me; I am tired of bearing it. And if this night the Angel of Death were to come and call me hence, I would raise my hands and say: God be praised! I am not a coward and I have enough strength to put an end to my life, but such an act is incompatible with morality."

Death had him cornered. The Angel of Death stood at the door, like old Lampe, saying, "It is time." And time continued to pass over Königsberg.

Time continued to pass over Königsberg and would wake him up with the loud crowing of a neighborhood cock. He tried to buy the cock, but the neighbor declined his offer. "Ah, you've got normal ears," Kant sighed. "I have metaphysical hearing!" In the morning fog, in torrents of rain, the cock would flap its black wings: It is time, it is time!

. . . at six o'clock, sunk in his armchair, he was still spreading a symmetrical net of concepts on the windowpanes of his study. In this spider web of categories and forms, as though reflected in a crystal globe, the lines of the tower extended the faded sky, and the clouds swayed helplessly. But the cock kept flapping its wings—it is time—and the growing of the trees outside the window made him uneasy. Their slender trunks, as though the hands of some gigantic sundial, cast a shadow on the windowpanes of his study: it is time!

The poplars were cut to save the philosopher's shaky sense of reality, which was based on longstanding habits. This execution performed on nature was authorized by the decision of the town council and Kant's express wish since "man converses with nature as a judge with a defendant." This sentence was dictated by the need to save the whole system, which required that the sphere rolled down the inclined plane by Galileo run at the speed he had forecast. There was a certain weakness in this gesture not unlike that of the Persian despot who had the sea whipped after losing a battle.

Sunk in his armchair, Kant again was able to look at the ruins of the Königsberg castle, the clouds and the pale sky. But the spider web spread on the windowpane no longer caught the shadows and glints—it was empty. If Lampe had opened the study door, he would have found everything in its proper place: the silk curtain, the desk, the profile on the wall, the portrait of Rousseau, the high back of the armchair, and the white hands resting on its shiny wooden arm. Kant no longer mastered reality. Outside the window the trunks of the cut-down trees were turning red, and a few rusty leaves of ivy stuck out against the yellow sky at sunset. The leaves silvered by a September frost were stiff, as though cut from a sheet of tin.

In vain Kant tried to make the final connection among concepts. "The tortures of Tantalus," he jotted down on 21 September 1798, and discouraged, he put aside the manuscript of a recently begun work in which he was attempting to mark out the transition from the metaphysical basis of the natural sciences to physics. The black profile appeared for a moment outlined against the background of the yellow sky; it hung in the intersection of the window frame. The head had sunk down into the shoulders; the bony elbows and lace ruffles resembled frayed wings.

The tragedy of Icarus—Max Scheler explained—lies in the fact that the closer Icarus drew to the sun, the more his wax wings melted away.

4

EDGAR: Why, then your other senses grow imperfect
       By your eyes' anguish.
       . . . O, matter with impertinancy mixed!
       Reason in madness!

His memory failed him by degrees, and he lost the sight of his left eye. In vain he bent over the expiring stream of memory; in this small, slimy rivulet, only the remnants of images were still fluttering: the red of the walls, the clouds, the window frames, and a scrap of the green curtain. He tried to console himself (not without reason) by means of increased activity of the right eye, but his gait was now more unsteady. With his body half-turned, he cautiously protected his right arm as though it were a broken wing. In the manner of Egyptian drawings, he glided down the lime-tree alley, flat as his own shadow.

The glittering autumn light gilded his withered profile. On his left hand, there was darkness, his temple was engulfed in blue shadows, and the edges of the eyelid half-drooping over his unseeing eye turned red. In his impaired sight, the field of vision narrowed like the moon in her first quarter, in the narrow crescent of light the branches darkened and the yellow leaves rustled. Indifferent and downcast, Kant passed by the familiar trees and houses. Ivy climbed the brick walls in the burghers' neat gardens, and in the deep green, withered roses, stifled by the flourishing ivy, still did not stop reddening. Pumpkins ripened in rows, and dahlias struggled in the parched grass, pulling their bulky roots out of the soil, and sunflowers bent their heavy heads through the railings of the fences. In their round faces, the circles of ripened seeds were already exposed, and golden dust scattered amidst the shadows of the railings made intersections beneath the feet of the passersby. Sad and weary, his legs trembling, Kant stepped on the grill of black and gold. "It is beautiful indeed . . . this verdure and these flowers, but such is the case every year, every year. . . ." In expectation of a great change, he had developed an aversion to the immutable course of nature. "Such is the case every year, . . . every year," he repeated in the spring of 1802.

Without regret Kant was bidding adieu to *his* world. "Why am I reluctant to make way for the new world which is coming and why drag on my sickly and excessively prolonged existence through so many privations? Why should my case cause any disturbance in the tables of mortality . . . and make dependent on the force of will what until now has been called destiny?"

He wrote this sentence down as though he held Marcus Aurelius's stylus in his hand rather than a quill. Without regret he was bidding adieu to the world, and it appeared that he was only waiting for the "occasion" to "make way."

Once it happened that Kant fell down during his daily stroll. Two ladies, whom he had just passed, hastened to his aid. "What harm could possibly result from the fall of such a light body?" he jokingly reassured the distressed ladies and politely declined their kindly proffered arms. With a red rose in his withered hand, he resembled the statue of Arnobius consumed by time, before which Condillac in vain had waved a crimson rose in order to bring its bronze skull to life. Leaning on his walking stick, Kant fell into deep thought, as though he had to make an important and final decision, and after a moment, with a gesture bespeaking old-fashioned gallantry, he handed the rose to one of the ladies. It was in this manner that he finally parted with the past. Now expectation was all that was left him.

The year 1803 found Kant in a sad and enfeebled state; "to have one foot *here* and the other in eternity is like being an angel in the Koran, whose one eyebrow is 8,000 miles away from the other," he complained. During the day he would doze off in his armchair, but in the evening when he was taken off to bed, he would sigh, "Oh, gentlemen, you are young and strong. You see my misery . . . when you reach my age, you will be as weak as I am. The Bible says that man's life lasts at most seventy years, and the best of it is weariness and labor."

He passed uneasy nights and was visited by evil dreams. Evil dreams, like bats, flew out of the Homeric underworld through the gate of horn. Their membranous wings flapped in the bedroom with eternally closed shutters, and their round, ruby eyes glittered in the darkness. Horrified, he would wake up and fall asleep again. Images stained with blood, as though pages torn from *King Lear,* floated through his strained imagination like leaves in the wind. At daybreak he would laugh, mock the phantoms of the night, and keep writing in his notebook, "Avoid bad dreams." Alas, they returned every single evening. At night his weakened psychic inhibitions failed to dominate his imagination; in the daytime his overtaxed memory failed him. It is true that he could still recite by rote Kepler's tables of logarithms, but he grew confused while doing the simplest mathematical calculations, and sometimes he could not find the simplest words of everyday usage. At dinner he would frequently repeat over and over again the same stories, and thus instead of providing entertainment, he saddened his table companions by the spectacle of his increasing mental debility. Pedantic as usual, he would write down on various scraps of paper funny anecdotes about Lampe, Napoleon, and Frederick the Great, but all in vain: his notes would slip out of his trembling hands, he would hem and haw, grow lost in thought, and lose the thread of the story. Finally, he said, "I am old and helpless, gentlemen," and sank into silence. His overexhausted memory at this point cast up only leftovers: scraps of folk melodies heard in childhood, and odds and ends of school Latin. The first words of a tale from a school text-book kept coming back with amazing persistency: *Rusticus senex cum adpropinquatem mortem sentiret* . . . He did not remember the lines that followed, so he kept reciting the words in reverse order: *sentiret, mortem, adpropinquatem, cum, senex.* Next he would link words together in a nonsensical way: *forceps*—cow, *rusticus*—moustache, *nebulo*—it's you.

As his memory faded, his sense of the unity of his psyche grew less stable, his consciousness became blurry, and time raced by faster and faster. *Eheu . . . fugaces . . . fugaces . . .* the words slipped away and the days slipped away and he could no longer keep up in his pursuit of them. The days flowed by like the pages of a book hurriedly leafed through by a reader anxious to get to the end. Only when a cup of black coffee brightened his mind for a moment would he speculate on the coming resolution of a complicated plot: what will happen next? He did not know what to think of a future life. "Nothing, or nothing definite," he confessed to one of his friends. Since his mind had fewer and fewer bright moments, he demanded coffee more and more insistently. He nagged like a child and begged with clasped hands. He excitedly greeted a steaming cup of coffee in the language of Columbus: "I see land! I see land!" He had the impression that he saw on the surface of this black ocean the outlines of Charon's boat and its white sail—a symbol of hope. Bending over a cup of coffee, he now saw the distant contours of the other shore.

Once it happened that he fell asleep in his armchair. The small flame of a candle that had been lit just as dusk was falling still quivered in the yellow light pouring through the windowpanes, and the dark cherry polish of the chairs glittered in the bronze shadows. Dusk was slowly thickening in the corners of the study, and the golden circle above the candlestick grew sharply etched in the expiring light of the winter sun. The glow of the candle refracted from the frame of Rousseau's portrait scattered luminous dust on the walls, placing a border around the black profile.

The shadow swayed, veiled the light for a moment, and then burst into flames. What happened was simply that his head fell forward on his chest and bent over the table, and the flame of the candle licked his cotton nightcap. In this feeble flame, in the smell of burning cotton, the world was ablaze: trees, mountains, and oceans were burning. The fire spread over the starry sky, and the stars, blackened by the smoke, fell into the fire and night, like birds circling over a burning house. The fire gained possession of an edifice raised up with such difficulty: the powerful links between concepts were cracking apart, the interconnections among categories, scorched and consumed by the white-hot fire, gave way with a crash and collapsed. In the red and the gold, in the gray coils of smoke, Kant abandoned his house, lonely and driven out, as King Lear had been:

> Blow, winds, and crack your cheeks!
> Rage! Blow!
> . . . You sulph'rous and thought executing fires,
> Vaunt-couriers of oak-cleaving thunderbolts,
> Singe my white head!
> . . . I tax not you, you elements, with unkindness:
> I never gave you kingdom . . .
> . . . Here I stand your slave,
> A poor, infirm, weak and despised old man:
> But yet I call you servile ministers,
> That will with two pernicious daughters join
> Your high-engendered battlers 'gainst a head
> So old and white like this.

* * *

> . . . he sighed, his face a thing of pallor,
> And down his cheeks streamed many tears,
> And when he kissed the shining mirror,
> To stone he turned, a man of fears.

(Adam Mickiewicz, "Forefathers' Eve") *

In the very last days of his life, Kant jotted down in his notebook:

> Every day has its own worries,
> And a month has thirty days.
> So what follows from this is simple,

---

*Trans. G. R. Noyes, versified by Marjorie B. Peacock, in *Slavonic and East European Review* 17 (1939).

And you can say for sure,
That the happiest month is February.

But that particular February had only twelve days for Kant. On the seventh of February—Hasse* writes—he invited us for the last time. He was carried to the table, but scarcely had he swallowed a single spoonful of soup, when he asked to be carried back to bed. He was nothing but a skeleton now, and his exhausted body sunk into the bed as into the grave. On the eleventh, in the evening, his eyes were glassy, and his face absolutely serene. "I asked him," Wasianski recounts, "if he knew me. He was speechless, but he turned his face toward me, and made signs that I should kiss him. Deep emotion thrilled me . . . I had never seen him confer this mark of love upon anybody except once, and that was a few weeks before his death, when he drew his sister to him and kissed her. The kiss which he now gave to me was the last memorial that he knew me. . . . There were all the signs of death being close at hand . . . about one o'clock in the night he himself made a movement toward the spoon from which I collected that he was thirsty . . . but the muscles of his mouth had not strength enough to retain it, so that he raised his hand to his lips, until with a rattling sound it was swallowed . . . then he said, in a way that I was just able to understand, 'It is well' (*Es ist gut*). These were his last words. . . . The whole body and extremities were already growing cold and the pulse intermittent . . . at a quarter after three o'clock . . . the pulse was no longer perceptible to the touch in his hands, feet, or neck. . . . About ten o'clock in the forenoon he suffered a remarkable change; his eye was rigid and his face and lips became discolored by a cadaverous pallor. . . . It was near eleven o'clock when the moment of dissolution approached. His sister was standing at the foot of the bed, his sister's son at the head, and I was kneeling at the bedside for the purpose of still observing the fluctuations in the pulse. . . . The breath grew feebler . . . then it became wholly intermittent. And the upper lip was slightly convulsed; after this, there followed one feeble respiration or sigh. . . ."

Eleven o'clock had passed. If Wasianski had approached Kant's lips with an open watchcase in order to catch the philosopher's last sigh upon it, he would have seen, as though in a mirror, upon this

*Königsberg resident and friend of Kant's.

surface—unblemished by the slightest breath—the vaulted forehead, the blue eyelids, the bony nose, and the withered lips—the face of Immanuel Kant.

AUTHOR'S NOTE

The artistic aims of the present essay are contained in the title, *Portrait*, and thus are those of the art of painting. Since Kant's life was proverbially colorless and monotonous, the author had to overcome a good many difficulties, in that *ex definitione* all elements lying outside the art of painting, such as psychological analysis, explication of texts, or historical commentary, had to be carefully excluded. *The transposition of concepts into images was the goal of this essay.* That is why it is preceded by an extensive introduction in which the art of painting is discussed. These pictorial aims have determined not only the form of the essay but also its scope, which necessarily had to be concise so that it could be taken in at one glance, like a painting. This was likewise the origin of the persistent recurrence of a certain number of central themes. The purpose of these repetitions was to create an abstract of the whole in the reader's memory, that is, to keep ever-present in the reader's consciousness themes that naturally pass out of sight during the reading. That is why the sentence that serves as the beginning reappears at the end. The iteration of motifs (the window, the ruins of the castle, the green silk curtain) also had as its purpose to accentuate the tragic monotony of the life of Königsberg thinker. These same goals obliged the author to make the use of a play of lights and shadows almost to the point of exaggeration.

But how else—remaining within the framework of these aims— would it be possible to show the loss of the sense of reality that tormented the philosopher? That is precisely why the trees outside the window are compared to patches of paint on a watercolor that is still damp, and Kant walking down the lime tree alley is likened to "flat," two-dimensional Egyptian drawings.

Since the loss of the sense of reality has been mentioned, a word of further explanation is in order. Is it neuropathy? Undoubtedly, in Kant's fragile, asthenic physical constitution, the complicated lines of a repressed psychosomatic neurosis are manifested, easily detectable in the maniacal ritual of his daily life, in his eccentricities, and in his rigid habits. A psychologist with a volume of Pierre-Marie-Félix Janet's classic works in his hand would readily find in Kant's biography a series of symptoms which constitute the phenomenon of "psycho-astheny," and he could, without any difficulty, formulate clinical terms for the Kantian "critiques":

> La perte de la fonction du réel—for the first
> L'amour exagéré de l'honnêteté—for the second
> Les émotions sublimes—for the third

He would even be able, following Callicles's example, to find in the Kantian critique of law a manifestation of weakness that avoids doing battle by taking shelter in the shadow of the sword and scales of the blind goddess.

Undoubtedly . . . that may be . . . but it was precisely such explorations that I wanted to avoid. And not only because the psychological origins of a work do not indicate its objective value; that the philosophical and cultural value of Kant's "critiques" lies beyond the reach of the psychologist's curiosity is perfectly obvious. I was guided primarily by the necessity of maintaining proper distance and tact in dealing with one of the greatest thinkers who ever lived. It was for that reason that in the climactic sections when describing Kant's hours of philosophical meditation I appeal to the unbearable "overfamiliarities" which the authors of "psychological biographies" cannot do without.

And besides, if Kant actually was a neurotic, he was one who knew how to cope with his weakness. Contrary to all appearances, it may be that Kant was not even an "eccentric." "An eccentric," Kant used to say, as though anticipating the inquisitiveness of his future biographers, "apes a man of character." Those things that have the traits of what is called eccentricity are only "leftovers," a sort of "by-product" of the powerful internal labor whose fruits were "the critiques." For above all, Kant was "a man of character." How badly mistaken Janet is when he writes:

> . . . quand on a vu beaucoup de scrupuleux, on en arrive à se demander avec tristesse si la spéculation philosophique n'est pas une maladie de l'esprit humain.

When one has seen a good many psychiatrists who have not escaped the fate of their paitents, it would be possible, following Janet's erroneous path, to ask in sadness whether psychiatry too by some chance *n'est pas une maladie de l'esprit humain.* In a similar fashion, the discovery of America could be "disqualified" since Columbus was a paranoiac.

Nevertheless, a weakened sense of reality, which is to some extent the central theme of the various pictorial goals of this essay, deserves a commentary. But since Kant was a metaphysician, our arguments will also be of a metaphysical nature. If he was tormented by a weakened sense of reality, Kant, as is befitting a philosopher, mourned the loss of the "consciousness of principles" upon which reality is founded.

Kant was not a man inclinded to confessions, but in the confessions of another thinker, Théodore-Simon Jouffroy, we find the history of the "philosophical loss of a sense of reality" which, it seems, can throw light on the problem we are considering. Jouffroy, a noble thinker whose name is mentioned in the history of philosophy only *en passant,* alongside his more or less original considerations, left us a few moving pages worthy of Descartes' pen. They deserve to be cited here:

> The day had come when, from the interior of that calm edifice of the religion which had sheltered me at my birth, and under whose shadow my early youth had passed, I had heard the wind of doubt which from all sides beat upon its walls to their foundations. I shall never forget that December evening when the view that hid my own disbelief from me was torn in two. I still hear my own steps in that narrow and bare room where I had continued to pace back and forth long after the time for sleep; I still see that moon, half-veiled by clouds, which from time to time lit the room's cold tiles. The hours of the night were passing without my noticing it; I followed my thought with anxiety, which was descending layer after layer into the depths of my consciousness and frittering away all the illusions which until now had been hindering my sight and which from moment to moment made its windings more and more visible to me.
>
> In vain I tried to take hold of my last beliefs as a shipwrecked sailor grabs hold of the remnants of his ship; in vain—horrified by the unknown void in which I was about to be carried—I

hurled myself for the last time along with my beliefs toward my
childhood, my family, my country, toward all that was dear and
sacred for me; the inflexible current of my thought proved
stronger: it forced me to abandon all: family, parents, memories,
beliefs; the test continued growing more obstinate and severe as it
approached its goal and it did not stop until it had reached it.
Then I knew that there was nothing more standing upright in my
very depth. It was a frightful moment, and when finally toward
the morning I threw myself on the bed totally exhausted, I
seemed to feel that my first life, so radiant and full, became extinguished, and behind me another life opened, a gloomy, depopu-
lated one, where henceforth I was to live *alone, alone* with my
fatal thought which had just exiled me there, and which I was
tempted to curse. The days which followed this discovery were
the saddest in my life. It would take too long to tell what feelings
shook me then. Although my intelligence did not consider its
work without a certain pride, my soul could not adapt to a state
unsuited to a human weakness; by violent returns it sought to
regain the shores which it had lost; in the ashes of its past beliefs it
found again sparks, which seemed at certain moments to ignite
faith. But convictions, overthrown by reason, can be raised up
only by reason, and those gleams were quickly extinguished.

And further:

These were entire days, entire nights of meditation in my room; it
was such an exclusive and prolonged concentration of my attention on interior facts, where I was trying to find the answer to all
questions, that *I lost all feelings of external things, and when I
returned to them in order to eat and drink, it seemed to me, that I
was leaving the real world, and entering a world of illusions and
phantoms.*

The connection between losing one's faith and, if it can be expressed this way, an *inverted* sense of reality, as discussed in Jouffroy's memoirs, is so obvious that it is not worthwhile stressing the
point.

The rationalist Jachmann assures us that Kant was "a true admirer of God" (*ein Gottesverehrer*). Borowski's impressions are
quite different, since he speaks of a loss of faith during Kant's early
years. Much has been written on this subject. There have been
numerous interpretations of Kant's opus, some honest, some guid-

ed by ill-will, and the pronouncements of Kant's friends have often
been the subject of critical comparison, but if Kant's style is scrutinized, there is no way of denying the justice of Heine's literary
expertise:

> After repeated and thorough study of Kant's chief work, I fan-
> cied I perceived everywhere visible his polemic against the exis-
> tent proofs of the existence of God, and I would discuss it at
> greater length were I not restrained by religious sentiment. The
> mere fact that I see someone discussing the existence of God
> arouses in me a strange anxiety, a dismal dejection, such as I once
> experienced at New Bedlam in London when I lost sight of my
> guide and found myself surrounded by nothing but
> madmen . . . Did he perhaps, just by destroying all the proofs for
> the existence of God, intend to show us clearly how awkward it is
> not to be able to know anything about the existence of God? In
> this matter he acted almost as wisely as a Westphalian friend of
> mine who had smashed all the lamps in Grohnder Street in Göt-
> tingen, and then, standing in the dark, delivered a long lecture to
> us on the practical necessity of lamps, which he had broken scien-
> tifically only in order to show us that we could see nothing with-
> out them . . .

Who knows whether we do not find in Jouffroy's confessions a
sketch of Kant's unspoken drama? Perhaps in the eternally barricaded windows of his bedroom, the shutters had been banging,
blown about by "the wind of doubt," which, as it filled out the sail
of the green curtain, bore off the great recluse to the dark flood
waters unbounded even by unknown lands. What frightful loneliness! *Raz Boga net tak kakoizhe ya i general?*—one of Dostoevsky's heroes protested indignantly, not without reason.

There is still another major problem connected with the question of a weakened sense of reality: *the problem of power*. First, a
few words of explanation: Kant organized his life so as to have as
little contact with reality as possible and to control the tempo of his
life, as Galileo did by forecasting the speed of a sphere rolling down
an inclined plane. He had tried to avoid all collisions with reality so
as to preserve the ingenious structure of his life and system. He
wanted to endow his life with the same order he imposed on the
"masterless" world: the fog, the wind, the trees, and the clouds.
Undoubtedly Kant knew that he was no master of the rain and the

wind that wrestled with the eternally barricaded shutters of his bedroom, and he knew that he did not rule the revolutions of the heavens above Königsberg. Undoubtedly, but—now looking at the matter from a psychological (I stress *psychological*) point of view— since Kant had reduced the shape and development of the world to the various forms experienced by a subject, then, in the depths of his soul, subconsciously, he could not help but suffer over the unforeseeable—in the common, ordinary sense of the word— structure of phenomena. That is why he schematized and organized the course of his daily life in such a way that no unforeseen accident could destroy the prearranged sequence of events.

That is why Kant was so alarmed by the growing of the trees outside the window, that is the reason why whenever he was tormented by frightful nightmares, he jotted down: "Avoid bad dreams." To say, "Avoid bad dreams," is like telling a poplar tree, "Wither," or a cloud, "Dissolve." One must be totally devoid of any psychological sensitivity to fail to notice in that short sentence written "as a reminder" a craving for power which would have liked to regulate the revolutions of the heavenly bodies and to chart the course of the flight of swallows. And that is why Kant's life was a true drama: *during the day he could not master the external world, at night he could not master his own imagination.* In the chaos of his unbridled imaginings, Kant was alone, and in lonely solitude he watched the incomprehensible shadows outside his window—the swaying branches of the trees.

It is one thing to accept Kantian philosophy as a system of concepts, it is another thing to become emotionally attached to it. Our understanding of Kant is quite different while we are reading *The Critique of Judgment* than it is during a stroll when we are not thinking about "categories," but about the green slopes of the hills and the glittering windings of the Isère river. Imperceptibly coloring our emotional attitude, consciousness of the fact that *we* endow those trees with the principles of their existence and that *we* are the lawmakers of this world that is reflected in the windings of the river, gives us that special joy that Monsieur Jourdain experienced in Molière's caricature when he discovered that he was speaking prose.

In speaking of the subconscious, Freud refers to the Kantian "thing-in-itself," not without very good reason.

Man, the creator of phenomenal reality, as a rule finds within himself, as Schopenhauer did, that mysterious *Ding an sich*, and the Isère valley lying at his feet, the glistening windings of the river, the clouds and the mountains—not only has this world been organized by man, it has also been *created* by him. And this is why it is so difficult to free oneself from the temptations of Kantian philosophy, once we have looked at the world through Kant's eyes, rather than those of Saint Francis.

On the pages of *The Critique*, the signs of the zodiac are revolving, and so are lights and shadows; trees are growing, clouds pass across the sky, water flows—but beyond that screen, riverbeds are running dry, trees are rotting; reality is condemned to death.

And Kant, sunk in his armchair, looks at the ruins of the Königsberg castle, the slender poplars, the helpless clouds: he knows that the lights are going out, that the ruins of the Königsberg castle are crumbling, and the poplars are withering away—he knows that all that remains are his hands, multiplied by the hands of those who are turning the pages of his *Critique of Pure Reason*. The dry, senile hands cover the world with the green silk curtain hanging over the window of his modest study.

Bouquéron, 15 December 1941

TRANSLATED BY JADWIGA KOSICKA

Zygmunt Kubiak

Pascal

Whenever I repeat to myself the sentence that Blaise Pascal died three hundred years ago, the stress invariably falls on the word "died." At such moments I do not think of Pascal as a great writer, or even as a great man. I simply think of him as a man, as one of the vast nation of the dead—those who "are our elders in death."

The great and famous men of the past are for us little more than cardboard figures. They drag behind them the refuse of dates and of the various cultural trends of a given epoch. They are reduced to a chapter in a handbook, or an entry in a encyclopedia. It is not so with Pascal. One can think about him in virulently historical terms only if one does not know anything about him and has never read his *Pensées*.

"When we see a natural style," Pascal writes in one of his notes, "we are astonished and delighted; for we expected to see an author, and we find a man."* No one could possibly better characterize Pascal's own work than he did with these words.

But it should stressed that in Pascal's work "a natural style" means not only a style of writing but above all a way of thinking. Let us quote another passage: "Man is full of wants: he loves only those who can satisfy them all. 'This one is a good mathematician,' one will say. But I have nothing to do with mathematics; he would take me for a proposition. 'That one is a good soldier.' He would

---

*Unless otherwise noted, all quotations from Pascal come from Blaise Pascal, *Pensées*, trans. W. F. Trotter (New York: Modern Library, 1941).—TRANS.

take me for a besieged town. I need, then, an upright *man* who can accommodate himself generally to all my wants."

In his writings Pascal is fond of stressing the word *man*. Thus he lets us know that he speaks not as a philosopher, not as a specialist in some discipline (however broad it may be), but simply as one of us facing the business of life and the mystery of death.

This is precisely the crux of Pascal's *Pensées;* their author, one of the greatest philosophers that ever lived, has nothing of the professional philosopher about him.

I often ponder the following question: take a philosopher—a materialist or an idealist, or any other "ist" for that matter—who has developed a system of his own, published a number of books, and, to his own satisfaction, succeeded in axiomatizing certain theses of metaphysics (or of the materialistic philosophy of nature) and in splitting the essence into still more variables than have hitherto been known, and imagine that he suddenly became besieged by doubts as to the validity of the very bases of the doctrine he has promulgated (let us suppose that Hegel at the end of his life came to the conclusion that his concept of "the objective Spirit" was fallacious). Would such a philosopher be capable of rejecting and totally disowning everything (literally everything) that he had previously accomplished? The question is a naive one, but it returns to haunt me whenever, with a dread typical of a layman, I think about the great philosophical systems, the great intellectual structures (or should I say rather the great verbal and linguistic structures?) which have been formulated by men and which then come to shape their lives.

Pascal renounces all philosophical systems. From his garden filled with things human, he throws out all magical "philosopher's stones." With one stroke of his pen he crosses out the divisions and classifications of Scholastic philosophy and all codified moral systems: "Why should I undertake to divide my virtues into four rather than into six? Why should I rather establish virtue in four, in two, in one? Why in *Abstine et sustine* rather than into 'Follow Nature,' or 'Conduct your private affairs without injustice,' as Plato, or anything else? But there, you will say, everything is contained in one word. Yes, but it is useless without explanation, and when we come to explain it, as soon as we unfold this maxim which contains all the rest, they emerge in that first confusion which you desired to avoid."

Is there a need to state even more clearly why I esteem Pascal so much? For his giving us an example—a splendid, unattainable example of what truly free thought is.

The question of "free thought" is beset by very serious misconceptions. We assume, quite naively, that it suffices to rebel against some sort of authority in order to think freely. But we seem to forget that we are much more severely and restrictively hindered by conventions that we are not aware of. We also seem to overlook the fact that often—while rebelling against the authorities—we are forever going round and round in a closed circle circumscribed by the very act of rebellion and the obsessions that go along with it. There are many striking examples of this in the history of human thought. In his rebellious thinking Voltaire remained throughout his entire life a slave of these obsessions. They forced him to make disparaging remarks about Joan of Arc despite all the historical evidence to the contrary and, in defiance of common sense, to consider religious reformers as frauds and charlatans.

Truly free, genuinely skeptical thought is the rarest of things. Especially if it is thought committed to paper. Once a person decides to write his thoughts down, he is constantly aware of the eyes of posterity which will read his text. A multitude of secondary considerations—deeper and more difficult to detect than any opportunistic external calculations—entwine and fetter human thought from the very moment of its inception. And even if a person jots down his reflections one moment and commits them to the fire the next, he is not entirely indifferent as to how he looks in his own judgment. Do not a fair number of pessimists scan their despair with rounded phrases that make us ask, are they not, by chance, standing in front of a gilded mirror engaged in self-contemplation in the melancholy of their own eyes?

All this is precisely what Pascal brings to our attention. Stating, for example, that by nature men wish to have admirers, he promptly adds: "Even philosophers wish for them. Those who write against it want to be praised for having written well; and those who read it desire the glory of having read it. I who write this have perhaps this desire, and perhaps those who will read it. . . ."

"I who write this . . ."—Pascal is perpetually on guard. He never excludes himself from the territory submitted to doubt. But let us pay closer attention to the next part of this sentence: "I . . . have perhaps this desire. . . ." I have in mind, of course, the little word "perhaps." It is the most important, the most telling word in the entire passage. Had he written "I have this desire," it would have been only a bit of masochism (something akin to the attitude of a Dostoevsky hero, who delightedly repeats, "Yes, I *am* a swine . . ."), or else a case of hypocritical humility (a frequent failing among philosophers). For in fact, at this particular moment Pascal is trying to free himself from dependence on public admiration. He knows that his desire to do so is sincere. But he also knows how complex the problem of sincerity is. The little word "perhaps," which his pen has produced almost unbidden, indicates that Pascal is not standing in front of a mirror, nor is he spitting in his own face, he is simply observing: observing himself the way he does everything around him—unmercifully, unsparingly.

Pascal is the first great—and the greatest of them all—modern philosopher of suspicion, a relentless analyst of our captive existence in the world. The phrase "philosophizing with a hammer," created by the author of *Twilight of the Idols*, could more aptly be applied to Pascal.

With his hammer Pascal beats on everything and strips reality naked. The skepticism of this most radically skeptical of all philosophers is the antithesis of the smiling, devoutly pinkish skepticism of various *esprits forts*. "Do they profess to have delighted us by telling us that they hold our soul to be only a little wind and smoke, especially by telling us this in a haughty and self-satisfied tone of voice? Is this a thing to say gaily? Is it not, on the contrary, a thing to say sadly, as the saddest thing in the world?" Those skeptics can pronounce such a thesis gaily because they do not know what they are saying. The thesis in question is not of the slightest interest to them; they have never confronted it. They are advancing it solely for the sake of contradicting some old ladies (of various sorts) who (equally thoughtlessly) preach a totally opposite thesis. They are slaves to the old ladies; they possess neither their own life, nor their own death. Whereas the author of the *Pensées*, by beating with his hammer and stripping reality naked, grasps every thesis in its real shape and its real dread.

Through his skepticism Pascal arrives at the only thing that can never be called into question: the bare description of the human situation.

When I consider the short duration of my life, swallowed up in the eternity before and after, the little space which I fill, and even can see, engulfed in the infinite immensity of spaces of which I am ignorant, and which know me not, I am frightened, and am astonished at being here rather than there, why now rather than then. Who has put me here? . . .
The eternal silence of these infinite spaces frightens me. . . .

Here are the words from the *Pensées* put into the mouth of a man in despair whom Pascal wishes to address—words so passionate that we can sense the feelings that author himself must have gone through:

I know not who put me in the world, nor what the world is, nor what I myself am. I am in terrible ignorance of everything. I know not what my body is, nor my senses, nor my soul, not even that part of me which thinks what I say, which reflects on all and on itself, and knows itself no more than the rest. I see those frightful spaces of the universe which surround me, and I find myself tied to one corner of this vast expanse, without knowing why I am put in this place rather than at another of the whole eternity which was before me or which shall come after me. I see nothing but infinities on all sides, which surround me as an atom, and as a shadow which endures only for an instant and returns no more. All I know is that I must soon die, but what I know least is this very death which I cannot escape.

Such a state of soul, immortalized in the *Pensées*, brings to mind the experiences of another sage, Omar Khayyám, who came from distant Persia. Recalling his name now may even be timely, because quite recently—in 1959—a hundred years had elapsed since Europe first learned of Khayyám. He was introduced by the English poet Edward FitzGerald, who made a brilliant translation of the *Rubáiyát* by the Persian sage. It soon had achieved an enormous popularity and went into many printings. One bound copy of the *Rubáiyát* with a pearl-studded cover went to the bottom of the ocean along with the doomed *Titanic*.

As for Omar Khayyám: he lived in the eleventh century and was (like Pascal) a great mathematician and, above all, a seeker of the Truth. He wrote the *Rubáiyát* at the end of his life, when he had come to doubt whether science and philosophy could ever reveal to him the truth about man's destiny.

> Into this Universe, and *Why* not knowing,
> Nor *Whence*, like Water willy-nilly flowing;
>   And out of it, as Wind along the Waste,
> I know not *Whither*, willy-nilly blowing.

> Up from Earth's Centre through the Seventh Gate
> I rose, and on the Throne of Saturn sate,
>   And many a Knot unravell'd by the Road;
> But not the Master-knot of Human Fate.*

Omar Khayyám, also like Pascal, was frightened by "the eternal silence of these infinite spaces." At such moments of dread he would write his aphorisms, while sitting in the tower of the astronomical observatory in the Persian town of Merv, or hiding in the garden raising a goblet of wine to his lips in order "to quench the fire of Anguish."

> The Ball no question makes of Ayes and Noes,
> But Right or Left as strikes the Player goes;
>   And He that toss'd you down into the Field,
> *He* knows about it all—HE knows—HE knows!

Such a state of soul has nothing in common with nihilism. Likewise it has nothing in common with Sartre's doctrinarianism or with Schopenhauer's pessimistic doctrine (and by the way, I esteem Schopenhauer far more than I do today's pessimistic doctrinarians). It has also nothing in common with the attitude of those philosophers who hold the doctrine that thought has emerged from matter. Neither Pascal nor Khayyám, with all their sadness and doubt, has even come close to atheism. Both are far too consistent skeptics for that. If I had to choose in Pascal's *Pensées* the aphorism that seems to me the most brilliant, I would select this one: "Atheism shows strength of mind, but only to a certain degree."

*Quotations are from Edward FitzGerald, *The Romance of the Rubáiyát* (London: Allen & Unwin, 1959).—TRANS.

I recently read a monograph on astronomy written by a contemporary physicist, Fred Hoyle, in which he addresses materialists in more or less the following fashion: You claim that you can tell a lot about the universe. But take one step further and consider the following question: Why is the universe here at all? (a childish, but singularly acute formulation). That's right—try to answer that first of all!

Khayyám and Pascal, the two mathematical geniuses, after having made their physical observations and after gazing at the stars, say the same thing that Faust will declare years later:

> And well I know that ignorance is our fate
> And this I hate.

Man can learn nothing—that is, nothing really essential, nothing really decisive—about his fate from either science or philosophy.

But at least let us keep awake. That is the lesson taught by those sages who are philosophers of human pride.

In Khayyám's *Rubáiyát* and Pascal's *Pensées*—from the ruins of cognition, against the background of the unfathomable universe—there emerges the figure of man who refuses to submit and who revolts against nothingness: against the humdrum of everyday existence and its superficially important occupations, against the pressure of drab illusions so widespread among men (for whom any shiny trinket is more valuable than the truth), against the whole swindle of an average human life—a life that ensnares us in a net of petty deals and petty ambitions until the moment when we are swallowed by the grave. Thought, independent, free and alert— although so infirm and constantly knocking against the wall of mystery—is the sole force with which man can challenge the universe in its material aspect, the universe (and life) as an indifferent force of inertia: "Man is but a reed, the most feeble thing in nature; but he is a thinking reed. The entire universe need not arm itself to crush him. A vapour, a drop of water suffices to kill him. But, if the universe were to crush him, man would still be more noble than that which killed him, because he knows that he dies and the advantage which the universe has over him; the universe knows nothing of this."

In his garden Omar Khayyám spoke with ardor:

Ah Love! could you and I with Him conspire
To grasp this sorry Scheme of Things entire,
  Would not we shatter it to bits—and then
Re-mould it nearer to the Heart's desire!

Whereas Pascal at the end of his despair meets the Jesus of the Gospels, the heavenly Friend who knows everything about the torment of existence (after Pascal's death a scrap of paper was found by his side containing the record of that great mystical experience, the famous words "Joie, joie, pleurs de joie . . ."). We can read about that meeting in Pascal's *Mystère de Jesus:*

Jesus suffers in his passion the torments inflicted upon him by men, but in his agony he suffers the torments which he inflicts on himself: *turbare semetipsum . . .*

Jesus seeks some comfort at least from his three dearest friends, and they sleep . . .

Jesus is alone on earth, not merely with no one to feel and share his agony, but with no one even to know of it . . .

He suffers this anguish and abandonment in the horror of the night . . .

Jesus will be in agony until the end of the world. There must be no sleeping during that time . . .

While Jesus remains in agony and cruellest distress let us pray longer . . .

—"Take comfort; you would not seek me if you had not found me."

"I thought of you in my agony; I shed these drops of blood for you . . ."

"It is tempting me rather than testing yourself to wonder if you would do right in the absence of this or that. I will do it in you if it happens . . ."

"Do you want it always to cost me the blood of my humanity while you do not even shed a tear?"

"I am a better friend to you that this man or that, for I have done more for you than they, and they would never endure what I have endured from you, and they would never die for you, while you were ebbing faithless and cruel, as I did, and as I am ready to do, and still do in my elect . . ."*

*This passage is from Pascal, *Pensées,* trans. A. J. Kraislsheimer (Baltimore, Md: Penguin Books, 1966), pp. 312–14.—TRANS.

Pascal, the totally skeptical philosopher, is an ardent admirer of the Bible; half of his *Pensées* is devoted to its analysis, because the Bible is something entirely different from all the systems of philosophy. I am at a loss how to put it into words but I feel it very strongly: to my mind, the Bible is above all a record of experiences and not a record of any kind of thesis. Yes, experiences: Moses really was in the wilderness (for forty years) and thirsted for water; the prophets really were cast into deep pits. And the Apostles really broke bread together.

Now when I reread my notes written on the margins of Pascal's *Pensées*, I realize that they are quite chaotic. But who said that everything that is written has to be totally coherent?

Are Pascal's *Pensées* always totally coherent? Fortunately, they are not.

It is said that Pascal had no time to compose his work and that the *Pensées* are only the notes for it. But I strongly suspect that he would never have composed his work in such a way that it could be included in a list of well-made treatises. He wrote down in his notes only what he had fully reflected upon, had really been bothered by or truly convinced of.

Would he ever have decided to fill the empty spaces with texts indispensable for a balanced composition but which would have been experienced to a lesser degree, and therefore less authentic? Would he have decided to trim and chip away all the complications and contradictions?

"O, qui dira les torts de la rime!" complained Verlaine of the tyranny of rhyme in poetry. This could be applied with greater justification to the art of the essay: O, who can ever describe the evil brought about by composition, by the literary necessity of composition! O, what blockhead—not a slave, as in Verlaine's complaint, but a blockhead (I suspect it was one of my beloved Greeks)—has stipulated that every essay, every treatise must have a beginning and an end (I should add: an effective and strong but above all a satisfying beginning and end); and that all the holes in the middle which at a given moment we are unable to fill honestly and sincerely should be filled with cotton wool rather than left as gaping holes. O composition, mother of half-truths, schoolmistress of self-deceptions!

For that reason I shall not attempt to compose these incoherent notes of mine jotted down on the margins of Pascal's work—the only reading of Pascal for which I was competent. Throw them into the fire unless they can be of some use to someone.

(1963)

TRANSLATED BY JADWIGA KOSICKA

Zygmunt Kubiak

From Saint Augustine

Leafing through Saint Augustine's *Confessions* I again chanced upon the passage that almost everyone seems to know, even though it is quoted out of context: "Sero te amavi, pulchrituda tam antiqua et tam nova, sero te amavi." "I have learnt to love you late, Beauty at once so ancient and so new! I have learnt to love you late!"*

I have always felt—it would be difficult not to feel—that this passage has a certain magnificence, an extraordinary power, the power of style and of something more than style. But it is only now that I have suddenly understood what this power consists of. While reading these words of Augustine's, I remembered another passage, which I had likewise known for a long time, the famous cry that rings out in one of the chapters of Nietzsche's *Thus Spake Zarathustra:* "For I love you, O Eternity!"

Both say almost the same thing. (Writing "Beauty at once so ancient and so new," Augustine has in mind Eternal Beauty.) But how differently they express it! As soon as we reflect upon the fundamental difference between these two passages, a ray of understanding suddenly illumines the situation.

Just as Nietzsche does, one can cry out at any point in space and at any moment in one's life. One can suddenly fall in love with eternity or with nothingness—fall in love just like that, for no reason at all. One can drink a cup of coffee and exclaim, "For I love you, O Eternity!" One can open a window, disclosing a starry

*Saint Augustine, *Confessions*, trans. R. S. Pine-Coffin (Baltimore, Md.: Penquin Books, 1961).—TRANS.

192 •

night, and exclaim, "For I love you, O Eternity!" One can climb a mountain, or even a small hill, and amid the wind that makes the tree sway and one's hair flutter cry out to empty spaces, "For I love you, O Eternity!"

But that other cry—Augustine's cry—falls to the earth with the weight of a boulder: "Late!" Augustine says. "Sero te amavi, sero te amavi . . ." Only now—why only now, only today, here, why precisely here? Here, at this very spot. Here, where I stand at this very moment. ("Here I stand," that is what Luther, that troubled monk, will exclaim centuries later in a speech at the Diet of Worms.)

Nietzsche's cry is the cry of an independent man, independent in the strict sense of the word: a man independent of a given space and time. Whereas Augustine drags a chain behind him; we can hear it clanking in his words. The chain of reality. Augustine—at that very spot, at that moment—drags everything behind him: all the past and all thinking about the future, all his experiences, all the bodies he has touched, and even the pears he has stolen in his childhood. For that reason he cannot exclaim so freely, "For I love you, O Eternity!" He wears a collar around his neck. He is a slave to reality.

Don't you think that he could not fall in love with the eternity that Nietzsche loved for the same reason? An empty eternity filled with silence and a void of an eternal, aimless circle of events? Nietzsche feared neither suffering nor the void. He repeatedly said that he feared neither suffering nor the void. Now I recall yet another passage from his works, a passage where, I believe, I have caught the greatest of the European philosophers of the absurd unawares.

In *Ecce Homo* Nietzsche cites reverentially the refrain of a song composed by Lou Salome and insists on having the words engraved on his tombstone as the epitome of his lifelong credo: "If you have no more happiness to give me, well then! you still have suffering!" Such is the philosopher's challenge addressed to the world and to life: "You still have suffering!" Does not this beautiful refrain of the song strike a false note, false through and through? If someone says "you still have suffering!" it means that he has no idea what suffering is. (Modern thought, even the thought of many great writers, abounds in pseudosuffering!) The only real suffering is what makes us cry out: "No more! No more! No more!"

And yet at the end of his life Nietzsche had to face suffering. When he was lying in the grip of madness, abandoned by all, constantly visited by disconnected, fragmentary hallucinations, finally forsaken by that stylistic genius which throughout his life had helped him to lessen to some extent the dread of the void, since he could write so splendidly about it . . . When he was lying there . . .

(1963)

TRANSLATED BY JADWIGA KOSICKA

Andrzej Kijowski

Postscripta to Saint Augustine's *Confessions*

"Anyone, provided he can be amusing, has the right to talk of himself." This is the opening sentence of Baudelaire's intimate journals. "My heart laid bare," he called them, in which he confessed to "vaporization of the Ego," fear of disappearance without a trace, abhorrence of the abyss into which death was sucking him.

Anyone, the first passerby, whoever it may be, has the right to talk of himself. Nowadays it is the main subject and motif of literary creativity. Think how many authors take pen in hand solely to impress the public with the singularity of their fate and character and to divulge secrets that no one is interested in. In the past this was a privilege to which a writer became entitled at the end of his life; only after gaining recognition from his readers for his works had he the right to talk about himself, and, "surrendering to the expressed desire of the esteemed public," as the old Goethe did, present them with his autobiographical *Dichtung und Warheit* (Poetry and truth). Nowadays gloomy young men and melancholy young ladies appear one after the other—a Jack Kerouac, a Sylvia Plath, a Marek Hłasko, a Stachura—to make their confession and then disappear. For many of them, confession, competing with the confessions of others in frankness and despair, remains their only work. Confession made at the beginning of one's creative life is an act of self-destruction. What is there to write about afterward? Baudelaire started to write his "intimate journals" when his physical and mental strength was ebbing and he felt "the wind of the wing of madness pass over me." Many young people who have started their creative life by "laying their heart bare" have also paid for it with their lives. Autobiography is often a prelude to suicide. The Angel of Death has spread his wings over prose and poetry in which the bare "I" reigns supreme.

In his *Confessions* Saint Augustine reveals his faith, not himself. It is an act not of self-destruction but of self-salvation. Augustine knows that by talking about himself he is close to conceit, so he addresses God instead of the reader, telling him how he, God, has saved Augustine by giving him the grace of faith. He tried to find God by way of philosophy, in other words, by "things that are made," but he came to understand that the truth he was looking for cannot be found through the senses. Therefore he abandoned the materialistic doctrine of the Stoics, who (through the writings of Cicero) had shaped his philosophical formation, and he became engrossed in Neoplatonic idealism, which reached him in its Manichaean version. Thus he became introduced to the idea of evil, which had obstructed his path to God: "I was burning with anxiety to find the source from which evil comes."*

Ontology was the basis of his philosophic inquiry. Regarding all things as substances, he could not reconcile the substance of God with the substance of evil; he was able to sigh freely only when he finally understood that evil is not a substance. But from this ontological curse, Greek in origin, which saddled him with problems inconceivable for us today (for instance, where does God "pour" the remainder of his substance which heaven and earth are unable to absorb?), Saint Augustine was freed only when he found a new cognitive principle: the inner experience of Truth. Or simply the grace of faith.

We do not have to face such ontological dilemmas as Augustine did because we do not think in ontological terms any more. For us, what exists is not what has substance, but what is verifiable and what can be useful. We think in empirical and pragmatic terms, constantly enlarging the sphere of the verifiable and our understanding of the useful. In the sphere of the verifiable we have included the unconscious, that is, the mystery of the individual and the collective; we know how to investigate, describe, and reconstruct it through the structures of language. We are also able to deal with the category of

*All quotations from Saint Augustine are from *Confessions,* trans. R. S. Pine-Coffin (Baltimore, Md.: Penguin Books, 1961).—TRANS.

the useful on a scale both infinitely large and infinitely small, in quasi-divine interrelations and analogies between macro- and micro-cosm, in temporal dimensions which recede to nothing in the sphere of infinity. There order is already Providence, and a trace of thought appears to be a trace of the living God.

But between the profound experience of God and the mysteri-ous plans of Providence there lies our world, the world of evil, about which we, like Saint Augustine, ask: Where does it come from? Did God create it or does he merely tolerate it? Is it a special manifestation of his will, or is it rather a proof that he does not exist? In the face of evil we ask: Who has created whom? If God is man's creation, a purely verbal existence, begotten by man's fears and doubts, then like man God is helpless in the face of evil. If man is God's creation for his everlasting glory and use, begotten by his will, and if God is good, where then does evil come from? When-ever like the Manichaeans we came to the conclusion that evil comes from outside man and has its own independent existence, we abandoned our faith in the Lord of good and evil who reigns over the heavens and the void and it seemed to us that we knew what evil was when we were told what it springs from: for example, from the struggle for survival. We tried to find a universal answer to the question of where evil comes from and to provide a key capable of instantly unlocking all the mysteries. Thus we have explained the course of history and the fate of the individual, the development of social systems and of the human heart as the result of the class struggle. And in this way we were like those philosophers, brought up on Greek ontology as Augustine was, who attempted to curb evil by understanding what its substance was, and those theolo-gians who, by giving it the name of an appropriate demon, knew what to do with it: to conjure and exorcise it. It seemed to us that by studying the nature of social relations we were learning the truth about man's inner nature, and that individual guilt was a derivative of collective guilt, and individual suffering a derivative of the suf-fering of all of humanity. Therefore individual happiness—we thought—depends on the general welfare; so we found the social system to be the source of ethics. And if evil did not disappear with the change in social system, we asked what made man so prone to it, why did he seem to derive so much pleasure from inflicting suffering on himself and on others, why was death, which he feared so much, so appealing to him at the same time? And to all these questions we would find an almost Manichaean answer, maintaining that evil, which originates in itself, is just as much as good a point of departure in the search for Truth. We have relativized good and evil, truth and falsehood. We have been and still are in the same perplexity as Saint Augustine, although we do not reason in categories of substance: we consider good and evil to be equivalent forces. And we know, as Saint Augustine did, that from this perplexity, from the vicious circles of multifarious human reality in all its plentitude, which cannot be explained or changed by a single turn of the philosophic key, we can be saved only by the inner experience of truth which comes from outside, the given truth, the truth revealed to us, to which we turn in faith.

According to Saint Augustine, faith is a medicine.

It cures doubt, that mortal sickness of the soul. A doubting soul is a dying soul: "In so far, then, as I thought the death of His body unreal, the death of my own soul was real; and the life of my soul, because it doubted His death, was as false as the death of His flesh was true."

Faith restores life to the soul. For the soul lives if it rejoices. Joy is the life of the soul. Joy is an announcement of an act of cognition. In joy we get to know God. Every man strives for that disposition; he has the right to it, desires it, and deserves it, and it comes to him as a gift: "I learned to rejoice with awe in my heart." This joy is man's defense, his argument and his warranty: "For even if a man inwardly applauds God's disposition, how is he to resist that other disposition in his lower self?" This "other disposition," the "disposition in his lower self" or natural law, is the law of the Prince of this world who is the enemy of God and of man. By conforming to his law we elude grace, reject redemption, and despise and stifle joy in us because we consider it unworthy of us.

We despise joy because we do not consider it to be a sign of the truth but an obscuring of it. What are you trying to achieve, we ask the soul, consolation or truth? If what you need is primarily consolation, then you are ready to accept it in any form. If what you crave is primarily joy, you will attend every Sabbath and accept every invitation extended to you. You will take part in the *Fackelzug* (torchlight procession) under the banner *Kraft durch Freude* (strength through joy), go to stadiums, where you, my soul, will applaud and yell at the top of your voice, go to noisy jazz sessions, take part in drug- or sex-induced hallucinations, and in all of them you will say that you have experienced the truth. And to free yourself from the anguish of thinking and doubting, you are ready to believe every absurdity offered you by the first dema-gogue, charlatan, clown, or policeman trained in psychology. "The enemy of our true happiness . . . wants me to divorce my joy from the truth and place it in man's duplicity." "The enemy of our true happiness" tempts us also with false joy, and how are we to tell it from true joy? Adam Zagajewski has said of his protagonist that he feels a sense of elation whenever he learns the truth. Yes, something like that does happen, but can we be certain that truth will always manifest itself that way? Augustine says that true joy is in peace and that peace is in God. God is in his Church. Hence the road of truth and peace to eternal joy leads through the Church, thus it is equiva-lent to obedience. By saying "No rest has my soul but in God's hands," he lays the cornerstone for the edifice of culture, whose principle, whose module, is obedience to the faith, and whose ar-chitectonic style is joy, even ecstatic, collective joy, at times sacred, at times ominous (the Crusades!), but serving merely as a harbinger of a still-higher joy, the joy of the heart that has found God. Thus the edifice so established and built has endured for ten centuries.

And what centuries they were! Augustine did his writing in an age when peace of the heart in God was the only peace man could be granted, and the certitude of God's truth was the only certitude in the midst of the lawlessness and cruelty with which the world was filled when, on the ruins of Rome plundered by the barbarians, a new moral and judicial order for the future of Europe was being born. Everything, starting with the principle of the division of power and ending with the dogmas of faith, had been called into question and seriously undermined. Roman Christianity was, after all, a part of the declining order, but it was to be revived later in the Germanic and Anglo-Saxon countries. But one thing was certain: God is the supreme good; even the barbarians believed that. The Vandals besieging Hippo, the seat of Augustine's congregation, were also Christian, but of the Arian creed. The Christians of that period murdered one another over the dogmas of faith and religious rituals, as Muslims and Hindus still do today. Calling for peace of the heart in God and obedience to the faith in the one universal

Church of Christ, the bishop of Hippo called on every single human being and all of humanity: abandon all your worries, seek and find peace in yourselves, and peace shall reign on earth.

For the next ten centuries European culture was conceived in the spirit of Augustine, aiming at the joy and peace of faith, until the critical period of the Renaissance and Reformation, during which there was a revival of the Stoic ethos of doubting reason against which Augustine had fought throughout his life. Doubt was once again considered the highest intellectual virtue, and anxiety the measure of a philosopher's true worth. The humanistic crown of martyrdom and glory was woven out of the sufferings of reason as it fought against every temptation of consolation. The later centuries, down to our own time, have kept adding new torments to this humanistic crown of cognitive suffering.

Augustine, a disciple of the Stoics, took this crown off; and he knew well both the pains and delights it provides. He knew that reason wants to believe. It wants to believe in a rational love that encompasses the totality of being and creates out of itself a series of particular beings, setting them the task of discovering their origin as the aim of their existence. He knew the drama of reason that refuses to believe. It refuses to believe when instead of awakening in itself the same love that created the world, which is the higher goal of knowledge, it surrenders to a lower goal: that of success for the questing intellect. Then that gives way to an even lower goal: freedom for the questing intellect; and that to an even lower one: social recognition as an intellectual. "For I had now begun to wish to be thought wise. I was full of self-esteem, which was a punishment of my own making. I ought to have deplored my state, but instead my knowledge only bred self-conceit." Higher goals give way to lower ones, for everything that man does for his own glory ends in degradation. Man's works are subjected to the law of gravity. Man draws around himself a circle of knowledge in order to find within it the proof of his own power. But it is an illusory power since it is measured on a scale devised by man himself. On that scale success is the only measure. In conformity to it we have built a new culture whose cornerstone is freedom of the cognitive mind, and whose style is suffering; the edifice of a tormented culture in which the most profound initiation is heroic self-destruction as a new type of saintliness and martyrdom.

"I wanted to be just as certain of these things which were hidden from my sight as that seven and three make ten. . . .

"But I wanted to be equally sure about everything else, both material things for which I could not vouch by my own senses, and spiritual things of which I could form no idea except in bodily form. If I had been able to believe I might have been cured."

Yearning for certain knowledge is a sickness; faith is a cure for it.

The Church teaches and cures; it redeems and heals. Like Christ. The recurring motif in the teachings of Christ is the equation faith equals health, truth equals life. "I am . . . the truth and the life," "Whoever lives and believes in me shall never die," "Go, your faith has made you well."

Faith in the medicine that he prescribes is a demand that every doctor has always made and still makes today. Faith is the will to live. Christ is not a doctor like other doctors; he does not say, whoever believes in me shall be cured, but "whoever believes in me shall never die." He demands faith such as no one yet has ever had, faith that is the will to eternal life.

There were no atheists in the world that Augustine lived in, or in the world that Christ lived in—which in a cultural sense were essentially the same world. But the religion of a Greek, a Persian, a Jew, a Scythian, or a Roman—were he a scholar, a civil servant, or the emperor himself—did not require faith; it belonged to the natural order, as did the state and all its institutions. Gods and emperors, good and evil spirits, and good and bad civil servants made up one world. A God requiring faith is an innovation of Christianity. The Christian revolution is a revolution of faith. As to the nature of faith, the Christians were involved in frightful controversy that divided them the way different conceptions about social systems divide mankind today: did Christ possess two natures, or only one; was he resurrected in body and soul, or only in soul; how will we be resurrected—will we be saved by our deeds and by faith, or by faith alone; is Satan equal to God, or was he created by God along with the angels? The corpus of the Catholic faith was in its formative stage. Mankind still hesitated as to how to read the message that had been bequeathed to it. There was, however, one point on which Christians were in agreement, namely, that an act of faith is the key to eternity, the secret of life, and a gift from God. And therefore they waged wars about the nature of that faith. The Christian revolution was bloody and lasted a very long time. It was still going on when Augustine wrote his *Confessions*. The burning flame of this revolution can be felt on every page.

Having rejected the official doctrine of the state that he had served as a functionary, Augustine confessed his faith in Christ. The town of which he was bishop was besieged by proponents of the two natures of Christ who had been killing clergy obedient to Rome. The faith and its tenets were for Augustine in actual fact a matter of life.

Now, as I am writing these words, faith has again become a matter of life. Not because a confession of faith is threatened by death, but because it has ceased to be a cornerstone of the secular structure: the state, culture, or even the family. It has ceased to be an object of transmission and imposition. It has become the object of a free choice that every person, every Christian, has to make in a dialogue with his own reason and the God of his heart. Everyone experiences to the fullest the absurdity of faith and the absurdity of the lack of faith. As did Saint Augustine: "I wanted to be certain of these things which were hidden from my sight" "for I began to realize that I believed countless things which I had never seen."

We know even more about this than Augustine. The sphere of our faith has spread to all the fields of specialization in which we are not specialists (and their number is constantly on the rise since the number of special fields keeps on growing), each equipped not only with its own method of inquiry but also with its own language. Specialists in other fields have gained a superiority over us similar to that which the monks of old who wrote and spoke Latin had over the unlettered barbarians. Our entire worldview is based on faith, much as was the worldview of those barbarians. I believe in atomic particles and their terrifying force, in vitamins and their medicinal properties, in viruses and in antibiotics, in the laws of the market, in statistical surveys, and in the rightness of public opinion. I believe in the microscope, the telescope, and the stethoscope, and in those who use them. I believe that the bank won't steal my money, that the post office will deliver letters addressed to me, that my doctor will surgically remove the diseased part of my stomach and will not confuse my X rays with someone else's, that the pharmacist won't poison me, and that the plumber replaced the right pipe in the wall. I believe in the same way as I am believed when I am doing the talking. Every specialist believes in other specialists because no longer are there specialists who know everything. The scope of faith is not limited to knowledge; faith is a force to be used by whoever is in power. For the source of power nowadays is information, and access to coded data, to accurate figures, to the true version of events, to personal files, is what the *sacrum* of the royal seal used to be in the past. Aren't the reactions of the masses mystical? And what about the reactions of the stock exchanges and the banks? Is faith not capable of disturbing the world's order when it causes, for example, an outbreak of panic in the monetary markets? All of our knowledge about the world is not much more verifiable than that of a medieval theologian's about the supernatural world, the only difference being that our knowledge relates to matters the average person understands, such as health, money, politics. But a medieval theologian would have been utterly baffled by the phrase "work quota," just as we are by Augustine's problems with substance.

Faith has not been eliminated in favor of verifiable and useful knowledge; it has only changed its field. Faith changes its field as do the fields of science and research methodology, the techniques of ruling and administration, and the areas of major concern, which move with the current of human hopes and fears.

Our choice is between the absurdity of unverifiable knowledge and the absurdity of revealed faith.

We do not choose between faith and disbelief, but between greater and lesser faith.

In the past people have suffered and died for an "iota" or a conjunction. They would say: we believe in this, and not in that—"that" is absurd. That the Son of God had come down to earth they had no difficulty believing because God is all-powerful, but not that God can be contained in human nature, because what is greater cannot be contained in what is smaller. God is all-powerful, but he cannot be illogical. They had no difficulty in believing in the Trinity, but that the Holy Ghost issues from both the Father and the Son was incomprehensible, because it contradicted the principle of the excluded middle. It was evident that man would be resurrected after death both in body and soul, but it was unclear whether the righteous would enjoy eternal bliss even before the end of the world or would have to wait in the abyss for the Last Judgment. For how can a person be "cleared" before the court passes judgment? God is all-powerful, but he cannot be in contradiction to Roman law.

From our perspective these dilemmas—and many more to follow!—belong, as it were, to the external, temporal order of faith. Today our concern is not with the pronouncements of faith but with the very possibility of faith at all. If it is not possible, it can make no pronouncements; and if it is possible, it speaks in the language of mysteries, and consequently every dogma is a sign marking the spheres of faith on the map of human knowledge.

The difficulty that faith encounters nowadays lies not only in the fact that it has an enemy in empirical science (which after all is based on faith) but in the fact that it has been blocked on all sides by false faiths. The revolution of faith has spread to all the spheres of human culture which Christianity has penetrated both openly and covertly, and, like any creative idea, it has produced its imitations. As the domain of religion has narrowed and its influence on the secular life has decreased, *quasi-religious* forms of consciousness, culture, and power are created that are scarcely distinguishable from the truly religious ones.

And alongside faith there is a *quasi faith*.

Augustine spoke only about that faith which is medicinal and cures doubt—"the deadly malady of the soul." Between true faith and its imitation there is the same difference as between medicine and poison; the former cures, the latter kills. The former can be recognized by the joy and peace of heart it offers, the latter by the despair it brings its adherents.

"For when I look for you, who are my God, I am looking for a life of blessed happiness."

By becoming one with God we enter into the unique rhythm of his life: "Why is it that in this part of your creation which we know there is this ebb and flow of progress and retreat, of hurt and reconciliation? Is this the rhythm of our world? Is this what you prescribed when from the heights of heaven to the depths of earth, from the first beginnings to the end of time, from the angel to the worm, from the first movement to the last, you allotted a proper place and a proper time to good things of every kind and to all of your just works?" A proper place and a proper time, history and evolution are God's designs and his works. The spatiotemporal basis of the world is God's law, which we can fathom through faith. Through faith we get to know the world in a proper way. Through faith, recognizing the law and its giver, we live in a proper way in the world of nature and participate in the world of history. The joy of faith is the joy of a proper, full knowledge; the joy of faith is the joy of a proper, full life.

A life in freedom. Complete freedom exists only in God, since outside of him it is circumscribed by man's tendency toward evil. The freedom found in God is open to goodness, which is limitless, while evil is limited. "I was enslaved since I did not want what you wanted."

In freedom from God man constantly desires something new, in slavery to God I want what God wants, and God is the *constans* of evolution, history, and man's fate: "For you are always the same, because all those things which are neither unchangeable nor endure for ever are for ever known to you and your knowledge of them is unchangeable." God is not identical with Being; he is outside Being, he establishes its order and manifests himself through it, but remains a mystery. "I scrutinized all these riches beyond number and stood back in awe, for without you I could see none of them, and I found that none of them was you. Nor was I myself the truth." So God is not a hypostasis either of my love or of my creative will; he is not an idea of mine, rather I am an idea of his. God is within me and outside of me, but he is not me: "On all sides You were like a rampart." Always present, as the thought of a creator is present in his work; the work owes its creator everything, but it is the creator who enjoys the work's independent existence. The same applies to man; he has only what he was given, but he is free to do what he wants to with that gift. God and man exist on separate planes linked only by the command that comes from God: "Give me the grace to do as you command, and command me to do what you will!"

God is the sole guarantor of unity and immutability—the unity and immutability of the universe, the unity and immutability of the soul. Thanks to God the world fulfills its aims, and thanks to God the human personality achieves cohesion and authenticity. "I groaned aloud in the weariness of my heart . . . my heart was buffeted hither and thither by winds blowing from opposite quarters."

A man who breaks the covenant with God breaks the covenant with himself; he who ceases to recognize God ceases to recognize himself. Evil, wickedness, is not a substance but "a perversion of the will when it turns aside from You, O God, who are the supreme substance, and veers towards things of the lowest order, being bowelled alive and becoming inflated with desire for things outside itself." This perversion consists of inflicting pain on oneself, of nonacceptance of faith: nineteenth-century humanistic Promethean heroism has become transformed into the academic heroism of the independent philosopher and the bohemian heroism of the *poète maudit*. "The soul is nurtured solely by what gives it true joy"—that is precisely what an intellectual is not free to do.

Man in revolt has lost his identity, but Augustine says, "I know no other content but clinging to God, because unless my being remains in him, it cannot remain in me." In God we seek what we are lacking: immutability and unity. "Your being knows and wills unchangeably; your knowledge is and wills unchangeably." Note the transposition of attributes: God's knowledge *wants* and is thus simultaneously will; the will *knows* and is thus simultaneously knowledge; God is the unity of will and knowledge ("Your being knows and wills unchangeably") and that is what man tries to achieve in his existence, eternally split and suffering on account of this split between will and knowledge. Thus he cries out, "For you my soul thirsts like a land parched with drought," and "No rest has my soul but in God's hands; to him I look for deliverance."

What is it, then, that prevents man from resting and finding what he seeks? It is "our own weight": "I was dragged away from you by my own weight and in dismay I plunged again into the things of this world." God is the actual center of gravity. There are then two forces of gravity: one good, the other evil. In this spiritual physics we can detect a trace of Manichaeanism.

How to overcome one's own weight? How to "cling to God"? Through obedience. Once man refuses to obey God, "things" begin to take over his mind. He is torn apart between two gravitational fields; one pulls him to God, the other to the world of things. Man must understand and recognize that he, along with the entire world of things, the entire natural order and reality that he himself has created, exists within God and that in all of nature he alone can discover this through Christ—who is simultaneously here and there: within reality—as the Incarnated Word—and outside it—as the Word of God that was before all time began. Man is the subject of his own actions, but at the same time he is the object of God's thought; man is within God because he exists and because he exists only in God. But man does not know who he is unless God reveals it through his Son who is the Word. Man comes to know himself by listening to the Word. He comes to know himself by obedience; through obedience he becomes a Godly man—a Son—just as the Son through obedience became a man.

There is a rational will in the universe, a creative and active will, known to all of nature and with which she works harmoniously, since nature is linked to it by the power of the inner laws imposed upon her without asking her consent. There is no freedom in nature. A star, flower, insect, or horse cannot refuse the activities that are assigned them, nor can they refuse to exist at all. They cannot commit suicide, whereas man can.

Man has freedom of choice. He can cooperate with the universal will or not. He can be slothful. He can depend on someone else's will, that is, live by the toil of others, or in slavery. He can live beneath his abilities, in other words, fail to fulfill his tasks in the universal scheme. His callings are not as clear as for all of nature. He has to find them, fathom them. He is the only existence in nature that has not enough time to learn how to live. An ant knows what to do as soon as it emerges from the egg, and it never errs thereafter; a bird leaving the nest is a mature bird; but an old man dies lamenting that he has never understood what his calling was. In order to grasp it, man must act in concert with the rational, creative, active will, with what is immutable; he must find the center of universal gravity and discover in himself that order which rules the cosmos: he must forge his will and his knowledge into one, he must surrender himself. Man is the only creature in all of nature authorized to collaborate with her for the pleasure of it—that is to say, out of love, which consists of obedience, humility, and faith.

Man reaches up to God from the depths of his suffering, which cannot be compared to anything else in this world since it is conscious suffering.

God reaches man from the vast height of his elevation, which cannot be compared to anything else in this world since no one is equal to God.

God and man meet in an act of love; the grace of God with the humility of man. "You, Lord, who are so high above us, yet look with favor on the humble." "Grant me, Lord, to know and understand whether a man . . . must know You before he can call You to his aid."

The search for God is unlike a scientific investigation; it lacks the impartiality that characterizes the scientific attitude. Only he who wants to find God searches for him, and he who wants to find him has already found him. He who asks whether God exists already betrays an inner need for certainty that such is actually the case.

The God for whom I search is within my reach, but I am not aware of it because I do not know how to call him. I search for him not as an archaeologist searches for ruins that have been buried in the sands, not as a philologist establishes the original version of an ancient text, not as a mathematician or a physicist searches for a formula. I search for him as a blind man searches for an object that he knows is somewhere in the room, or as a poet searches for a metaphor to express something he already knows: the blind man knows he will find the object since he put it in the room himself, and the poet knows he will find the metaphor since all the circuits have started flashing in his brain. Searching for God is actually searching for the words that express him; I search for words so that with their help I can explain to my reason about my new love and bring out into the open what until then has been my heart's secret. Reason is a link between me and other people; it translates the culture of my heart, which is my secret, into the language understood by the culture of my epoch and the nation I belong to. The search for God is a search for a rational and social expression of the love that my heart has already surrendered to. This love is grace; the rest is work. And this love is all-important: "For it is better . . . to find You and leave the question unanswered than to find the answer without finding You."

Augustine was a child when Rome appeared to be regaining its long-lost power and glory. Its ancient temples were refurbished, its old customs were restored, its legions marched off to conquer Persia. He was a young man when the Visigoths inflicted on the Romans at Hadrianopolis a defeat from which the empire never recovered. The prime of his youth was spent under the reign of

Theodosius the Great, who had united all the Roman territories for the last time, but upon whose death the final division into the Western and Eastern empires took place. He had just turned forty and became an observer of the collapse of the Western Empire during Honorius's reign. He was past fifty when the Visigoths conquered Rome, the Saxons Britain, the Vandals Spain, and the Goths Gaul. He was seventy-five years old when the Vandals attacked his native Carthage. He died in beleaguered Hippo, of which he was the bishop, thirty-six years before the Germanic warrior occupied the Capitol and announced to the world the end of Rome. Thus he was an eyewitness to the greatest catastrophe in history.

The son of a devout Christian mother, he was spared the experience of the persecution of Christians during his lifetime. He was too young to experience personally the Christian desertions and betrayals of faith during the reign of Julian the Apostate, who restored the official cult; thus the vacillation that his father displayed in religious matters and the postponing of his own baptism can perhaps be explained by the administrative pressures prevailing at the time. Augustine began his life as an adult just at the moment of the final triumph of the Christian religion. He was thirty-eight years old when the emperor Theodosius banned the pagan cults. Thus he belonged to the first generation of Christians who could profess their faith without fear. In choosing Christianity, he was choosing the official religion of the state. By entering the service of the Church, he was giving all his strength to the institution that in the disintegrating empire was the sole element of moral and social order, and on the level of the community and the city often the sole element of administrative regularity. As opposed to the state, which was becoming increasingly abstract, the Church was *real.*

So the dilemma that Augustine had to face was all the more difficult. He wanted his choice to be concerned with the truth, and only with the truth, so as to be as heroic as the choice once made by Saul of Tarsus, and then by the generations of martyrs and followers, the model of which has been forever fixed in the Gospel according to Matthew (19.21), in a conversation that Christ had with the rich young man: "Go, sell what you possess." Which means sacrifice all that you consider the most precious!

This is and always will be an absurd choice, and it cannot have any characteristics of practical reason. There must be something absurd about it, if not on a political plane, then on a moral one; if not on a material plane, then on an intellectual one. "Go, sell what you possess" also means destroy what you consider the most precious. It also means do something that will absolutely astonish you. Do something that brings you to the brink of suicide, in keeping with the words "Whoever loses his life for my sake will find it."

Augustine was a rhetorician. For money he would compose and deliver speeches and lectures, take part in philosophical deliberations, public disputes, and elocutionary competitions. He was, accordingly, a *literary* man. He would say what was expected of him and in a fashion that would appeal to the public. Nowadays he would write for the weeklies, do books on commission, go on lecture tours, appear on television, participate in literary competitions by invitation only. To be a rhetorician, to be a penman, as he put it, means "to sell one's soul": "Men give voice to their opinions, but they are only opinions, like so many puffs of wind that waft the soul hither and thither and make it veer and turn." A professional literary man is a functionary of the cultural conventions protected by the institutions characteristic of the period.

Augustine rejected the convention that belonged to the cult of the dying state: he became a priest. He chose the socio-spiritual reality of the Church. He rejected fiction in favor of the truth authenticated by the blood of Christ and that of the martyrs. He rejected conventional rhetoric and elected to serve the Word of Life. It was an *existential* choice. In this new service Augustine achieved the "equation of Life and Existence," that is, the equation of Being and the awareness of Being, which—as he put it—can be attained only in God and which contains the promise of salvation. Only in God "is there no difference between existence and life," only God and the redeemed soul really exist.

The heroism of this choice did not entail either physical or civil risk. For many centuries since Augustine the heroic has been based, and still is based, on the confrontation with reason, for which faith is but "folly." By choosing the truth of the gospel and the reality of the Church, Augustine chose the peace for which his heart longed but from which his reason recoiled and his own mental culture was alienated. Augustine believed in the Incarnated God because he wanted to believe; and yet as a Christian he wanted to believe in him with the same certainty with which he doubted him as a philosopher. He wanted to reconcile the new culture of Christ with the old culture into which he was born and by which he had been formed. Out of this drama was born Augustine's theology of radical, desperate solutions, a theology of trust and obedience, a suicidal theology expressed in the following words from the *Confessions:* "Those who look for the Lord will cry out in praise of him, because all who look for him shall find him, and when they find him they will praise him. I shall look for you, Lord, by praying and . . . I shall believe in you."

He wanted to know exactly what was happening to him during the process of transformation and why he was undergoing such a transformation. This was the source of his introspection, which in turn made him into a true writer, who, in order to be born, first had to die as a "penman," a "rhetorician," a "vendor of words."

And what a teller of stories he was! He tells us about his opportunistic father; his mother so naively pious that her fondness for religious ceremonies (agapes) led her to alcoholism; his own ambitons, habits, and desires; a mistress whom he mistreated; a beloved son; friends whom he also loved, although he saw them as the source of his weaknesses. One of them, a certain Alypius, Augustine writes, was willing to "make terms with death," that is, he intended to be married.

This Alypius, moreover, had developed a strong craving for gladiatorial shows, and that proved to be the source of his spiritual downfall: "The din had pierced his ears and forced him to open his eyes, laying his soul open to receive the wound which struck it down . . . he was no longer the man who had come to the arena, but simply one of the crowd he had joined."

This has a familiar ring for us: the law of the crowd, the force of gravity, the deceptive charm of the spectacle, the intoxication with the strength of others. The ancients probably lived more in the crowd than we do and were more dependent on it than we are. Cultural conventions must have been more coercive than our own. We are not yet forced to go to watch sports events; the ancients were. Only by realizing this can we imagine how important those silent gatherings in the name of the Lord must have been, in a circle of trusted friends, near the dead, making the customary offerings of food, tasting the food and rejoicing that the Lord risen from the dead was with them. If only we knew what they gained spiritually in this fashion, as compared to the losses they suffered every single day by being among crowds passively submitting to the meaningless rituals orchestrated by the state which nobody believed in any more, not even the emperor himself, or to the gruesome and idiotic entertainments overflowing with blood and sex.

If only we knew! . . . But don't we know it all only too well? The difference is that Augustine tells it superbly, but unfortunately we cannot tell our story to him.

He tells us about inner anxiety, of being perpetually torn between the good and bad sides of his nature: "Day after day I postponed living in You, but I never put off the death which I died each day in myself." He admits how difficult it was for him to abandon the woman he loved, his career, the money. Subtly he warns us against too hasty renunciations, for "to return to them later would be a disgrace." He complains of a constant lack of time, money, and books, and of his inability to reconcile practical life with the search for the truth, especially since he cannot renounce either the truth or life. We are well acquainted with this too, as we are with the feeling of "being driven by futile trifles"; "I longed for a life of happiness, and yet, while I fled from it, I still searched for it."

Because we are free to choose between the absurdity of temporality and the absurdity of transcendency.

The absurdity of temporality means a career, fictitious success, a family, offspring; we die still troubled by such strivings.

In this context the story of the happy drunkard is worthy of special attention. One day Augustine was commissioned to write a speech in praise of the emperor. He had resolved that

> it should include a great many lies which would certainly be applauded by an audience who knew well enough how far from the truth they were. I was greatly preoccupied by this task and my mind was feverishly busy with its harassing problems. As I walked along one of the streets in Milan I noticed a poor beggar who must, I suppose, have had his fill of food and drink, since he was laughing and joking. Sadly I turned to my companions and spoke to them of all the pain and trouble which is caused by our own folly. My ambitions had placed a load of misery on my shoulders and the further I carried it the heavier it became, but the only purpose of all the efforts we made was to reach the goal of peaceful happiness. This beggar had already reached it ahead of

us, and perhaps we should never reach it at all. For by all my laborious contriving and intricate manoeuvres I was hoping to win the joy of worldly happiness, the very thing which this man had already secured at the cost of the few pence which he had begged.

Of course, his was not true happiness. But the state of felicity which I aimed at was still more false . . . . They will say that it was drunkenness that made the beggar happy, while my soul looked for happiness in honor . . . . It was not true honor, any more than the beggar's joy was true joy, but it turned my head even more. That very night the beggar would sleep off his drunkenness, but mine had been with me night after night as I slept and was still with me in the morning when I woke, and would still be with me night and day after that . . . . There was a difference too between the beggar and myself. He was certainly the happier man, not only because he was flushed with cheerfulness while I was eaten away with anxiety, but also because he had earned his wine by wishing good day to passersby while I was trying to feed my pride by telling lies.

Augustine knew the voracious craving for success, but we, belonging to a similarly ritualized culture, are consumed by it on an infinitely larger scale owing to the attention that technological means and mass media accord to any success. Augustine and his listeners knew that the speech was a lie; Alypius and thousands of spectators in the amphitheater knew that the show was revolting. So do we, sitting in our cinemas, in front of our TV sets, at literary evenings and commemorative celebrations. We know that we listen to rubbish, watch rubbish, applaud rubbish, and create rubbish, delighting in the applause and the prizes that we get for such rubbish. Here are our rituals, and how similar to their Roman counterparts. And like Augustine we are unable to disengage ourselves from them. And what is there left besides such rituals? Social death.

But we are also well acquainted with envy similar to that which Augustine experienced when he saw the happy drunkard: we envy the good-for-nothings, the Gypsies, the tramps, the proletarians, and the savage barbarians. Artists and intellectuals are comforted by the myth of the free man who is happy. For there are no men more captive than artists and intellectuals; they are hired to *simulate* freedom.

For that reason, those desirous of freedom pursue that kind of career, consider it the most precious thing in the world, and cannot be persuaded to give it up. By simulating freedom, we are closest to it. Or at least we think that we are. "But if I had then been asked to choose between the life which that beggar led and my own," Augustine writes, "I should have chosen my own life, full of fears and worries though it was. This would have been an illogical choice."

The absurdity of temporality versus the absurdity of transcendence; a faith in unclear, unattainable, unverifiable things, a life well beyond our spiritual means. Who among us deserves the saintliness to which we aspire, if we aspire at all? Who among us understands the words with which he expresses his faith, if he expresses any faith at all? Who among us while professing his faith is convinced that he professes it fully and that he is as filled with it as he is filled or has been filled with desire for things of this world? Do we not make others laugh with our renunciations and our pious practices, do we not feel like laughing at them ourselves? In reality, is faith not "folly in the eyes of the world" and does this "folly" not hurt us? How often are we rewarded for it with peace and joy? And how many bitter and empty moments do we spend in devotion and faith? Not one of us could withstand the pressure of transcendence, the weight of grace, were it not for the Church, and that is precisely what it is for. Augustine tells us that the Church arose from the needs of the heart; he tells us what happiness he would have had if he could have shared his spiritual solitude with a circle of friends in a "commune" which they had established for that purpose (the story of that commune reads like a story of a student commune in our day) and how he had decided to exchange that sophisticated, academic commune on the margin of society for the Church, for the congregation of the faithful, and the pride of spiritual aloofness for the humility of a servant.

Augustine was perhaps the first among Christian writers to work out a psychology of faith and of disbelief. He had noticed that aestheticism is one of the consequences of a lack of faith. Describing a certain Manichaean rhetorician, Augustine says, "I did not trouble to take what he said to heart, but only to listen to the manner in which he said it—this being the only paltry interest that remained to me now that I had lost hope that man could find the path that led to You."

Lack of faith is the death of the soul; those "paltry interests" are no more than the soul's phantomlike impulses. And all literature from which the spirit of faith has absented itself is phantom-like; it is a literature that has lost the most important among its many goals, which is the redemption of man from the dread of anxiety and eternal death. Beauties of prosody and composition are a compensation that the spirit pays itself in exchange for the loss of its true goals. In literature only what serves some higher purpose is endowed with eternal life. And the highest of purposes is the search for God's signs in nature and history.

And the search for God's signs in man. The art of introspection comes from the Stoics. But it was Christianity that gave the process of character development new dynamics: the dynamics of "the history of the soul." It created a new occasion for observation and a new principle. The salvation of the soul is this new occasion, and confession is its new principle. A Christian giving an account of his life and that of his fellow men recounts the soul's adventures on its way to God. It is a kind of spiritual plot; evil constantly leads the soul astray, good constantly rescues it at the last moment, all ends in a happy denouement: the soul reaches its goal—God who waits for it. If *The Odyssey* were retold as an allegory of the soul's wanderings in search for God who awaits it on a heavenly Ithaca, the result would be *The Divine Comedy*. If retold in prose, in conformity with the real world, the result would perhaps be *The Human Comedy*. That is why the great European novel from Balzac to Dostoevsky, which deals with the split in man between the absurdity of temporality and the absurdity of transcendency, has its patron in Augustine, who infused the Greco-Roman form with a new spirit.

He infused literature with a new spirit because he understood why literature bored him so much and seemed so sterile. Because it has become something external placed inside the human heart. A conventionalized literature is like an intruder in a family, the members of which cease to live and communicate in their customary way, assuming instead the language and manners of the newcomer. The boredom that literature produces is the sadness of a heart that has been disinherited.

Boredom, sadness. Is it the sadness of the epoch, or a personal sadness? Is it the sadness of a man who does not find the sought-for means of expression in contemporary forms or the public response he seeks, or is it the sadness of a man who has captured the essence of the word and come to know its natural poverty?

Augustine's sadness and Augustine's boredom are the sadness and boredom of a man watching mankind in its death throes. Therefore he addresses God in an open, despairing letter. He writes about himself, his peers, his loves, and his amusements, about pride, the paths of thought, the longings of the heart. He tells God how he searches for him, how he imagines him, and what he expects from him.

But God knows everything that man tells him. A man talking to God merely checks his ability to tell the truth, which God knows better than he does. A writer surrenders to God's truth and serves it by translating God's knowledge and sensitivity into his own language. He tells everything to God, who knows everything. So he must be truthful and accurate, because God verifies his work; he must be lucid and tell his story well, so God won't be bored reading a novel whose ending he already knows. Teach us this art, saintly colleague from Carthage!

(1985)

TRANSLATED BY JADWIGA KOSICKA

P · A · R · T   T · H · R · E · E

Stanisław Jerzy Lec

Aphorisms

It isn't easy to live after death. It takes a lifetime.

Mankind deserves sacrifice—but not of mankind.

To God what is God's, to Caesar what is Caesar's. To humans—what?

He who has a good memory can forget more, more easily.

Dark windows are often a very clear proof.

How should we train memory to learn to forget?

Abel was the first to discover that dead victims do not protest.

Only the dead can be resurrected. It's more difficult with the living.

When confronted with his murderer the corpse
didn't identify him.

The first condition of immortality is death.

I know why Jews are considered wealthy—they
pay for everything.

You can divide people in many ways. Said the
astonished executioner, "I just divide them into
heads and bodies."

Don't shout for help at night. You may wake
your neighbors.

I dreamt of a slogan for contraceptives: "The
unborn will bless you."

Are naked women intelligent?

"What do you do," asked a friend, "when you
find, in your own bed, your wife's lover with
another woman?"

Tell me whom you sleep with and I shall tell you
whom you dream of.

His life was broken. Now he has two separate
and very pleasant lives.

What becomes of a devil who ceases to believe in
   God?

Optimists and pessimists differ only on the date
   of the end of the world.

Don't tell your dreams. What if the Freudians
   come to power?

Perhaps God chose me to be an atheist?

Illiterates have to dictate.

Open Sesame—I want to get out.

I prefer the sign NO ENTRY to the one that says
   NO EXIT.

                                                  (1967)

                    TRANSLATED BY JACEK GALAZKA

Jan Błoński

The Poor Poles Look at the Ghetto

On more than one occasion Czesław Miłosz has spoken in a perplexing way of the duty of Polish poetry to purge the burden of guilt from our native soil, which is—in his words—"defiled, blood-stained, desecrated."* His words are perplexing, because one can only be held accountable for the shedding of blood that is not one's own. The blood of one's own kind, when shed by victims of violence, stirs memories, arouses regret and sorrow, demands respect. It also calls for remembrance, prayer, justice. It can also allow for forgiveness, however difficult this may be. The blood of the other, however, even if split in a legitimate conflict, is quite another matter, but it also does not involve desecration. Killing in self-defense is legally condoned, though it is already a departure from Christian moral law: Christ ordered Peter to put away his sword. Whenever blood is spilt it calls for reflection and penance. Not always, however, can it be said to desecrate the soil.

What Miłosz means here is neither the blood of his compatriots nor that of the Germans. He clearly means Jewish blood, the genocide which—although not perpetrated by the Polish nation—took place on Polish soil and which has tainted that soil for all time. That collective memory which finds its purest voice in poetry and literature cannot forget this bloody and hideous stigma. It cannot behave as if it never happened. Occasionally one hears voices, especially among the young, who were not emotionally involved in the trag-

*Ewa Czarnecka, *Podróżny świata: Rozmowy z Czesławem Miłoszem: Komentarze* (1983), p. 119.

edy, saying, "We reject the notion of collective responsibility. We do not have to return to the irrevocable past. It is enough if we condemn this crime in toto as we do with any injustice, any act of violence." What I say to them is this: "Our country is not a hotel in which one launders the linen after the guests have departed. It is a home which is built primarily on memory; memory is at the core of our identity. We cannot dispose of it at will, even though as individuals we are not directly responsible for it. We must carry it within us even though it is unpleasant or painful. We must also strive to expiate it."

How should this be done? To purify after Cain means, above all, to remember Abel. This particular Abel was not alone, he shared our home, lived on our soil. His blood has remained in the walls, seeped into the soil. It has also entered into ourselves, into our memory. So we must cleanse ourselves, and this means we must see ourselves in the light of truth. Without such an insight, our home, our soil, we ourselves will remain tainted. This is, if I understand correctly, the message of our poet. Or at any rate, this is how Miłosz sees his duty, while calling upon us at the same time also to assume this obligation.

How difficult this task is can be seen from Miłosz's celebrated poem "Campo dei Fiori." At the heart of it there is the image of the merry-go-round which was—by chance, but what a coincidence!— built in Krasiński Square in Warsaw just before the outbreak of the ghetto rising. When the fighting broke out, the merry-go-round did not stop; children, youngsters, and passersby crowded around it as before:

> At times wind from the burning
> would drift dark kites along
> and riders on the carousel
> caught petals in mid-air.
> That same hot wind
> blew open the skirts of girls
> and the crowds were laughing
> on that beautiful Warsaw Sunday.*

Miłosz compares "the happy throng" to the crowd of Roman vendors who—only a moment after the burning at the stake of

*Translated by Louis Iribarne and David Brooks in Czesław Miłosz, *The Collected Poems 1931–1987* (New York: Ecco Press, 1988), pp. 33–34.

Giordano Bruno—went merrily about their business as before, enjoying their "rose-pink fish" and "baskets of olives and lemons" as
if nothing had happened. He ends the poem with reflections on
"the loneliness of the dying," who have the word of the poet for
their only consolation. It is only the word, the poet seems to be
saying, that can preserve what can still be saved. It purges the memory by voicing a protest against the passing away and "the oblivion / born before the flames have died."

The act of remembering and mourning fixes in the memory the
image of the stake in the middle of the marketplace or that of a
merry-go-round on the grave. The success of the poem itself—
which is often quoted and has been translated into many languages—is clear proof of that. In its Hebrew version, the poem
may appear as evidence of the hostile indifference of the Poles in
the face of the Holocaust. Years later Miłosz wonders "whether
there really was such a street in Warsaw. It existed and, in another
sense, it did not. It did exist because there were indeed merry-go-
rounds in the vicinity of the ghetto. It didn't because in other parts
of town, at other moments, Warsaw was quite different. It was not
my intention to make accusations."* The poem, he concedes, is
too "journalistic," allowing one to draw conclusions too easily. It
simplifies truth and by so doing soothes the conscience. Worse, the
poet discovers that he has written "a very dishonest poem." Why?
Because—I quote—"it is written about the act of dying from the
standpoint of an observer." So it is; the piece is so composed that
the narrator, whom we presume to be the poet himself, comes off
unscathed. Some are dying, others are enjoying themselves, all that
he does is "register a protest" and walk away, satisfied by thus
having composed a beautiful poem. And so, years later, he feels he
got off too lightly. Matched against the horrors of what was occurring at the time, he says, the act of writing is "immoral." "Campo
dei Fiori" does not succeed in resolving the conflict between life
and art. Miłosz adds in his defense that the poem was composed as
"an ordinary human gesture in the spring of 1943," and, of course,
we must immediately concede that it was a magnanimous human
gesture. During that tragic Easter, it saved—as someone put it
somewhat grandiloquently—"the honor of Polish poetry." We

*In Czarnecka, *Podróżny świata*, pp. 63–64.

agree with the poet, though, that the last word on the subject has yet to be spoken.

This agonizing over a poem may perhaps help us understand why we are still unable to come to terms with the whole of the Polish-Jewish past. Here then I shall abandon literature and draw directly on my personal experience. Perhaps, on reflection, not even very personal, as almost everybody who has traveled abroad, especially in the West, must have had this question put to him at one time or other: "Are Poles anti-Semites?" Or more bluntly: "Why are Poles anti-Semites?" I myself have heard it so many times, and so many times I have tried to explain, that I could attempt a thumbnail sketch of some twenty or so of such conversations:

—Are Poles anti-Semites?

—Why do you put your question in this way? There are Poles who are anti-Semites, some others who are philo-Semites, and a growing number who do not care either way.

—Well, yes, of course, but I am asking about the majority. Poles have always had a reputation for being anti-Semites. Could this be an accident?

—What do you mean by "always"? Wasn't it true that at a time when Jews were expelled from England, France, and Spain, it was in Poland and not elsewhere that they found refuge?

—Yes, maybe, but that was a long time ago, in the Middle Ages. At that time Jews were the objects of universal contempt. But at least since the mid-eighteenth century in Europe, there has always been a problem of Polish intolerance.

—But it is exactly at that time that Poland disappeared from the map of Europe!

—Polish society, however, continued to exist, and the Jews could not find their place within it. Why?

—We were under foreign rule; we had to think of ourselves first.

—This is precisely what I mean. Why could you not think of yourselves together with the Jews?

—They were too numerous. We did not have sufficient resources. We could not provide for their education, judiciary, administration. Jews didn't even speak Polish; they preferred to learn

Russian or German. But there were enlightened people among us who advocated the course of assimilation and strove to bring the two communities together.

—But why? Why couldn't Jews simply remain Jews? You were also responsible for pograms, why?

—It is not true, the first pograms took place in the Ukraine and they were provoked by the czarist police. . . .

And so such discussions continue:

—When you regained independence, the fate of Jews did not improve. On the contrary, anti-Semitism became even more vicious.

—You can't change society in only twenty years, and besides that, was it not much the same elsewhere in Europe at the time? In the aftermath of the First World War we received many Jews from Russia and after 1934 from Germany.

—That may be true, but you still treated them as second-class citizens. During the war you saved too few.

—There is in Israel a place commemorating people who saved Jews during the war. Thirty percent of the names on that list are Polish names.

—But the percentage of Jews who survived the war in Poland is low, the lowest in Europe in relation to the total number of the population.

—In 1942 there were four Jews for every eight Poles in Warsaw. Now, how is it possible for the eight to hide the four?

—It was indeed the Poles who used to identify Jews and passed them on to the Germans and to the police, which was, let us not forget, Polish.

—In every society there is a handful of people without conscience. You have no idea what the German occupation in Poland was like. To hide one Jew meant risking the life of one's whole family, children included.

—Yes, that's true, but there were equally brutal repressions for the underground activities, and a great number of people were involved in them. Following the war Jews did not wish to remain in Poland.

—Indeed. It was difficult for them to live surrounded by memories.

—It was difficult for them to live among Poles who did not wish to give them back their houses and shops and threatened and even killed some of them. Have you not heard of the pogroms in Krakow and Kielce?

—The pogrom in Kielce was a political provocation.

—Even if it was, so what? It did find a response. Ten thousand people besieged the Jewish house in Kielce. Ten thousand people can't be provocateurs.

—Jews were sometimes a target not for being Jews but for sympathizing with Communists.

—In 1968, is it because they were Communists that they had to leave Poland?

And so on, indeed endlessly. The debates of historians resemble this discussion. The same arguments and events—only more carefully documented—appear time and again. There is a vast body of literature, both of a personal and a documentary nature, of which we have very little idea in Poland. We should, however, know it better, because it also refers to us. It contains a wide range of viewpoints and opinions. There are books whose authors do not hide that they are motivated by hate. We cannot afford to ignore them; they are born of personal experiences whose authenticity cannot be doubted. And, besides, haven't we ourselves produced works that are equally full of hatred, sometimes hysterical hatred, toward Jews?

There are also many books that are cautious and, as far as possible, devoid of partisanship. These books carefully remind us of the intellectual as well as the material conditions of Polish-Jewish coexistence. They take into account the terror, unimaginable today, of life under the German occupation and a certain moral degradation of the society which was a direct result of life under this enormous pressure. This, in fact, was not a uniquely Polish experience; it also happened elsewhere.* They make a tacit assumption that the tragedies of Eastern Europe cannot be measured by the yardstick of, say, the English experience. When the skies are literally falling in, even a kick

---

*The victim cannot accept that he was not only wronged but also humiliated and demeaned by his persecutor, that he was unable to stand up to the inhumanity of it all. In the years 1944–48, Polish opinion was not able to acknowledge the disintegration of all norms and the moral debasement of a large part of our society in the aftermath of the war. The drastic treatment of these themes by writers such as Borowski and Różewicz aroused indignation.

can be an expression of sympathy and compassion. The truth, however, remains difficult to determine and difficult to accept. Two years ago I attended a discussion in Oxford between some foreign and some Polish specialists, and I must confess that it was a distressing experience. For us as well as for the Jewish participants, I suppose. We were a long way from agreeing with each other, but that is not the aim of such conferences. I was continually aware of what was not being said there and what was the main reason why these discussions—friendly, for the most part—were painful for all concerned. It was later that I came to the conclusion that this was due to the sense of a kind of contamination, a feeling of being somehow soiled and defiled, which is what Miłosz had in mind in the passage noted above.

And that is why I would like to go back once more to the poet. In 1943 Miłosz wrote another poem about the destruction of the ghetto, a poem entitled "A Poor Christian Looks at the Ghetto." It is more ambiguous, perhaps more difficult to understand. It opens with an image of destruction:

> It has begun: the tearing, the trampling on silks,
> It has begun: the breaking of glass, wood, copper, nickel,
>   silver, foam
> Of gypsum, iron sheets, violin strings, trumpets, leaves,
>   Balls, crystals.

And later:

> The roof and the wall collapse in flame and heat seizes
>   the foundations,
> Now there is only the earth, sandy, trodden down,
> With one leafless tree.

The city was destroyed, what remained is the earth, full of broken shells and debris. It is also full of human bodies. In this earth, or rather under it:

> Slowly, boring a tunnel, a guardian mole makes his way,
> With a small red lamp fastened to his forehead.
> He touches burned bodies, counts them, pushes on.
> He distinguishes human ashes by their luminous vapor,
> The ashes of each man by a different part of the spectrum.

Who this mole is, it is difficult to say. Is he a guardian, perhaps a guardian of the buried? He has got a torch, so he can see; better at any rate than the dead can see. And the poet himself, he is as if among the buried. He lies there with them. He fears something. He fears the mole. It is a striking, startling image:

> I am afraid, so afraid of the guardian mole,
> He has swollen eyelids, like a Patriarch
> Who has sat much in the light of candles
> Reading the great book of the species.

And so this mole has the features of a Jew, poring over the Talmud or the Bible. It seems more likely that it is the Bible, as this alone deserves the name of "the great book of the species," meaning, of course, the human species.

> What will I tell him, I, a Jew of the New Testament,
> Waiting two thousand years for the second coming of
>   Jesus?
> My broken body will deliver me to his sight
> And he will count me among the helpers of death:
> The uncircumcised.*

It is a terrifying poem; it is full of fear. It is as if two fears coexist here. The first is the fear of death; more precisely, the fear of being buried alive, which is what happened to many people who were trapped in the cellars and underground passages of the ghetto. But there is also a second fear: the fear of the guardian mole. This mole burrows underground but also underneath our consciousness. This is the feeling of guilt which we do not want to admit. Buried under the rubble, among the bodies of the Jews, the "uncircumcised" fears that he may be counted among the murderers. So it is the fear of damnation, the fear of Hell. The fear of a non-Jew who looks at the ghetto burning down. He imagines that he might accidentally die then and there, and in the eyes of the mole who can read the ashes, he may appear "a helper of death." And so, indeed, the poem is entitled "A Poor Christian Looks at the Ghetto." This Christian feels fearful of the fate of the Jews but also—muffled, hidden even from himself—he feels the fear that he will be

*Translated by the author in *Collected Poems 1931–1987*, pp. 64–65.

condemned. Condemned by whom? By people? No, people have disappeared. It is the mole who condemns him, or rather *may* condemn him, this mole who sees well and reads "the book of the species." It is his own moral conscience that condemns (may condemn) the poor Christian. And he would like to hide from this mole-consciousness, as he does not know what to say to him.

Miłosz, when asked what or who is represented by this mole, declined to answer. He said that he had written the poem spontaneously, not to promote any particular thesis. If this is so, the poem would be a direct expression of the terror that speaks through images, as is often the case in dreams and also in art. It makes tangible something that is not fully comprehended, something that was and perhaps still is, in other people's as much as in the poet's own psyche, but in an obscure, blurred, muffled shape. When we read such a poem, we understand ourselves better, since that which has been evading us until now is made palpable. As for myself, I have—as probably every reader does—filled in the gaps in my own reading of "A Poor Christian." I hope, however, that I have not strayed too far from the intentions of the poet.

Here I return to the hypothetical conversation, that simplified summary of dozens of arguments and discussions. What is immediately striking here? In the replies of my fictitious Pole one detects the same fear that makes itself felt in "A Poor Christian." The fear that one might be counted among the helpers of death. It is so strong that we do everything possible not to let it out or to dismiss it. We read or listen to discussions on the subject of the Polish-Jewish past, and if some event, some fact that puts us in a less-than-advantageous light, emerges, we try our hardest to minimize it, to explain it away and make it seem insignificant. It is not as if we want to hide what happened or deny that it took place. We feel, though, that not everything is as it should be. How could it have been otherwise? Relations between communities, like the relations of two people, are never perfect. How much more relations as stormy and unhappy as these. We are unable to speak of them calmly. The reason is that, whether consciously or unconsciously, we fear accusations. We fear that the guardian mole might call to us, after having referred to his book: "Oh, yes, and you too, have you been assisting at the death? And you too, have you helped to kill?" Or at the very least: "Have you looked with acquiescence at the death of the Jews?"

Let us think calmly: the question will have to be asked. Everybody who is concerned with the Polish-Jewish past must ask these questions, regardless of what the answer might be. But we—consciously or unconsciously—do not want to confront these questions. We tend to dismiss them as impossible and unacceptable. After all, we did not stand by the side of the murderers. After all, *we* were next in line for the gas chambers. After all, even if not in the best way possible, we did live together with the Jews; if our relations were less than perfect, the Jews themselves were also not entirely without blame. So do we have to remind ourselves of this all the time? What will others think of us? What about our self-respect? What about the "good name" of our society? This concern about our "good name" is ever-present in private and, even more so, in public discussion. To put it differently, when we consider the past, we want to derive moral advantages from it. Even when we condemn, we ourselves would like to be above—or beyond—condemnation. We want to be absolutely beyond any accusation, we want to be *completely* clean. We want to be also—and only—victims. This concern is, however, underpinned by fear—just as in Miłosz's poem—and this fear warps and disfigures our thoughts about the past. This is immediately communicated to those we speak to. We do not want to have anything to do with the horror. We feel, nevertheless, that it defiles us in some way. This is why we prefer not to speak of it all. Alternatively, we speak of it only in order to deny an accusation. The accusation is seldom articulated but is felt to hang in the air.*

Can we rid ourselves of this fear? Can we forestall it? I think not, as it lies, in all truth, in ourselves. It is we ourselves who fear the mole who burrows in our subconscious. I think that we shall not get rid of him. Or at least we shall not get rid of him by forgetting about the past or taking a defensive attitude toward it. We must face the question of responsibility in a totally sincere and honest way. Let us have no illusions: it is one of the most painful questions we are likely to be faced with. I am convinced, however, that we cannot shirk it.

*That is why there are so few literary works that treat the theme of the attitude of Polish society to the Jewish Holocaust. It is not only because literature is rendered speechless in the face of genocide. The theme is too hot to handle; writers have felt that they came into conflict with their readers' sensibility.

We Poles are not alone in grappling with this question. It may be helpful to realize this. Not because it is easier to beat one's breast in company. Not because in this way the blame may appear less weighty. Rather, because in this way we shall be able to understand it better. To understand both our responsibility and the reason why we try to evade it.

We read not so long ago about John Paul II's visit to the synagogue in Rome. We are also familiar with the Church documents in which—already at the time of Pope John XXIII—the relationship between Christians and Jews, or rather between Christianity and Judaism, was redefined, it was hoped for all time. In the pope's speech as well as in these documents one aspect is immediately clear. They do not concern themselves with attributing blame or with considering the reasons (social, economic, intellectual, or whatever) that made Christians look upon Jews as enemies and intruders. One thing is stated loud and clear: the Christians of the past and the Church itself were wrong. They had no reason to consider Jews as a "damned" nation, the nation responsible for the death of Jesus Christ, and therefore as a nation that should be excluded from the community of nations.

If this did happen, it was because Christians were not Christian enough. The Church documents do not state, we "had to" defend ourselves, we "could not" save Jews or treat them as brothers. They do not attempt to look for mitigating circumstances (and these can be found). Jews, being monotheists, were "beyond the pale" already in antiquity. In the Middle Ages what cemented Europe together was religious unity. Let us bear in mind that the Church was, on the whole, more tolerant than the secular rulers. Nonetheless, all this does not change the basic situation and must be put aside. Instead, what has to be stressed is that the Church sustained hostility toward Jews, thereby driving them into isolation and humiliation. To put it briefly, the new Church documents do not attempt to exonerate the past; they do not argue over extenuating circumstances. They speak clearly about the failure to fulfill the duty of brotherhood and compassion. The rest is left to historians. It is precisely in this that the Christian magnanimity of such pronouncements lies.

I think we must imitate this in our attitude to the Polish-Jewish past. We must stop haggling, trying to defend and justify ourselves.

Stop arguing about the things that were beyond our power to do, during the occupation and beforehand. Nor place blame on political, social, and economic conditions. But say first of all: Yes, we are guilty. We did take Jews into our home, but we made them live in the basement. When they wanted to come into the drawing room, our response was—Yes, but only after you cease to be Jews, when you become "civilized." This was the thinking of our most enlightened minds, such as Orzeszkowa and Prus. There were those among the Jews who were ready to adhere to this advice. No sooner did they do this, than we started in turn talking of an invasion of Jews, of the danger of their infiltration of Polish society. Then we started to put down conditions like that stated *expressis verbis* by Dmowski, that we shall accept as Poles only those Jews who are willing to cooperate in the attempts to stem Jewish influences in our society. To put it bluntly, those who are willing to turn against their own kith and kin.

Eventually, when we lost our home, and when, in its premises, the invaders set to murdering Jews, did we show solidarity toward them? How many of us decided that it was none of our business? There were also those (and I leave out of account common criminals) who were secretly pleased that Hitler had solved for us "the Jewish problem." We could not even welcome and honor the survivors, even if they were embittered, disorientated, and perhaps sometimes tiresome. I repeat: instead of haggling and justifying ourselves, we should first consider our own faults and weaknesses. This is the moral revolution that is imperative when considering the Polish-Jewish past. It is only this that can gradually cleanse our desecrated soil.

What is easy in the case of words is, however, more difficult in practice. A precondition is a change in the social awareness of the problem. For our part, we often demand of Jews (or their friends) an impartial and fair assessment of our common history. We should, however, first acknowledge our own guilt and ask for forgiveness. In fact, this is something they are waiting for—if, indeed, they are still waiting. I recall one moving speech at the Oxford conference in which the speaker started by comparing the Jewish attitude to Poland to an unrequited love. Despite the suffering and all the problems that beset our mutual relations, he continued, the Jewish community had a genuine attachment to their adopted

234 •

JAN BLOŃSKI

country. Here they found a home and a sense of security. There
was, conscious or unconscious, an expectation that their fate would
improve, the burden of humiliation would lighten, the future
would gradually become brighter. What actually happened was exactly the opposite. "Nothing can ever change now," he concluded.
"Jews do not have and cannot have any future in Poland. Do tell
us, though," he finally demanded, "that what has happened to us
was not our fault. We do not ask for anything else. But we do hope
for such an acknowledgment."

This means on the Polish side the acceptance of responsibility.
Here enters for the last time the guardian mole and asks: "Full responsibility? Also a shared responsibility for the genocide?" I can
already hear loud protests. "How can that be? In God's name, we
didn't take part in the genocide." "Yes, that is true," I shall reply.
Nobody can reasonably claim that Poles as a nation took part in the
genocide of Jews. From time to time one hears voices claiming just
that. We must consider them calmly, without getting angry, which
might be taken as a mark of panic. To me, as for the overwhelming
majority of people, these claims are unfounded. So why talk of genocide? And of shared responsibility? My answer is this: participation and shared responsibility are not the same thing. One can share
the responsibility for the crime without taking part in it. Our responsibility is for holding back, for insufficient effort to resist. Who
of us could claim that there was sufficient resistance in Poland? It is
precisely because resistance was so weak that we now honor those
who did have the courage to take up this heroic risk. It may sound
rather strange, but I believe that this shared responsibility through
failure to act is the less crucial part of the problem we are considering. More significant is the fact that if only in the past we had behaved more humanely, had been wiser, more magnanimous, genocide would perhaps have been "less imaginable," would probably
have been considerably more difficult to carry out, and almost certainly would have met with much greater resistance than it did. To
put it differently, it would not have met with the indifference and
moral turpitude of the society in whose full view it took place.

A question arises immediately whether this could be said not
only of the Poles but equally well of the French, the English, the
Russians, the whole of the Christian world. Yes, indeed, it can.
This responsibility is, indeed, our common responsibility. But it

cannot be denied that it was in Poland where the greatest number of Jews lived (more than two-thirds of the world's Jewry are Polish Jews, in the sense that their forefathers lived in the territories belonging to the Polish republic in the period before the Partitions). Consequently, we had the greatest moral obligation toward the Jewish people. Whether what was demanded of us was or was not beyond our ability to render, God alone must judge and historians will continue to debate. But, for us, more than for any other nation, Jews were more of a problem, a challenge we had to face.

To refer once more to the realm of literature: nobody understood this better than Mickiewicz. The thoughts and the vision of our romantic poet were more farsighted than that of any of his contemporaries. Unlike the majority of those who were well disposed to the Jews, Mickiewicz held the deep conviction that Israel, "the older brother," should not only enjoy the same privileges in Poland as everybody else but also at the same time retain the right to remain distinct in religion and custom. This was also Norwid's attitude; as far as we can judge, Słowacki was of the same opinion. So at the very least, our literary greats stood on the side of truth and justice. The thinking of Mickiewicz was indeed visionary: he seems to have been aware that only such a path could save the Jews (if only partially) from extinction, and us from moral turpitude. It would have been a truly extraordinary path to take and one that would have merited the epithet *messianic* in the proper sense of the word. Reality, unfortunately, took exactly the opposite form to that dreamt of by the poets. It was nowhere else but in Poland, and especially in the twentieth century, that anti-Semitism became particularly virulent. Did it lead us to participate in genocide? No. Yet when one reads what was written about Jews before the war, when one discovers how much hatred there was in Polish society, one can only be surprised that words were not followed by deeds. But they were not (or very rarely). God held back our hand. Yes, I do mean God, because if we did not take part in that crime, it was because we were still Christians, and in the last moment we came to realize what a satanic enterprise it was. This still does not free us from sharing responsibility. The desecration of Polish soil has taken place, and we have not yet discharged our duty of seeking expiation. In this graveyard, the only way to achieve this is to face up to our duty of viewing our past truthfully.

(1987)

Gustaw Herling

The Shadow Hour

Punctually at five o'clock a lone stag made his appearance among the snow-covered bushes on the peak of one of the heights. He seemed to listen for something and scoured the bottom of the valley with his glance. In the end he must have seen us, huddled in a cluster by the fence surrounding the feeding station, because he quickly disappeared behind the rim of the peak, as if he had sunk to his knees in the snow or dropped down in sudden panic. The lenses of the field glasses misted over, and it was turning dark. The twilight shadow hour seeped slowly into the clear frosty air, like blue ink dropping evenly into a silvery basin of water.

We were in a small valley encompassed by a crown of hills near the German-Austrian border. Winter was harsh that year: snow covered the earth with a thick mantle, and stags and hinds were often found dead on the heights. For several weeks an emergency feeding station had been in operation here. On the tree-sheltered site they filled troughs with chestnuts and set out bundles of hay in baskets. Everyday at half past five the starving animals came down into the valley. Sometimes it was a fairly small herd and only from the hill that ran straight down to the feeding point; sometimes they came down all the hills at once, sweeping across the white patch of level ground; and occasionally, when there was no other access, even leaping over the frozen band of the highway.

At half past five silence enveloped the entire vicinity: nary a sign of life nor a quiver on the hills, only an occasional lobe of snow would drop from an overladen branch, a veil of dust marking its course. There was a sharp frost, and evening now poured into the

silvery basin, no longer in drops but in a steady stream. Suddenly—
as six o'clock approached—the master of ceremonies shouted in a
high falsetto: *Ruhe!*

We saw them only at mid-slope. The hinds came first, and after
them the stags. Stopping every few steps, plowing stiffened forelegs
into the snow, flinging their heads up to one side at every ominous
or suspicious sound, drawing back timidly, dodging or jumping to
one side of the track or the other, they flowed down with the
twilight in a shadow ballet. When they reached the feeding place,
the darkness blurred and soon absorbed them.

Who knows why that scene so distinctly calls to mind a period I
always used to remember as if through a smudgy pane: my last
winter in Poland?

＊ ＊ ＊

Toward the end of October 1939 I returned from Warsaw to
my family home in the Kielce area for a farewell visit. I had already
made up my mind to cross over to the other side of the Bug River
and then take the route north or south to the West.

Our Dark Pool, embraced by the arms of an alderwood dam,
grew darker still in the twilight of autumn days. From a distance
the wind-furled leaves of water lilies stood out like water hens.
Wild ducks shot up from islets of rushes and reeds, desperately beat
the air with their wings, and flew off in the direction of Ostrowek;
there they abruptly ended their flight and dropped bricklike into
the bullrushes along the shore. The meadow beyond the dam was
bare. Bare too were the neighboring groves, which had only recently swarmed with summer holidayers. An unwartime peace
reigned all around, Germans were rarely seen, and the only thing
that troubled the calm of the dam was the water splashing through
the openings in the sluice gates and running over the rotten planks
of the floodgate. Level fields, a grimy leaden sky, mounds of black
earth, smoke over the potato fields, here and there a small solitary
figure on the horizon, the melancholy of nature going to sleep.
Trains packed with soldiers moved across the distant moors. All
you could hear from the dam on Dark Pool was the drawn-out
train whistle.

A month later I stepped off the train in Małkinia with a throng of fugitives.

Along the demarcation line and on both sides of it, there was a margin of freedom at the time to make a final choice before the loops of the net were drawn fast. Like fish scared off by pursuit, people dodged between the wings of the closing net. They would rush one way and then flee back again in the opposite direction. It was hard to make comparisons, because below a certain level everything seemed equally bad. People were seen off in Małkinia by kicks and blows from German policemen, and on the opposite bank of the Bug they were greeted by Soviet guard dogs and soldiers' gunshots. People camped out in the fields day and night, asking the muddy waves of the river what to do, lighting fires, knocking at peasant cottages for food, and guessing the future from the stars in a sky livid with the first frosts. On rainy nights the smugglers took fate into their own hands: snakelike files of small black dots wound around crossings that were thought to be less heavily patrolled; if there were no orders to maintain silence, you could hear people meeting and exchanging the names of cities, names that for some already evoked the specter of loss but to others still offered hope of deliverance.

The possibility of choice, even so limited and illusory, made that expanse mournfully attractive. People like me, with a view to a farther destination, were in the minority. Most of the fugitives clutched convulsively at their last chance to make a change without leaving Poland. The price they paid was constantly keeping their knapsacks and bundles closed in readiness, and keeping their ears alert for any kind of news at any time of day or night. Their eyes learned to read the faces of strangers at a distance, as if they were secret dispatches. Their trembling fingers crushed out one cigarette after another. Their hearts beat to a quickened rhythm.

One night, after several days of waiting, our strung-out retinue of shadows luckily dodged a Russian border station, guided on for a long time by an uncertain barking of dogs.

* * *

Life in Białystok was concentrated on the main street, where the Soviet side of the Border Zone set up its central post office and transit hub. In the human stream flowing up and down, people looked for relatives, friends, and occasional letter carriers. Sheets of paper brought from afar and furtively handed over in haste provided news of their near ones in a style the concision and expressiveness of which could never be matched by a pen that was in the service of imagination alone. People exchanged objects, valuables, and money, depending on which direction they were going. They passed information back and forth in a way that sounded like stock exchange quotations. When they shook hands in greeting, they did not know if it was simultaneously a farewell.

It was early December, the first snow was flaking down. The air was still charged with the dampness of the autumn, and moist petals of snow melted quickly and flowed in dirty streaks down the red banners slung across the street in honor of the advent of the New Power; down gigantic portraits of the Ruler; and over a plaster model of the monument to the Invincible Army. Loudspeakers uninterruptedly poured out the same words over and over again, words that were trampled at once into the glassy gray mud slick under the feet of passersby, muffled in the press of furs, sheepskins, and army coats, and buried by the sawdust of the never quieting buzz of human voices. The smell of vodka, sour soup, and half-baked bread came out of the doorways.

I found a corner to sleep in at the lodgings of a painter I knew. He lived with his wife and brother in a not very large room right on the main street of the town. This arrangement did not last long. My host was engaged in painting an enormous image of the Leader onto separate squares of cloth, transferring the image from photographs that were issued to "artists" together with the commission. The trial mounting of these portraits needed space. In time, the gradual assemblage of the parts of the face on the walls began to dislodge the tenants. I spent my last night in that room between the Eye and the Nose, and I damaged the Nose, albeit slightly, when I got up from my bedding in the dark to attend to my bodily needs. The next morning I read a silent eviction order in the eyes of the portraitist. Thus it was that I became one of the first sacrifices—in a mild form for the time being, however—to the Cult of Personality in the zone occupied by Gogol's countrymen.

My attempts to join one of the "subscription" groups planning to escape to Kaunas were ultimately unsuccessful: the amount of money I had was too small. I would have to seek my fortune in Lvov.

The charm of Lvov (reputedly greater still in winter than in the other seasons of the year) was at first hard to glimpse through the scaffolding of banners, slogans, models, and portraits. The whole country beyond the Bug River seemed plastered over with newsprint and battened with pasteboard and planks, like a store being totally overhauled.

Lvov was then living in a state of nerves bordering on hysteria. People would look around before uttering a single word that might be slightly audacious, they often changed sleeping places, intimate friends would talk in whispers, and very reluctantly did anyone divulge temporary addresses. An exception of sorts was the Scotch Coffee House, which was occupied from morning to late at night by men of letters. There was a gentlemanly something about the table talk there, something untouched by the war. Conversation quieted down after the first writers were arrested. They drank coffee and smoked cigarettes with the same expression in their eyes that I was accustomed to seeing among the wanderers in the Border Zone.

I passed my nights differently here—sometimes in the Tramworkers Settlement in the Gabrielówka Quarter, sometimes in the Engineers' House on Abrahamowicz Street, and sometimes on the bare floor of crowded rooms whose addresses I no longer remember. I spent my days trying to find a "way out." But the need to keep intact what was already so modest a sum for my "passage" made me look for possible occasional work. And the need to legalize my position in the event of an extended stay made me seek some kind of document. I succeeded only in the latter.

The lower-rung Soviet authorities made no secret of their weakness for "artists" and "writers." Lvov already had an official Western Ukrainian Writers' Association headed by a certain Pancz, a man from Kiev whom the authorities considered "reliable." A distinguished majority of the habitués of the Scotch were members, chiefly (when they were not Communists) out of consideration for the indispensable housing authorization. Ostap Ortwin learned the lesson. In the tiny room of the former Polish Writers' Association on Ossolińscy Street he began to draw up housing authorizations in Russian in the names of those who applied for them. What stood out in these documents, of course, was the magic word "writer" without further specification. Membership in one of the two competing associations soon became something on the order of an implicit political statement. People would say meaningfully: so-and-so belongs to Pancz or he belongs to Ortwin; and it was known in a small circle of initiates that some, those who were more skeptical in the face of the tortuous course of history and more cautious in looking into the future, belonged to Pancz *and* to Ortwin. Before the proceedings in Ossoliński Street could be assessed in the proper place and manner, there were dozens of Ortwinian housing authorizations circulating around the city, thanks solely to the word "writer," to dazzle the eyes of the minor officials of the billeting offices. I was not then a writer, all I had to my credit were a couple of student essays accepted for publication in periodicals, but Ortwin treated my "apprentice" status with Olympian calm and required only two signatures of recommendation for my application. Maria Dąbrowska and Juliusz Kleiner kindly provided them. I received my housing authorization from the hands of Parnicki: it was certainly one of the last he issued, because the next day they arrested the author of the novel *Aetius, the Last of the Romans*. I did not make use of the permit in Lvov, but later it served me several times as a safe conduct in the course of my wanderings.

When there was no further doubt that I would not find either "transit" or employment in Lvov, I again decided on the northern route. I had very little faith in going north through Volhynia, and I often stopped on the road without any particular aim. I circled round, I turned back, I looked into cities and towns I knew nothing about, I was almost a tourist. At night I sought shelter mainly in railway stations—in Lutsk, Luninets, and Horyn. That may be why what I have preserved from that barren interval is chiefly memories of dim and stuffy waiting rooms, peasants sleeping wherever they happened to drop—on benches, on tables, on the floor— frightened and disturbed by the chronic sleeplessness of newcomers from the Border Zone, Red Army men hugging their rifles as they dozed on wooden footlockers, and an earthy, tattered sky over the roofs when one went out for a while to take a breath of fresh air.

And thus I reached Lida. The smugglers there simply shrugged their shoulders, spitting scornfully at the sight of my money, and advised me to drink it all up in good company in the course of a single evening. I did not take their advice, but I finally realized that, so miserably endowed, I would never find a chink in that vicious circle. At night I slept upright in the chair of a barber shop. In the morning my own face in the mirror appalled me. There were two ways out: back across the Bug River or on to the job in Grodno that someone mentioned in a letter I received when I was still in Lvov.

* * *

A small Polish theatrical enclave had been formed that winter in Grodno. Two theaters had been set up: a playhouse under the direction of Aleksander Węgierko and a puppet theater, the State Puppet Theater of Western Belorussia, under the direction of Władysław Jarema, a brother of the painters Józef and the recently deceased Maria. They did not ask for very high qualifications of the people who helped the master carpenters in the workshop of the puppet theater. My work involved cutting out and modeling the easiest pieces of the marionettes and, should the need arise, replacing actors in bit parts. My earnings were enough to pay for a bed in a dormitory, meals in the mess hall, and small expenses.

If it is true that you recognize prosperity only by contrast, then Grodno was the epitome of prosperity to me. I liked my job too, and with a touch of irony it even seemed to be the one best suited to my new situation. To some degree, the war had turned us all into marionettes; so it was some relief and a ploy of humiliated pride to call into being one's own puppets and manipulate them while looking through the opening in the frosted window of the workshop at the green-gold onion atop the Orthodox church in Grodno.

At the beginning I went to stay in a quiet sleepy tenement a few steps from the Szypowski confectionery shop. We got together after work at Szypowski's in the early evening, to drink tea with saccharine, to puzzle out the next moves of the stage managers of history, and to plan the next step for our own marionette selves. Tidings of the outside world reached us obliquely, as if through a thick pane that obscured the light: someone had been arrested, someone else had disappeared, someone managed to throw a scrap of paper out of the window of a train of deportees being sent to the East.

My roommate was Edward Boyé. His status was that of court translator to Węgierko. Boyé would sit at his desk in the morning, unwashed, hung over, coughing, and cursing, averse to all of humankind, and rummaging idly among his papers: like the philosophers' stone, a Russian translation of Lope de Vega's *El perro del hortelano* occupied the place of honor.

Every evening I went with this translator of Boccaccio, Cervantes, and Aretino to the Communal Restaurant, where for a while under the Soviet system of bulk sales each customer was served sixteen small mugs of beer. We usually sat alone facing each other, saying little, turning our heads, obstinately drawing down the icy yellowish liquid, which in the lower regions of the body immediately turned into a rather warmer liquid of the same color. Habitués of the Communal Restaurant frequently made room for additional mugs without getting up from the table, in cross fire, heedless of the look of the place or their trousers. On these occasions Boyé would mutter sententiously, "Diuretic, that Russian beer."

A month later I moved to a cheaper room in the small house of a retired inspector of schools, an old bachelor, right on the Neman River. My new roommate was an unemployed circus fakir, Jasha, who as an artist had also been steered to the puppet theater. There was no chance in the realm of lifeless figurines for this young Belorussian to display his dazzling art. But we did take advantage of one of his skills: walking barefoot over glowing coals on the callous-hardened soles of his feet. While we were at work in the theater, he would stand in line insensitive to the cold and wait for bread for the whole troupe.

Every day came new evidence that there were places in the Eye of the Cyclone that for a time were spared the fury of the elements. When I would go back to the house at night, the ice on the river gleamed with quivering shafts of light, the little houses on the shore slept under hoods of snow, and slippery footpaths snaked around. It might have been an illustration for an old-fashioned winter's tale. Before going to sleep, Jasha would show off the circus numbers for which he did not find spectators elsewhere. In the next room, our pensioner paced around the table like Pushkin's cat around the oak tree, and sometimes he knocked on our door to ask, "Is there no news?" "It won't be long before it starts," he always said as he went off, "it won't be long before it starts." Until one night, we didn't find him in the house. The next day his disappearance briefly provided us with one topic of conversation at Szypowski's.

* * *

One day probably in the middle of March Jarema enigmatically whispered that the NKVD had been making inquiries after me. Whatever actually occurred, I detected in his voice a wish that I hasten my plans for the future.

Thanks to loans, I finally found two smugglers willing to chuck me into Lithuania. One of them was named Mickiewicz. These were the auspices under which I began my . . . road to Russia. Our little wagon avoided the toll barrier on the north side of Grodno and proceeded barely ten kilometers. The police car caught up with it in an empty field, where such operations attracted no one's attention. My Mickiewicz was in the service of the NKVD.

Three years later I met him as a corporal in the desert in Iraq, which showed that he ultimately followed in the footsteps of his victims. I looked him over in silence for a long time and saw the blood drain from his face. Then, still without a word, I walked on.

But this is where the evocative echo from my valley breaks off, that valley into which the shadows of my last winter in Poland run down from the hills at the hour of twilight. But why write this in the introduction to a book that is free of any addiction to reminiscence? . . . In a certain sense the present volume is the fruit not just of my readings but of my wanderings around the world. So let it be preceded by the words of the Pirandello sonnet that hangs on the wall in his family home outside Agrigento:

> se penso al punto in cui la vita mia
> si aprì piccola al mondo immenso e vano:
> da qui—dico—da qui presi la via . . .

When I think of the point at which my life opened small onto the immense vain world: this—I say—this is where I started from.

Naples, April 1963

TRANSLATED BY RONALD STROM

Aleksander Wat

Reading Proust in Lubyanka

This essay is made up of a taped section, a separate sketch found in Wat's papers, and a part of the taped text that he reworked.

We had no Communist literature the entire time, no Marxist literature at all. I was in many cells where prisoners were given books, at least a few, and everyone confirmed that they were never given that sort of book. My fellow prisoners had a very intelligent explanation for that: it was simply to keep the investigators, who were not terribly intelligent, from being nailed to the wall by Marxist arguments. There was no shortage, however, of religious literature. I read Solovyov there and a great many others. I read the church fathers, Saint Augustine on the Kingdom of God.

As I'll explain later, the books I read in Lubyanka made for one of the greatest experiences of my life. Not because they allowed me an escape but because, to a certain extent, they transformed me, influenced and shaped me greatly. It was the way I read those books; I came at them from a completely new angle. And from then on I had a completely new understanding, not only of literature but of everything.

Literature is insight and synthesis, which means that poetry, ultimately, is heroic. Naked, weak, hungry, trembling, endangered by all the elements, all the beasts and demons, the cavemen performed that act of heroism for consolation, in the deepest sense of the word. And at that time there in Lubyanka this seemed to me the essence of literature and the source of its legitimacy in the world. Consolation for a weak, naked caveman.

A SKETCH FOUND IN WAT'S PAPERS

As I've already mentioned, *Swann's Way* was in that first batch of books. My first book in a year. To my surprise and, later, almost to my horror, I realized that my entire value system had not been destroyed but had simply been left outside the prison walls. All my knowledge of people and society, all the circuitous paths of psychological inquiry, my industrious study of the passions, my over-sophistication—everything in which I had taken so much delight—in Lubyanka seemed atrophied, pretentious, and irritating at times. After the misery of Zamarstynów Prison what did I care about a satire on the Verdurins' salon? What did I care about a world enclosed in a salon like a ship in a bottle; what did I care about lifeless thoughts turned into elegant conversation? It was absorbing, of course, and helped to kill time. But everything in that book that was not poetry, that did not have poetry's energy and movement, was just costume drama.

Swann's Way did not emerge diminished from that reading. Quite the contrary, I was more charmed than ever by the power of its energy, its beauty of movement. The poetry in *Swann's Way* made everything intimate, an "inward vibration," and was all the more unusual in that it played off the outermost layers, the epidermis of the sensibility. And what was of more importance to me was that in its experience of time past, the book was, first and foremost, a state of constant agony in which nothing had yet died but everything was dying. An unbroken moment suspended between life and death, a final breath hellishly protracted beyond all measure—it is that alone that gives the book its depth and stirs the reader to his depths; without this, Proust's entire work would be no more than an enormous fresco of vanity, in both senses of the word. While reading *Swann's Way*, I began to discover a model for the agony I was suffering in prison, and Proust's long sentences and time periods recaptured their original power for me. An exchange of form and power—the archetypal relationship between author and reader. As if in mockery, it was everything flimsy about Proust—his quasi-Balzacian side, his descriptions of human life in "decadent capitalism"—that Anatolii Lunacharsky praised in his introduction and that was seen as the sole justification for publishing the book. Like all Marxist critics, Lunacharsky, the last of the

Bolshevik aesthetes, did not write about the work itself but treated it as a sociological "trot." When reading his introduction, I realized that I was repelled as much by communism's reduction of everything to the flat and the linear as by its atrocities.

By the way, the clichés used in introductions by Marxists— "subjectively reactionary but objectively progressive"; "a genius conditioned by the limitations of his time" or "his class," and so on—are sordid and arrogant, but, after all, they have saved and continue to save literature in those countries where, as Gobineau put it, "the inquisitor functions as a critic."

Machiavelli, in the Academy edition, was also in that first batch of books. Not long after that I happened on a large selection of his letters, a prerevolutionary edition containing his correspondence and a detailed biography. At one point I had read Machiavelli like *tout le monde*, through the prism of the epithet "Machiavellian"— "the genius of political corruption," "the severe masculine world of the condottieri . . . *virtu*. . . ." Machiavelli the poet came as a real revelation to me in Lubyanka. Not because of his verse itself, which was rather weak, but because he was a poet. "Dichterisch wohnt der Mensch auf dieser Erde" (Hölderlin). A poet of action, Machiavelli tried to make his earth *dichterisch*.

That book came to me at just the right moment. On the dunghill of Zamarstynów I had trained myself in hatred and disgust for politics, all and any. We had seen its ugly pockmarked face; it had come to the old refined city of Lvov from the Bolshevik steppes, the plains of Muscovy, and that was the source of our suffering. We heaped abuse on the politics of Poland, on the politics of the West, embroiled in a thousand petty intrigues like those that tore Machiavelli's Italy apart, that weakness that had helped give rise to two monstrous waves of barbarism.

It would be an exaggeration to say that reading Machiavelli in Lubyanka cured me of the hatred and disgust for politics I had acquired in Zamarstynów. That still comes back in me to this day and sometimes literally chokes me and makes me stammer; to write on political subjects is torture for me, but I was always doomed to have to speak my piece. The power and glory of reading come from those moments of illumination, when it clarifies the obscure, when it breaks things into their parts, but it is powerless against strong feelings. Once strong feelings have taken root in us, reading can only influence the direction they grow in, inhibiting or enhancing them, raising them to a higher level. Reading Machiavelli restored my equilibrium; I regained my sense of proportion and distinction, albeit sporadically—and what more could I have asked for? I learned to distinguish between politics as collective fate and as political instrument. Machiavelli showed me politics against a different sky, against stars that could not be seen from prison.

"Politics is fate." When, in 1808, at a gathering of kings in Erfurt, Goethe praised Voltaire's *Mahomet* as a *Schicksalstragödie*, the emperor Napoleon interrupted him to say, "A tragedy of fate? That's part of the past now. *Politik ist das Schicksal.*"

Machiavelli and his city-state were faced with the same hopeless task as the Athenians of the fifth century: how to safeguard the polis, the beauty and harmony of its logic, when, by the nature of things, large groups, large numbers, were fated to enter history, and vast dark forces came into play threatening the polis with subjugation and degradation to the conquerors' own low level. Machiavelli then became the poet of politics as Plato had once been its teacher. But, as opposed to Plato, Machiavelli was no longer able to believe in educating the rabble: "A corrupt people is unable to maintain the freedom it had once secured for itself." He no longer believed that the Ideal could be realized, and he believed neither in the wisdom of the philosophers nor in the virtue of the knights. The prince had to be educated.

Dramatic circumstances attended the writing of *The Prince:* [Machiavelli was] thrown into a dungeon, subject to torture that he bore with courage and with such sarcasm at his own expense that he could say when writing from prison in supplication to powerful people, "I acted so well that I felt a certain tenderness toward myself."

Released, finally released to a miserable little village, he described his life in a letter to Francesco Vettori: "In the afternoon I go to the inn, play dice and backgammon with the innkeeper, the miller, the butcher; we argue over pennies, exchange the most obscene of insults, and cheat each other. And thus do I defend myself against Fortune's spite . . . content that it has cast me low, as it peers at me to see if I blush with shame."

He would return home in the late afternoon, cast off his stinking clothes, don courtly attire, and then settle his accounts with

Livy and Seneca, whom he treated as equals. In those evening disquisitions after his days at the inn, he wrote *The Prince*, a crystal of poetry and logic, in one burst of genius.

Machiavelli, our contemporary, with our passion for self-degradation—"Content that Fortune has cast me so low. . . ." He put the entire *esperienze delle cose moderne* to the test and in that he resembles the people of today. When in one letter he describes with scrupulous naturalism an adventure in the dark with a lame, festering old prostitute, one suspects that this could have been Baudelaire's model for *The Jewess*. "For a long time now I have not been saying what I think and not thinking what I say, and, if a true word escapes me, I wrap it in so many lies that it cannot be found," writes Machiavelli to Francesco Guicciardini, a ready-made epigraph—and perhaps an epitaph as well, for Russian or Polish writers under communism.

Nowadays one speaks of "Stalin's Machiavellianism," a single phrase that joins the height of Renaissance thought and virtue (*virtu*) with Tartar customs. Although at that time I was still avoiding making any allusion to Stalin, since the principal accusation and perhaps even the cause of my arrest was my prewar statements about him (as numerous witnesses, my colleagues, had testified), in the cell I did read aloud the passage in which Machiavelli advises the Prince to commit all the atrocities he will have to commit right at the beginning, in one fell swoop, or else end up in a vicious circle of constantly renewed atrocities.

A SECTION OF WAT'S MEMOIRS

The pendulum of prison time swings between agony and nothingness, but in Lubyanka time has other laws and moves in a different way. But books brought us back to life, immersed us in the life of free people in the great and free world. We took fictional reality naively, like children listening to fairy tales. Could that have been the reason they gave us books in that laboratory of prison existence, where every detail had been thought out, quite possibly even by Stalin himself? Perhaps the experience of two such antithetical realities is supposed to induce a schizophrenic dissociation in a prisoner, rendering him defenseless against the investigation.

Could this be one means by which the investigator fires the desire to live, which is otherwise extinguished in a prisoner? I had a great desire to live because I found Nietzsche's *amor fati* in every trifle in every book, even the pessimistic ones. The more pessimistic the book, the more pulsating energy, life energy, I felt beneath its surface—as if all of literature were only the praise of life's beauty, of all of life, as if nature's many charms were insufficient to dissuade us from suicide, from Ecclesiastes, and from Seneca's "better not to have been born at all but, if born, better to die at once." I came across books that I had read before prison and that had sapped me of my will. For example, *Notes from the Underground*. But there in my cell even those books sang hosannas. In Lubyanka freedom seemed a hundred times more alluring and a hundred times more desirable than in Zamarstynów, where I had hit bottom. Could that have been the influence of the books I read? And wasn't that the investigator's intention: to fire the prisoner's desire for freedom so that he would be ready to do anything that was required of him?

But no doubt the secret behind our being given books was less complicated than that. Perhaps in Stalin's ark, which contained the prototypes for everything—wealthy collective farms, model cattle feeders, the most modern factories—there was also a place for a model prison in which the prisoners had a right to culture. Perhaps Stalin's personal fondness for reading as well as his Byzantine sense of decorum were significant here. Or perhaps this was an instance of chance and disorder in his global strategy. Or perhaps all the above operating together.

And so I think that reading had a twofold effect in Lubyanka, whether that was the investigator's intent or not. This isn't just speculation on my part; I observed its effect on my cell mates. Primarily, books stimulated a keen desire for life, life of any sort, at any cost, to live and move with the Rastignacs, Rostovs, and even the heroes of *Notes from the Underground,* an insatiable desire to live in freedom even if that were the miserable freedom of the camps. I encountered many prisoners who had been pulled out of the camps for a review of their trials; despite their having no faith in being released and despite the great wretchedness of camp life, they would still grow nostalgic about being able to move freely about the camp, about the chance to work and be in contact with large numbers of people. A second and opposite effect of reading was that it disordered a prisoner's mental structure by causing him to experience two entirely different realities simultaneously: the world of books—free, full of movement, light, change, colorful, Heraclitean—and the world where time stood still, lost all sensation in captivity, and faded into a dirty gray. The sum total of both opposed effects worked to the investigator's advantage because it disturbed the victim's entire soul.

But reading had the opposite effect on me. It marshaled my intellectual and spiritual resources and made me stronger. It truly was like touching the earth for Antaeus. No doubt that was because what I primarily filtered out from books, any sort of book, was the poetry they contained, and it was only in prison that I became aware of a certain banal truth, one that I had often doubted, namely, that I am a poet.

I am not a poet because I write poems (besides, I only did so in periods that were few and far between) or because I composed poems in prisons to condense my spiritual states. And not because I had loved poetry since I was a child and had a high respect for excellent verse. Both of those factors, though important, were secondary, incidental, here.

And not because I had wanted to make my life into a work of art, a poem. On the contrary. I never could bear the Oscar Wilde brand of dandyism, and there were times when I had felt a need for the ugly, the low, a need to go slumming. And my early reading of *A Seducer's Diary* and Kierkegaard's *Either/Or* had made me aware of my natural aversion to "aesthetes." In my early youth, I wanted to end up as a drunk in the gutter, a *clochard* (and I came close to it in my dadaist phase) or, alternatively, as a hermit philosopher living in the extreme poverty that I thought probably lay in store for me anyway. I also had long phases in which I needed to take refuge in mediocrity, and that was bad, very bad. On the whole, my life was a patchwork affair, and there was no question of its being a work of art.

In Zamarstynów not only did I examine my past in the light of conscience, an old habit of mine, but I undertook a spectrum analysis of all my failures, sins, disgraces—both those I could remember and those I had to wrest from oblivion because that truly was a *dies irae, dies illa.* . . . And everything that had been hidden away came up to the surface. It was then that I became fully aware that I had always experienced things as a poet. Mine had not been the philosopher's life: at the university I had concluded once and for all that it was pointless to dream of universal knowledge, *mathesis universalis;* I had lost faith in that, and partial, relative truths held no attraction for me. Mine was not a religious life either, a search for God, as one critic has imputed: heaven is either taken by storm or step by step and even in my religious ecstasies in Soviet prisons and sporadically later on in Communist Poland, I was passive toward religion.

But my life, oh, my life, had been a constant search for an enormous dream in which my fellow creatures and animals, plants, chimeras, stars, and minerals were in a preestablished harmony, a dream that is forgotten because it must be forgotten, and is sought desperately, and only sporadically does one find its tragic fragments in the warmth of a person, in some specific situation, a glance—in memory too, of course, in some specific pain, some moment. I loved that harmony with a passion: I loved it in voices, voices. And then, instead of harmony, there was nothing but scraps and tatters. And perhaps that alone is what it means to be a poet.

And so Lubyanka made me sensitive to everything; in poetry, novels, works of philosophy (we had books by Solovyov and Losky there), and in the handbook on minerology I read, I read both the poetry and the reflections they contained. As two sides of the same thing, since poetry without reflection is empty, just word games, and reflection without poetry is blind, its bearings lost. I said "reflection" but it would have been more accurate to say "philosophy," as a consolation for life's misery, as it appeared to Boethius in prison—in a robe with the letters T (*Theoria*) and P (*Praxis*) embroidered at the bottom. "Two sides" of what? Human fulfillment? Spiritual life in the state of becoming? The modus of existence? Consolation? In the end when asking myself those questions I applied to poetry what Saint Augustine had said about time: "When no one asks what it is, I know what is is; if someone asks me, I don't know." *Nescio:* and if asked what poetry is, I wouldn't know either, even though its substance was so self-evident as to be almost palpable in Lubyanka. I could detect its presence with my fingertips, even though poetry's spiritual content is perhaps even purer than that of religious experience, since the latter contains psychological elements—a person's feelings toward his father, his relationship to nature, and so forth. Poetry, however, can feed on those elements too, but it can also do without them. Perhaps poetry can do without everything and is a state of nirvana, not meaning nothingness but, on the contrary, the highest fullness. "*Gesang und Dasein*," I repeated after Rilke, and that was enough for me.

That was what I thought and felt about poetry in Lubyanka. Clearly my views have changed a great deal since that time, but still now, if asked to, I can't define what poetry is. For me it is still a state and not a fact, the highest value in literature and language. I would replace the poet's fashionable clamor to *réinventer la poésie* with the simpler but more difficult *réinventer le poète*.

Even when reciting poems to myself in Zamarstynów, where it was a crime to possess a scrap of paper, I knew poetry was a consolation, and something more than that as well: a wretched creature, subjected to misery of every sort, struggles toward beauty from the abdominable depths of his misery. . . . Let the critics discourse on the structure of poetry, linguistic entropy, metonymy—poetry fulfills itself when it is an act of heroism. That lesson on the ontological meaning of poetry was not lost on me. When we go back to the twenty, fifty, or hundred greatest works of world literature that we read as young people, we cannot, nor do we wish to, be freed from the charms of that initial reading. Still, we were prematurely exposed. What could we have known of their roots in human life? Under conditions like those in Lubyanka—cut off from the world, aware of the vast roaring world outside, the deathly hush inside, where time slows terribly while we continue to grow terribly old biologically—under those conditions we sought to recover our initial freshness of perception, the way Adam saw when he saw that "it was good."

Here I should interject that my experience was very much my own, and not typical. Not because I had been devouring books all my life or that the history of my childhood and youth could be told by the books I read, or that for my last seven years as a free man I had been the literary director of Gebethner and Wolff. I had acquired such a taste for analyzing and restructuring other people's work that I had stopped writing myself (or perhaps it was the other way around, and I had become an editor in order to stop writing). I felt in charge only when I had taken hold of the actual end of the thread and could see an entire work unravel into its components. And I gradually became cynical about what I considered the spurious integrity and unity of a given work; it was nothing but a skillfull montage of various elements and tricks. In Lubyanka, to my joy, I rediscovered the sense of integrity—the whole that "precedes" the parts and is their soul. I had fully recovered my ability to see things synthetically.

(1977)

TRANSLATED BY RICHARD LOURIE

Jan Kott

Journey to the East

1

It was the best tea we had had: almost completely transparent yet aromatic. I still remember its taste and fragrance, like that of dried apricots; no, like that of dried apricots steeped in alcohol. It was Yunnan tea, late autumn 1944. "A bad year," said our host, "but one of the best harvests." Later, after dinner, we drank a Szechuan tea—harvested the previous year—out of porcelain tea bowls so fragile it seemed to us our fingers would crush them. This tea was dark and bitter. "That winter was full of hope and the late harvest has its value among connoisseurs." On shelves of all sizes stood jars of various proportions, some quite tiny, others enormous; all bearing calligraphic characters in red or black ink. All of them held tea.

This had been our first invitation to a Chinese home, and the only such visit during our almost two-month stay in China. It wasn't until just shortly before our departure that I had realized how unusual it was and what efforts and interventions it had probably required. One needed special permission—from the very top—to invite foreigners into one's home. Even if they were from the people's democracies and official delegations, permission would have to be sought weeks in advance. The parents of Fu Tsong knew that Smendzianka was traveling in China with the Polish delegation. Their son the pianist had received first place for his playing of the mazurkas at the Chopin competition in Warsaw. He had also won a one- or two-year scholarship. Regina Smendzianka was one of the most promising pianists of her generation and had even played with Fu Tsong on occasion. She and Fu Tsong were friends, and he asked her to pay a visit to his parents in Peking. They in turn asked her to dinner and because she did not want to go alone, she asked me to accompany her.

In those days of fall 1954 Peking was easier to get to than Vienna or Berlin. West Berlin, that is. China was closer than Yugoslavia, particularly during Khrushchev's time, a year or so after Stalin's death. In Poland people were being released from prisons, in Russia from labor camps. Even in the Party there were whispers, faint it is true, about torture as a common practice during inquisitions. After Ilya Ehrenburg's *The Thaw* appeared in 1954, the word "thaw" was making the rounds. China opened its doors to delegations. But not only to delegations. To some sort of new hope. Or perhaps it was not hope at all, but a sudden restoration of the old faith.

China had been front-page news for five years. My memory returns to those years with reluctance. "You remember in order to forget," L. repeats, "but others will not let you forget." I remember that day well. Peking had been liberated and all Party and union members had been summoned to Warsaw's Polytechnic. Everything was in red: banners, armbands, walls papered with red cloth and crepe. The color red still seemed fresh to me then. As did the singing of the Internationale at the close . . . which dragged on. I am tone-deaf but that didn't stop me from singing with the entire auditorium until I went hoarse: "We have been naught, we shall be all. 'Tis the final conflict. . . ."

I don't remember where we had gathered in Lodz when Berlin fell in May 1945. That was over forty years ago. I remember only that we fell into one another's arms, and that many of us were still in the striped clothing of concentration camps. And again we sang the Internationale, once, twice, then again and again. The Polish flag was raised next to the red one on the Brandenburg Gate, but only red flags were displayed in Lodz. Over all the loudspeakers came the voice of Voivode Dąb-Kocioł (the old titles were still being used or perhaps he was already being called city council chairman): "We have finally lived to see the day when the Polish soldier has become the gendarme of Europe."

At Party headquarters that evening, bottles of lemonade and vodka, mustard glasses, and thickly sliced sausage were arranged on tables covered with packing paper and red crepe. There were two orchestras. I danced with, or rather cuddled, some young girl. She said her husband did not return home nights. Z., a friend of mine, tore her out of my arms—I did not want to let her go. "Do you know who that is?" I didn't. "You've gone crazy!" he said. "That's Moczar's wife." Moczar was the head of security in Lodz. Security worked mainly at night, in keeping with its custom, as did the NKVD (People's Commissariat of Internal Affairs). No wonder he didn't get home until dawn.

I ran out of there without another glance and returned to the empty Writers' House on Bandurski Street. Everyone celebrated the fall of Berlin until morning of the next day. A few months later I came across the following lines in Stendhal's *Voyage en Italie:* "Upon entering a new city I always first pose three questions: What are the addresses of the twenty wealthiest merchants? What are the names of the ten most beautiful women? And what is the name of the man who can have me hanged without trial?"

In the home of Fu Tsong's parents we also talked of Stendhal. And even about his travels in Italy. But we spoke mainly about music and about Stendhal's fascination with Cimarosa—Fu Tsong's mother was also a pianist. Our hosts spoke French and English fluently. Fu Tsong's mother was translating Balzac; his father, a professor of Western literature, was a Shakespeare scholar. The conversation slowly turned to politics. They hated Chiang Kai-shek. They called his rule an occupation; they were forced to go into hiding. Now they were full of hope. They spoke of teams of doctors being sent out into the villages for the first time, of millions of textbooks to teach reading and writing, of the freedom which did not exist but which was on its way. . . . I had not yet heard the phrase "a hundred flowers," but Fu Tsong's parents had probably already heard of this new Chinese flower bed.

We returned late at night through an empty Peking. Only rarely did a blue-clad bicyclist holding a lantern zip by in a white gauze mask. I distinctly remember the long streets endless as country roads bordered by walls—usually of clay—beyond which one could occasionally make out the shadowy outline of a cluster of houses. This return from the outskirts through an empty Peking

after conversation about music and hope reminded me of yet another return through a dark countryside and empty streets. Then,
too, I was returning at night from conversation about music and
hope. Then, too, I drank strong tea, except that it was from a thick
glass. But then the roles had been reversed: it was I who had spoken
of faith, for the host had had none.

That had been seven years before the trip to China. I had also
been part of a delegation of writers and artists, this time to Moscow
for the celebration of the thirtieth anniversary of the Revolution.
We were received by Russian writers, but Pasternak was not among
them. I asked about him. They told me that he was ill. I asked for
his address, but no one knew it. I got a message to contact two
Moscow friends. I found them, and they told me to declare myself
ill with the flu on a specified day and to wait in my hotel. At midnight we arrived at Pasternak's dacha in Peredelkino. He was translating Słowacki's *Maria Stuart*. He did not speak Polish but he
understood it, and he asked about his Polish friends and how things
were going there. I spoke about the doctors in the villages, about
publishing poetry in tens of thousands of volumes, and about our
being able to write whatever we wanted. We drank very strong tea.
Pasternak simply smiled. "All of you are like birds singing in a tree.
Each sings its own song. Until one morning you all wake up in
cages—perhaps even golden cages. Each cage will be labeled. One
'Former Futurist'; another, 'Recalcitrant Symbolist'; a third, 'Idealist'; and a fourth, 'Vulgar Materialist.' And a banner proclaiming
'Enemies of the People!' will hang over them all." In farewell, Pasternak gave me a copy of his last volume of poems, *The Breadth of
the Earth*, with the dedication *S proshchanyem schastya* (with my
wishes of happiness). This was a little book, of no more than eighty
pages in a dark cardboard cover, in an edition of about five thousand. When I got back to Warsaw, I saw an enormous banner
stretched across the front of the new House of Writers, right across
from the Column of Sigismund Vasa and the ruins of the Royal
Castle: "Writers—the Engineers of Human Souls."

2

On the way to Peking we stopped for a day and a night in
Moscow. In the morning we walked to the mausoleum in Red

Square. Stalin was already in it. I had seen Stalin seven years ago in the Bolshoi Theater at a performance of *Swan Lake*. We were sitting somewhere in the topmost balcony together with delegates from other "brother people's republics." Stalin sat in the loge right next to the stage with his marshals. Their decorations glittered, but from the upper gallery both Stalin and his generals looked like little figures set stiffly behind the red plush railing, smaller even than the ballerinas on the large stage, who froze after their pirouettes, their white skirts still floating in the air.

More than the Opera, however, I wanted to see the stations of the new metro. The Polish paper *Tribune of the People* (*Trybuna ludu*) constantly wrote about the marble, mosaics, and statues of Moscow's metro. "Ya khochu posmotryet na vash metropolit" (I want to take a look at your metropolitan). Comrade Apletin, into whose special care we were entrusted, looked at me oddly. "You will get an answer tomorrow." I was amazed. To see the metro? What could the problem be? The closest metro station was two blocks from our hotel. I did not get an answer the next day, nor the day after. "You must wait," said Apletin. "There will be an answer." The answer did indeed come. On the third day we left in a special black Volga. In half an hour the houses vanished, and we found ourselves driving through fields on an empty road. I didn't understand what was going on. "They are probably taking us to some secret station outside of Moscow," I thought. "And that's why we needed the passes." We had received three pieces of paper with gigantic round seals stamped on them. Apletin said not a word throughout the entire journey. In an hour we turned onto a side road leading through alder and birch groves, fluttering their last leaves. We drove through a gate and stopped in front of something that looked like an enormous manor house, somewhat dilapidated but still bearing traces of its former glory. We were greeted by two cassocked Orthodox priests with enormous beards almost to their waists. We were led through corridors and rooms—full of old people who were dressed in what seemed to be dark women's dresses—into a large room where the Metropolitan and Patriarch of all Russia received us in a gold chain and cross.

We were served sweet wine and sweet cakes with raisins, and the conversation was just as sugarcoated. Until I abruptly asked, "What does your Holiness think of the churches that have been

changed into museums of atheism?" The Metropolitan and Patriarch of holy Russia looked at us with eyes suddenly dancing with
light, or perhaps they were just reflecting the candles in the tall,
triple-armed candelabrum, and shook his white beard: "Museums
of atheism in the churches? I have heard of no such thing. Sometime in the past, perhaps, in the twenties. . . ."

We were silent for most of the return trip. It was only as we
entered Moscow that I said, "You must take great comfort in your
Metropolitan. . . ." Comrade Apletin gave me a searching glance,
and his eyes seemed to sparkle: "In the Caucasus there is an old
saying. Just because two people sleep under one blanket does not
mean they have the same dreams." Long after our departure, Apletin was still the laughing stock of Moscow for taking the Polish
writer who wanted to see the metro to the Metropolitan.

I remember little else of my first trip to Moscow except for
those two visits—to Pasternak and the Patriarch. Except for perhaps Zofia Nałkowska's hats, both with flowers, one with a veil
and some sort of broad blue ribbon. Nałkowska was the grande
dame of all the regimes and we were taken to see one or two factories. As we walked through a double row of women at one of
them—a chocolate and praline factory named after Feliks
Dzerzhinsky—we heard the women in dirty white aprons and ba-
bushkas whisper, "The czarina is coming."

The flight from Moscow to Peking in small prop planes took
close to two days, and we spent the night in Omsk. There was a
strange hotel in the marketplace, straight out of Gogol. And perhaps from that same time. The couches, spreads, and drapes of red
plush full of water spots and burn holes looked as if they had not
been dusted in years. In the room stood an enormous golden samo-
var that was still steaming as I opened the door. We were awakened
before dawn. Our plane was waiting but would not start. Then
suddenly it started up, moved and went dead again. We were asked
to get out. Around us was the steppe, empty to the horizon, not a
tree, not a trace of a single human presence. The pilot—dressed in a
sheepskin coat—got under the body of the plane, then went back to
his cabin and came out again with a heavy hammer. He got under
the wheels and began to pound away rhythmically, like the peasants of bygone days when their carts broke down. But he did get
the plane off the ground.

It was still night as we flew over the Gobi Desert: all black craters in a ring of silver light, just like the surface of the moon in telescopic photographs. Years later I visited the Negev Desert, with its browns, violets, and all possible yellows. God could not show himself in it in human form, but he could be a voice from the burning bush echoed in the rose columns of Solomon. The Gobi, though, is like the moon, an inhuman landscape.

Almost immediately afterward the plane descended. China. The earth looked like a garden. There wasn't an empty spot on it. The land was divided into small sparkling rectangles, all of the same size. These must have been rice fields still flooded with water.

This two-month stay in China was the most monotonous of all my travels. We lived in a newly constructed hotel for foreign guests. Each of us had a suite of two or three rooms, but one could not lock the door even in the bathroom: all the doors were without keys and without locks. We were never alone. Whenever we went out, our guides went with us. They clutched at our arms, always touching us, as if they feared we would trip or lose our way. This constant touching gave us a tormenting sense of claustrophobia, even in open squares.

Our guides and guardians, men and young women, were all dressed in navy drill pants and jackets buttoned to the neck. All of them spoke a decent Russian, some of them even knew a little English. But they never spoke to us individually; there were always at least two others present at every conversation. Only one of our guides, probably the youngest—she looked like a little girl, but then all the women looked much younger than their age—lingered with us a while in the evening or remained to talk in the corridor with M., the only painter in our group. One day she showed up dressed in white socks with narrow colored stripes at the top. In a stroke of naive girlish coquetry she must have shortened her pants by half an inch. She vanished that afternoon and we never saw her again.

Every evening at supper we were asked whom we would like to meet. We named writers, artists, musicians. Our chief guardian smiled, nodded, and methodically wrote our desiderata in his thick notebook. Yet the next day we were inevitably led to a kindergarten, house of culture, or model factory. They all seemed exactly alike. The ritual meeting in a kindergarten or in the Academy of

Sciences, in a shoe factory or in the House of Writers, was always the same. On one side of the long table in an auditorium always displaying the same portraits sat our delegation of "progressive" writers and artists. On the other side sat five, seven, or sometimes even nine older men, quite beefy for Chinese, all in the same navy jackets buttoned to the neck, except better cut and sewn of cord or wool. Green tea was poured from enormous thermos bottles.

"We have invited you so that we may learn from you, because your revolution is older than ours. . . ." At this the head of our delegation, seasoned with having presided over countless Party assemblies, answered (never changing the word order or intonation): "And we, comrades, have come to learn how in five years you have succeeded in liberating your heroic and industrious nation from centuries of . . ." After which there would always be a round of applause and the most rotund of our hosts would say: "And we must both learn from comrades in our brother nation the Soviet Union, the fatherland of the world proletariat. . . . We now ask for your questions, which we will answer comrade-to-comrade—concealing none of our past mistakes."

Regina was the first to break the silence: "How much does a pound of rice cost?" Our hosts conferred with one another for a few minutes in a whisper. All that reached us was "shu-shu-shu." Finally, the skinniest one would say: "Rice has no one price. Before the Revolution, the coolies in Shanghai . . ." The thing that most amazed us was that we never received a straight answer to anything: each question and every reply, whether in the model kindergarten or the Academy of Sciences, were scrupulously recorded in thick notebooks by at least two Chinese, and those who recorded were always lean.

In the evenings we were often joined by the French delegation. It consisted only of women, very progressive women. They were enthralled with the kindergartens. "C'est extraordinaire," they would say breathless with excitement. "Ces pauvres Chinois ont des maternelles et des orphélinats. . . ." But we had had enough orphanages and tea-filled thermos bottles. We were never allowed to go out unescorted. We wanted to see the city. "Why?" exclaimed our guide in a gentle voice, as if he were speaking to children. "We have already shown you the National Museum, the Imperial Palace, the Imperial Gardens. . . ." "But we just want to

walk around!" Our guide was dumbfounded. Two days later, unexpectedly, we were allowed out of our cars. We were inundated
by diminutive Chinese from all sides, but we were finally able to
walk the streets of the city. Behind us, no farther than twenty feet
away, drove the sad cavalcade of cars from which we had been
released for an hour.

After a month in Peking, we left to continue our travels in
China. We were a few thousand miles from Tibet. In this country,
which for centuries has called itself "the center of the world," a
thousand miles is "close." At an altitude of about ten thousand
feet, our breath quickened and it seemed to us we could almost hear
our hearts beat. Jungle surrounded the small village we visited.
Here there was a school for boys and girls from a tribe that apparently knew neither animal husbandry nor metalworking. The girls
did not attend school voluntarily, but those caught in the jungle
were trained to be midwives. One of them sat with us at supper. I
will never forget her eyes. There was no fear in them. There was
nothing in them. They were a deep dark blue and as liquid as the
eyes of a doe. Yet they were completely vacant.

Then we journeyed to the south. To this day I remember the
clatter of wooden thongs in Canton, which reached us at the highest floors of our hotel, faded only at midnight, started up again
before dawn, diminished briefly in the drowsy and humid hours of
the afternoon, and then grew stronger again, rising together with a
light breeze from the sea. In Canton we rediscovered—I cannot call
this by any other name—the smell of the human body, concealed
and cryptic in the north. In Peking only the children—in bright red
quilted jackets, caps adorned with tiny bells, and pants that were
split in the back—possessed corporeality with their laughing,
scampering and falling on every scrap of unoccupied earth; they
were the only living beings in that sea of blue drill buttoned to the
neck who would break suddenly from the universal torpor of meetings that lasted for hours to chase a buzzing fly.

In Canton on the streets of the old city one smelled grease and
sharp spices, the houses crowded onto the streets, or rather the
street forced its way into the houses; there were basements, gates,
dwellings with windows wide open or without windows at all, or
dwellings of crates where one could see the huddled bodies in the
flickering light of kerosene or oil lamps. Children and scrawny cats

scampered around. Fish were fried on little iron stoves or boiled in kettles.

One morning when we were being led out for a walk at the seashore, two children ran up to us. The boy was probably around seven years old, the girl about nine. Both were in rags but with that subtle and almost crippled beauty of all the southern races of Asia. They extended their hands to us. "Look at these begging children," said our guide. "There are no children like this anywhere else in all of China."

Most vividly of all, however, I remember Shanghai. Along the entire length of the shore, crammed together, were miles of concrete, ten- or twelve-story buildings, one right next to the other like clenched fists, with gates of iron bars and grated windows like enormous bomb shelters. One could still read the half-faded names of English and American companies, Swiss and Dutch banks, trade and travel corporations from all over the world. Yet directly across the street everything was frail and see-through: scaffolding of bamboo, bundles hung something like pendulums on rhythmically bending bamboo poles, junks on the shimmering sea with sails white as sheets stretched on slender bamboo masts.

We lived in an old hotel in what was formerly the old French quarter. Shanghai, like territories within central Africa, had been divided into automonous sectors by the colonial powers after the Boxer Rebellion. Our hotel had been the setting for André Malraux's *Man's Fate*. At night it seemed to me that I heard the footsteps of the terrorist Ch'en (who believed that if everything is subject to destruction, then the only thing that remains is to leave a deep crater in the earth) stalking the corridors.

We were shown a park in the old English quarter—with dense and lush lawns like those at Oxford—where a sign in two languages still read: "Dogs and Chinese Not Allowed." In the Museum of the Revolution we looked at a wall covered with pictures of marching coolies, thousands of them, each behind his own fragile rickshaw as if it were a tank; the instruments of torture, an ax, steel cages with spikes in the middle, chains; the faces of the murdered, beheaded or hanged. It seemed to me that I had again found Ch'en from *Man's Fate* among them and Garin, the Bolshevik commissar from Malraux's *The Conquerors*.

At the formal reception organized for us by the city I met Chang. Someone had told me about her on the first day of our visit. Shanghai had been taken barely a year before our arrival. Chang's job had been to "comb" the town. She was born in the second year of the Long March. People said that she had been enrolled into the Party as a child. She was the youngest colonel or perhaps even general. At this reception, she was dressed in ordinary army fatigues with no insignias except for a single red star.

She was tall for a Chinese from the north, with practically no eyes—just two slits, two slanted cuts. When she relaxed, her eyes absorbed all the light like two lenses. Her look was intense. We began to talk. Our conversation was straightforward from the very beginning. And from the outset we felt a mutual attraction. "I'll come see you," she said. She came to my hotel room late that night. She brought a bottle of Russian cognac and two glasses. She was probably the only woman in the entire city who could get away with something like this.

She was undoubtedly curious about a man from another world. She had only been to Moscow. But she had another reason for this conversation. She knew everything about me that she needed to know: that I had joined the Party during the occupation, that I had been a member of the delegation to Moscow . . . she believed that I was higher and more entrenched in the Party than I really was.

She began to talk about Orwell. She had not read him—where and in what language could she have?—but she had heard the name and knew the titles of his works. She asked me to tell her about *Animal Farm* and *1984*. But this was merely the preface to the real exchange. It wasn't until a year or two later that I realized what Colonel Chang had really been after with her army shirt unbuttoned and a glass of cognac in her hand. She asked me about factions in our Central Committee. She was cautious and did not actually use the words "pro-Russian factions" but that was what she wanted to know.

I was also careful or simply naive, and I certainly knew far less than she did about Soviet advisers in the army and the work of internal security. Yet one has to pay even for half-truths in such encounters. She could not tell me that she didn't know the price of rice or how much of it could be bought by a porter after working a twelve-hour shift. I asked about the rural communes. "At first we overreacted. Big landowners were tried in the villages and were usually stoned on the spot. We put an end to this. Now we put the rich peasants to work as swineherds." I asked Chang about prostitution. In Shanghai apparently there had been ten or possibly twenty thousand whorehouses before the liberation. Until just recently, double rows of teenage girls crammed the narrow streets all the way down to the port. Our minister of culture had returned from a trip to Shanghai two months before we left on our trip to China. He had asked his hosts to take him to a bordello. "All are being disinfected," he was told.

"We put two hundred girls on a small barge," said Chang. "When the barge drifted out to sea, sailors unplugged two holes underneath. Then they set off in a small skiff. The barge sunk before they reached the port. That same evening all the bordellos shut down. The next morning, hours before sunrise, girls stood in long lines outside of offices that recruited workers for harvesting tea and carrying baskets of silt to the rice fields. . . ." After this there was nothing but a long silence. Perhaps Colonel Chang felt she had said too much. She took the remaining cognac and left.

Shanghai was the last leg of our trip. A week later we left Peking, stopping in Ulan Bator. Camels grazed on the air strip in small herds right next to the hangars. To one side of the airport stretched the steppe, on the other loomed a city—a city of tents extending to the horizon. "We are finally in Europe!" There was not only bitter humor in this exclamation, but a deep sigh of relief.

3

A year or so after our return from China, Warsaw was visited by Chou En-lai. He spoke of letting "a hundred flowers" blossom, and we, too, wrote about this campaign with a new fascination. Not a year had passed when we discovered that of the hundred flowers, only one remained. It was then that I ran across Smendzianka. "I've got bad news," she said. "Fu Tsong has not heard from his parents in weeks. He fears they have been arrested or . . ." her voice dropped, "that they've been taken to work in the fields." The season of "a hundred flowers" was over. The Cultural Revolution was beginning. I ran into Smendzianka a few weeks later. "The Chinese Embassy is demanding that Fu Tsong return immediately."

All of Warsaw adored Fu Tsong: his colleagues and professors, men and women, Poles and foreigners. I met him at a party. He had fingers like ivory. Even a year of physical work would mean the end of his career as a pianist. But what could one do? Fu Tsong could not ask for asylum in Poland. The Ministry intervened, and even the Foreign Department of the Central Committee tried to do something. His scholarship was good for one more year. The Chinese nodded, admitted that all the arguments were absolutely reasonable, and then insisted that Fu Tsong return immediately. Pressure was increasing. From then on, two "guardians" never left Fu Tsong for a minute.

Finally, arrangements were made with the embassy that Tsong's concert in Poznan would be his last. The plane to Poznan left at ten in the morning. Fifteen minutes later a plane left the same airport for London. Fu Tsong bade his guardians farewell and got on the wrong plane. This was probably the first and last instance of cooperation between English, Soviet, and Polish intelligence, who normally sniffed at one another like ferocious dogs and watched each other like hawks. They had come to an agreement to usher to safety in the West a young Chinese pianist with fingers like batons of ivory.

The news from China grew frightening. The Cultural Revolution was in full swing. Polish students returning from China brought us firsthand information. They talked about the "water drop" method. Professors, writers, or artists who were accused of "aloofness from the working masses" were visited by one of the Red Guards at seven in the morning. At the universities these were usually the professor's own students. Dressed in a navy drill jacket buttoned to the neck, the young man would repeat courteously but without respite the errors the scholar or writer had committed and insist that he publicly pronounce his self-criticism. In an hour another young man in the same navy jacket buttoned to the neck showed up and gently repeated the lecture about the errors the professor had committed. . . . An hour later came a third, then a fourth, fifth, on into the night, day after day, week after week. This kind of persuasion led many to jump out the window in the third week of treatment or to drown themselves in wells in keeping with the old Chinese custom. "Asia," said the young scholar who told me this story. "This couldn't happen here." I recalled the feeling of relief when we had landed in Ulan Bator.

In 1949 or 1950 the Marxist offensive aimed at the universities in Poland got underway, at first in the departments of philosophy and Polish literature. A two-day conference on the subject "Marxist Literary Criticism" was organized in Warsaw and the older professors and younger faculty were invited to participate in open and frank discussion. M., who cut her teeth at *The Forge (Kuźnica)* in Lodz,* had organized and prepared the conference. She had slightly prominent cheekbones; large, wet lips that were always pressed tightly together; and hair always combed smooth. She wore a blouse buttoned high at the neck or one of those old-fashioned white collars. She looked like a nineteenth-century feminist. We agreed that on the first day I would speak immediately after Roman Ingarden.

The auditorium was full. Ingarden spoke very slowly, calmly and clearly. He repeated his literary theory of the intentional and imaginative levels in a literary work. On the board he drew a chart with all the divisions and their signs. He covered the whole blackboard with his writing, down to the very corner at the bottom. When he finished, there was a timid applause, mainly in the back of the room. I waited a moment and then stepped onto the dais next to the podium. I walked unhurriedly to the board and wiped it clean slowly and systematically, from top to bottom, until everything that Ingarden had written was erased. Then I walked back to the podium: "Now we can begin the scientific theory of literature from the very beginning." I received long and sustained applause. After my lecture M. came up to me and kissed me with her wet lips: "You were magnificent! There was great romantic irony in what you did!" (M. had just begun studying romanticism.) The secretary of the Cultural Sector of the Party also came up to me: "You have a future before you, comrade professor."

4

Some thirty years later the first small group of Chinese students arrived at the State University of New York in Stony Brook, where I was teaching. They came mainly to study computers and physics, but there was one doctoral student in comparative literature. She

---

The Forge was a post–World War II weekly named after an eighteenth-century Polish political club. The founders of *The Forge* wanted to link themselves to the traditions of the Polish Jacobins.

was extremely bright. In a few weeks she was conducting classes in linguistics and tutorials for freshmen. In Peking she had also been an assistant professor at the Institute of Foreign Languages.

Cheung rarely spoke. Perhaps she was distrustful or simply shy. She knew that I was from Poland and maybe that is why I was the first person to whom she told her story. Her father was a historian who wrote about the French Revolution and had gone into hiding during the time of the Kuomintang. Her mother was a sociologist and must have been a good scholar since she was invited to Harvard twice. But she was not allowed to go. During the Cultural Revolution they were all sent to work on farms: she, her parents, and her brother. But each to a commune in a different part of the country. Cheung was nine years old, her brother seven. For months they had no news of each other, and for a long time they were not allowed to write letters. They did not even know each other's addresses. They all returned after three years.

"What was it like?" I asked. "It wasn't too bad," she replied. "My work was light. Six hours. In the afternoon I attended school for three more. The only problem was catching up when I got back in order to get into the university."

I invited her to lunch one day in the cafeteria on campus. Our lunch was nothing out of the ordinary: roast chicken with rice. Cheung ate very slowly and did not leave a single grain of rice on her plate. After eating she carefully picked every crumb from the tablecloth. I pretended not to see this, but Cheung turned her head away. At about the same time Fu Tsong left England to visit his mother. His father was no longer alive. I never found out whether he had died while working in the commune or afterward. One of our mutual friends wrote from London that Fu Tsong was taking his mother a generous supply of English Breakfast tea.

Santa Monica, December 1987

TRANSLATED BY LILLIAN VALLEE

Stanisław Lem

Reflections on My Life

As I write this autobiographical essay, I am aware of two opposed principles that guide my pen. One of those two extremes is chance; the other is the order that gives shape to life. Can all the factors that were responsible for my coming into the world and that enabled me, although threatened by death many times, to survive unscathed in order finally to become a writer—moreover, one who ceaselessly strives to reconcile contradictory elements of realism and fantasy—be regarded only as the result of long chains of chance? Or was there some specific predetermination involved, not in the form of some supernatural *moira,* not quite crystallized into fate when I was in my cradle but in a budding form laid down in me—that is to say, in my genetic inheritance was there a kind of predestiny befitting an agnostic and empiricist?

That chance played a role in my life is undeniable. In the First World War, when the fortress of Przemyśl fell, in 1915, my father, Samuel Lem, a physician in the Austro-Hungarian Army, was taken prisoner by the Russians, and was able to return to Lemberg (now Lvov), his native city, only after nearly five years, in the wake of the chaos of the Russian Revolution. I know from the stories he told us that on at least one occasion he was to be shot by the Reds on the spot for being an officer (and therefore a class enemy). He owed his life to the fact that when he was being led to his execution in a small Ukrainian city he was noticed and recognized from the sidewalk by a Jewish barber from Lemberg who used to shave the military commander in that city and for this reason had free access to him. The barber interceded for my father (who was then not yet my father), and he was allowed to go free and was able to return to Lemberg and to his fiancée. (This story, made more complex for aesthetic reasons, is to be found in one of the fictitious reviews—of "De Impossibilitate Vitae," by Cezar Kouska—in my book *A Perfect Vacuum.*) In this instance, chance was fate incarnate, for if the barber had happened to pass through that street a minute later my father would have been irrevocably doomed. I heard the tale from him when I was a little boy, at a time when I was unable to think in abstract terms (I may have been ten) and was thus unable to consider the respective merits of the categories of chance and fate.

My father went on to become a respected and rather wealthy physician (a laryngologist) in Lvov. I was born there in 1921. In the rather poor country that Poland was before the Second World War, I lacked nothing. I had a French governess and no end of toys, and for me the world I grew into was something final and stable. But, if that was the case, why did I as a child delight in solitude, and make up the rather curious game that I have described in another book—the novel *The High Castle,* a book about my early childhood. My game was to transport myself into fictitious worlds, but I did not invent or imagine them in a direct way. Rather, I fabricated masses of important documents when I was in high school in Lvov: certificates; passports; diplomas that conferred upon me riches, high social standing, and secret power, or "full power of authority," without any limit whatsoever; and permits and coded proofs and cryptograms testifying to the highest rank—all in some other place, in a country not to be found on any map. Did I feel insecure in some way? Threatened? Did this game perhaps spring from some unconscious feeling of danger? I know nothing of any such cause.

I was a good student. Some years after the war, I learned from an older man who had held some position or other in the prewar Polish educational system that when the IQs of all high-school students were tested—it must have been around 1936 or 1937—mine was over 180, and I was said to have been, in the words of that man, the most intelligent child in southern Poland. (I myself suspected nothing of this sort at the time of the test, for the results were not made known to us.) But this high IQ certainly was of no help in surviving the occupation of the *Generalgouvernement* (to which administrative unit Poland had been reduced by the Germans). During that period, I learned in a very personal, practical way that I was no "Aryan." I knew that my ancestors were Jews, but I knew nothing of the Mosaic faith and, regrettably, nothing at all of Jewish culture. So it was, strictly speaking, only the Nazi legislation that brought home to me the realization that I had Jewish blood in my veins. We succeeded in evading imprisonment in the ghetto, however. With false papers, my parents and I survived that ordeal.

But, to return to my childhood in prewar Poland, my first reading matter was of a rather curious nature. It was my father's anatomy books and medical texts, in which I browsed when I was still hardly able to read, and I understood them all the less since my father's professional books were in German or in French. Only the fiction in his library was in Polish. Pictures of skeletons, of neatly dissected human skulls, of human brains precisely sketched in many colors, of intestines in preserved condition and embellished with magic-sounding Latin names, provided my earliest contacts with the world of books. Hunting through my father's library was, of course, strictly forbidden to me, and it attracted me precisely because it was forbidden and mysterious. I must not forget to mention the actual human bone that was kept behind the glass doors of my father's bookcase. It was a skull bone—*os temporale*—that had been removed during a trepanation; perhaps it was a relic from the time when my father was studying medicine. I held this bone, without any particular feelings, several times in my hands. (I had to steal my father's key to be able to do this.) I knew what it was, but I wasn't frightened by it. I only wondered about it in a certain way. Its surroundings—the rows of big tomes of medical textbooks— appeared quite natural to me, for a child, lacking any real yardstick, is unable to differentiate between the banal or commonplace and the unusual. That bone—or, rather, its fictional counterpart—is to be found in another novel of mine, *Memoirs Found in a Bathtub*. In this book, the bone became a whole skull, cleanly dissected from a corpse, that was kept by a doctor in a ward—one of the many stations in the hero's odyssey through a labyrinthine building. A complete skull like this was owned by my uncle, my mother's brother, who was also a physician. He was murdered two days after the Wehrmacht marched into Lvov. At that time, several non-Jewish Poles were also killed—mostly university professors—and

Tadeusz Boy-Żeleński, one of the best-known Polish writers. They were taken from their apartments during the night and shot.

Now, then, what objective, extrinsic connection—i.e., not one imagined by me and consisting solely of associations—could there be between a little boy's fascination with the parts of a human skeleton and the era of the Holocaust? Was this apparently significant and fitting omen a matter of chains of chance, purely of coincidence? In my opinion, it was. I do not believe in manifest destiny or predetermination. In lieu of a preestablished harmony, I can well imagine (upon the basis of the experiences of my life) a preestablished disharmony, ending in chaos and madness. In any case, my childhood was certainly peaceful and Arcadian—especially when compared with what happened in the following years.

I grew into a bookworm and read everything that fell into my hands: the great national poems, novels, popular-science books. (I still remember that a book of the kind that my father gave me as a gift sold for seventy zlotys—the price was written inside—and that was a fortune in those days; for seventy zlotys you could buy a whole suit. My father spoiled me.) I also—I can still remember it— looked with keen interest at the male and female genitalia reproduced in my father's anatomy books. The female pubis struck me especially—as something spiderlike, not quite nauseating but certainly something that could hardly have a connection with erotic feelings. I believe that I was later, during my adolescence, sexually quite normal. But since my subsequent studies in medicine included gynecology, and since I was, for a month, an obstetrician in a hospital, I associate the pornography of today not with sexual longing and with copulative lust but with the anatomical pictures in the tomes of my father, and with my own gynecological examinations. The thought that a male may be highly excited by the mere sight of female genitalia strikes me as very peculiar. I happen to know perfectly well that this is a case of libido—of the instincts built into our senses and programmed by evolution—but the desire for sex without love strikes me as something comparable to an irresistible urge to eat salt and pepper by the spoonful because dishes without salt and pepper lack full flavor. I feel no repulsion but no attraction, either, as long as there is no specific erotic bond of the kind that is called "love."

As an eight-year-old boy, I fell in love with a girl. I never uttered as much as a word to the girl, but I observed her often in a public garden near our house. The girl had no inkling of my feelings, and most probably never even noticed me. It was a burning, long-lasting love affair dissected, as it were, from all actual circumstances—even from the sphere of any kind of wishful thinking. I was not interested in becoming her friend. My emotions were restricted to worshiping her from afar: aside from that, there was absolutely nothing. May the psychoanalysts make what they will of these feelings of a small boy. I do not comment further on them, because I am of the opinion that such an episode can be interpreted in any way one chooses.

At the beginning, I mentioned the opposites of chance and order, of coincidence and predestination. Only as I wrote the book *The High Castle* did the thought cross my mind that my fate—my profession as a writer—was already budding in me when I looked at skeletons, galaxies in astrophysical tomes, pictures of reconstructions of the monstrous extinct saurians of the Mesozoic, and many-colored human brains in anatomical handbooks. Perhaps these external circumstances—these impulses and sensuous impressions—helped to shape my sensibility. But that is only speculation.

I not only imagined fantastic kingdoms and domains but also made inventions and mentally created prehistoric animals unheard of in paleontology. For instance, I dreamed up an aircraft shaped like a giant concave mirror, with a boiler situated in the focus. The circumference of the mirror was studded with turbines and rotors to provide lift, as in a helicopter, and the energy for all that was to be derived from solar radiation. This unwieldy monstrosity was supposed to fly very high, far above the clouds, and, of course, only during daytime. And I invented what had already existed for a long time without my knowing it: the differential gear. I also drew many funny things in my thick copybooks, including a bicycle on which one rode moving up and down, as on a horse. Recently, I saw something like this imaginary bicycle somewhere—it may have been in the English periodical *New Scientist*, but I am not quite sure.

I think is it significant that I never bothered to show my designs to other people; indeed, I kept them all secret, both from my parents and from my fellow pupils, but I have no idea why I acted in this way. Perhaps it was because of a childish affection for the mysterious. The same was the case with my "passports"—certificates and permits that, for instance, allowed one to enter subterranean treasure troves. I suppose also that I was afraid to be laughed at, for, although I knew that these things were only a game, I played it with great seriousness. I divulged something of this childhood world in the book that I have already mentioned, *The High Castle*, but it contains only a small part of my memories. Why only a small part? I can answer such a question at least partly. First, in *The High Castle* I wanted to transport myself back into the child that I had been, and to comment on childhood as little as possible from the position of the adult. Second, during its gestation period the book generated a specific normative aesthetic similar to a self-organizing process, and there were certain memories that would appear as dissonances in this canon. It was not the case that I intended to hide certain things because of, say, a feeling of guilt or of shame but, rather, that there were memories that would not fit into the pattern that I presented as my childhood. I wanted—something impossible to attain—to extract the essence of my childhood, in its pure form, from my whole life: to peel away, as it were, the overlying strata of war, of mass murder and extermination, of the nights in the shelters during air raids, of an existence under a false identity, of hide-and-seek, of all the dangers, as if they had never existed. For, indeed, nothing of this had existed when I was a child, or even a sixteen-year-old high school boy. I gave an indication of these exclusions in the novel itself. I do not remember exactly where, but I signaled that I had to or wanted to keep certain matters out by dropping a parenthetical remark that every human being is able to write several strikingly different autobiographies, according to the viewpoint chosen and the principle of selection.

The meaning of the categories of order and chance for human life was impressed upon me during the war years in a purely practical, instinctual manner; I resembled more a hunted animal than a thinking human being. I was able to learn from hard experience that the difference between life and death depended upon minuscule, seemingly unimportant things and the smallest of decisions: whether one chose this or that street for going to work; whether one visited a friend at one o'clock or twenty minutes later; whether one found a door open or closed. I cannot claim that in following my instinct for self-preservation I always employed a minimax strategy of extreme cautiousness. To the contrary, I exposed myself to danger several times—occasionally when I thought it necessary but in some cases through mere thoughtlessness, or even stupidity. So that today, when I think of such idiotically reckless patterns of behavior, I still feel wonder, mingled with bewilderment, about why I acted as I did. To steal ammunition from the so-called *Beutepark der Luftwaffe* (the depot where the German Air Force stored its loot) in Lvov and to turn it over to somebody totally unknown to me—somebody of whom I knew only that he was a member of the Resistance—I considered to be my duty. (I was in a position to do so since, as an employee of a German company, I had access to this depot.) But when I was instructed to transport something—a gun, in this case—from one place to another just before curfew, and was told, strictly, not to use the tram (I was supposed to walk), it happened that I nevertheless disobeyed the order and climbed onto the footboard of a tram, and that a "Black One"—a Ukrainian policeman who was a member of the auxiliary police of the German occupational forces—jumped onto the footboard behind me and put his arm around me to reach for the door handle. It could have meant an ill end for me if the policeman had felt the gun. My act was insubordination, thoughtlessness, and folly all in one, but I did it anyway. Was it a challenge to fate, or only foolhardiness? Up to this day, I am not sure. (I am better able to understand why I visited the ghetto several times—risky though this was—when it was open to visitors. I had friends there. As far as I know, all, or nearly all, of them were transported to the gas chambers of Belzec in the fall of 1942.)

At this point, the question arises whether what I have reported so far is relevant at all, in the sense of having any direct, causal relationship to my profession as a writer, or to the kind of writing I have done—excluding, of course, autobiographical works like *The High Castle*. I believe that such a causal relationship exists—that it isn't mere chance that I attribute in my work such a prominent role to chance as the shaper of human destiny. I have lived in radically different social systems. Not only have I experienced the huge differences in poor but independent, capitalist (if one must call it that) prewar Poland, the Pax Sovietica in the years 1939–41, the German occupation, the return of the Red Army, and the postwar years in a quite different Poland, but at the same time I have also come to understand the fragility that all systems have in common, and I have learned how human beings behave under extreme conditions—how their behavior when they are under enormous pressure is almost impossible to predict.

I remember well my feelings when I read *Mr. Sammler's Planet,* by Saul Bellow. Now, I thought that book very good—so good that I have read it several times. Indeed. But most of the things that Mr. Bellow attributed to his hero, Mr. Sammler, in recounting his experiences in a Poland occupied by the Germans, didn't sound quite right to me. The skilled novelist must have done careful research before starting on the novel, and he made only one small mistake—giving a Polish maid a name that isn't Polish. This error could have been corrected by a stroke of the pen. What didn't seem right was the "aura"—the indescribable "something" that can be expressed in language perhaps only if one has experienced in person the specific situation that is to be described. The problem in the novel is not the unlikeliness of specific events. The most unlikely and incredible things did happen then. It is, rather, the total impression that evokes in me the feeling that Bellow learned of such events from hearsay, and was in the situation of a researcher who receives the individual parts of a specimen packaged in separate crates and then tries to put them together. It is as if oxygen, nitrogen, and water vapor and the fragrance of flowers were to be mixed in such a way as to evoke and bring to life the specific mood of a certain part of a forest at a certain morning hour. I do not know whether something like this would be totally impossible, but it would surely be difficult as hell. There is something wrong in *Mr. Sammler's Planet;* some tiny inaccuracy got mixed into the compound. Those days have pulverized and exploded all narrative conventions that had previously been used in literature. The unfathomable futility of human life under the sway of mass murder cannot be conveyed by literary techniques in which individuals or small groups of persons form the core of the narrative. It is, perhaps, as if somebody tried by providing the most exact description of the molecules of which the body of Marilyn Monroe was composed to convey a full impression of her. That *would* be impossible. I do not know, of course, whether this sort of narrative inadequacy was the reason that I started writing science fiction, but I suppose—and this is a somewhat daring statement—that I began writing science fiction because it deals with human beings as a species (or, rather, with all possible species of intelligent beings, one of which happens to be the human species). At least, it *should* deal with the whole species, and not just with specific individuals, be they saints or monsters.

It is likely that, after my beginner's attempts—that is to say, after my first science-fiction novels—I revolted for the same reason of narrative limitations against the paradigms of the genre as they developed and became fossilized in the United States. As long as I didn't know current science fiction—and I didn't know it for a long time, because up to 1956 or 1957 it was almost impossible to get foreign books in Poland—I believed that it had to be a further development of the starting position taken by H. G. Wells in *The War of the Worlds*. It was he who climbed into a general's position, from which it was possible to survey the whole human species in an extreme situation. He anticipated a future filled with disasters, and I must admit that he was correct. During the war, when I read his novel several times, I was able to confirm his understanding of human psychology.

Today, I am of the opinion that my earliest science-fiction novels are devoid of any value (regardless of the fact that they had large editions everywhere and made me world-famous). I wrote these novels—for instance, *The Astronauts,* which was published in 1951, and was about an expedition to the planet Venus from a simplistically utopian Earth—for reasons that I can still understand today, although in their plots and in the kind of world they depicted they were contrary to all my experience of life at the time. In these books, the evil world of reality was supposed to have suffered a sea change into a good one. In the postwar years, there seemed to be only this choice—between hope and despair, between a historically untenable optimism and a well-justified skepticism that was easily apt to turn into nihilism. Of course, I wanted to embrace optimism and hope!

However, my very first novel was a realistic one, which I wrote perhaps in order to rid myself of the weight of my war memories—to expel them like pus. But perhaps I wrote this book also in order not to forget; the one motive could well go together with the other. The novel is called *The Hospital of Transfiguration,* and it is about the fight of the staff of a hospital for the insane to save the inmates from being killed by the German occupiers. One German reviewer ventured the opinion that it was a kind of sequel to Thomas Mann's *The Magic Mountain*. What was in Mann only a portent—only the distant hint of a then nearly invisible lightning, since the horrors to come were still hidden behind the horizon of the times—proves to be in my novel the final circle of Hell, the logical outcome of the predicted "decline of the West" in the mass exterminations. The village, the hospital for the mentally ill, the professional staff: none of the places and characters ever existed; they are all my invention. But mentally ill persons—and many others—were indeed murdered by the thousands in occupied Poland. I wrote *The Hospital of Transfiguration* in 1948, my last year as a student. It could not appear until 1955, however, since it didn't conform to the then already reigning standards of socialist realism. In the meantime, I was, as I can say without exaggeration, very busy.

In 1946, we—my father, my mother, and I—moved from Lvov to Krakow, having lost all our possessions in the course of the war. My father, who was seventy-one years old, was forced, because of these reverses, to work in a hospital; there was no possibility that he could set up his own practice. We all lived in a single room in Krakow, and my father didn't have the means to buy his own equipment. Purely by chance, I learned how I could financially help our family: I wrote several long stories for a weekly dime-novel series that featured a complete story in each issue. Considered as thrillers, they weren't so bad. Aside from that, I wrote poems; they appeared in *Tygodnik powszechny*, the Krakovian Catholic weekly. And two novellas—not science fiction proper but on the margin of fantasy—plus some odds and ends in various publications. But I did not take my writing very seriously.

In 1947, at the age of twenty-six, I became a junior research assistant for an organization called Konwersatorium Naukoznawcze (the Circle for the Science of Science), founded by Dr. Mieczysław Chojnowski. To him I presented my most dearly held works: a theory of brain functions invented by me, and a philosophical treatise. He called both nonsense but took me under his tutelage. Thus, I was forced to read logic textbooks, scientific methodology, psychology, psychometrics (the theory of psychological testing), the history of natural science, and many other things. Although it was apparent that I couldn't read English, I had to do the best I could with English-language books. These books proved so interesting that I had to crack them, dictionary in hand, as Champollion cracked his hieroglyphs. Since I had learned French at home and Latin and German in school, and had picked up some Russian, I somehow managed to get along. But to this day I can understand only written English. I can neither speak the language nor understand it when it is spoken. For the monthly *Zycie nauki* (The life of science), I compiled surveys of scientific periodicals from the standpoint of the science of science. By doing so, I became involved in the wretched Lysenko affair, for in my survey I synopsized the controversy between him and the Soviet geneticists in what an official report from the ministry in charge of Polish universities called "a tendentious manner." I held Lysenko's doctrine of the inheritance of acquired characteristics to be ridiculous, and I was proved right after several years, but my taking this position had rather painful consequences for our monthly. Something similar happened a little later, when I perceived in Norbert Wiener's and Claude E. Shannon's cybernetics a new era not just for technological progress but also for the whole of civilization. At that time, cybernetics was considered in our country to be a fallacious pseudoscience.

In those years, I was particularly well informed about the latest developments in the various sciences, for the Krakovian circle functioned as a kind of clearinghouse for scientific literature from the United States (and, to some extent, from Canada) coming in to all the Polish universities. From the book parcels received I could borrow all the works that stirred my interest, including Wiener's *The Human Use of Human Beings*. At night, I read everything voraciously, so that I could pass on the books as soon as possible to the people who were supposed to get them. On the basis of this reading, I wrote those of my novels that I can still acknowledge without shame—*Eden* (1959), *Solaris* (1961), *The Invincible* (1964), etc. They incorporate cognitive problems in fictions that do not oversimplify the world, as did my earliest, naive science-fiction novels.

My father died in 1954, and toward the end of the fifties I was able to acquire for us—myself and my wife—a small house on the southern outskirts of Krakow, which we still have. (Close to this house, a larger house, in a larger garden, is in the process of being built for us as I write these words.) In the late sixties, I first made contact with my future literary agent and kindred spirit, Franz Rottensteiner, from Vienna. Both of us were then writing many critical, often polemical essays for Anglo-American science-fiction "fanzines" (i.e., the amateur magazines published by the aficionados of science fiction), mostly for Bruce Gillespie's Australian *Science Fiction Commentary;* that resulted in a certain popularity for both of us, even if it was of a negative sort, in the science-fiction ghetto. Today, I am of the opinion that we wasted our efforts. In the beginning, it was totally incomprehensible to me why so many authors were erecting, *viribus unitis*, a common prison for science fiction. I believed that, according to the law of large numbers alone, there had to be among so many a considerable group at the top, as far as both writing abilities and scientific qualifications were concerned. (For me, the scientific ignorance of most American science-fiction writers was as inexplicable as the abominable literary quality of their output.) I was in error, but it took me a very long time to recognize it.

As a reader of science fiction, I expected something like what is called, in the evolutionary processes of nature, "speciation"—a new animal species generating a diverging, fanlike radiation of other new species. In my ignorance, I thought that the time of Verne, Wells, and Stapledon was the beginning, but not the beginning of the decline, of the sovereign individuality of the author. Each of these men created something not only radically new for their time but also quite different from what the others created. They all had enormous room for maneuvering in the field of speculation, because the field had only recently been opened up and was still empty of both writers and books. Each of them entered the no-man's-land from a different direction and made some particular province of this *terra incognita* his own. Their successors, on the other hand, had to compromise more and more with the crowd. They were forced to become like ants in an ant hill, or industrious bees, each of which is indeed building a different cell in the honeycomb but whose cells are all similar. Such is the law of mass production. Thus, the distance between individual works of science fiction has not grown greater, as I erroneously expected, but has shrunk. The very thought that a Wells or a Stapledon could have written, alternately, visionary fantasies and typical mysteries strikes me as absurd. For the next generation of writers, however, this was something quite normal. Wells and Stapledon are comparable to the people who invented chess and draughts. They discovered new rules for games, and their successors have applied these rules with only smaller or larger variations. The sources of innovation have gradually become depleted; the thematic clusters have become fossilized. Hybrids have arisen (science fantasy), and the patterns and schemata of the literary form have been applied in a mechanical and ready-made way.

To create something radically new, it was necessary to advance into another field of possibilities. I believe that in the first period of my career I wrote purely secondary things. In the second period (*Solaris, The Invincible*), I reached the borders of a field that was already nearly completely mapped. In the third period—when I wrote, for example, reviews of nonexistent books and forewords to works that, as I put it, ironically, in an interview, would be published "sometime in the future but that do not exist yet"—I left the fields already exploited and broke new ground. This idea is best explained by a specific example. A few years ago, I wrote a small book entitled *Provocation*. It is a review of a fictitious two-volume tome ascribed to a nonexistent German historian and anthropologist, whom I call Aspernicus. The first volume is titled *Die Endlösung als Erlösung* (The final solution considered as redemption), the second *Fremdkörper Tod* (Foreign body death). The whole thing is a unique historicophilosophical hypothesis about the as yet unrecognized roots of the Holocaust, and the role that death, especially mass death, has played in the cultures of all times up to the present day. The literary quality of my fictitious criticism (which is rather long, or it wouldn't have filled even a small book) is beside the point here. What counts is the fact that there were professional historians who took my fancy for the review of a real book, as is attested to by attempts on the part of some of them to get hold of the book. To my mind, *Provocation*, too, is a kind of science fiction; I am trying not to limit the meaning of the name of this category of writing but, rather, to expand it.

Nothing I've ever written was planned in an abstract form right from the start, to be embodied later in literary form. Nor can I claim that it was my intention to find other fields for development—that I set out with the intention of seeking them out for my imagination. But I can say something about the conception of an idea, the gravid state, the pains of giving birth, though I do not know the genetic makeup of the embryo or know how it is transformed into a phenotype—the finished work. Here, in the realm of the "embryogenesis" of my writing, considerable differences have developed in the course of some thirty-six years.

My earliest novels (which I acknowledge as my own only with some discomfort) I planned and constructed according to a complete design. I wrote the novels in the *Solaris* group in a similar manner, which I myself cannot explain. The terminology of birth that I have used above may sound inappropriate, but it is somewhat apt. I am still able to point to passages in *Solaris* and *Return from the Stars* where I found myself, during the writing process, in the position of a reader. When Kelvin, the narrator of *Solaris*, arrives at the station hovering over the planet Solaris and finds it empty of human beings, and when he starts his search for the crew and encounters the scientist Snow, who goes into a state of panic when he sees Kelvin, I had no idea why nobody had expected his arrival or why Snow behaved in this peculiar manner; indeed, I had no idea at all that some "living ocean" would cover the whole plant. All this was divulged to me in the same manner that it becomes clear to the reader in the course of reading the book—with the sole difference that it was I who created the novel. And in *Return from the Stars* I faced a wall when the returning astronaut frightens one of the first women he meets, and then the word "betrization" is used: that's the treatment that human beings have undergone in the future world to rid them of their aggressive impulses. I didn't know at first exactly what the word should mean, but I knew that there must be some unbridgeable difference between the civilization that the man left when he flew to the stars and the one that he found upon his return. The metaphor that takes its terms from the lexicon of embryology is thus not nonsense, for a woman who is with child knows that she carries an embryo, but she has no idea how the embryo is transformed from an ovum into a child. Considering myself to be a rationalist, I dislike such confessions, and I should prefer to be able to say that I knew everything I was doing—or, at least, a good deal of it—beforehand, and that I planned and designed it, but *amicus Plato, sed magis amica veritas*.

Nevertheless, something can be said about my creative method. First, there is no positive correlation between the spontaneity of my writing and the quality of the resulting work. I gave birth to *Solaris* and *Return from the Stars* in a similar manner, but I think that *Solaris* is a good book and *Return from the Stars* a poor one, because in the latter the underlying problems of social evil and its elimination are treated in a manner that is too primitive, too unlikely, and perhaps even false. (Even if the evil done to others with full intent could be suppressed pharmacologically—the book's main premise—no chemical or other influence upon the brain could cause the unintended evil effects of all social dependencies, conflicts, and contradictions to disappear from the world in the same manner that an insecticide can eliminate vermin.) Second, creative spontaneity is not a guarantee that there will be sure development of a whole narrative—i.e., a plot that can be finished without applying force. I have had to put more stories aside unfinished or drop them into the wastebasket than I have been able to submit to publishers. Third, this process of writing, which is characterized by the signs of a creation by trial and error, has always been arrested by blocks and blind alleys that forced me to retreat; sometimes there has even been a "burning out" of the raw materials— the manifold resources necessary for further growth—stored somewhere in my skull. I was not able to finish *Solaris* for a full year, and could do it then only because I learned suddenly—from myself— how the last chapter had to be. (And then I could only wonder why I hadn't recognized it from the beginning.) And, fourth, even what I wrote spontaneously never received its final shape in the first thrust of work. I have never written a larger work (it is different with short stories) in a "linear" way right to the end in one sweep; rather, in the pauses between writing sessions—it is for purely physiological reasons impossible to sit at the typewriter all the time—I had new ideas that enriched what was already finished or was to be written soon; changed it; and complicated it with some new turn or complexity of plot.

Practical experience—the result of wrestling with my writing over the years—has taught me never to force what I am working on if it has not ripened at least partly but, rather, to let it rest for some time (which may amount to periods of months, or even years) and let the thing mill around in my head. (A gravid woman knows that an early birth bodes nothing good.) This situation has put me on the horns of a dilemma, however, for, like nearly all writers, I often try to invent excuses for not writing. As is well known, laziness is one of the main barriers hindering everyone in his work. If I waited until I carried something in its definite form around in my head, I would never create anything.

My method of creating (which I should like to call, rather, my behavior as a writer) has changed during the years, if only very slowly. I have learned to avoid the pure spontaneity of beginnings which motivated me to write something even when I had not the slightest idea what would come of the thing—its plot, its problems, its characters, etc.—because the instances in which I was unable to finish what I had begun were on the increase. Perhaps the imaginative space that was given me became gradually emptied, like a territory rich in oil, from which the black gold at first fountains in the air everywhere in geysers, no matter where one begins to drill; after some time, one has to use ever more complicated tricks and apply pressure to drive the remaining reserves up to the surface. The center of gravity of my work, then, gradually shifted in the direction of the gaining of a basic idea, a conception, an imaginative notion. I ceased to sit down at my typewriter whenever I had a quite small but ready beginning; instead, I started to produce an increasing number of notes, fictitious encyclopedias, and small additional ideas, and this has finally led to the things I am doing now. I try to get to know the "world" to be created by me by writing the literature specific to it, but not whole shelves of reference works of the sociology and the cosmology of some thirtieth century, not the fictitious minutes of scientific expeditions or other types of literature that express a zeitgeist, the spirit of a time and a world, alien to us. After all, this would be an endeavor impossible to accomplish during the short life span of a human being. Nor do I now do what began in the first place rather as a joke—write criticism in the form of the reviews of nonexistent books or forewords to them (*A Perfect Vacuum, Imaginary Magnitude*). I do not publish these things any longer but use them to create my own knowledge of another world, a knowledge entirely subservient to my literary program—in other words, to sketch a rough outline that will be filled in later. I surround myself, so to speak, with the literature of a future, another world, a civilization with a library that is its product, its picture, its mirror image. I write only brief synopses or, again, critical reviews of sociological treatises, scientific papers, and technical reference works, and I describe technologies that have taken the place of literature after its final death, just as television has made obsolete the *cinématographe* of Lumière, and three-dimensional television will make obsolete the TV sets of today. There are also historicophilosophical papers, "encyclopedias of alien civilizations" and their military strategies—all of them, of course, in a kind of shorthand, or I would need the longevity of a Methuselah to create them. It may well be that I will publish something out of this "library for a given purpose" independently of the work for which it served as a frame and a source of information.*

And where do I get all these facts, which I adorn with such enchanting titles as "The Trend of Dehumanization in Weapon Systems of the 21st Century" or "Comparative Culturology of Humanoid Civilizations"? In a certain sense, from my head; in another, not. I have invented several picturesque similes to illustrate for myself and others what my working method is like:

(1) A cow produces milk—that is certain—and the milk doesn't come from nothing. Just as a cow must eat grass in order to be able to produce milk, I have to read large amounts of genuine scientific literature of all kinds—i.e., literature not invented by me—and the final product, my writing, is as unlike the intellectual food as milk is unlike grass.

(2) Just as the ape in Wolfgang Köhler's psychological experiments wasn't able to reach a banana hanging very high, and made a scaffold from junk—boxes lying around, etc.—in order to be able to climb up to the banana, I have to build up in subsequent moves and attempts an informational "scaffold" that I must climb up to reach my goal.

(3) The last simile is somewhat drastic and may appear to be very primitive, but it nevertheless contains some grain of the truth. A water closet has a reservoir that must be filled, and when the lever or

*Michel Butor once expressed the opinion that a team of science-fiction writers should cooperate in the construction of a fictitious world, because such an undertaking is beyond the powers of any single individual. (This was supposed to explain the poor quality, the one-dimensionality of the existing science fiction.) I did not take those words of Butor's seriously when I read them. And yet I have, although many years later and by myself, tried to realize the basic essence of this idea as described above. And in Borges, too—in his "Tlön, Uqbar, Orbis Tertius"—you can read of a secret society that creates a fictitious world in all its particulars, with the intent of turning our world into the imagined one.

button is pushed all the water flushes down in one stream. Thereafter, the reservoir is empty for a time, and until it has been filled again no impatient pushing of the button or the lever will cause the small Niagara to flush forth again. As far as my work is concerned, this image is appropriate, in that if I did not keep enriching my fictitious library there would come a state of depletion, and after that I would not be able to get anything more out of my mind—my information storehouse. I wrote *A Perfect Vacuum*—it contains fifteen fictitious book reviews—nearly without a pause, and after that my reservoir was empty. Indeed, the comparison can be dragged a little further. Just as, if you push the button of a toilet too soon, there will flush down only inadequate Niagaras, I can squeeze a little more from my head after the writing of a book like *A Perfect Vacuum*. But I will not be satisfied with the stuff gained this way, and I cast these remnants aside.

My working methods are additionally complicated and enriched by my having from time to time written quasi-scientific works that were not intended as scaffoldlike supports for fiction but meant seriously as independent books on the theory of literature (but they are along empirical lines that are alien to specialists in the humanities). And I have produced *Science Fiction and Futurology* (1970), which is an acerbic criticism and theory of science fiction; and skeptical futurology, like *Summa Technologiae* (1964), which doesn't amass many speculations about the wonderful or terrible things of the near future but, rather, attempts to pursue a few radical ideas to their utmost limits; and the *Dialogues* (1957), about the horizons and chances of cybernetics implicit in the system; and essays on various topics, such as *Biology and Values* (1968) and *Applied Cybernetics: An Example from the Field of Sociology* (1971)*—a discussion of the pathology of socialism. Later, it

---

*I shall add the autobiographical element in my discursive writings to this enumeration. In brief, I am a disenchanted reformer of the world. My first novels concerned naive utopias, because in them I was expressing a desire for a world as peaceful as that described in them, and they are bad, in the sense in which a vain and erroneous expectation is stupid. My monograph on science fiction and futurology is an expression of my disappointment with a fiction and a nonfiction that pretend to be scientific, when neither of them turns the attention of the reader in the direction in which the world is in fact moving. My *Philosophy of Chance* is a failed attempt to arrive at a theory of the literary work based on empiricism; it is successful inasmuch as I taught myself with the help of this book what factors cause the rise and decline in the fortunes of literary works. My *Summa Technologiae*, on the other hand, is proof of the fact that I am not yet a despairing reformer of the world. For I do not believe that mankind is for all time a hopeless and incurable case.

turned out that several of the ideas that occurred to me during the writing of these works and that I used as hypotheses and examples—i.e., much of what I encountered on my chosen intellectual way during the process of writing—could also be put to good use in fiction. At first, this happened in a totally unconscious manner. I noticed it only when it was pointed out to me; that is, my critics discovered the similarities and were of the opinion that I oscillated with full consciousness between serious discussion and fantastic literature, when I myself was not aware of such a seesawing. Once my attention was drawn to this phenomenon, I sometimes browsed in my own books with an eye toward this possibility of exploitation or cross-fertilization.

In looking back, I see clearly that in my middle period as a writer I wrote fiction without any regard for the existence of some continuity between the imagined worlds and our world. In the worlds of *Solaris, Eden,* and *Return from the Stars,* there are no immediately obvious transitional stages that could connect these states of civilization with the obnoxious state of things on earth today. My later work, on the other hand, shows marked signs of a turning toward our world; that is, my later fictions are attempts to establish such connections. I sometimes call this my inclination toward realism in science fiction. Most likely, such attempts, which to some extent have the unmistakable character of a retreat (as a renunciation of both utopia and dystopia, extremes that are either repugnant to me or leave me cold, just as is the case for a physician when he faces someone incurably ill), spring from the awareness that I must soon die, and from the resulting desire to satisfy, at least with hypotheses, my insatiable inquisitiveness about the far future of mankind and the cosmos. But that is only a guess; I wouldn't be able to prove it.

In response to a request to write his autobiography, Einstein emphasized not the historical circumstances of his life but, rather, his most beloved offspring—his theories—because they were the children of his mind. I am no Einstein, but in this respect I nevertheless resemble him, for I am of the opinion that the most important parts of my biography are my intellectual struggles. The rest, not mentioned so far, is of a purely anecdotal character.

In 1953 I married a young student of medicine. We have a son of fifteen, who likes my novels well enough but modern music—

pop, rock and roll, the Beatles—his motorcycle, and the engines of automobiles perhaps even more. For many years now, I have not owned my books and my work; rather, I have become owned by them. I usually get up a short time before five in the morning and I sit down to write: I am writing these words at six o'clock. I am unable now to work more than five or six hours a day without a pause. When I was younger, I could write as long as my stamina held out; the power of my intellect gave way only after my physical prowess had been exhausted. I write increasingly slowly—my self-criticism, the demands I put upon myself, have continued to grow—but I am still rather prolific. (I know this from the speed with which I have to throw away used-up typewriter ribbons.) Less and less of what comes into my mind I consider to be good enough to test as suitable subject matter by my method of trial and error. I still know as little about how and where my ideas are born as most writers do. I am also not of the opinion that I am one of the best exegetes of my own books—i.e., of the problems characteristic of them. I have written many books of which I haven't said a word here, among them *The Cyberiad*, the *Fables for Robots* (in *Mortal Engines*), and *The Star Diaries*, which on the generic map of literature are to be found in the provinces of the humorous—of satire, irony, and wit—with a touch of Swift and of dry, mischievous Voltairean misanthropy. As is well known, the great humorists were people who had been driven to despair and anger by the conduct of mankind. In this respect, I am one of those people.

I am probably both dissatisfied with everything that I have written and proud of it: I must be touched by arrogance, but I do not feel anything of it. I can notice it only in my behavior—in the way that I used to destroy all my manuscripts, in spite of many attempts and requests to get me to deposit these voluminous papers in a university or some other repository to preserve them for posterity. I have made up a striking explanation for this behavior. The pyramids were one of the wonders of the world only while there was no explanation of how they were erected. Very long, inclined planes, on which bands of workers hauled up the stone blocks, possibly on wooden cylinders, were leveled once the work was finished, and thus today the pyramids rise up in a lonely way among the shallow sand dunes of the desert. I try to level my inclined plane, my scaffolds and other means of construction, and to let stand only that of which I need not be ashamed.

I am not sure whether what I have confessed here is the pure truth, but I have tried to adhere to truth as well as I could.

(1984)

TRANSLATED BY FRANZ ROTTENSTEINER

Leszek Kołakowski

Modernity on Endless Trial

If we are to believe Hegel—or Collingwood—no age and no civilization is capable of conceptually identifying itself. This can be done only after its final demise, and even then, as we know too well, such an identification is never certain or universally accepted. Both the general "morphology" of civilizations and the description of their constitutive characteristics are notoriously controversial and heavily loaded with ideological biases, whether they express a need for self-assertion by comparison with the past or a malaise in one's own cultural environment and the resulting nostalgia for the good times of old. Collingwood suggested that each historical period has a number of basic ("absolute") presuppositions which it is unable clearly to articulate and which provide a latent inspiration for its explicit values and beliefs, its typical reactions and aspirations. If so, we might try to spot and to uncover those presuppositions in the life of our ancient or medieval ancestors and perhaps build on this basis a "history of mentalities" (as opposed to the "history of ideas"), but we are in principle prevented from revealing them in our own age, unless, of course, the owl of Minerva has already flown out and we are not aware of our living in the twilight, at the very end of an epoch.

And so, let us accept our incurable ignorance of our own spiritual foundation and be satisfied with the survey of the surface of our "modernity," whatever the word might mean. Whatever it means, it is certain that modernity is as little modern as are the attacks on modernity. The melancholic "ah, nowadays . . . ," "there is no longer . . . ," "in olden days . . . ," and similar expressions contrasting the corrupted present with the splendor of the past are probably as old as the human race; we find them in the Bible and in *The Odyssey*. I can well imagine Paleolithic nomads angrily resisting the foolish idea that it would be better for people to have permanent dwellings or predicting the imminent degeneration of mankind as a result of the nefarious invention of the wheel. Mankind's history conceived as a degradation belongs, as we know, to the most persistent mythological topics in various parts of the world, including both the symbol of the exile and Hesiod's description of the five ages. The frequency of such myths suggests that, apart from other possible social and cognitive functions, they voice a universally human, conservative mistrust of changes; a suspicion that "progress," on second thought, is no progress at all; a reluctance to assimilate transformations, however beneficial in appearance, of the established order of things.

The changes go on, nonetheless, and they usually find a sufficient number of enthusiastic supporters. The clash between "the ancient" and "the modern" is probably everlasting and we will never get rid of it, as it expresses the natural tension between structure and evolution and this tension seems to be biologically rooted; it is, we may believe, a characteristic of life as such. It is obviously necessary for any society to have the forces both of conservation and of change, and it is most doubtful whether any theory will ever work out reliable tools whereby we could measure the relative strength of those opposite energies in any given society, add and subtract them from each other like quantifiable vectors, and build on this basis a general schema of development, endowed with predictive power. We can only guess what gives some societies an ability to assimilate rapid changes without falling apart, what makes others be satisfied with a very slow pace of movement, in what exact conditions development or stagnation leads to violent crises or to self-destruction.

Curiosity—that is, a separate drive to explore the world disinterestedly, without being stimulated by danger or physiological dissatisfaction—is, according to students of evolution, rooted in specific morphological characteristics of our species and thus cannot be eradicated from our minds as long as the species continues to remain itself. As both Pandora's most deporable accident and the adventures of our progenitors in paradise testify, the sin of curiosity was the main cause of all the calamities and misfortunes that have befallen mankind, and it was unquestionably the source of all its achievements.

The exploration impulse has never been evenly distributed throughout various civilizations. Generations of scholars have asked the question, why has the civilization that emerged from joint Greek, Latin, Judaic, and Christian sources proved so uniquely successful in promoting and spreading rapid and accelerating changes in science, technology, art, and social order, whereas many cultures survived for centuries in almost stagnating conditions, affected only by barely noticeable changes or sunk into slumber after short-lived eruptions of creativity?

There is no good answer. Each civilization is a contingent agglutination of various social, demographic, climatic, linguistic, and psychological circumstances, and any search for one ultimate cause of its emergence or decline seems very unpromising. When we read studies that purport to show, for example, that the Roman Empire collapsed because of the widespread use of lead pots, which resulted in the poisoning and damaging of the brains of the upper classes, or that the Reformation can be accounted for by the spread of syphilis in Europe, we cannot forbear from strong doubts about the validity of such explanations. On the other hand, the temptation to look for "causes" is hard to resist, even if we guess that civilizations arise and crumble under the impact of uncountable factors, independent of each other, and that the same may be said about the birth of new animal or plant species, about the historical location of cities, the distribution of mountains on the surface of the earth, or the formation of particular ethnic tongues. By trying to identify our civilization we try to identify ourselves, to grasp the unique collective "Ego" which would be necessary and whose nonexistence would be as little conceivable as my own nonexistence is for me. And so, even though there is no answer to the question, why is our culture what it is? it is unlikely that the question might be deleted from our minds.

"Modernity" itself is not modern, but clearly the clashes about modernity are more prominent in some civilizations than in others and nowhere have they been as acute as in our time. At the beginning of the fourth century, Iamblichus stated that the Greeks are by nature lovers of novelty (Φύσει γὰρ Ἕλληνές εἰσί νεωδεροποιοί, *Egyptian Mysteries*, 7.5) and disregard tradition—in contrast to the barbarians; yet he did not praise the Greeks for that reason, quite the contrary. Are we still heirs of the Greek spirit in this respect? Is our civilization based on the belief (never expressed in so many words, to be sure) that what is *new* is good by definition? Is this one of our "absolute presuppositions"? This might be suggested by the value judgment usually associated with the adjective *reactionary*. The word is clearly pejorative, and one hardly finds people who would be ready to use it to describe themselves. And yet to be reactionary means nothing more than to believe that the past was in some of its aspects, however secondary, better than the present. If to be reactionary means automatically to be wrong—and the adjective is almost invariably employed on this assumption—it appears that one is always wrong in believing that the past might have been better in whatever respect, which amounts to saying that whatever is newer is better. And yet we hardly ever state our "progressism" in such a bold manner. The same ambiguity haunts the very word *modern*. In German the word means both "modern" and "fashionable," whereas English and other European tongues distinguish the two meanings. And yet the Germans might be right; it is not clear how the distinction should be defined, at least in areas where both adjectives are usable. To be sure, in some cases those words are not interchangeable; in expressions like "modern technology," "modern science," "modern industrial management," the word *fashionable* would not do, but it is hard to explain the difference between "modern ideas" and "fashionable ideas," "modern painting" and "fashionable painting," or "modern clothes" and "fashionable clothes."

In many instances the concept "modern" seems to be "value free" and neutral, not unlike "fashionable": modern is what is prevailing in our time; and indeed the word is often used sarcastically (like in Chaplin's *Modern Times*). On the other hand, the expressions "modern science" and "modern technology" strongly suggest, at least in common usage, that what is modern is thereby better. The ambiguity of meaning reflects perhaps the ambiguity, just mentioned, that haunts our attitude to changes: they are both welcomed and feared, both desirable and cursed. Many companies, in advertising their various products, employ both phrases like "good old-fashioned furniture" or "a soup according to Grandma's recipe" and "an entirely new soap," "an exciting novelty in washing powder technology." Both kinds of tricks seem to work. I do not know whether the sociology of advertising has produced an analysis of how, where, and why these apparently contradictory slogans prove to be successful.

Having no clear idea what "modernity" is, we have recently tried to escape forward from the issue by talking about "postmodernity" (an extension or an imitation of the somewhat older expressions "postindustrial society," "postcapitalism," etc.). I do not know what "postmodern" is and how it differs from "premodern," nor do I feel that I ought to know. And what might come after the "postmodern"? The postpostmodern, the neopostmodern, the neoantimodern? When we leave aside the labels, the real questions remain, why is the malaise in the comfort of modernity so widely felt, and where are the sources of those aspects of modernity that make this malaise particularly painful?

How far back modernity may be extended depends, of course, on what we believe is constitutive in the meaning of the notion. If it is big industry, rational planning, the welfare state, and the subsequent bureaucratization of social relationships, the life of modernity is to be measured by decades rather than by centuries. If we think, however, that the foundation of modernity is in science, it would be proper to date it to the first half of the seventeenth century, when the basic rules of scientific inquiry were elaborated and codified and when scientists realized—thanks mainly to Galileo and his followers—that physics was not to be conceived as a rapport with experience but rather as an elaboration of abstract models never to be perfectly embodied in experimental conditions. Yet nothing prevents us from probing more deeply into the past: the crucial condition of modern science was the movement toward the emancipation of secular Reason from Revelation, and the struggle for the independence of the faculties of arts from theology in medieval universities was an important part of this process. The very distinction of natural and divinely inspired knowledge, as it was worked out in Christian philosophy from the eleventh century onward, was, in its turn, the conceptual foundation of this struggle, and it would be difficult to decide what came first: the purely philosophical separation of two areas of knowledge or the social process whereby the intellectual urban class with its claims to autonomy was established.

Shall we then project our "modernity" onto the eleventh century and make Saint Anselm and Abelard its—respectively, unwilling and willing—protagonists? There is nothing conceptually wrong with such an extension but nothing very helpful either. We can go indefinitely far, of course, in tracing back the roots of our civilization, but the question so many of us have been trying to cope with is less, when did modernity start? and more, what is the core—whether explicitly expressed or not—of our contemporary widespread *Unbehagen* (malaise) *in der Kultur?* Anyway, if the word *modernity* is to be useful, the meaning of the first question has to depend on the answer to the latter.

And the first answer that naturally comes to mind is summed up, of course, in the Weberian *Entzauberung* (disenchantment) or in any similar word covering roughly the same phenomena.

We experience an overwhelming and, at the same time, humiliating feeling of déjà vu in following, and participating in, contemporary discussions about the destructive effects of the so-called secularization of Western civilization, the apparently progressing evaporation of our religious legacy and the sad spectacle of a godless world. It appears as if we suddenly woke up to perceive things that the humble, and not necessarily highly educated, priests have been seeing—and warning us about—for three centuries and that they have repeatedly denounced in their Sunday sermons. They kept telling their flock that a world that has forgotten God has forgotten the very distinction between good and evil, has made human life meaningless and sunk into nihilism. Now we, proudly stuffed with our sociological, historical, anthropological, and philosophical knowledge, discover the same simple wisdom, which we try to express in a slightly more sophisticated idiom.

I admit that by being old and simple, this wisdom does not necessarily cease to be true, and indeed I do believe it to be true (with some qualifications, though). Was Descartes the first and the main culprit? Probably yes, even on the assumption that he codified philosophically a cultural trend that had already paved its way before him. By equating matter with extension and thereby abolishing real variety in the physical universe, by letting this universe infallibly obey a few simple and all-explanatory laws of mechanics, and by reducing God to its logically necessary creator and support—a support, however, that was constant and thus robbed of significance in explaining any particular event—he definitively, or so it seemed, did away with the concept of Cosmos, of a purposeful order of Nature. The world became soulless, and only on this presupposition could modern science evolve. No miracles and no mysteries, no divine or diabolical interventions in the course of events, were conceivable any longer; all the later and still continuing efforts to patch up the clash between the Christian wisdom of old and the so-called scientific worldview were bound to be unconvincing for this simple reason.

To be sure, it took time before the consequences of this new universe were unfolded. Massive, self-aware secularity is a relatively recent phenomenon. It seems from today's perspective, however, that the erosion of faith, inexorably advancing in educated classes, was unavoidable. Faith could have survived, ambiguously sheltered from the invasion of rationalism by a number of logical devices and relegated to a corner where it seemed both harmless and insignificant. For generations, many people could live without realizing that they were denizens of two incompatible worlds and could protect, by a thin shell, the comfort of faith while trusting Progress, Scientific Truth, and modern technology. The shell was eventually to be broken, and this was ultimately done by Nietzsche's noisy philosophical hammer. His destructive passion brought havoc into the seeming spiritual safety of the middle classes and demolished what he believed was the bad faith in those who refused to be witnesses to the "death of God." In passionately attacking the spurious mental security of people who failed to realize what had really happened, he was successful because it was he who said everything to the end: the world generates no meaning and no distinction between good and evil, reality is pointless and there is no other hidden reality behind it, the world as we see it is the Ultimum, it does not try to convey a message to us, it does not refer to anything else, it is self-exhausting and deaf-mute.

All this had to be said, and Nietzsche found a solution or a medicine for the despair: this solution was madness. Not much could have been said after him on the lines he had laid out. It might have appeared that it was his destiny to become the prophet of modernity.

In fact, he was too ambivalent to assume this task. On the one hand he affirmed—under duress—the irreversible intellectual and moral consequences of modernity and poured scorn on those who timidly hoped to save something from the old tradition. On the other hand he denounced the horror of modernity, the bitter harvest of progress; he accepted what he knew—and said—was terrifying. He praised the spirit of science against the Christian "lies," but, at the same time, he wanted to escape from the misery of democratic leveling and sought refuge in the ideal of a barbarous genius. Yet modernity wants to be satisfied in its superiority and not torn asunder by doubt and despair.

Therefore Nietzsche did not become the explicit orthodoxy of our age. The explicit orthodoxy is still the patching up. We try to assert our modernity but to escape from its effects by various intellectual devices in order to convince ourselves that meaning can be restored or recovered apart from the traditional religious legacy of mankind and in spite of the destruction brought about by modernity. Some versions of liberal pop theology contribute to this work. So do some varieties of Marxism. Nobody can foresee for how long and to what extent this work of appeasement may prove successful. But the just-mentioned intellectuals' awakening to the dangers of secularity does not seem to be a promising avenue in getting out of mankind's present predicament. Not because such reflections are false but because they might be suspected of being born of an inconsistent manipulative spirit. There is something alarmingly desperate in intellectuals who have no religious attachment, faith, or loyalty proper but who insist on the irreplaceable educational and moral role of religion in our world and deplore its fragility, to which they themselves eminently bear witness. I do not blame them either for being irreligious or for asserting the crucial value of religious experience; I simply cannot persuade myself that their work might produce changes they believe desirable, because to spread faith, faith is needed and not an intellectual assertion of the social utility of faith. And modern reflection on the place of the Sacred in human life does not want to be manipulative in the sense of Machiavelli or of the seventeenth-century libertines who admitted that while piety was necessary for simpletons, skeptical incredulity suited the enlightened. Therefore such an approach, however understandable, not only leaves us in the place we were before but is itself a product of the same modernity it tries to restrict, and it expresses modernity's melancholic dissatisfaction with itself.

We ought to be cautious, however, when we make judgments about what in our culture expresses modernity and what the antimodern resistance. We know from historical experience that what is new in cultural processes often appears in disguise of the old, and vice versa—the old may easily put on fashionable clothes. The Reformation was ostensibly and self-consciously reactionary: its dream was to reverse the corrupting effects of the centuries-long development in theology, in the growth of secular Reason, in institutional forms of Christianity, and to recover the pristine purity of faith of apostolic times; but by doing away with the accumulated tradition as a source of intellectual and moral authority, it in fact encouraged a movement that was exactly opposite to its intention; it liberated the spirit of rational inquiry into religious matters because it made Reason—otherwise violently attacked—independent from the Church and tradition. Romantic nationalism often expressed itself as a nostalgic quest for the lost beauty of the preindustrial world, but by thus praising the praeteritum it contributed greatly to the eminently modern phenomenon which is the idea of the nation-state; and such a superbly modern product as nazism was a monstrous revival of those romantic reveries, thereby perhaps disproving the notion that we can properly measure modernity on the axis "tradition-rationality." Marxism was a mixture of an unequivocal enthusiasm for modernity, rational organization, and technological progress with the same yearning after the archaic community, and it culminated in the utopian expectation of the perfect world of the future in which both sets of values would be implemented and make a harmonious alloy; the modern factory and the Athenian agora would somehow merge into one. Existential philosophy might have appeared a highly modern phenomenon—which it was in its vocabulary and conceptual network—yet from today's perspective it seems instead a desperate attempt to revindicate the idea of personal responsibility in the face of a world in which progress consists in human persons' becoming, with their assent, no more than media whereby anonymous social, bureaucratic, or technical forces express themselves and people are unaware of the fact that in thus letting themselves be reduced to irresponsible instruments of the impersonal work of "society" they rob themselves of their humanity.

And so, the "cunning reason" of history probably has not stopped operating and nobody can guess, let alone have any certainty about, whether his own contribution to the collective life is to be seen in terms of modernity or of the reactionary resistance to it; nor, for that matter, which of them deserves support.

We might look for comfort in the idea that civilizations are able to take care of themselves and to mobilize self-correcting mechanisms or to produce antibodies that fight the perilous effects of their own growth. The ground of this analogy is not quite reassuring, though: after all, we know that the symptoms of a disease are often the organism's attempts at self-cure; most of us die as a result of the self-defense devices that our bodies employ to combat external dangers. Antibodies can kill. So might the unpredictable cost of self-regulation kill a civilization before it regains the sought-after equilibrium. It is true, no doubt, that criticism of our modernity, that is, of the modernity associated with, or perhaps put into movement by, the industrialization process, began as soon as this very modernity and that it has kept spreading since. Leaving aside the great eighteenth- and nineteenth-century critics of modernity— Vico, Rousseau, Tocqueville, the romantics—we know in our age a number of outstanding thinkers who in various ways pointed out and deplored the progressing loss of meaning in the manipulation-prone *Massengesellschaft* (mass society). Husserl attacked, in philosophical terms, the inability of modern science meaningfully to identify its own objects, its satisfaction in phenomenalist exactitude which improves our predictive and controlling power over things but is gained at the expense of understanding. Heidegger spotted the root of our sinking into impersonality in the oblivion of metaphysical insight. Jaspers associated the moral and mental passivity of seemingly liberated masses with the erosion of historical self-awareness and the subsequent loss of responsible subjectivity and of the ability to base personal relationships on trust. Ortega y Gasset noticed the collapse of high standards in art and humanities as the result of intellectuals' being compelled to adjust themselves to the low tastes of the masses. So did, in spuriously Marxist terms, the members of the Frankfurt school.

The critique of modernity, whether literary or philosophical, might be seen, in its immense variety, as a self-defense organ of our civilization, but so far it has failed to prevent modernity from advancing at an unprecedented speed. The lament seems all-pervading; whatever area of life we reflect upon, our natural instinct is to ask, what is wrong with it? and indeed we keep asking, what is wrong with God? with democracy? with socialism? with art? with sex? with the family? with economic growth? It seems as though we all live with the feeling of an all-encompassing crisis without being capable, however, of identifying clearly its causes, unless we escape into easy one-word pseudosolutions ("capitalism," "God has been forgotten," etc.). Optimists often become very popular and are listened to avidly, but they are met with derision in intellectual circles; we prefer to be gloomy.

It seems to us sometimes that it is less the content of changes and more their dizzy pace that terrifies us and leaves us in a state of never-ending insecurity, as we feel that nothing is certain or established any longer and that whatever is new is likely to become obsolete in no time. There are still living among us a few people who were born on an earth where there were no cars and no radios and electric light was an exciting novelty; during their lifetime how many literary and artistic schools have been born and died away, how many philosophical and ideological fashions have arisen and gone, how many states were built or perished! We all participate in those changes and we bemoan them nonetheless, as they seem to deprive our life of any substance we could safely rely upon.

I was told that near a Nazi extermination camp, where the soil was superbly fertilized with the ashes of uncountable cremated bodies of the victims, the cabbage grew with such tremendous rapidity that it had no time to form a head and produced instead a stem with separate leaves; apparently it was not edible. This might serve as a parable for thinking about the morbid tempo of progress.

We know, of course, that we must not extrapolate the recent curves of growth—some of them exponential—in various areas of civilization, and that the curves have to decline one way or another or perhaps turn into S curves; we fear, however, that the change might come too late or be caused by catastrophes that will destroy civilization by healing it.

It would be silly, of course, to be either "for" or "against" modernity *tout court*, not only because it is pointless to try to stop the development of technology, science, and economic rationality, but because both modernity and antimodernity may be expressed in barbarous and antihuman forms. The Iranian theocratic revolution was clearly antimodern, and in Afghanistan it is the invaders who carry in various ways the spirit of modernity against the nationalist and religious resistance of poor tribes. It is trivially true that very often the blessings and the horrors of progress are inseparably tied to each other and so are the enjoyments and the miseries of traditionalism. When I try, however, to point out the single most dangerous side of modernity, I tend to sum up my fear in one phrase: the disappearance of taboos. There is no way that we could distinguish between "good" and "bad" taboos, artificially support the former and remove the latter; the abrogation of one, on the pretext of its "irrationality," results in a "domino effect" and in a withering away of the others. Most sexual taboos have been abolished and the remaining few—like the interdiction of incest and of pedophilia—are under attack; enough to think that in various countries there are groups openly advocating their "right" to engage in sexual intercourse with children, that is, their right to rape them, and demanding—so far unsuccessfully—the abolition of corresponding legal sanctions. The taboo expressed in the respect for the bodies of the dead seems to be a candidate for extinction; and although the technique of transplanting organs has saved many lives and will doubtless save many more, I find it difficult not to feel a sympathy with people who anticipate with horror a world in which dead bodies will be no more than a store of spare parts for the living or raw material for various industrial purposes; perhaps respect for the dead and for the living—and for life itself—are inseparable. Various traditional human bonds which make communal life possible and without which our existence would be regulated only by greed and fear are not likely to survive without a taboo system, and it is perhaps better to believe in the validity of even apparently silly taboos than to let them all vanish. To the extent rationality and rationalization threaten the very presence of taboos in our civilization, they corrode its ability to survive. But it is quite improbable that taboos—which are barriers erected by instinct and not by conscious planning—could be saved, or selectively saved, by a rational technique; in this area we can only rely on the uncertain hope that the social self-preservation drive will prove strong enough to react to their evaporation and that this reaction will not come in barbarous form.

The point is that in the normal sense of "rationality" there are no more rational grounds for respecting human life and human personal rights than there are, say, for forbidding the consumption of shrimp among Jews, of meat on Friday among Christians, and of wine among Muslims. They are all "irrational" taboos. Any totalitarian system that treats people as exchangeable parts in the state machinery, to be used, discarded, or destroyed according to the state's needs, is in a sense a triumph of rationality. Still, it is compelled, in order to survive, reluctantly to restore some of those "irrational" values and thus to deny its rationality, thereby proving that perfect rationality is a self-defeating goal.

(1986)

Jerzy Grotowski

Performer

The Performer, with a capital letter, is a man of action. He is not a man who plays another. He is a dancer, a priest, a warrior: he is outside aesthetic genres. Ritual is performance, an accomplished action, an act. Degenerated ritual is a spectacle. I don't want to discover something new but something forgotten. Something which is so old that all distinctions between aesthetic genres are no longer of use.

I am a *teacher of Performer*. I speak in the singular. A teacher is someone through whom the teaching passes; the teaching should be received, but the manner for the apprentice to rediscover it, *to remember*, is personal. How does the teacher himself come to know the teaching? By initiation, or by theft. Performer is a state of being. A man of knowledge, we can speak of him in reference to Castaneda if we like the romantic color. I prefer to think of Pierre de Combas. Or even of Don Juan as described by Nietzsche: a rebel who should conquer knowledge; even if he is not cursed by others, he feels different, like an outsider. Hindu tradition tells of *vratias* (the rebel hordes). *Vratia* is someone who is on the way to conquer knowledge. A man of knowledge has at his disposal *the doing* and not ideas or theories. The true teacher - what does he do for the apprentice? He says: *do it*. The apprentice fights to understand, to reduce the unknown to the known, to avoid doing. By the very fact that he wants to understand, he resists. He can understand only after he *does it*. He *does it* or not. Knowledge is a matter of doing.

danger and chance

If I use the term: warrior, you can refer it again to Castaneda, but all Scriptures also speak of the warrior. You can find him in the Hindu tradition as well as in the African one. He is somebody who is conscious of his own mortality. If it's necessary to confront corpses, he confronts them, but if it's not necessary to kill, he doesn't kill. Among the Indians of the New World it is said, that between two battles, *the warrior has a tender heart, like a young girl.* To conquer knowledge he fights, because the pulsation of life becomes stronger and more articulated in moments of great intensity, of great danger. Danger and chance go together. There is no real class if not in regard to real danger. In a moment of challenge appears the rhythmization of human impulses. The ritual is a moment of great intensity; provoked intensity; life then becomes rhythmic. Performer knows to link body impulsion to sonority (the stream of life should be articulated in forms). The witnesses then enter into intense states because, as they say, they have felt a presence. And this is owing to Performer, who is a bridge between the witness and something. In this sense, Performer is *pontifex*, a maker of bridges.

Essence: etymologically, it's a question of being, of *be-ing*. Essence interests me because in it nothing is sociological. It is what you did not receive from others, what did not come from outside, what is not learned. For example, conscience is something which belongs to essence; it is different from the moral code which just belongs to society. If you break the moral code you feel guilty, and it is society which speaks in you. But if you do an act against conscience, you feel remorse - this is between you and yourself, and not between you and society. As almost everything that you possess is sociological, essence seems to be a little thing, but it is yours. In the fifties, in Sudan, there were young warriors in the villages Kau. For the warrior with organicity in full, the body and essence can enter into osmosis: it seems impossible to dissociate them. But this is not a permanent state, it lasts only for a short period. In Zeami's words, it's *the flower of youth.* However, with age, it's possible to pass from the *body-and-essence* to the *body of essence.* That is the outcome of a difficult evolution, the personal labor, which in some way is the task of each one. The key question is: what is your process? Are you faithful to or do you fight against your process? The process is something like the destiny of each one, his own destiny, which develops (or: which just unfolds) with time. So: *what is the quality of your submission to your own destiny?* You can catch the process if what you do is in keeping with yourself, if you don't *hate what you do*. The process is linked to essence and virtually leads to the *body of essence*. When the warrior is in the short time of osmosis *body-and-essence,* he should catch his process. When you adjust to the process, the body becomes non-resistant, nearly transparent. Everything is in lightness, in evidence. With Performer, performing can become near process.

the I-I

It can be read in ancient texts: *We are two. The bird who picks and the bird who looks on. The one will die, the one will live.* Busy with picking, drunk with life inside time, we forget to *make live* the part in us which looks on. So, there is the danger to exist only inside time, and in no way outside time. To feel looked upon by this other part of yourself (the part which is, as if it were, outside time) gives another dimension. There is an I-I. The second I is quasi virtual; it is not -in you- the look of the others, nor any judgement; it's like an immobile look: a silent presence, like the sun which illuminates the things - and that's all. The process of each one can be accomplished only in the context of this still presence. I-I: in experience, the couple doesn't appear as separate, but as full, unique.
In the way of Performer - he perceives essence during its osmosis with the body, and then works the process; he develops the I-I. The looking presence of the teacher can sometimes function as a mirror of the connection I-I (this connection is not yet traced). When the link I-I is traced, the teacher can disappear and Performer continue toward the *body of essence;* that which can be recognized in the photo of Gurdjieff, old, sitting on a bench in Paris. From the image of the young warrior of Kau to that of Gurdjieff, is the way from the *body-and-essence* to the *body of essence*.
I-I does not mean to be cut in two but to be double. The question is to be passive in action and active in the look (reversing the habit). Passive: to be receptive. Active: to be present. To nourish the life of the I-I, Performer must develop not an organism-mass, an organism of muscles, athletic, but an organism-channel through which the forces circulate.
Performer should work with a precise structure; making efforts, because persistence and respect for details are the rigour which

allows him to make present the I-I. The things to be done must be precise. *Don't improvise, please!* It is necessary to find the actions, simple, yet taking care that they are mastered and that they endure. If not, they will be not simple, but banal.

what I recall

One access to the creative way consists of discovering in yourself an ancient corporality to which you are bound by a strong ancestral relation. So you are neither in the character nor in the non-character. Starting from details you can discover in you somebody other - your grandfather, your mother. A photo, a memory of wrinkles, the distant echo of a color of the voice enable you to reconstruct a corporality. First, the corporality of somebody known, and then more and more distant, the corporality of the unknown one, the ancestor. Is this corporality literally as it was? Maybe not literally - but yet as it might have been. You can arrive very far back, as if your memory awoke. That is a phenomenon of reminiscence, as if you recall Performer of the primal ritual. Each time I discover something, I have the feeling it is what I recall. Discoveries are behind us and we must journey back to reach them. With the breakthrough - as in the return of an exile - can one touch something which is no longer linked to origins but - if I dare say - to *the origin?* I believe so. Does essence stay in the background of the memory? I don't know at all. When I work close to essence, I have the impression that memory actualizes. When essence is activated, it is as if very strong potentialities are activated. The reminiscence is perhaps one of these potentialities.

the inner man

I quote: *Between the inner man and the outer man there is the same infinite difference as between the heaven and the earth.*
                 When I was in my first cause, I did not have God, I was my own cause. There, nobody asked me to where I tended, nor what I was doing; nobody was there to question me. What I

wanted, I was it and what I was, I wanted it; I was free from God and from all things.

When I came out (flowed out) all creatures spoke of God. If someone asked me: - Brother Eckhart, when did you come out of the home? - I was still there just a moment ago. I was myself, I wanted me myself and knew me myself, to make the man (which here below I am).

This is why I am unborn, and by my mode unborn, I cannot die. What I am by my birth will die and vanish, because it is devolved to time and will decay with time. But in my birth were born also all creatures. They all feel the need to rise from their life to their essence.

When I return, this breakthrough is much more noble than my coming out. In the breakthrough - there, I am above all creatures, neither God, nor creature; but I am what I was, what I should remain now and for ever. When I arrive - there, nobody asks me where I come from nor where I have been. There I am what I was, I do not increase nor diminish, because I am - there, an immobile cause, which makes move all things.

NOTE: One version of this text (based on the conference of Grotowski) was published in May 1987 by ART-PRESS in Paris, with the following note by Georges Banu: «What I propose here is neither a recording, nor a summary, but notes carefully taken, as close as possible to the formulas of Grotowski. It should be read as indications of a trajectory and not as the terms of a program, nor a document - finished, written, closed. The echoes of the voice of the hermit can arrive to us even if his acts remain secret.» The sub-titles (except the last: "the inner man") are of the editor of ART-PRESS. The above text has been reworked and extended by Grotowski. To identify "Performer" with the participants of the Workcenter would be an abuse of the term. The matter is rather of that case of apprenticeship which, in all the activity of "teacher of Performer" does not occur but rare times.

Original French text translated by Thomas Richards

Witold Gombrowicz

Selections from *Diary*

1955

Wednesday

Yes, this was more or less the vacuum which that joyful writing breathed, even though it was the clamor of a hundred mouths in comparison with the silence of today's gagged ones. I have already said: I will not gauge the height of our flight by the depth of our fall. During those years in Poland, I felt as if I were in something that wants to be, but cannot, that wants to express itself, but is unable to. . . . What a curse! All the frustrations around me! Yet the human material was good and certainly no worse than any other European material. They looked like capable creatures, stuck doing shoddy work, inhibited by something impersonal, superior, interhuman, and collective emanating from the milieu. Entire social classes right out of a sarcastic dream: the landed gentry, the peasantry, the urban proletariat, officers, ghettos . . . Polish thought, Polish mythology, the Polish psyche . . . an inept and inefficient Polishness, which permeated the heritage that delineated us like a subtle fume. . . . I returned from visiting my country brothers upset by the diabolical dissonance; yet in the city, cafés scuffling helplessly with destiny awaited me, and people like a sandy forest full of gnarled trees.

The hope of a slow perfection, gradual development and attainment, could have been a guiding light, but should I have waited? I could not agree to have my life be a mere introduction to life. Was I to serve in literature only as a temporary stopgap, so that I could make possible the appearance of the independent Polish word in one or two hundred years? In that case it was not worth sitting down to write. Art that is incapable of ensuring its creator an authentic existence in the spiritual sphere is only an unceasing shame, a humiliating testimony to a bungled job. Each second I saw how one of my "friends" tamed a faith for himself, an ideological or aesthetic position, in the hope that in the end he would become a real writer. This approach inevitably ended in a series of grimaces, a pyramid of claptrap, and an orgy of unreality.

Either a person is someone or not—one cannot fabricate oneself artificially. In independent Poland, the artificial fabrication of existence became an ever more frequent substitute for a genuine existence: these intellectuals and artists tried to be someone with this *arrière-pensée* in order to simply be. To believe in God not because it is a necessity of the soul but because faith strengthens. To be a nationalist not from nature and conviction but because it is necessary to a good life. To have ideals not because one carries them in one's blood but because they "organize things." All of them searched feverishly for some sort of form so they wouldn't disintegrate . . . and I would have had nothing against this, if they had had the courage to admit what they were doing and if they had not deceived themselves.

This, however, was naive self-delusion. I, therefore, finally broke off all relations with people in Poland and with what they were producing. I withdrew into myself, determined to live only my own life, whatever it was, and to see only with my own eyes. I thought that if I were capable of being myself, then I would discover solid ground beneath my feet. Shortly thereafter, however, it became obvious that this extreme individualism could not, alone, make me any more real or creative. It solved nothing, and least of all, it did not loosen my tongue. For what was this "I" on which I wanted to base my work? Was it not formed by the past and the present day? Wasn't the way I was a consequence of Polish development? Nothing of what I did, said, thought, or wrote satisfied me and you probably know this feeling: when you notice that you are constantly saying that which you don't want to say because the text you wrote sounds pretentious, stupid, false. For all the perversions of your upbringing, influences that shaped you, habits with which you were vaccinated, because all of your immaturity in the face of the main issues of being and culture make form impossible. I could not find a form to express my reality. I could not, in general, describe this reality, find my place. In these conditions I could only—and this is what I wrote in *Ferdydurke*—pretend to be a writer (modeled on other colleagues).

There is only one insurmountable difficulty in this thing—that even Solomon cannot draw something from nothing. Be oneself? Yes, but if one is immaturity? . . .

Nevertheless a thought that I never doubted guided me: that if I am, then I have the eloquence of a fact, something which is . . . in and of itself, that if I was, I had the right to speak and this voice had the right to be heard.

It was then that I looked at that entire inadequacy of Polish expression in literature from another vantage point. This is what appeared to me.

This literature surely did not re-create reality—even though it was reality, even in its very powerlessness. Imagine an author who sets out to write a play, for example. If he isn't in the position to afford the appropriate honesty, spiritual doggedness, his work will be a mere pile of aborted words. This play, however unimportant and undramatic as a work, will, nevertheless, be a real play insofar as it is a testimony of defeat and the author, worthy of derision as an author, will, nevertheless, be deserving of sympathy and maybe is even great and dramatic as a man who could not find a way of expressing himself.

Poland's real reality, therefore, did not express itself in books, which were not of it—they were next to it—but in the fact that books did not express us. Our existence was dependent on the fact that we did not have an existence adequately crystallized. Our form consisted of its inappropriateness to us. So where had Polish writers made their mistake? In trying to be that which they could not be—formed individuals, when instead they were people in the process of being formed . . . and that they desired, in poetry and prose, to pull themselves up to the level of the European, more crystallized nations, regardless of the fact that this condemned them to everlasting inferiority—as they could not compete with that more polished form.

Therefore it seemed paradoxical to me that the only means by which I, a Pole, could become a fully valuable phenomenon in culture was this one: not to hide my immaturity, but to admit it; and with this admission to break away from it; and to make a steed out of the tiger that was devouring me up to now, which steed (if I could mount it) could take me farther than those Western folks who were "delineated." . . . At first glance, this does not look threatening as a program or rallying cry—behold, one more caprice of the intellect, seeking ways out . . . but when I penetrated its consequences (while writing *Ferdydurke*), I distinctly noticed their devastating perversity. What did this mean? One simply had to turn everything upside down, beginning with the Poles themselves. To turn the complacent, preening Pole, so enamored of himself, into a creature equally aware of its inadequacy and ephemerality—and turn this keenness of vision, this ruthlessness in not concealing weaknesses, into a strength. Not only would our approach to history and national art have to undergo annihilation, but our entire notion of patriotism would get transformed at its base. More, a lot more, our entire attitude toward the world would have to change and our assignment then would no longer be working out some sort of specific Polish form, but the acquisition of a new approach to form as something that is endlessly created by people and never satisfies them. In addition: one has to demonstrate that everyone is like us, that is, one has to reveal the complete inadequacy of the civilized man in the face of the culture which is too much for him.

It was a matter of no less than exchanging a man who had form for a man (this also pertains to a nation) who produces form—a dry recipe, but one that suddenly and unexpectedly changes the entire Polish way of being in the world. As for me, I did not concern myself with the mad enormity of this revolution. Even today I do not ask if it is pertinent to suggest something like this in Polish culture, which, decimated and made to heel, is pulled in exactly the opposite direction (for dialectic thought in totalitarian practice changes into dogmatic thought). The programs did not frighten me because a program did not move me but an inner need did. An artist is not here to reason, he is not here to arrange syllogisms, he exists to create a picture of the world. He does not refer to someone else's reason, only to someone else's intuition. He describes the world as he feels it and expects that the audience will feel it in the same way and will say: yes, that's it, that is reality and it is more real than that which I have been calling reality up to now—even though perhaps both, the artist and the audience, would not know how to prove logically why this is more real. For me it was enough that a breath of authentic life suddenly refreshed me at this very thought. I strove in this direction blindly simply because each step made my word stronger and my art more real. I did not concern myself with all the rest. The rest—sooner or later—will create itself.

1956

Monday

Existentialism.

I don't know how existentialism would be able to become something more than a toy in my hands, and change into serious-ness, death, doing oneself in. I write down my opinion of existen-tialism here, not out of respect for my own dilettante's opinions, but out of respect for my own life. Describing, as best as I can, my spiritual adventures (as if I were describing my corporeal adven-tures), I cannot bypass two bankruptcies which have occurred in me: the existential and the Marxist. I confirmed the crash of exis-tential theory in myself not long ago by discussing it during my little course of philosophy . . . *contre coeur*, as something already dead.

I wrote *Ferdydurke* in the years 1936–37, when no one knew anything about this philosophy. In spite of this, *Ferdydurke* is exis-tential to the marrow. Critics, I will help you in determining why *Ferdydurke* is existential: because man is created by people and because people mutually form themselves. This is precisely exis-tence and not essence. *Ferdydurke* is existence in a vacuum, that is, nothing except existence. That is why, in this book, practically all the basic themes of existentialism play fortissimo: becoming, creat-ing oneself, freedom, fear, absurdity, nothingness . . . with the single difference that in addition to the typical existential "spheres" of human life, like Heidegger's banal and authentic life, Kierke-gaard's aesthetic, ethical, and religious life, or Jaspers's "spheres," there is yet another sphere, namely, the "sphere of immaturity." This sphere or "category" is the contribution of my private exis-tence to existentialism. Let us say it right off: this is what separates me the most from classical existentialism. For Kierkegaard,

Heidegger, and Sartre, the more profound the awareness, the more authentic the existence. They measure honesty and the essence of experience by the degree of awareness. But is our humanity really built on awareness? Doesn't awareness—that forced, extreme awareness—arise among us, not from us, as something created by effort, the mutual perfecting of ourselves in it, the confirming of something that one philosopher forces onto another? Isn't man, therefore, in his private reality, something childish and always beneath his own awareness? And doesn't he feel awareness to be, at the same time, something alien, imposed and unimportant? If this is how it is, this furtive childhood, this concealed degradation are ready to explode your systems sooner or later.

It is not worth carrying on about *Ferdydurke*, which is a circus and not a philosophy. It remains a fact, however, that even before the war, I was like a cat walking my own paths through existentialism. Why, then, when I became familiar with the theory later on, was it of no use to me at all? And why, now, when my existence grows more monstrous with each year, so very mixed with dying, and beckons me, forces me to seriousness, why is their seriousness of no use to me at all?

I might forgive those professors the twisting intestines of their thinking which does not want to be thinking, their leaps from logic into alogic, from abstraction into the concrete and vice versa. Their thought, that retching thought, really is "that which is not and is not that which it is"—that is how deeply their splitting contradictions penetrate. A self-destructive thought, which creates the impression that we are using our hands to cut off our hands. Their works are one cry of desperate impotence, the most artful expression of failure, and it is here that beating one's head against the wall becomes the only remaining method. Yet I might forgive them this, this might even suit me. I might even be able to handle the purely professional reproaches put to them by their colleagues, concerning, for example, the relation subject-object or their being handicapped by classical idealism or their illicit ties to Husserl. Perhaps I have already become accustomed to the thought that philosophy has to be a failure and I know that we can only dispense thought that has been dashed to pieces, after all, we know that a rider who mounts this horse has to fall off. No, I am not demanding. I am not asking for absolute answers to absolute questions. I would be happy in my poverty with even a dialectical scrap of truth, which would cheat this hunger for even a moment. Yes, if this could satisfy me even temporarily, I would not refuse even this regurgitated nourishment.

I would be satisfied all the more easily since, I have to admit, even though this philosophy is bankrupt in its very points of departure, nevertheless, it can become immensely fertile and enriching as an attempt to systematize our profoundest knowledge about man. After discarding this specific scholasticism that speculates in the abstract (this is what existentialism hates, but what it thrives on), something very important, something concretely, practically important remains: a certain construct of man, resulting from the profoundest, most authentic confrontation possible between consciousness and existence. The various theses of the existentialists will perhaps turn out to be a professorial ranting, but the existential man, such as they saw him, will remain the great acquisition of consciousness. This is certainly an abysmal model. Falling into this abyss, I know that I will not reach the bottom, but nevertheless it is not alien, it is the abyss of my nature. And perhaps this metaphysics of man and life will lead to nothing. It is, nevertheless, an unavoidable necessity in our development, something without which we could not reach a certain maximum of ours, that highest and most profound effort that must be attained. So many of the loose intuitions that are so abundant in the air we breathe that they visited me almost daily are here woven into a system, organized into a whole that is desperately lame and barely alive, but some sort of whole, nevertheless. Existentialism, whatever else it may be, is founded on our essential anxiety. It liberates our metaphysical *dernier cri*. It hones the ultimate half-truth about us to such a degree that Heidegger's or Jaspers's man must replace the other anachronistic models and it imposes itself on the imagination and delineates our frame of mind in the cosmos. Here, therefore, existentialism becomes a dread and proud power, along the lines of those great acts of self-delineation, which every so often model the face of humanity. The only question is: How long will this last model suffice? Our tempo is accelerated, resulting in lighter and more fleeting definitions.

My relationship with existentialism is tormentingly unclear and tense. It intrudes into my existence, but I don't want it. And it is not I who am in this predicament. Strange. Philosophy, exhorting to authenticity, leads us into gigantic falsehoods.

Tuesday

We told each other our dreams. Nothing in art, even the most inspired mysteries of music, can equal dreams. The artistic perfection of dreams! How many lessons this nocturnal archmaster gives to us, the daily fabricators of dreams, the artists! In a dream everything is pregnant with a dreadful and unfinished meaning, nothing is indifferent, everything reaches us more deeply, more intimately than the most heated passion of the day. This is the lesson: an artist cannot be restricted to day, he has to reach the night life of humanity and seek its myths and symbols. Also: the dream upsets the reality of the experienced day and extracts certain fragments from it, strange fragments, and arranges them illogically in an arbitrary pattern. It is exactly this lack of sense that has the profoundest meaning for us: we ask why, in the name of what, is our ordinary sense destroyed. Gazing at the absurd as at a hieroglyph, we try to decipher its reason for being, of which we know only that it is, that it exists. . . . Art, therefore, also can and should upset reality, take it apart into elements, build illogical new worlds of it and in this arbitrariness is hidden a law, which in disturbing sense has it, so that the madness that destroys our external sense leads us into our internal meaning. The dream reveals the abysmal idiocy of the task set for art by those classical minds that prescribe that art ought to be "clear." Clarity? Its clarity is the clarity of night, not day. Its brightness is exactly like that of a flashlight that extracts just one object out of the darkness, immersing the rest in an even more bottomless night. It should be, beyond the boundaries of its light, dark like the pronouncements of the Pythia, veiled, not spelled out, shimmering with a multiplicity of meanings and broader than precision. A classical clarity? The clarity of the Greeks? If this seems clear to you then it is because you are blind. Go at high noon to take a gook look at the most classical Venus, and you will see the darkest night.

Thursday

How should I explain why existentialism did not lead me astray?

Perhaps I was close to choosing an existence that they call authentic—in contrast to a frivolous temporal life, which they call
banal. That is how great the pressure of seriousness is from all
sides. Today, in today's raw times, there is no thought or art that
does not shout to you in a loud voice: don't escape, don't play,
don't poke fun at yourself, don't run away! Fine. I, too, in spite of
everything, would also prefer not to lie to my own being. I, therefore, tried this authentic life, full of loyalty to existence in myself.
But what do you want? It can't be done. It can't be done because
that authenticity turned out to be falser than all my previous decep-
tions, games, and leaps taken together. I, with my artistic temperament, don't understand much theory, but I do have a nose when it
comes to style. When I applied maximum consciousness to life, in
an attempt to found my existence on this, I noticed that something
stupid was happening to me. Too bad, but no way. It can't be
done. It seems impossible to meet the demands of *Dasein* and simultaneously have coffee and croissants for an evening snack. To
fear nothingness, but to fear the dentist more. To be consciousness,
which walks around in pants and talks on the telephone. To be
responsibility, which runs little shopping errands downtown. To
bear the weight of significant being, to instill the world with meaning and then return the change from ten pesos. What do you want?
I know how these contrasts come together in their theories.
Slowly, gradually, from Descartes through German idealism, I
grew accustomed to their structure, but laughter and shame toss me
about at the sight of it with equal strength, as in the first days, when
I was still completely naive. And even if you were to "convince"
me a thousand times over, there would still always be some elementary, unbearable ridiculousness in this!

This is impossible to bear, especially in existentialism. As long
as philosophy speculated in isolation from life, as long as it was
pure reason reeling off abstractions, it was not violence, affront,
and ridiculousness to such a degree. Thought simply was, life simply was. I could tolerate Cartesian or Kantian speculations because
they were only the work of the mind. I, on the other hand, sensed
that beyond consciousness is being. I felt elusive in being. Basically
I never treated these differently than as an exclusive creation of a
certain power of mine, the power of reasoning, which, however,
was only one of my functions, which was, in an ultimate sense, an

expansion of my vitality. And so, because of this, I did not have to surrender. But now? Existentialism? Existentialism wants to get at all of me, it no longer appeals only to my cognitive powers, it wants to penetrate me in my deepest existence, it wants to *be* my existence. Here, therefore, my life bolts and begins to kick. Intellectual polemics with existentialists really amuse me. How can you polemicize with something that strikes at your being? This is no longer just a theory, but a rapacious act of their existence in relation to your existence and one does not answer this with arguments but with living differently than they would like you to and so categorically differently that your life becomes impenetrable to them.

Historically speaking, the plunge of the human spirit into this existential scandal, into its specific helpless rapacity and wise stupidity, was probably inevitable. The history of culture indicates that stupidity is the twin sister of reason, it grows most luxuriously, not on the soil of virgin ignorance, but on soil cultivated by the sweat of doctors and professors. Great absurdities are not thought up by those whose reason hovers over daily affairs. It is not strange, therefore, that the most intense thinkers were the producers of the greatest idiocies. Reason is a machine that purifies itself dialectically, but this means that dirt is appropriate to it. Our rescue from this dirty imperfection of reason was that no one has ever taken reason too seriously—beginning with the philosophers themselves. As for me, I can't believe that Socrates, Spinoza, or Kant were real peple and completely serious ones at that. I claim that an excess of seriousness is conditioned by an excess of frivolity. Of what were these majestic conceptions born? Curiosity? Accident? Ambition? Gain? For pleasure? We will never know the dirt of their genesis, their hidden, intimate immaturity, their childhood or shame because even the artists themselves are not allowed to know about this. . . . We will not know the roads by which Kant-the-child and Kant-the-adolescent changed into Kant-the-philosopher, but it would be good to remember that culture or knowledge is something much lighter than one would imagine. Lighter and more ambivalent. Nevertheless, the imperialism of reason is horrible. Whenever reason notices that some part of reality eludes it, it immediately lunges at it to devour it. From Aristotle to Descartes, reason behaved calmly for the most part because it judged that everything could be understood. Beginning with the

Critique of Pure Reason, however, and then Schopenhauer, Nietzsche, Kierkegaard, and others, it began to delineate terrain inaccessible to thinking and to discover that life ridicules reason. This, reason could not bear and from then on, its torments, which reach tragicomic heights in existentialism, begin.

It is here that reason meets, face-to-face, the greatest and most elusive of sneerers, life. Reason discovered and made that enemy concrete, one could say that they thought long and hard until they thought up something about which they could no longer think. That is why one is overwhelmed with shame in the face of the creations of this freak reasoning: here, as if by the strength of some sort of maliciousness, repulsive perversion, and greatness in a demonic twist, reason becomes a great ridiculousness, profundity leads to the dregs of impotence, accuracy strikes at stupidity and the absurd. Horrified, we see that the more seriousness, the less serious! This did not happen to us to this extent with other philosophers. They grew closer to ridiculousness in proportion to their penetration into the terrain of life and, in this way, Nietzsche is more comical than Kant. Yet laughter was not yet a necessity when regarding them, for this thought was isolated, at least to a point, and it did not engage us. It was only when the theoretical problem became a "mystery" of Gabriel Marcel that the mystery turned out to be ridiculous to the bursting point!

Let us attempt to delineate the nature of this ridiculousness. It is not just a matter of this desperate contrast between an "ordinary reality" and their ultimate reality, a contrast so massive and devastating that no analyses can patch it up. Our laughter in this is not only laughter planted with both feet in "common sense," no, it is worse because it is more spasmodic, it is independent of us. When you, existentialists, speak to me of consciousness, fear, and nothingness, I burst with laughter not because I don't agree with you, but because I must agree with you. I agreed and, lo and behold, nothing happened. I agreed but nothing changed in me, even by an iota. The consciousness that you injected into my life entered my bloodstream and instantly became the life that now shakes me in spasms of giggles, the ancient triumph of the element. Why am I forced to laugh? Simply because I also revel in consciousness. I laugh because I delight in fear, play with nothingness, and toy with responsibility. Death does not exist.

Tuesday

In spite of this I have to say that I do not believe that any culture, art, or literature can afford to bypass existentialism. If Polish Catholicism, or, too, Polish Marxism, fence themselves off from existentialism with an unwise disregard, they will become a blind alley, a provincial backwater.

On Sunday, Duś and I drove out into the neighborhood to visit.

The lady of the house, an Englishwoman (and the wife of a wealthy stockbroker from Buenos Aires, who bought a small parcel of land here and on it built a chalet) treated me right off with a strange aggressiveness, which was all the more unusual as I was a complete stranger to her. You, sir, must be an egotist. I smell the egotist in you! . . . After which she does not stop letting me know something more or less like this: You imagine that you are someone, but I know better! You are a pseudointellectual, a pseudoartist (if you were worth something, you would be famous!), which is to say, you are a parasite, a drone, a theoretician, a lunatic, anarchist, a tramp, and, certainly, a swaggerer! You must work! Live for society! I work, I sacrifice myself, I live for others, but you are a sybarite and a Narcissus!

To those "I's" with which she destroys my egotism, I add another few: I am an Englishwoman! I am distinguished! Look how honest I am and casually impertinent! I have grace! I am charming, amusing, aesthetic, and also, moral! I have my own mind! Not just anyone appeals to me!

Once, Sabato or Mastronardi, I no longer remember which, told me that at a certain party, an *estanciero* (a person otherwise well brought up) walked up to a well-known Argentine writer and said: You, Sir, are a numbskull! When asked what specifically in the writing of this particular author aroused such abomination in him, he admitted that he had never read him and had upbraided him *por las dudas,* just in case, so that he would not think "too highly of himself."

This phenomenon has its name here. It is called the "Argentine defensive." The defensive of this lady, who was rather likable although a bit mannered, was not serious because one could see that she wanted to be appealing and that she wields this genre because she considers it charming and distinguished. Sometimes, however, an Argentine becomes truly discourteous in a defensive, a rare thing in this polite country.

Monday

I feel that there is no way to ignore existentialism or to bypass it with any kind of dialectic. I believe that the artist or writer who has not come face-to-face with its initiations hasn't the slightest notion about the current day (Marxism will not save him). I also believe that the lack of this experience, the existential experience, in Polish culture, which is bound firmly between the frameworks of Catholicism and Marxism, will once again retard it in relation to the West, by some fifty to a hundred years.

One cannot leap over existentialism, one must vanquish it. Yet one will not vanquish it with discussion because it does not lend itself well to discussion. It is not, after all, an intellectual issue. Existentialism will be overcome only by the passionate and categorical choice of another life, another reality. By choosing this other reality, we become that reality. Generally speaking, in the future we should bid farewell to the methods of "objective" discussion, persuasion, and argumentation. We will not untie our Gordian knots with our intellect. We will cut through them with our own lives.

I resist the theoretical and systematic existentialism of philosophers because the world from which it issues is opposed to my life, it does not fit my life. To me, existentialists are dishonest people: this feeling is stronger than reason. Notice that I am not doubting their avenues of thought or the intuition by which they arrived at this doctrine. I am disregarding it because of its results, which, as existence, I cannot come to terms with or assimilate in any way. I say, therefore, that it is not for me and I push it away. At the instant that I dispose of their existential night of the single consciousness by passionate decision, I return a normal, concrete world to life and this is the world in which I can breathe. The point here is not at all to prove that this world is the most real reality. The point is the blind, stubborn affirmation of the temporal world in spite of that intuition, as the only thing in which is life is possible, as the only thing which is compatible with our nature.

We must be aware of existentialism just as we had to make ourselves aware of Nietzsche or Hegel. What's more, we have to extract everything we can from this—all conceivable depth and wealth. Yet we cannot believe it. Of course, we should wield this knowledge for it is the best knowledge we can attain, nevertheless, he who believes in it is grotesquely stiff, inertly ponderous, awkward and clumsy! Let us retain this awareness on a remoter plain, as an auxiliary device. Even though existentialism may blind us with flashes of the highest revelation, we have to disregard it. We should treat it with disdain. This is no place for loyalty.

TRANSLATED BY LILLIAN VALLEE

Czesław Miłosz

Nobel Prize Lecture

1

My presence here, on this tribune, should be an argument for all those who praise life's God-given, marvelously complex unpredictability. In my school years I used to read volumes of a series then published in Poland—"The Library of the Nobel Laureates." I remember the shape of the letters and the color of the paper. I imagined then that Nobel laureates were writers, namely, persons who write thick works in prose, and even when I learned that there were also poets among them, for a long time I could not get rid of that notion. And certainly, when, in 1930, I published my first poems in our university review, *Alma Mater Vilnensis*, I did not aspire to the title of writer. Also, much later, by choosing solitude and giving myself to a strange occupation—that is, to writing poems in Polish, while living in France or America—I tried to maintain a certain ideal image of a poet, who, if he wants fame, wants to be famous only in the village or the town of his birth.

One of the Nobel laureates whom I read in childhood influenced to a large extent, I believe, my notions of poetry. That was Selma Lagerlöf. Her *Wonderful Adventures of Nils*, a book I loved, places the hero in a double role. He is the one who flies above the earth and looks at it *from above* but at the same time sees it in every detail. This double vision may be a metaphor of the poet's vocation. I found a similar metaphor in a Latin ode of a seventeenth-century poet, Maciej Sarbiewski, who was once known all over Europe under the pen name of Casimire. He taught poetics at my

university. In that ode he describes his voyage—on the back of
Pegasus—from Vilno to Antwerp, where he is going to visit his
poet friends. Like Nils Holgersson, he beholds under him rivers,
lakes, forests; that is, a map, both distant and yet concrete. Hence,
two attributes of the poet: avidity of the eye and the desire to
describe that which he sees. Yet whoever considers writing poetry
as "to see and describe" should be aware that he engages in a quarrel with modernity, fascinated as it is with innumerable theories of
a specific poetic language.

Every poet depends upon generations who wrote in his native
tongue; he inherits styles and forms elaborated by those who lived
before him. At the same time, though, he feels that those old means
of expression are not adequate to his own experience. When adapt-
ing himself, he hears an internal voice that warns him against mask
and disguise. But when rebelling, he falls in turn into dependence
on his contemporaries, various movements of the avant-garde.
Alas, it is enough for him to publish his first volume of poems to
find himself entrapped. For hardly has the print dried when that
work, which seemed to him the most personal, appears to be en-
meshed in the style of another. The only way to counter an obscure
remorse is to continue searching and to publish a new book, but
then everything repeats itself, so there is no end to that chase. And
it may happen that leaving behind books as if they were dry snake
skins, in a constant escape forward from what has been done in the
past, he receives the Nobel Prize.

What is this enigmatic impulse that does not allow one to settle
down in the achieved, the finished? I think it is a quest for reality. I
give to this word its naive and solemn meaning, a meaning having
nothing to do with philosophical debates of the last few centuries.
It is the earth as seen by Nils from the back of the gander and by the
author of the Latin ode from the back of Pegasus. Undoubtedly,
that earth *is* and her riches cannot be exhausted by any description.
To make such an assertion means to reject in advance a question we
often hear today, "What is reality?" for it is the same as the question of Pontius Pilate: "What is truth?" If among pairs of opposites
which we use every day the opposition of life and death has such an
importance, no less importance should be ascribed to the opposi-
tions of truth and falsehood, of reality and illusion.

2

Simone Weil, to whose writings I am profoundly indebted, say, "Distance is the soul of beauty." Yet sometimes keeping distance is nearly impossible. I am "a child of Europe," as the title of one of my poems admits, but that is a bitter, sarcastic admission. I am also the author of an autobiographical book which in the French translation bears the title *Une autre Europe*. Undoubtedly, there exist two Europes, and it happens that we, inhabitants of the second one, were destined to descend into "the heart of darkness" of the twentieth century. I wouldn't know how to speak about poetry in general. I must speak of poetry in its encounter with peculiar circumstances of time and place. Today, from a perspective, we are able to distinguish outlines of the events which by their death-bearing range surpassed all natural disasters known to us, but poetry, mine and my contemporaries', whether of inherited or avant-garde style, was not prepared to cope with those catastrophes. Like blind men we groped our way and were exposed to all the temptations the mind deluded itself with in our time.

It is not easy to distinguish reality from illusion, especially when one lives in a period of the great upheaval that began a couple of centuries ago on a small western peninsula of the Eurasian continent, only to encompass the whole planet during one man's lifetime with the uniform worship of science and technology. And it was particularly difficult to oppose multiple intellectual temptations in those areas of Europe where degenerate ideas of dominion over men, akin to the ideas of dominion over Nature, led to paroxysms of revolution and war at the expense of millions of human beings destroyed physically or spiritually. And yet perhaps our most precious acquisition is not an understanding of those ideas, which we touched in their most tangible shape, but respect and gratitude for certain things that protect people from internal disintegration and from yielding to tyranny.

Precisely for that reason, some ways of life, some institutions, became a target for the fury of evil forces—above all, the bonds between people that exist organically, as if by themselves, sustained by family, religion, neighborhood, common heritage. In other words, all that disorderly, illogical humanity, so often branded as ridiculous because of its parochial attachments and loyalties. In many countries, traditional bonds of *civitas* have been subject to a gradual erosion, and their inhabitants become disinherited without realizing it. It is not the same, however, in those areas where suddenly, in a situation of utter peril, a protective, life-giving value of such bonds reveals itself. That is the case of my native land. And I feel this is a proper place to mention gifts received by myself and by my friends in our part of Europe and to pronounce words of blessing.

It is good to be born in a small country where Nature was on a human scale, where various languages and religions cohabited for centuries. I have in mind Lithuania, a country of myths and poetry. My family in the sixteenth century already spoke Polish, just as many families in Finland spoke Swedish and in Ireland English; so I am a Polish, not a Lithuanian, poet. But the landscapes and perhaps the spirits of Lithuania have never abandoned me. It is good in childhood to hear words of Latin liturgy, to translate Ovid in high school, to receive a good training in Roman Catholic dogmatics and apologetics. It is a blessing if one receives from fate school and university studies in such a city as Vilno. A bizarre city of baroque architecture transplanted to northern forests and of history fixed in every stone, a city of forty Roman Catholic churches and of numerous synagogues. In those days the Jews called it a Jerusalem of the North. Only when teaching in America did I fully realize how much I had absorbed from the thick walls of our ancient university, from formulas of Roman law learned by heart, and from history and literature of old Poland, both of which surprise young Americans by their specific features: an indulgent anarchy, a humor disarming fierce quarrels, a sense of organic community, a mistrust of any centralized authority.

A poet who grew up in such a world should have been a seeker for reality through contemplation. A patriarchal order should have been dear to him, a sound of bells, an isolation from pressures and the persistent demands of his fellow men, the silence of a cloister cell. If books were to linger on a table, they should be those that deal with the most incomprehensible quality of God-created things; namely, Being, the *esse*. But suddenly all this is negated by the demoniac doings of history, which acquires the traits of a bloodthirsty deity.

The earth which the poet viewed in his flight calls with a cry, indeed, out of the abyss and doesn't allow itself to be viewed *from above*. An insoluble contradiction appears, a terribly real one, giving no peace of mind either day or night, whatever we call it: it is the contradiction between being and action, or, on another level, a contradiction between art and solidarity with one's fellow men. Reality calls for a name, for words, but it is unbearable, and if it is touched, if it draws very close, the poet's mouth cannot even utter a complaint of Job: all art proves to be nothing compared with action. Yet to embrace reality in such a manner that it is preserved in all its old tangle of good and evil, of despair and hope, is possible only thanks to a distance, only by soaring *above* it—but this in turn seems then a moral treason.

Such was the contradiction at the very core of conflicts engendered by the twentieth century and discovered by poets of an earth polluted by the crime of genocide. What are the thoughts of one of them, who wrote a certain number of poems that remain as a memorial, as a testimony? He thinks that they were born out of a painful contradiction and that he would prefer to have been able to resolve it while leaving them unwritten.

3

A patron saint of all poets in exile, who visit their towns and provinces only in remembrance, is always Dante. But how the number of Florences increased! The exile of a poet is today a simple function of a relatively recent discovery: that whoever wields power is also able to control language and not only with the prohibitions of censorship but also by changing the meaning of words. A peculiar phenomenon makes its appearance: the language of a captive community acquires certain durable habits; whole zones of reality cease to exist simply because they have no name. There is, it seems, a hidden link between theories of literature as *écriture*, of speech feeding on itself, and the growth of the totalitarian state. In any case, there is no reason why the state should not tolerate an activity that consists of creating "experimental" poems and prose if these are conceived as autonomous systems of reference, enclosed within their own boundaries. Only if we assume that a poet constantly strives to liberate himself from borrowed styles in search of reality is he dangerous. In a room where people unanimously maintain a conspiracy of silence, one word of truth sounds like a pistol shot. And, alas, a temptation to pronounce it, similar to an acute itching, becomes an obsession which doesn't allow one to think of anything else. That is why a poet chooses internal or external exile. It is not certain, however, that he is motivated exclusively by his concern with actuality. He may also desire to free himself from it and elsewhere, in other countries, on other shores, to recover, at least for short moments, his true vocation—which is to contemplate Being.

That hope is illusory, for those who come from the "other Europe," wherever they find themselves, notice to what extent their experiences isolate them from their new milieu—and this may become the source of a new obsession. Our planet, which gets smaller every year with its fantastic proliferation of mass media, is witnessing a process that escapes definition, characterized by a refusal to remember. Certainly, the illiterates of past centuries, then an enormous majority of mankind, knew little of the history of their respective countries and of their civilization. In the minds of modern illiterates, however, who know how to read and write and even teach in schools and at universities, history is present but blurred, in a state of strange confusion. Molière becomes a contemporary of Napoleon, Voltaire a contemporary of Lenin.

Moreover, events of the last decades, of such primary importance that knowledge or ignorance of them will be decisive for the future of mankind, move away, grow pale, lose all consistency, as if Friedrich Nietzsche's prediction of European nihilism found a literal fulfillment. "The eye of a nihilist," he wrote in 1887, "is unfaithful to his memories: it allows them to drop, to lose their leaves. . . . And what he does not do for himself, he also does not do for the whole past of mankind: he lets it drop."

We are surrounded today by fictions about the past, contrary to common sense and to an elementary perception of good and evil. As the *Los Angeles Times* recently stated, the number of books in various languages that deny that the Holocaust ever took place and claim that it was invented by Jewish propaganda has exceeded one hundred. If such an insanity is possible, is a complete loss of memory as a permanent state of mind improbable? And would it not present a danger more grave than genetic engineering or poisoning of the natural environment?

For the poet of the "other Europe," the events embraced by the name Holocaust are a reality so close in time that he cannot hope to liberate himself from their remembrance unless perhaps by translating the Psalms of David. He feels anxiety, though, when the meaning of the word Holocaust undergoes gradual modifications, so that the word begins to belong to the history of the Jews exclusively, as if among the victims there were not also millions of Poles, Russians, Ukrainians, and prisoners of other nationalities. He feels anxiety, for he senses in this a foreboding of a not distant future when history will be reduced to what appears on television, while the truth, because it is too complicated, will be buried in the archives, if not totally annihilated. Other facts as well, facts for him quite close but distant for the West, add in his mind to the credibility of H. G. Wells's vision in *The Time Machine:* the earth inhabited by a tribe of children of the day, carefree, deprived of memory and, by the same token, of history, without defense when confronted with dwellers of subterranean caves, cannibalistic children of the night.

Carried forward as we are by the movement of technological change, we realize that the unification of our planet is in the making, and we attach importance to the notion of international community. The days when the League of Nations and the United Nations were founded deserve to be remembered. Unfortunately, those dates lose their significance in comparison with another date, which should be invoked every year as a day of mourning, although it is hardly known to younger generations. It is 23 August 1939. Two dictators then concluded an agreement provided with a secret clause by virtue of which they divided between themselves neighboring countries that possessed their own capitals, governments, and parliaments. Not only did that pact unleash a terrible war; it reestablished a colonial principle according to which nations are no more than cattle, bought, sold, completely dependent upon the will of their instant masters. Their borders, their right to self-determination, their passports, ceased to exist. And it should be a source of wonder that today people speak in a whisper, with a finger to their lips, about how that principle was applied by the dictators forty years ago.

Crimes against human rights, never confessed and never publicly denounced, are a poison that destroys the possibility of a friendship between nations. Anthologies of Polish poetry publish poems of my late friends Władysław Sebyła and Lech Piwowar, and give the date of their deaths: 1940. It is absurd not to be able to write how they perished, though everybody in Poland knows the truth: they shared the fate of several thousand Polish officers disarmed and interned by the then accomplice of Hitler, and they repose in a mass grave. And should not the young generations of the West, if they study history at all, hear about 200,000 people killed in 1944 in Warsaw, a city sentenced to annihilation by those two accomplices?

The two genocidal dictators are no more, and yet who knows whether they did not gain a victory more durable than those of their armies? In spite of the Atlantic Charter, the principle that nations are objects of trade, if not chips in games of cards or dice, has been confirmed by the division of Europe into two zones. The absence of the three Baltic states from the United Nations is a permanent reminder of the two dictators' legacy. Before the war, those states belonged to the League of Nations, but they disappeared from the map of Europe as a result of the secret clauses in the agreement of 1939.

I hope you will forgive my laying bare a memory like a wound. This subject is not unconnected with my meditation on the word *reality*, so often misused but always deserving esteem. Complaints of peoples, pacts more treacherous than those we read about in Thucydides, the shape of a maple leaf, sunrises and sunsets over the ocean, the whole fabric of causes and effects, whether we call it Nature or History, points toward, I believe, another, hidden reality, impenetrable though exerting a powerful attraction that is the central driving force of all art and science. There are moments when it seems to me that I decipher the meaning of afflictions that befell the nations of the "other Europe," and that meaning is to make them the bearers of memory—at the time when Europe, without an adjective, and America possess it less and less with every generation.

It is possible that there is no other memory than the memory of wounds. At least we are so taught by the Bible, a book of the tribulations of Israel. That book for a long time enabled European nations to preserve a sense of continuity—a word not to be mistaken for the fashionable term *historicity*.

During the thirty years I have spent abroad, I have felt I was more privileged than my Western colleagues, whether writers or teachers of literature, for events both recent and long past took in my mind a sharply delineated, precise form. Western audiences confronted with poems or novels written in Poland, Czechoslovakia, or Hungary, or with films produced there, possibly intuit a similarly sharpened consciousness, in a constant struggle against limitations imposed by censorship. Memory thus is our force; it protects us against a speech entwining upon itself like the ivy when it does not find a support on a tree or a wall.

A few minutes ago I expressed my longing for the end of a contradiction that opposes the poet's need of distance to his feeling of solidarity with his fellow men. And yet, if we take a flight *above* the earth as a metaphor of the poet's vocation, it is not difficult to notice that a kind of contradiction is implied, even in those epochs when the poet is relatively free from the snares of history. For how to be *above* and simultaneously to see the earth in every detail? And yet, in a precarious balance of opposites, a certain equilibrium can be achieved thanks to a distance introduced by the flow of time. "To see" means not only to have before one's eyes. It may mean also to preserve in memory. "To see and to describe" may also mean to reconstruct in imagination. A distance achieved thanks to the mystery of time must not change events, landscapes, human figures, into a tangle of shadows growing paler and paler. On the contrary, it can show them in full light, so that every event, every date, becomes expressive and persists as an eternal reminder of human depravity and human greatness. Those who are alive receive a mandate from those who are silent forever. They can fulfill their duties only by trying to reconstruct precisely things as they were and by wresting the past from fictions and legends.

Thus, both—the earth seen from above in an eternal now and the earth that endures in a recovered time—may serve as material for poetry.

4

I would not like to create the impression that my mind is turned toward the past, for that would not be true. Like all my contemporaries, I have felt the pull of despair, of impending doom, and reproached myself for succumbing to a nihilistic temptation. Yet, on a deeper level, I believe, my poetry remained sane and in a dark age expressed a longing for the Kingdom of Peace and Justice. The name of a man who taught me not to despair should be invoked here. We receive gifts not only from our native land, its lakes and rivers, its traditions, but also from people, especially if we meet a powerful personality in our early youth. It was my good fortune to be treated nearly as a son by my relative Oscar Miłosz, a Parisian recluse and visionary. Why he was a French poet could be elucidated by the intricate story of a family as well as of a country once called the Grand Duchy of Lithuania. Be that as it may, it was possible to read recently in the Parisian press words of regret that the highest international distinction had not been awarded half a century earlier to a poet bearing the same family name as my own.

I learned much from him. He gave me a deeper insight into the religion of the Old and New Testaments and inculcated a need for a strict, ascetic hierarchy in all matters of mind, including everything that pertains to art, where he considered it a major sin to put the second-rate on the same level with the first-rate. Primarily, though, I listened to him as a prophet who loved people, as he says, "with old love worn out by pity, loneliness and anger," and for that reason tried to address a warning to a crazy world rushing toward a catastrophe. That a catastrophe was imminent I heard from him, but also I heard from him that the great conflagration he predicted would be merely a part of a larger drama to be played to the end.

He saw deeper causes in an erroneous direction taken by science in the eighteenth century, a direction that provoked landslide effects. Not unlike William Blake before him, he announced a New Age, a second Renaissance of imagination now polluted by a certain type of scientific knowledge, but, as he believed, not by all scientific knowledge, least of all by the science that would be discovered by men of the future. And it does not matter to what extent I took his predictions literally: a general orientation was enough.

Oscar Miłosz, like William Blake, drew inspiration from the writings of Emanuel Swedenborg, a scientist who earlier than anyone else foresaw the defeat of man hidden in the Newtonian model of the universe. When, thanks to my relative, I became an attentive reader of Swedenborg—interpreting him not, it is true, as was common in the romantic era—I did not imagine I would visit his country for the first time on such an occasion as the present one.

Our century draws to its close, and largely thanks to those influences, I would not dare to curse it, for it has also been a century of faith and hope. A profound transformation of which we are hardly aware, because we are a part of it, has been taking place, coming to the surface from time to time in phenomena that provoke general astonishment. That transformation has to do, and I use here words of Oscar Miłosz, with "the deepest secret of toiling masses, more than ever alive, vibrant and tormented." Their secret, an unavowed need of true values, finds no language to express itself, and here not only the mass media but also intellectuals bear a heavy responsibility.

But transformation has been going on, defying short-term predictions, and it is probable that in spite of all horrors and perils, our time will be judged as a necessary phase of travail before mankind ascends to a new awareness. Then a new hierarchy of merits will emerge, and I am convinced that Simone Weil and Oscar Miłosz, writers in whose school I obediently studied, will receive their due. I feel we should publicly confess our attachment to certain names because in that way we define our position more forcefully than by pronouncing the names of those to whom we would like to address a violent no. My hope is that in this lecture, in spite of my meandering thought, which is a professional bad habit of poets, my yes and no are clearly stated, at least as to the choice of succession. For we all who are here, both the speaker and you who listen, are no more than links between the past and the future.

(1980)

Stanisław Barańczak

Tongue-tied Eloquence: Notes on Language, Exile, and Writing

Occasioned by Reading Josef Škvorecký

1

Among many hilarious, outrageous, sublime, crazy, profound, or otherwise memorable scenes that fill the pages of Josef Škvorecký's unparalleled *The Engineer of Human Souls*, one brief episode seems to me particularly pregnant with meaning. One of the novel's minor characters, Milan, a recent Czech defector granted asylum in Canada, is throwing a housewarming party. Except for his Canadian girlfriend, all the guests are, not unexpectedly, Czech émigrés:

> Someone is telling a joke about the Prague policeman who drowned trying to stamp out a cigarette a passer-by had tossed in the river. There is loud laughter.
> Barbara hands Milan his glass.
> "I suppose he's telling jokes?"
> "That's right."
> "Well," says Barbara deliberately, "couldn't you translate them for me?"
> "They're only word games. My English isn't good enough."
> "Then how about making an effort? Your English is good enough for some things."
> But Milan ignores her . . .*

---

*Josef Škvorecký, *The Engineer of Human Souls*, trans. Paul Wilson (London: Pan Books, Picador, 1986), p.141.

. . . and, bad conversationalist as he might seem, he is right to do so. On the list of things that are the hardest to translate into another language, jokes come a close second after rhymed poetry (whereas love entreaties, as Barbara pretends not to realize, are among the easiest, if they require any translation at all). This is particularly true when the jokes are Eastern European and told anywhere west of the Iron Curtain. Though no intellectual giant, Škvorecký's Milan understands that instinctively and immediately.

More sophisticated minds sometimes need a dozen years to grasp this simple truth. I have in mind the example of a famous Eastern European wit, the poet Antoni Słonimski, who in pre-1939 Poland had been nearly idolized by the readers of his side-splitting feuilletons published in every issue of the most popular literary weekly. At the outbreak of war he took refuge in the West and spent the next twelve years in London, but in 1951, of all moments, he decided to come back to Poland for good. Asked many years later why he had chosen to do so, he gave a disarmingly frank answer: in England, he was unable to tell a joke. No, he had no qualms about living under capitalism, especially since Stalinism anno 1951 was hardly a more attractive option. No, he had nothing against the English and their ways either: in fact, he was a declared Anglophile all his life. And no, he did not really feel lonely, or materially underprivileged, or socially degraded. What he could not stand was that whenever he tried to tell a joke to an English friend, he somehow was not funny.

For a while, he was determined to do anything in his power to succeed. He worked doggedly on his English and prepared all his jokes beforehand, endlessly chiseling their fine points and rehearsing for hours on end; once, before meeting some natives he particularly wished to impress, he stooped as low as to jot down a witticism on his cuff. All in vain; every joke of his was a flop. This would have been unbearable enough for a mere mortal. For Słonimski, who had spent twenty years building up his reputation as the wittiest man in Poland, this was sufficient reason to go back to the lion's den. There, hardships or no hardships, censorship or no censorship, he could at least sit down at his regular table in his favorite café, crack a joke, and hear his admirers laugh.

2

As told by Słonimski, this story of the return of the prodigal joker may well have been a joke in itself—the motives behind his decision were certainly more complex than that—but it says something about the expatriate's experience that usually escapes definition. And it says even more about the experience of the expatriated writer. After all, works of literature, just as jokes, are essentially "word games," as Škvorecký's Milan would have it. Easy for Robert Frost to say that poetry is what is lost in translation! Squarely settled in his homeland, he wrote for an audience that shared both his experience and his language, and it was of secondary concern to him just how much of what he intended to say was lost on some distant Chinese or Chilean reader. A writer who lives in exile has to care much more about what is "lost in translation." His foreign readers are within earshot, since he lives among them; if they don't laugh at his translated word games, it hurts.

Of course, he may choose to stay forever on the safe side, that is, to lock himself up in the comfortable cell of his native language and write exclusively for the audience formed of his compatriots, either at home, or in the diaspora, or both. (Needless to say, this solution is only relatively safer: literature that deserves its name is always a risky business, and the fact that you share a language, literary tradition, experience, and whatever else with your reader does not necessarily mean that he gives a damn.) But once the writer decides to reach beyond his native language and familiar audience, once he lets the very problem of "translation" cross his mind (regardless whether technically he is to be translated by someone else, translates his works himself, or writes originally in the language of his adopted country), the balance sheet of gains and losses will always loom in his consciousness ominously and inexorably.

3

What makes things even more bothersome is that the whole process of balancing the necessary losses against the uncertain gains is a two-way street. Trying to adapt his work to a foreign culture, the writer living in exile has no choice but to make this work lose some of its original flavor—that seems an obvious price to pay.

Less obvious is the fact that this loss has its reverse side: being, after all, an outsider in the culture he tries to conquer, the writer sooner or later realizes that some of this culture's qualities are lost on him as well. While attempting to hammer the peg of his work into the hard, resisting log of a foreign culture, he cannot but damage both pieces of timber, that is, simplify to some extent both the work and the culture as he sees it.

Again, the telling housewarming-party episode in Škvorecký's novel illustrates this double point in a neatly symmetrical way. Barbara's failure to comprehend an Eastern European joke is paralleled by Milan's failure to appreciate an allusion to American cultural lore. Her playing with a jigsaw puzzle (to which she, left out of the Czech conversation, has resorted) is for him just "a Canadian habit"; for her, it's an echo of a mythical Hollywood shot, one heavy with the symbolism of rejection, loneliness, and disenchanted love:

> How could he know it? When "Citizen Kane" last played in Prague, Milan was not yet in this world.
> "You never give me anything I really care about," says Barbara, waiting against hope for Milan to understand.

But the line is lost on Milan, as well as the message that Barbara's quote was supposed to convey. An exiled writer similarly loses a considerable part of the intricate meaning of the culture he attempts to enter. He may try, for instance, to tell a typically absurd Eastern European story: yet in order to believe in the validity of such an undertaking at all he has to block out his awareness of the fact that his North American audience has been brought up on a tradition whose pragmatism excludes the very notion of the absurd. Thus, in trying to impose his own vision, his own set of values, his own symbolism upon the foreign culture, he unavoidably distorts it: not only by enriching it but also by ignoring some of its intrinsic laws. And the only difference between him and Milan is that he is more or less aware of his ignorance.

4

Natural human egotism being a factor, however, it is understandable that what strikes the exiled writer first and foremost is

TONGUE-TIED ELOQUENCE · 341

how much of his own message is "lost in translation" or untranslatable altogether. A short poem by my coeval and compatriot, the Polish author Ewa Lipska, expresses it better than any semantic analysis. The poem is entitled "To Marianne Büttrich"; we are not told who Marianne Büttrich is, but it is clear that she lives on the other side of the European Great Divide, presumably in West Germany:

> For a year now I've been trying
> to write you a letter.
> But
> the locusts of my thoughts
> are untranslatable.
>
> Untranslatable are the people on duty
> guarding my words and grammar.
> My hours are untranslatable
> into yours.
>
> The black lilacs behind the window.
> The unbuttoned gates. The yellowed cigarette end of a day.
> The dead eye in the peephole
> at six a.m.
>
> *Rilke is untranslatable too.*
> *Die Blätter fallen, fallen . . .*
> *Wir alle fallen . . . .*
>
> I've got so much to tell you
> but
> a tunnel is approaching
> my delayed train.
>
> A long whistle sounds.
>
> *I'm tried, Marianne,*
> *I'm leaving for the Bermuda Triangle*
> *to take a rest.**

*First published in Lipska's *Przechowalnia ciemności* (Warsaw: Warszawska Niezależna Oficyna Poetów i Malarzy, 1985).

Mind you, Lipska is not an exile (though she has visited the West) and she wrote this poem from the perspective of someone living in Poland in the 1980s. Still, there is no significant difference between her and the exiled writer as far as the notion of the fundamental untranslatability of Eastern European experience is concerned. If anything, the feeling of tongue-tied helplessness is stronger in the latter case. It is exacerbated by an inevitable clash of two facts. On the one hand, any writer who moves—either voluntarily or under pressure—from behind the Elbe line to the West is convinced that he has a special mission to carry out. His task, as he sees it, is to open the Westerner's eyes to what is going on "over there" and what threatens to engulf their free and well-to-do world as well. But on the other hand, precisely because he is now in direct touch with his new audience, he soon finds out, to his utter astonishment and horror, that the Westerners do not exactly desire to have their eyes pried open. Czesław Miłosz is a writer who should know about this: he came forward with one of the first such eye-openers when he defected in 1951 and soon afterward published his *Captive Mind,* to the boos of the largely pro-Stalinist Western European intellectual community. In his brief essay "Notes on Exile," written much later in America, he describes this sort of clash as a classic paradox: in his homeland, the writer's voice was listened to but he was not allowed to speak; in exile, he is free to say whatever he wishes but nobody cares to listen (and moreover, Miłosz adds, the writer himself may have forgotten what he had to say).

Granted, in real life the stable symmetry of this paradox sometimes wobbles. There are areas and periods of suddenly awakened or slowly growing interest in the part of the world the exiled writer came from, and his voice may come through with unexpected force. But even then his experience is hardly translatable in its entirety. Consider two skimpy lines from Lipska's poem: "The dead eye in the peephole / at six a.m." The Western reader's gaze will slide over this phrase as just another metaphor, perhaps a slightly macabre one: it may remind him of, say, a scene from *The Night of the Living Dead.* For the Polish, or Czech, or Russian, or Rumanian reader, the phrase's impact is much more direct and its meaning much more specific. In the "dead eye" he will recognize the blank stare of a secret policeman he may have seen more than once through the peephole in his own door, and "six a.m.," as the typical time for police raids, will refer him unequivocally to the notion of a home search and arrest. If fear is the common semantic denominator of these two readings, it is fear of two distinctly different sorts: the enjoyable and leisurely fear of a horror-movie goer versus the ugly, shabby, completely unalluring yet very genuine fear of a citizen of a police state. The former smells of popcorn; the latter reeks of cold sweat.

5

"Wer den Dichter will verstehen, muss ins Dichters Lande gehen" (Who wants to understand the poet must go to the poet's homeland): old Goethe's noble adage sounded perfectly empirical in his enlightened time, but we, in our post-totalitarian epoch, should know better. Our century has known too many pilgrims who went "to the poet's homeland" only to be given red-carpet treatment, courtesy of Intourist, and a watchful guide, courtesy of the KGB. As *Political Pilgrims,* the well-known book by Paul Hollander, has documented, under certain circumstances there is nothing more false than the so-called eyewitness account. If the eyewitness comes from a nation or system with no experience in matters of all-out deceit and especially if he is willing to be duped, it is enough to hand him a skillfully packaged reality, and voilà—in his account all the barbed wire miraculously disappears and citizens' happy faces shine all around. Attempts to penetrate the inscrutable East from outside usually stop at the first banquet table with a generous supply of caviar. It speaks volumes for the futility of such pilgrimages that exactly caviar was the most vivid memory Billy Graham brought home from his preaching tour of the Soviet Union a couple of years ago. During the same tour the sharp-eyed evangelist did not notice a ten-foot-long banner with precise data about the scope of religious persecution, nearly thrust into his face by some naive dissident.

Perhaps, then, the West would, ironically, be better off if it believed so-called literary fiction rather than the sort of facts that the conveniently myopic eyewitnesses provide? Perhaps things have gone so far, indeed, that the inhabitant of the West thirsting for firsthand knowledge of the Eastern Bloc is much less likely to obtain it by visiting one of the Bloc's countries than by reading a poem by Czesław Miłosz, a novel by Josef Škvorecký, or an essay by Joseph Brodsky?

6

What I am saying amounts to a praise of the cognitive potential of literature, which here, in this hemisphere swarming with deconstructionists, is a rather contemptible opinion to hold. Yet at the risk of sounding hopelessly backward, I hereby admit that I indeed believe in literature's power in naming reality—or, to put it differently, letting us hear and comprehend reality's many-voiced hubbub more subtly and fully than any other kind of account. In this sense, the testimony supplied by the literary imagination may weigh more on the witness stand than the evidence of our senses, especially when the evidence has been fabricated in order to fool us; and the imagination may be a more efficient interpretive tool than abstract reasoning, especially when we face a reality whose absurdity transcends rationalistic thinking. As a witness, literary fiction nearly always beats both being on the safe ground of supposedly hard facts and being in the clouds of ideological dogmas.

This also—perhaps above all—applies to the works of exiled writers. Their evidence has a special value despite the fact that their precarious balancing between two worlds, two cultures, two value systems, and two languages puts them, in more ways than one, at a special risk. For one thing, there is the aforementioned barrier of different experiences: the audience in the exiled writer's adopted country, even if not entirely indifferent, is often unable to understand not merely his interpretation of reality but simply what he speaks about. And quite naturally so, since neither the material of their own experiences nor their inherited way of viewing reality has prepared them to accept this sort of literary world. A world in which, for instance (to draw once again on Škvorecký's *Engineer of Human Souls*), it is perfectly possible that one day workers in a factory are called to a meeting, aligned in single file, and ordered to sign, one by one and with no exception, a petition demanding the execution of the nation's political leader whom they were told to worship only yesterday. For an American reader, this is an Orwellian fantasy; for a Czech writer, this is what in fact happened in his country and what he could have seen with his own eyes.

Yet different experiences, heterogeneous though they may be, can be forcibly brought together by the writer to reveal some common human denominator; they can be juxtaposed and compared, and their mutual differences can be defined, explained, and reflected upon. The more annoying thing about literature is that all this has to be done in this or that ethnic language, which naturally limits the defining, explaining, and reflecting to the writer's native audience. (Classical dancers are, obviously, better off in this respect: the language of their art is international. But then, I somehow cannot picture myself pirouetting in public. Toiling at my untranslatable manuscripts poses, I should think, a relatively smaller risk of making a fool of myself.)

The problem of translation rears its ugly head once again. If someone has ever tried to translate a literary text, his own or someone else's, he knows well that the chief difficulty of this endeavor lies not in the mere tedium of rummaging through dictionaries and laboriously substituting one word for another. The chief difficulty is that two different lanaguages are never a mirror reflection of one another; their seemingly corresponding parts never exactly match. The semantic ranges of supposedly equivalent words in fact only partially overlap; or a meaning may be expressed by three different synonyms in one language and five in the other; or a word has no counterpart in the other language at all; or the emotional tinge of a word disappears in its foreign equivalent. . . . And we are still on the level of separate words; what about phrases, sentences, verse lines, stanzas, paragraphs? What about the nation's accumulated historical experience that reflects itself in the elusive connotations of words and expressions, not to be found in any dictionary? What about complications of a literary and poetic nature that raise the elementary incompatibility of two language systems to the second and third power? There is no end to the translator's woe, and his most brilliant effort may result at best in an approximation that is more ingenious than other approximations.

But the author—particularly the author who lives in exile and harbors the ambition to conquer the minds of his foreign-tongued hosts—is not interested in approximations. He wants his one-of-a-kind message to come across in unaltered and unbent shape, just as he intended it to look and sound. In this situation, the translator is

346 · STANISLAW BARAŃCZAK

the author's adversary rather than his ally, a spoiler rather than helper, a necessary evil. Even if the translator is the author himself.

7

A glance at the contemporary literary scene makes one realize that the panorama of ways of dealing with this problem stretches between two extremes. One extreme solution, represented, I believe, by Milan Kundera, consists in minimizing the translator's potential interference. The author is to make his original work as translatable as possible—in fact, he makes himself write in a deliberately translatable, clear and unequivocal style, so that the translator will not be prodded into too many deviations from the intended meaning.

The other extreme, best illustrated by Kundera's opponent in other matters, Joseph Brodsky, consists in skipping translation altogether. Brodsky's literary evolution in exile—as an essayist, but also a poet—has aimed at achieving linguistic self-sufficiency, becoming capable of writing the most artistically complex works directly in the language of his adopted country, so that the translator's services would no longer be called for.

Both extreme solutions may be admired for their radical boldness, and in fact it is very rare that a writer dares adopt either of them in their pure form. The more common solutions can be located somewhere in between: these are the fairly usual cases of authors who, for instance, are capable of writing a decent essay or article in their second language, but who wisely refrain from writing poems or novels in it and instead rely on translators (at best trying to keep their arbitrariness in check by cooperating with them). Even though the Kundera and the Brodsky solutions have their respective advantages, the risk involved in either is indeed great. In the first case, the writer constantly faces the danger of losing his unique voice, slipping into some bland, abstract, international style, sounding like translationese even before the translation as such has been undertaken. In the other, the writer is constantly engaged in a high-wire act of imposture, usurpation of a language that will never be genuinely his own; and the more breathtaking the heights of stylistic bravado he manages to reach, the more painful may be the fall. Of course, both Kundera and Brodsky are artists masterful enough to dodge these dangers. Yet even they are not shielded from the criticisms of those whose opinions matter the most—the readers for whom the French or English of these authors' works is a native language.

This is also true of anybody who attempts to bypass the translation problem on a more limited scale, for instance by trying to write—like the author of these words—some relatively plain essayistic prose directly in his second language. Perfect bilingualism is not a very common ability even when it comes to you naturally (for instance, by virtue of having been raised by a nationally mixed pair of parents), much less when you try to attain it by learning. As a practical consequence, the exiled author who writes in his adopted language can do pretty well without a translator but, as a rule, he cannot do without an editor. No matter how hard he tries, and no matter how linguistically proficient he is, there will always be some wrongly used *the*'s or *a*'s, some misshapen syntactic patterns, some ill-fitting idioms that will expose his hopeless position as an eternal outsider. After all, even in Joseph Conrad's English some Polish turns of phrase occasionally occur. Or so I'm told by native speakers of English.

8

This, obviously, teaches you humility. The chief reason why the exiled writer tries to write in the language of his adopted country is his desire to accomplish his mission—that is, to get his message across to a broader audience. But, ironically, exactly by accomplishing his mission in this way he fails to accomplish it in another, arguably more important, sense. For his mission as a writer is not merely to get his message across but also to leave his individual imprint on this message; literature's essence is not so much the message itself as the endless spectrum of "word games" (to quote Škvorecký's Milan once more) in which the writer's uniqueness may be revealed. This is extremely hard, in fact almost impossible, to achieve if you write in a language that is not yours by birthright.

True, even though the absolutely perfect command of a language is something an outsider cannot really acquire, he can, through a lot of effort, finally attain a fluency and glibness that make him sound almost like a native writer. But literature is something more than glib writing. It also includes the right—and necessity—to violate glibness, to make light of rules, to speak in a novel way without bothering to be correct. In literature, a new thought cannot emerge but from a new way of speaking: in order to say anything relevant, you must break a norm. And this is precisely what an outsider cannot afford, since if breaking is to make any sense at all, you may break only the norms that bind *you*, not someone else. If a native writer purposefully violates language, it's called progress; if an outsider does it, it's called malapropism.

The exiled writer is someone who has left the cage of an oppressive political system; but if he is to remain a writer at all, he must never really leave another cage—that of his native language. There, he was gagged; here, he is tongue-tied. The ultimate irony: those who are the most tongue-tied may have the most to say.

(1989)

Wojciech Karpiński

The Blazon of Exile

> *My yearning ache, my recollections*
> *I swear to preserve with royal care*
> *ever since I adopted the blazon of exile:*
> *on a field of sable a starry sword.*
>
> —*Vladimir Nabokov, "The Blazon"*

Some writers have a strange power of lurking behind one's back. They appear uninvited. Like intruders they whisper into my ear in the street a few ever-recurring words. At night they come to my apartment and take out their books. Not necessarily those which are there on the shelves. One of them, Gombrowicz, has marvelously described his own brief adventure of this kind. On his arrival in Paris someone lent him the novels of Genet. And then it began. He looked out of the window in his hotel: the street was empty. He went out. Genet was winking at him with his back, leaning against a lamp post. A compromising situation. And a possibility of blackmail. He was fascinated by the poetry hidden in Genet's phantasmagorias. A shimmer of the picklock to a safe containing the secret of a difficult and thrilling beauty. And yet, he had not even read Genet's novels carefully; he became fascinated by a new tune, his own, perceived in a flash.

I have in mind an intrusion of a somewhat different kind. Somebody's words, remembered in shreds, transformed, impose themselves on the imagination and fashion my words after their own mold. Such power did Nabokov win over me. Not with *Lolita* or any particular English or Russian novel of his. With what then?

With his imagined imagination, accessible on the pages of his novels in a pale reflection, directly marked on a dozen pages of memoirs, in a few poems, in a couple of interviews, in one or two political statements, in his life, which flickers from behind his work.

He rejected biographical speculations. He enjoyed playing with style, gazing into the color and melody of words. He liked setting traps, inventing a false author or a doubly false hero. He was happy when swindlers and demagogues, searchers of ideologies, disciples of groups and trends, let themselves be enticed, unable to see the individual color, the delicate shade of existence. And yet, his games, his style, and the treacherous flashes of his construction fascinate me because I perceive in them the traces of his personality, the outline of his biography, the one and only, not to be reduced to anecdote, although connected with it.

On the pages of his novels I traced the hidden image of the author, entangled in lines shaped into other themes, like in those drawing puzzles where one has to find a cat or a dog hidden in the contours of a landscape. He was an individualist who took pride in not belonging to political parties, not participating in collective manifestations, but he interests me against the contrasting background of the epoch. I do not look for the reflection of that epoch or its mechanical denials, but for the testimony of the inner independence of an unusual man in unusual circumstances. Just as one used to imprint on letters one's family seal in red sealing wax, sometimes with blackened streaks, so Nabokov imprinted in his work his crest, the blazon of memory and imagination.

What would he have become—that fantastically talented youth, born in the last year of the nineteenth century, having an enormous fortune at his disposal, admired by his parents, writing conventional poems, and passionately searching for rare butterflies—what would he have become had not the sword of exile fallen on him, depriving him of the memories of childhood, fatherland, literary tradition?

If he wanted to remain true to himself, he had to invent his past, to re-create and transform Russia with his imagination. To be true to fiction, his fiction, as if to his country. In 1919 he sailed away on one of the last boats to leave the Crimea, which was being captured by the Bolsheviks. He did not go back to Russia again. But he never left it: his Russia existed in his reminiscences and in his language, on which he steadfastly worked. In Cambridge, where he studied English and French literature, he spent time playing ball and tennis and writing Russian poems. In a cold room at Trinity College, an issue of the *Times* was burning in the fireplace while he read Dahl's dictionary and noted down in his mother tongue phrases that fascinated him. He put down on paper new lines of his poems. Then he went to Berlin. He continued to write poems there and began to write novels.

In 1925 he wrote "The Blazon," a short description of his leaving Russia. I am very moved by that conventional poem. Not by its form, but by its, I would say, spirit-of-the-future aspect:

The Blazon

As soon as my native land had receded
in the briny dark the northeaster struck,
like a sword of diamond revealing
among the clouds a chasm of stars.

My yearning ache, my recollections
I swear to preserve with royal care
ever since I adopted the blazon of exile:
on a field of sable a starry sword.*

In our century so many exiles bade farewell to so many fatherlands. It is not the banal description that fascinates me in Nabokov but the oath thrown into the future. The starry sword becomes real only against the background of the imaginary biography made probable by the work. While in Berlin, Nabokov imbued with artistic brilliance the Crimean moment of farewell, throwing a glance forward to as yet nonexistent Parisian and American achievements. This inner openness would help him in the future to find the meaning of his confiscated past, and was its transformed wealth, its motherland. The singled-out moment, the acceptance of spiritual gift, the rejection of force, the choice of freedom.

Years later he mentioned the impetus that threw him out of Bolshevik Russia—the artistic and political impetus. He never ceased to be an exile. His political views did not change in the

*From *Poems and Problems* (New York: McGraw Hill, 1970), p.31.

slightest after he departed the Crimean shore. He took particular pride in the fact that he was quick to see through the essence of Communist tyranny. He saw in it a dream of low equality realized in blood, boredom, and humiliation. In 1927, on the tenth anniversary of the Bolshevik upheaval, he wrote one of his very few political texts. I read his statement as a supplement to "The Blazon." In a few pages he provided an exposition of political nobility and defined the sense of exile: "I have contempt for the idea that wants to turn people into ants; I have contempt for this attack against my free self, for this boring page in the festive history of mankind. I have contempt for the sickening taste of *petit bourgeois* smugness; I do not even wish to mention the blood that has been spilt. Silence, slight shudder of the nostrils will suffice. But in the days of their jubilee, let us celebrate the ten years of our freedom. We are the wave of our motherland, tossed on other shores; the motherland which could be as free as our dreams are. Exile does not always mean sadness. We are the free citizens of our dreams. Let us forget for a while the toils of our wandering and remember the bright moments: the solitude in a foreign electrified night on a bridge somewhere, in the street, in a station, vis-à-vis someone's face or a rhythm of words."

In his view people ought to be ethically equal, while spiritually they ought to have the right to full diversity. The political democrat in him was united with the artistic individualist. He had his eyes open to dangers threatening that unity: brute force lurks everywhere. The specter of Zoorland (the totalitarian imaginary country from his novel *Glory*), the imposed equality in slavery, visited him not only in the nightmares of imagination. As a youth he managed to save himself from the Bolshevik force. He then assumed the blazon of exile. On his sky after that shone the starry sword of Liberty.

He swore the oath of freedom and memory yet again. He succeeded in evading the Nazi force first in Paris; then, at the last moment, in May 1940, he set off on a boat from France for America. The sword of exile reached him again. Behind him he was leaving a spiritual fortune, the rich literary achievement of a Russian émigré. He faced a decision, perhaps even more difficult than that taken twenty years earlier. He did not write for money. His Russian books brought him little. He did not need many readers.

But he wished for some resonance, albeit in a narrow circle, albeit in his own mind. But the world of his references, the world of Russian émigrés, was becoming a double mirage. New storms tossed the waves of exiles ever farther from their dreamed-of motherland.

Nabokov in his interwar incarnation, as the fantastic fairy-tale bird Sirin (that was how he signed his books), achieved success in émigré circles. He had literary antagonists whom he irritated with his aesthetic attitude, but his talent evoked respect. Nina Berberova thus described in her memoirs the moment when *The Defense,* Nabokov's first truly masterful novel, appeared in *Contemporary Annals (Sovremennye zapiski)*: "I had the feeling that my generation of young exile writers, dispersed from Harbin, Shanghai to Paris, Berlin, San Francisco, ceased to be a lost generation, struggling round foreign cities in vain. We obtained a justification for our wanderings. Sirin-Nabokov exists, his prose which opened new vistas, his free imagination, his style so perfectly obedient to his artistic aspirations; hence we exist too."

Fate did not demoralize him with literary fame that came too early. He was always a step away from it. His first two novels, *Mashenka* and *King, Queen, Knave,* were speedily translated into German and brought him some money, but then came the crash of 1929 and it was difficult to secure further translations. This was followed by 1933 and the new waves of Zoorlandian conquests. There was no room for his books in that sort of world. English versions of *Camera Obscura* and *Despair* did appear; however, the publisher wanted to be a prompter and a nanny, suggesting changes, the need for a happy ending. No, that was not for him. A few of his works were published in French, among them the excellent *Despair,* excellently translated. The young philosopher and critic Jean-Paul Sartre, even then on the trail of false authenticities and blind denunciations, wrote a review about the uprooted émigré, about the emptiness and barrenness of Nabokov's work.

His last prewar years, spent in Paris, were the most difficult. Just before his departure for the States he lived in the rue Boileau. He was writing just then his first English novel, *The Real Life of Sebastian Knight,* as well as composing his last Russian novel, of which only fragments were to be published: *Ultima Thule* appeared in the last issue of *Contemporary Annals.* He knew that he would never return to Russia; he knew that he intended to go to the States. He tried new language instruments, new spells for a new exile. His English, a language he had known since childhood, always seemed to him a stone implement in comparison with the Russian tongue, marvelously pliable and obedient.

It was at that time, however, in the last Parisian and first American years, that, as a consolation, the Russian poetic muse granted him the greatest favors. In that period his best poems were conceived. One of them in particular, "Fame," I found close to my heart. It comes to me in rue Claude Lorraine, in rue Boileau, during Parisian walks, in the metro, or when I read a book. It returns with a shred of internal rhythm, with an agglomeration of words. Nabokov's poem is like an accelerated rush of thoughts and images averse to discipline. A poem for voices, written in the States during the war, probably on those autumnal New England days when the air becomes salty-transparent and the Indian-summer sun inflames not only maple trees but also the daydreamings of exiles. A poem summing up old experiences, sketching at a whirlwind pace a new variant of Nabokov's blazon.

He wrote in his essay on inspiration that imagination visits him unexpectedly, whispers into his ear a fragment, a few words, makes him hold an image before his eyes without revealing the reasons. Then it disappears. Sometimes it returns a few years later and allows him to perceive more. I would wish that fragments of "Fame" were written while he was still in Paris, in that last winter and spring of 1940. Maybe for a while he took off the sadness of the Paris days, the elegant strangeness of the city, and, enchanted by the brightness of Parisian twilight, he began to speak to himself the cruel and intoxicating words, in the rhythm of a march, then a run. How fast such transformations are achieved! Gone are the slender houses of cool Paris, rue Boileau, and the Exelmans metro station—the goal of his wandering; there comes the moment of the saved word and proud memory, the moment of an accelerated rhythm of the heart and imagination. Gone are the problems of the right of sojourn, work visas, gone are the émigré quarrels; there comes the moment of shady clouds and voices. Nabokov runs in the rhythm of words, bittersweet like Medusa's smile, sober like the labyrinths of his novels and vibrating like them. In a split second he puts on a royal cloak, and covered in it he goes not to the alchemist's or political scientist's lab, not to a port or Parisian bar, not even to the Exelmans metro station, the apparent goal of his wandering, but to his motherland, from which he has never been exiled, because he is her memory and imagination, the oath of allegiance and manifestation of liberty. The words compose themselves into a mysterious and promising rhythm, the run continues, but the imagination has dispersed among Parisian houses, hidden in the crowd which is being swallowed by the mouth of the metro. The not-yet-author, somewhat abashed, stops, pretending to have had an outward reason for his run—a bus, a familiar silhouette. The whispered words have lost their lightness; their sense has scattered or assumed hideous shapes. No, there can be no poem made out of that. The rhythms have disappeared.

It will return, soon it will return. Again he will run down a Parisian street, open his eyes wide on the New York night. Once more a conversation will flow, a voice, many voices. Conversation with whom? Whose voice? This what the poem "Fame" talks about. Who talks? The music. I strip the poem of its Russian melody, of its English disguise; it talks to me. I hear it sometimes in Polish; it has run far from the point of departure, but I recognize the same silhouette, the same accelerated tangle of threads.

The exile's artistic blazon assumed different concrete shapes, continued to remain in his imagination, once perceived with the power of artistic gaze on the black sky in the flicker of stars, enlivened and transformed with the strength of spiritual effort, transmitted to others, to everyone who is able to discern in himself the sign of presence and exile, separation and assent. Stars were coded in letters which then dispersed on the sky like stars. Even in moments of despondency he remained a poet and an exile.

His political blazon did not change either, even when the time came for the most difficult choice to be made. It was the year 1944. His brother found himself in a German concentration camp. The outcome of the war was still in the balance. Hitler's new rockets were falling on London. On the eastern front Nabokov's compatriots were paying an immeasurable tribute in blood. In those circumstances many Russian émigrés viewed Stalin and his despotic rule in a different light. Some wrote about two motherlands, talked about changes, cherished illusions about changes. Some émigrés, on the other hand, more or less explicitly sided with Hitler, taking the view that anything that might liberate Russia from Stalin's tyranny was worth accepting. For the same reasons (i.e., that one must think politically and choose), many during the war, and particularly in the immediate postwar period, chose—more or less explicitly—Stalin. They were driven to the door of his embassy by poverty, pity, despair, fear.

In that situation, faced with those temptations, Nabokov let loose, or rather shouted out, a purely political poem, exceptional in his writings, which meant an affirmation of the vows of freedom, a new acceptance of the blazon of exile:

> No matter how the Soviet tinsel glitters
> upon the canvas of a battle piece;
> no matter how the soul dissolves in pity,
> I will not bend, I will not cease
>
> loathing the filth, brutality, and boredom
> of silent servitude. No, no, I shout,
> my spirit is still quick, still exile-hungry,
> I'm still a poet, count me out!*

Years passed. The mustached tyrant found himself in a mausoleum from which he was then thrown out. To Nabokov at last came fame, offered him by a little girl with a Southern sounding name, Lolita. His life and views basically did not change. Asked in an interview about his attitude to contemporary Soviet Russia, he restated his old convictions: "Well, historically I am a 'White Russian' myself. . . . [I define my alienation from present-day Russia] as a deep distrust of the phony thaw now advertised. As a constant awareness of unredeemable iniquities. As a complete indifference to all that moves a patriotic Sovetski man of today. As the keen satisfaction of having discerned as early as 1918 the *meshchantsvo* (petty bourgeois smugness, Philistine essence) of Leninism. . . . I have practically no contact with [Soviet citizens] though I did once agree, in the early thirties or late twenties, to meet—out of sheer curiosity—an agent from Bolshevist Russia who was trying hard to get émigré writers and artists to return to the fold. He had a double name, Tarasov something, and had written a novelette entitled

Poems and Problems, p. 127.

Chocolate, and I thought I might have some sport with him. I asked him would I be permitted to write freely and would I be able to leave Russia if I did not like it there. He said that I would be so busy liking it there that I would have no time to dream of going abroad again. I would, he said, be perfectly free to choose any of the many themes Soviet Russia bountifully allows a writer to use, such as farms, factories, forests in Fakistan—oh, lots of fascinating subjects. I said farms, et cetera, bored me, and my wretched seducer soon gave up. He had better luck with the composer Prokofiev."*

I like the courage of Nabokov's opinions, though I am aware of dangers inherent in them. What do I value in him? The quick rhythm of thought, the crafty clarity of words and images, the bold privacy of imagination, the combining—in the background—of mythology and politics. I go back to several fragments of *The Gift,* to *Despair* and *Lolita,* to the affectionate descriptions in *Conclusive Evidence.* I compose the splinters of his books into a new mosaic. The borderline between prose and poetry is then obliterated. Godunov-Cherdintsev swears that he will perpetuate forever the uniqueness of the moment when, there, on the old bridge, he, a boy, was standing one evening with a girl, swallows were flying, and the boy asked, "Tell me, will you remember forever *that* swallow—not swallow in general, not those swallows, but the one that has just soared by us?" And she replied, "Of course I will remember." And the two of them cried. That opening of imagination opened the future before Nabokov, and made it easier for him to maintain contact with the past. He was able to achieve a sovereign and courageous attitude to time.

He moves me most as a defender and exemplar of exile. He gave exile the patent of nobility. He was not the first, but in the twentieth century he did this in a truly lordly fashion. In his writings I look for the *lettres de noblesse* of such an attitude. I find the clearest reflection of the blazon of exile on the pages of his memoirs and in a few poems and interviews. I do not agree with all his opinions. He paid a price for courage. He was on occasion carried by formulas. He wanted to shock the Philistines of spirit, those who had views different from his. I read with pleasure his flights of pride. A few words to the emissaries of the Viennese shaman? Dostoevsky, Balzac, Stendhal—

Strong Opinions (New York: McGraw Hill, 1973), pp. 96–98.

third-rate writers? I like it, or smile at it, as one reacts to the icono-clastic brilliance of a bright high school student. No, I do not regard *Death in Venice* as the embodiment of vulgar pretentiousness. On the contrary, that novella is an embodied myth, impossible to sum-marize in formulas. Nabokov's statement about the four doctors who evoke revulsion in him (Dr. Freud, Dr. Zhivago, Dr. Schweit-zer, and Dr. Castro) seems to me, to put it mildly, unjust. One can perhaps look for an explanation in the fact that when *Lolita* was climbing up the bestseller lists, its serious rival, sometimes victorious, was *Doctor Zhivago*. This is not a justification, however; well, the years of splendid isolation left their traces. For that matter, one can hardly expect a balanced appraisal from someone who staked his entire life on a different concept of artistic creation, paying heavily for that choice. And yet, years later, the two books would be placed side by side as two fairy tales of amorous infatuation, two oaths of loyalty by two poet-exiles with exposed sensibility, unable to find a place for themselves in the surrounding world and unwilling—in spite of everything—to abandon their search.

Nabokov was particularly unjust to Pasternak, as if he could not afford to be tolerant of a different vision of exile. Was he afraid that the legitimacy of his choice would be undermined? On being awarded the Nobel Prize, Pasternak was first prevented from ac-cepting it and then subjected to a humiliating mind-destroying treat-ment. He wrote a poem in which he asked what wrong he had done by making the whole world weep over the beauty of his native land. Soon afterward, Nabokov wrote a poem whose beginning is a pas-tiche of Pasternak's verses. "What wrong have I done and am I a seducer, a criminal by making the whole world dream of my poor little girl? I know that people are afraid of such as I and burn on the stakes for their machinations and, as if from poison concealed in a hollowed emerald, perish from my art. Still, how amusing that in the last paragraph, despite the repairers and the prohibitions of the age, the shadow of a Russian twig will sway on the marble of my hand." How moving that after so many years he returned in a dream to his native land and saw there the shadow of his monument. It seems that the malicious tone of the poem weakened the brakes he usually put on himself, and the final image exposes the exile's dreams.

The roads of exile run in different directions; different are the means by which exiled artists control their dreams. Nabokov belongs to writers who are exceptionally aware. He reacted with enmity to all forms of exhibitionism. All the more moving are the flickers of candor. The twig swaying over the marble of his hand, a heraldic ornament enclosed in words, the seal of a uniquely intimate and important experience—that is how exiles struggle with time which they do not accept, while believing, against the world, against others and themselves, that time will come to their side and that theirs will be a victory beyond the grave. That is how with their works they compose blazons of exile, monuments of freedom.

When I read Nabokov's words, distanced by irony, about "the last paragraph," I think about another poem, incomparably more moving, which also deals with a future monument on Russian soil. For a writer as aware as Nabokov, silence was a form of confession. He sometimes spoke with a lethal lack of deference about his contemporaries, but I have not found that he wrote anything about Anna Akhmatova. And yet it was she who continued, and with what splendor, his beloved Pushkinian line of Russian poetry; it was she who remained faithful and free, great. She carried in herself the untouched Russian speech over and above the physical terror and spiritual slavery. In *Requiem*, her oath of allegiance, she engraved with words, ethereal and at the same time made of stone, her own blazon of spiritual liberty. She too went through exile, though it took a different form from the fate of the émigrés, which she feared, as she saw in it the temptation of infidelity (and maybe that was why she was not always just with regard to it). Those closest to her were taken from her—some were killed, others imprisoned; she was condemned to total loneliness; attempts were made to make her renounce her elementary values: freedom of mind and loyalty of heart. In her hiding she saved the memory of affliction and the sovereignty of word. Maybe that is why I read her poems on inspiration with a double emotion: they were written by a great poetess, and with them she defended herself from annihilation.

All the writings of Akhmatova are a monument to loyalty and liberty. In the last poem from the *Requiem* cycle she speaks about the monument directly:

> Again the hands of the clock are nearing
> The unforgettable hour. I see, hear, touch

All of you: the cripple they had to support
Painfully to the end of the line; the moribund;

And the girl who would shake her beautiful head and
Say: "I come here as if it were home."

I should like to call you all by name,
But they have lost the lists. . . .

I have woven for them a great shroud
Out of the poor words I overheard them speak.

I remember them always and everywhere,
And if they shut my tormented mouth,

Through which a hundred million of my people cry,
Let them remember me also. . . .

And if ever in this country they should want
To build me a monument

I consent to that honour,
But only on condition that they

Erect it not on the sea-shore where I was born:
My last links there were broken long ago,

Nor by the stump in the Royal Gardens,
Where an inconsolable young shade is seeking me,

But here, where I stood for three hundred hours
And where they never, never opened the doors for me.

Lest in blessed death I should forget
The grinding scream of the Black Marias,

The hideous clanging gate, the old
Woman wailing like a wounded beast.

And may the melting snow drop like tears
From my motionless bronze eyelids,

And the prison pigeons coo above me
And the ships sail slowly down the Neva.*

Ahkmatova's words came true. Her monument in front of the prison, her agony station, stands in the eyes of everyone who has read her poems. Still, it is a different monument of her that can be perceived in the czar's gardens and in the Florence of her dreams, "delusive, perfidious, mean, longed-for," to which she will return. Those are the victories of exiles, all exiles; that is why with such great effort they compose their imaginary coats of arms; that is why in moments of weakness or frankness they dream about monuments and let others dream. Those are dreams of memory—not so much dreams of bronze and marble, of genealogies, as of the blazon of exile, of perpetuating imagination which will keep faith with memory and will carry on the effort of the free spirit. Monuments bequeathed in their works help society to retain memory and freedom, and when these values are threatened, to regain them in the future. The knowledge of those works enables one to undertake fruitful journeys in time and space. Some monuments speak to me with a particularly great power. I think of them with gratitude. Their diversity does not bother me. Nabokov on the Crimean shore, and in his Berlin apartment, and in the rue Boileau, and in an American motel, and among Swiss butterflies. Akhmatova in her sublet room waiting for news from prison and the appearance of the muse. Pasternak in a dacha near Moscow writing down forever a few views of the Russian soil. Solzhenitsyn in Rostov and Moscow, in Zurich and Vermont, looking for old traces and with difficulty learning a new, hard freedom.

In other countries, real and imaginary, other traces have allowed me to embark on fuller journeys. I watched other monuments: Nietzsche in a Turin street and on Alpine slopes; Valéry in Parisian drawing rooms, Kawafis in the shops, cafés, and haunts of Alexandria; Rilke learning to see and die in a Paris hospital, on the rocks at Duino, in the Muzot tower. Those shadows have found their home in my imagination. Even closer are the native shadows. Mickiewicz in the rue de Seine, Słowacki in the rue Ponthieu, Krasiński between the Colosseum and the Lateran. Imagination

*From *Requiem and Poem without a Hero*, trans. D. M. Thomas (London: Paul Elek; Athens: Ohio University Press, 1976), pp. 31–32.

rushes to more modern times, to Miłosz's San Francisco Bay, to Gombrowicz's calle Venezuela in Buenos Aires, to Herling's Neapolitan alleys running down to Chiaia, to Czapski's house hidden among the trees in Maisons-Lafitte. There is no need here for plaster, marble, or bronze figures set in artificial poses; all that is needed is imagination which enlivens imagination. It is here. It is on Promenada Street in Warsaw that Herbert's Mr. Cogito grapples with a shapeless monster; it is in Sèvres, not far from Paris, that trees stand so upright, so upright, ferns grow madly, and imagination travels to the imagined Lvov, and it is on the walls of Białołęka and Mokotów prison, where the leaders of Solidarity were interned after the proclamation of martial law, that I see the new blazon of freedom. . . . It is here, now, in Paris, in the street named after the painter in whom Nietzsche saw the model of calm, that the words found in exiled writers shape themselves in rhythm and sense, bring calm in moments of depression, somewhere on the old bridge, among people and problems, on a foreign electrified night.

(1985)

TRANSLATED BY BOLESLAW TABORSKI

Adam Zagajewski

From "The Little Larousse"

HOW TO LEAVE A HOUSE OF SLAVERY

In a procession, with banners, singing angry songs and hymns of revenge, waving clenched fists at the oppressors.

Or one could also leave a house of slavery English style, bidding farewell to no one, dressed for a brief outing, volume of poems in the pocket of a windbreaker. The morning is fair and the forecast calls for a long, beautiful day.

THOMAS MANN

Slender, boyish, smiling, elegantly dressed, a true gentleman. Lucky—success does not abandon him—even in emigration. Destiny watches over him just as it did over Joseph. Sometimes I think Thomas Mann, a writer whom I admire, was the embodiment of the spirit of the times. He was the spirit of the times in his own slender person. This would, after all, explain the steadiness of his successes, from the first to final book. Others may err, but the spirit of the times does not, nor does it have memory lapses. The public does not betray it—the public, too, is the embodiment of the spirit of the times, its feminine, receptive half.

My point is this: the early Thomas Mann comes out on the side of dark genius, music, becoming, indistinctness. He is—at that time—an opponent of democracy. Later, however, he moves to the opposite side, he begins to understand that only democracy, in its Western, rational edition, can be a safeguard against catastrophe,

• 363

murder, blood. He talks more and more of politics. He stops being the mysterious artist whose next book is impossible to foresee. He is tranformed into a public man, he expresses opinions, says things that are generally correct (almost too correct—after the last war he was known to express sentimental statements on the subject of communism). His last great novel, *Doctor Faustus,* derives the genealogy of this dark genius from the devil. The novel's narrator is Serenus Zeitblom, an affable humanist, someone who would have great prospects of success in municipal elections.

Right before our eyes the spirit of the times changes its clothes, removes its dangerous shirt and dons a tie, becomes one of us. The dark genius has nothing to look for in democracy. The devil planned democracy quite differently: it is to be the deck of a ship full of smooth, aerodynamic objects. When a storm or even a large wave appears, suddenly there turns out to be nothing to grab on to. Of course I, too, prefer democracy, but I am troubled by the alternative—either a dark genius or the just boredom of democracy. Democracy is familiar with compromise, but the dark genius—no. Nevertheless a new alloy of these two elements is necessary. Desired. Unlikely.

SOLITUDE IN POLAND? IMPOSSIBLE!

No one really wants a genuine, awful, solitary solitude; no one chooses it. A relative, measured solitude can be desirable. We may want to lock the door because guests appear in it too often. If, however, no one visits us, we can easily leave the gate wide open. So let us not speak of ultimate solitude but of the other, less unusual kind: it does not exist in Poland, nor can it. Yes, Norwid, as we know, was alone in his lifetime. It is painful to imagine him on a bustling Parisian street, alone. But he was not really lonely, and he knew it, rightly expecting that his grandchildren would study him avidly. Not only did he not cut himself off from the community of people thinking in Polish, but he even belonged to this community as one of its more important partners, only momentarily unheeded, seeing as how he expressed himself against the current of popular opinion, popular fallacies, popular condemnation. He was more deeply entrenched in this community than many others, he was a whirlpool, not a wave, and that is why people did not want to read him.

And Gombrowicz? There were in his life—which we know from his own lips—years of almost complete solitude, the first Argentine years and really Argentine years—sensual, mute. But Gombrowicz told us about them and offered us his solitude.

Polish culture has a communal character and it is at once splendid and painful. Awful and splendid. Every word belongs to everybody. Every silence becomes public property.

THE DANGERS AND PLEASURES OF SLAVERY

I will begin with the pleasures; I could speak of this lightly or darkly, with feigned frivolity or exaggerated sadness. Instead, I will try to speak to the point. Slavery—as I have already said—orders the cosmos, which is generally very chaotic and full of riddles. Moreover, slavery makes me innocent, for it is not I who have enslaved myself, only a certain malicious and intimately known demon. Slavery is responsible for concentrating my efforts on attempts to liberate myself, and I immediately feel slightly troubled at the thought that someday I may succeed in doing so. And all the more troubled because I am somewhat familiar with countries deprived—as the result of incomprehensible circumstances—of the weight of slavery. I know these countries a little and I have seen how unhappy their inhabitants are. They consume tranquilizers, undergo psychoanalysis, kill themselves. They lack will because they have never been deprived of it.

Those among them who are more sensible and energetic than their brothers and sisters have understood one should not sit with folded arms while not far from their borders lie captive countries. Some establish parties advocating a program of enslavement and enjoy great popularity. Others, on the contrary, write very interesting books about my captivity, and in their free moments read books devoted to the same subject written by their colleagues. Still others try to visit my country as often as possible and use every vacation to do so. Sometimes they take packages with them. Sometimes, to regain a sense of well-being, it is enough for them to have another look at the low, gray sky, policemen with angry faces, and churches filled with sad and pious multitudes.

The danger of captivity: one should imagine there is a 200-watt light bulb hanging directly over my face and shining straight into my eyes. There are two possibilities. I can have my eyes open, and then the light blinds me. If, on the other hand, I shut my eyes, I still see nothing because a pool of darkness created by the irritated nerve endings of the retina merely replaces the glare. These two states, glare and darkness, correspond to two phases of captivity. At first the cruel demon is able to gain control over me. Then, when I have liberated myself from his dictates, the same dark pool hangs suspended over me like a hawk, and I see neither the world nor myself beyond it. The dark pool is usually called (internal) freedom.

THE POSITIVISTS

I share some of the aversion religious thinkers have for positivism. Disregarding metaphysics leads to the impoverishment of mankind, which weakens the foundations of culture and makes man susceptible to new, frivolous, or even criminal faiths. Please have a look: in interwar Poland, a so-called Lvov-Warsaw school took shape—a philosophical school that rejected metaphysics, concerned as it was with research in logic. After the war, the Communists took over. They began to destroy the universities, religion, the economy. They were introducing the country to Lenin-Stalinist order.

One might have expected the representatives of the Lvov-Warsaw school to submit to the demands of the new authorities. After all, they don't believe in God, they have discarded metaphysics, they are analysts, they are led by no great star.

Rules of logical or semantic analysis, big deal! There is nothing thrilling or solid in them, nothing that would promise spiritual ballast. It would have seemed, therefore, that these professors of philosophy and logic—representatives of nonmetaphysical direction—would, after a brief moment of hesitation, join the ranks of dialectical materialists and together with them and Engels study the changing states of boiling water.

Yet nothing even close to this happened. In fact, their reaction was just the opposite; these people belonged to the most resolute and bravest defenders of intellectual integrity. The new rulers despised them. They were removed from their positions, and great care was taken so they could not exercise "a harmful influence upon the young."

What happened? It seems to me we are dealing with something that goes beyond systems, and even metaphysics changes nothing here—there were, for example, quite metaphysical patriot-priests. We are not dealing with -isms here, but with integrity, a fatal force that exists in some and that others sorely lack. Such events and surprises force reflection and pose questions, such as: do the great historicophilosophical systems that wield categories as basic as metaphysics lose something as small as a grain of sand—or as the human heart—that is, personal courage, decency? There are things in the world that philosophers are helpless in facing.

One of the last representatives of this school was the now deceased Professor Izydora Dąmbska. During martial law, in the fall of 1982, I took part in a session in which she—a weak, bent old woman with poor vision—also participated. She was asked in the name of what values did she and a handful of others resist the pressures brought to bear on them. It was simple, she said, straightforward. She seemed unable to understand that one could behave differently.

Metaphysicians, listen to the old woman. Marcus Aurelius is also listening to her carefully and with appreciation.

ELASTICITY

Gombrowicz taught elasticity, suppleness of thought. Gombrowicz is honored in Poland, especially by doctoral students. He has become the Messiah of doctoral dissertations and even of tenure. But beyond this, he is not taken seriously. It is a rare person who sees the use he can make of elasticity, pliancy of thought. Quite the contrary, people reason thus: this country is enslaved; let thought, therefore, be hard and utilitarian. Let some study the nineteenth century, others the Russian question, still others modern economic theory. Even though the days when Gombrowicz was universally considered a madman have passed, it occurs to almost no one that thought can be somewhat artistic, disinterested, outside of current theories; that it may have no purpose—except cognition, except to play with cognition the way a kitten plays with a ball of yarn. Meanwhile, it could turn out that elastic, pliant feline thinking leads us *now* to the freedom promised to our grandchildren by hard and utilitarian analyses. All this for our grandchildren. Communists said the same thing: "Comrades, we must tighten our belts, we are working for future generations."

THE OTHER BROTHERHOOD

Where should one seek fraternity? Not in political parties and not at great meetings where cigarette smoke clouds the future of the world. And if one were to find fraternity elsewhere? If one were to seek it in the reality existing in us, unnamed and divine, clothed in a thick layer of platitudes like roses covered with straw in winter? People need expeditions, discoveries, agreements that last—thanks to art—no more than a split second, like the flash of magnesium in the studio of a provincial photographer. A brotherhood lasts one-half second, yes, it is this minimalist program I propose to all those gathered. And so the hope arises that a brotherhood limited this way will not be followed by an epoch of terror lasting years.

There also exists, it is clear, a first and fundamental fraternity, the understanding among those who rescue and bring help, doctors and pilots. The members of this brotherhood may use a very modest vocabulary, because the sense of their actions is not contained in words. A good illustration of the laconic quality of rescuers is the famous sentence uttered by Stanley at the end of his long African expedition in quest of the lost traveler: "Doctor Livingstone, I presume?" He was not mistaken.

THE LITTLE LAROUSSE

In some parts of this book, I allow myself opinions and judgments aimed against the tyranny of history. I express them in the name of what is *un*historical in us, in the name of the unhistorical man, who in each of us is a next-door neighbor to a very historical man, shaped by the course of history in Poland and Europe like a pebble, worked smooth by waves. Someone gives me a *Little Larousse;* I leaf through it for hours and look at the pages (it reminds me of the pleasure of leafing through the prewar *Arct's Encyclopedia* in my postwar childhood days).

The Little Larousse, as everyone knows, is constructed so that the first part is like a dictionary and constitutes something of an overview of the structure of the world. Here, ladies and gentlemen, you will find the teeth of mammals, instructions for building a mower, an illustration of a sailboat and a gnu, a branch of magnolia and a pineapple, an illustration showing the production of iron or the construction of a combustion engine. The second half, however, is devoted to historical entries and it is mainly full of outstanding personalities, people of action with prominent chins, and the wide brows of thinkers and artists. There are also maps, photographs, and reproductions of cathedrals, sculptures, paintings, famous bridges and mosques—it turns out that all of them arose in time.

Between the two parts of the *Larousse* stretches a kind of no-man's-land: a buffer zone that is not supposed to allow a violent conflict between the dreamlike structure of the world and its feverish life. The mediators are the Romans, as the pink pages of the center section contain mainly Latin quotations.

Nevertheless, the historical section is the most fascinating! The teeth of mammals, which endure immobile in the lexical sections, bite here; designs come to life, sailboats plow through raging waters, motors growl, antelopes dart lightly but more quickly than the earth rotates, prominent chins pronounce lofty speeches, clouds of thought drift over wide brows. The grindstones of the world revolve and conduct their creative-destructive activities, bridges rise, church doors swing open, people crystallize, the great figures of painters and statesmen, prophets and discoverers of TB vaccines. That which is most important appears: people whose existences were strong.

RILKE'S DEATH

In a book written by J. F. Angelozz I came across the details of Rilke's death. Rilke died of leukemia. He suffered tremendously in his last days and hours. Dr. Haemmerli—the doctor who cared for the sick man—wrote this about his patient: "The thought of having to die was so terrible to him that he put it away, never once asking what disease he was suffering from and never once mentioning the possibility of dying." He died the morning of 29 January 1926 in a Swiss sanatorium near Valmont.

Who died in the sanatorium in Valmont? One of the greatest experts on death European art had produced. For years he had been absolving death in his poems and letters. He wanted it to become a part of life, wanted it to merge with life. His *Duino Elegies* were a triumph over death. Rilke dreamed about transferring visible things into a spiritual sphere, making them endure. He did nothing else throughout his life. Letters, poems, his novel about Malte are a never-ending attempt to domesticate life—and death, tranferring them to a safe place, changing them into an image, into thought.

And then Rilke dies: "The thought of death was so terrifying to him . . ."

In Switzerland, in a sanatorium, dies a fifty-one-year-old man whose vocation was the domestication of death. One of the renowned representatives of this calling, this profession. Reader, you are not allowed to think I am for a moment reproaching Rilke with weakness, a lack of courage. I am moved to think there is an ineradicable boundary between spiritual life and everyday life where the former, the freer of the two, develops, creating forms. If even Rilke . . . if even Rilke—in his final moment—does not find support in the fruits of his own spiritual work, does this mean that only a part of life—and a part of death—submits to a spiritual metamorphosis, while a hard, cruel layer hides beneath, indifferent to incantations, words, and images, the eternally frozen earth? This would suppose spiritual life, in creating new spaces in us, in offering to us the boundless riches of impressions and metaphors by dint of which we create new worlds, slanted worlds slipped between real things like bookmarks between pages, at the same time leaves in us someone who we have always been and will be, who does not submit to the transformations of the natural man, afraid of lightning bolts and death, a greedy wild man who seeks shelter, a dry cave, and, above all, the next day, another sunrise, because he absolutely does not agree to imagining the end, the last sunset, the last supper, the last caress, the last dream, the last cherry.

The division that art has long been accustomed to express through two figures—each Don Quixote has a Sancho Panza and each Don Giovanni a Leporello—fits quite well within the breast of one man, and does not need two actors at all.

Death does not want to be understood. What is comprehensible in death is only that lighter part of death belonging to life, the almost transparent part. Death has within it its own Leporello. His business, his passions and hatreds, his irritated ambition will never be known to us. That someone never speaks, he strikes.

THE HEGELIAN STING

In *The Captive Mind,* Czesław Miłosz writes about the Hegelian sting, that is, about paralyzing minds with the supposed unavoidability of dialectics—and the Red Army. The dispute about whether or not Miłosz is right continues. His opponents claim there was no sting, just fear, fear of fear, the desire for a career, the need for safety, money, and an apartment in Warsaw, or just good old conformity.

Yet the effects of the Hegelian kiss are still evident today. They do not appear in loyalty to the Communist party, but in a real Hegelian sympathy for generalities, things that are common, universal, social, for living in history, in the historical moment, in the conviction that an invisible umbilical cord joins us with our neighbors and with the neighbors of our neighbors, in the inability to express what is individual, ordinary, mute. We are joined by a chain of good will. We are shackled by the immortal plural. Always together, always holding hands, handing one another the same cigarette, the same book. The unusual, ingenious justification: Poland. Instead of trying to understand what the world really is, what death is and how it proceeds, where God resides, instead of liberating ourselves as individual men, facing a mystery, threatened by damnation, rubbing up against salvation, we have our tried and true way, the word we use to silence the lips of destiny: Poland. We live our life by cutting it up, by dividing it into little pieces instead of offering it the corner of eternity we have found, a moment of silence, not a transitory moment marked by hurry, anger. But perhaps we do not even need to offer, to dedicate. That will happen of its own accord, without our knowledge. The generosity of the gift is important, not its address.

HEGEL AND KEATS

In European tradition Hegel is usually opposed to Kierkegaard, a juxtaposition understandable both historically and

logically. One could take this choreography of pairing philosophers and writers even farther. Ultimately both Hegel and Kierkegaard were mad dialecticians. Moreover, Hegel was a detective,
believing, as apparently all policemen do, in the truism that all
criminals return to the scene of the crime. That is why he built a
system where, if I remember correctly, the Absolute calls the world
to life, leaves it, goes away, until it finally returns, really returns to
the scene of the crime where inspector Hegel is waiting with an
arrest warrant (it turns out he is God as well). Kierkegaard was
more modest, he circled Copenhagen aimlessly, read the Bible,
listened to Mozart—all in order to accuse him.

If one wants to find someone altogether different from the
Prussian philosopher, one must go elsewhere. To John Keats, for
example, the poet who died young. Keats believed things exist, that
some of them are beautiful. He believed, or rather he simply knew,
that the contours of objects are hard. If something is, then it is.
Meadows and forests really exist and our rapture is also no illusion
although it cannot last forever. A nightingale concealed in the
branches of a tree does not lead Keats to reflections of a theological
or historiosophic nature. Keats does not contradict the nightingale
and does not cast doubt on its sensual nature, because he hears its
song, he is intoxicated and happy.

Things exist, clouds move slowly across the sky, mountain
streams fall in a light foam over the cliffs, the pines sway in the
wind, their trunks creaking. Homage is due the world. The song of
a nightingale is at once final and ruthless and cannot be undermined, but it also conceals the vague desire to have some other song
respond, a poem by Keats, for example.

TO BE ENSLAVED

That we could find ourselves enslaved is possible. There is just
one thing to avoid at all cost—*becoming* a slave.

(1990)

TRANSLATED BY LILLIAN VALLEE

Adam Michnik

Don Quixote and Invective

For Stanisław Barańczak

1

Fifty years have passed since a certain German emigrant published an open letter in a New York paper that put him outside the
fold of official German life. His critics even claimed that he had put
himself outside the German nation. They argued, what good is a
writer who abandons his nation at so crucial a moment? What good
is a writer who attacks the German state in a foreign, hostile press
and thereby participates in anti-German propaganda financed by
the enemies of Germany? Does a writer like this, who allows himself megalomaniacal aspirations to govern souls in Germany, have
the right to expect his country to agree to publish his books? No!
The German people will not tolerate renegades spreading slander
about "brown terror" in a country they left in so mean-spirited a
way. Such emigrants slander Germany in order to ingratiate themselves with their foreign sponsors. Foreigners find the national revolution and rebirth in Russia a bitter pill to swallow—that is why
they attack the new order and its leaders. But they should have no
illusions: the German people will be deaf to the calumny and appeals of turncoats and subversives; the German people will not
permit others to blacken the names of their most cherished sons,
leaders of the Nationalist Socialist party, who run a legal government and conduct a policy of stabilization. The Germany governed
by Adolf Hitler does not want war—it wants order and peaceful

cooperation. Germany remembers well the Weimar epoch of anarchy, upheavals, strikes, unemployment, and the specter of hunger. There will be no going back to those times. Germany is undergoing normalization. The subversives are isolated.

They, these fair-weather patriots, also say that the German state is a threat to peace. It would be hard to come by a more flagrant lie. Germany—the chancellor of the Reich, Adolf Hitler, has declared this on several occasions—wants peace with everyone. Thoughts of expansion are alien to Germany. This peace must, however, be a just peace, free from dictates and interferences in internal affairs. That is why it is necessary to break with the ideologizing of international politics, with its attempt to blockade Germany, with its criminal plans to support the internal enemies of the German state or its traitorous emigrants. Against this background of interference in the internal affairs of Germany, no agreements are possible.

2

Thomas Mann, Nobel laureate in literature, knew the language of these arguments inside out. He couldn't stand nazism, and much earlier, in his well-known essay "Goethe and Tolstoy," spoke of it bluntly.

> I do not propose to dwell upon German fascism, nor upon the circumstances, the quite comprehensible circumstances, of its origin. It is enough to say that it is a racial religion, with antipathy not only for international Judaism, but also, quite expressly, for Christianity, as a humane influence; nor do its priests behave more friendly toward the humanism of our classical literature. It is a pagan folk-religion, a Wotan cult; it is, to be invidious—and I mean to be invidious—romantic barbarism. It is only consistent in the cultural and educational sphere, where it seeks to check the stream of classical education, to the advantage of the primitive German heritage.*

*Thomas Mann, *Essays of Three Decades*,trans. H. T. Lowe-Porter (New York: Alfred A. Knopf, 1971), p. 172. Most of the subsequent excerpts from Mann's letters are taken from *Letters of Thomas Mann, 1889–1955*, selected and trans. Richard and Clara Winston (New York: Alfred A. Knopf, 1971); the remainder (unavailable in English) have been translated from the Polish as cited by Michnik. Subsequent references, to either *Essays* or *Letters*, are in the text.—TRANS.

Mann did just the opposite. He defended the humanist tradition and classicism, the life of the spirit bequeathed by the past. Subsequent Nazi excesses made him realize he could not limit his reaction to a careless shrug of the shoulders. Nazi propaganda could count on being effective among the German people; it could also count on finding believers among disoriented foreigners. But these were not the only reasons for his concern. He realized that the status of an exile—especially within German tradition—was ambiguous: it meant breaking with collective national destiny and choosing a separate road. Such a decision is always difficult and always costly. Perhaps this was why he was reluctant to assume expatriate status right away?

Let us recall: he found himself in exile quite accidentally. In February 1933 he and his wife left Germany because Mann was giving a series of lectures abroad. In the course of his voyage, he stopped in Switzerland. That is where he learned of Hitler's seizure of power. He could not, nor did he want to, return to a totalitarian Germany. ("The question arises . . . whether the air there will be breathable for me," he wrote.) He did want to be present in Germany through his books, however. And thus while other refugees, including Mann's children and his brother Heinrich, engaged in anti-Nazi political activity, he, a Nobel laureate, the greatest name in modern German literature—*said nothing*.

Why did he keep silent? wondered German emigrants. He was often asked this question. One literary critic felt his silence was due to the "incapacity to make decisions and solve problems" that was so typical of liberalism when faced with "the irrational and anti-intellectual currents of the epoch." In a private letter Thomas Mann protested against this interpretation. He wrote:

I have sacrificed two thirds of my worldly possessions in order to be able to live in freedom outside the German frontiers. And even without engaging in furious polemics against the Third Reich, by being outside I am perpetually demonstrating against what is being done in Germany and to Germany today. It has seemed to me worthwhile to remain in contact with my German public, which by character and culture is in opposition to Hitler's system today and from which someday the countermovement against it can emerge. This contact would be immediately destroyed—that is, my books, which the Germans can still read, would have been banned at once—if I had drawn my sword more plainly than I have in any case done in my statements of recent years. (*Letters,* p. 237)

When on his sixtieth birthday, in 1935, he received many letters from Germany, he was pleased. "The hundreds of letters from Germany—yes, yes, from Germany, even from labor camps—have done my heart good. The need to demonstrate an inner freedom must be strong and widespread if the occasion was seized upon so readily."

Nonetheless these self-interpretations were received with a dose of skepticism. Mann was accused of allowing his silence to be used by semiofficial Nazi propaganda. People sneered at his concern for honoraria from German publishers, for saving his home in Munich and other material possessions. These were not completely groundless accusations. Everyone—even Thomas Mann—gives in not just to spiritual but also to completely prosaic temptations: the author of *The Magic Mountain* made no secret of this. In an April 1934 letter to another exile-friend, he wrote:

My abhorrence of conditions there, and my ardent desire to see the gang in control there go to hell one way or another in the shortest possible time, has not changed in the slightest. But I see less and less why I should be excluded from Germany for the sake of these idiots, or should leave them my belongings, house, and property. I am continuing my efforts to wrest these things from the hands of the Munich hoodlums; and since, to the disappointment of these same hoodlums, I was not expatriated during the latest deportations, there actually is some chance that I will regain possession in the foreseeable future. To have our own furniture would mean a great saving in rent for us, and it would also be a psychic reassurance to be surrounded by the objects of our previous life. But the chief point is that recovering them would be a triumph over the present tyrants of Munich and would willy-nilly have to be accompanied by the renewal of my passport. Then I could at least travel to the Memel area to see to our house there. I claim the right of such freedom of movement; I feel their denying me that freedom is an outrage. Isn't that a possible attitude, *too?* Do tell me whether you regard it as treasonous and unprincipled. (*Letters,* p. 216)

Thus he vacillated between temptations and desires. He deluded himself: he got nothing back. Can one hold his calculations and illusions against him? Wouldn't holding these things "against him" conceal some ugly feature of character that allows us to demand that others live as saints and exclusively according to our expectations?

I am inclined to answer this question in the affirmative. I am inclined to believe that in the secret ease with which we believe the most repugnant slander about emigrants, and how others can be controlled by the specter of material gratifications, lies one of the chinks through which totalitarian dictatorships secrete venom into human souls. Our aroused envy of exiles is supposed to reconcile us to our torturers. How sad this is. . . .

Mann was caught in the cross fire. The newly created Union of Reich Writers demanded he declare that he served literature in the spirit of "national authority." Emigrants were waiting for him to make a clear-cut break. Everyone held Mann's indecision against him. And he kept silent; he did not want to decide one way or another. Why? His reticence concealed other, unrevealed motives. Mann feared becoming reduced by politics. For so many years he had defended his status as an "apolitical man," as a writer independent of parties and doctrines, and had protected himself with his famous irony from the vulgarity, dirt, and Manichaeanism of the world of politics that one may assume he was well aware of the dangers awaiting a writer reduced to the political medium. He was writing *Joseph and His Brothers* at the time, and he wanted to offer this book to his German readers. He could do this only at the price of silence. Did he have the right to do this?

3

He pondered the question himself. He wrote about his doubts in private letters. Taken together they make an unusual, if unplanned, literary work and a fascinating chapter in the *Bildungsroman* that was his life. In August 1934 he wrote:

Daily events in Germany so sharply irritate my moral, critical conscience that work on my third volume has come to a total halt; I am on the point of setting it aside in order to devote myself to a political credo and polemic in which I relieve my heart and take revenge for all the spiritual injury inflicted on me during this year and a half. Maybe I can deliver a blow that the regime will feel. Of course I am miserable about the novel, which in any case has been delayed, and I know very well how many arguments there are against such an investment of time and energy. Is there even any sense in neglecting finer duties to argue against this rot? On the other hand, isn't it also a duty which the world would thank me for? In short, I vacillate and don't know what to put my hand to—a horrible condition. (*Letters*, p. 225)

He also wrote:

What concern is "world history" to me, I suppose I ought to think, so long as it lets me live and work? But I cannot think that way. My moral-critical conscience is in a state of constant exacerbation, and it is becoming more and more impossible for me to continue pursuing the, it may be, sublime game of novel writing until I have "rendered an accounting" and unburdened my heart of its concern, its perceptions, its pain, as well as its freight of hatred and contempt. . . . The time seems ripe for such a statement as I have in mind, and the moment might soon come when I would repent having delayed too long in silence. (*Letters*, p. 224)

He wrote as well, and this is an important remark, that he felt the world crisis as a crisis in his own life and work; this is how the main conflict of the epoch was reflected in him. As if he were justifying himself to us. And we? We say sometimes that the duty of an intellectual is to "testify to values." And we say too that realism, efficacy, should determine all public undertakings. Undoubtedly, both of these postulates are correct. In formulating them together, however, we seem to forget rather easily that this life strategy of a "golden mean" allows harmonious existence only when democratic norms of living together function, when pluralism and the principle of dialogue are the natural environment of human words and gestures. The essence of totalitarianism is the destruction of this natural environment. When the order of pluralism dies, the rules and criteria of normal existence die with it. Whoever lives in the old way and does not accept, or pretends not to accept, the existing changes, whoever wants to live in a totalitarian system according to rules formed by the order of democratic pluralism, is either a saint ripe for martyrdom or a hypocritical conformist ready for betrayal. He is a saint if he speaks the words whose natural result are a concentration camp; he is a flunky if in making gestures that seem apolitical on the surface, he registers acquiescence to totalitarian institutions.

In Mann's letters, there is the record of his ending a friendship on these grounds. When in 1918 his youngest daughter, Elizabeth-Veronica, was baptized, the presiding pastor was Kuno Fiedler, the godfather Ernst Bertram, Mann's friend, an essayist and literary historian, the author of a well-known book on Nietzsche. After the Nazis' accession to power, Kuno Fiedler "found himself" in prison, while Ernst Bertram found himself in "the new reality." The fate of Mann's two friends was symbolic of the alternatives of the time, a prison cell or intellectual self-enslavement.

Ernst Bertram tried in November 1933 to convince Mann not to submit to the exile propaganda that was villifying Germans in the eyes of the world, to discard the "distorting glasses" and look at the "new Germany" with faith in its future, to remember that certain painful excesses are simply the inevitable price of the "national revolution," for "you can't make an omelet without breaking eggs." Bertram tried to assure Mann that "everything was normal."

Mann answered his friend in a letter written in January 1934. He wrote with considerable respect and the same amount of resolve. He thanked Bertram for his "great epistolary effort," "that generous sacrifice of time and energy," and then he declared: "I shall not embark on a reply and an attempt at correction, for it would necessarily be endless and hopeless. We have moved too far apart, and arguing back and forth can only cause more sadness on both sides."

He assured Bertram that Hitler's propaganda was demonizing the emigrants' significance, and that his conception of their role and influence was greatly exaggerated. "If the whole world has not yet reached a proper understanding of the grace and dignity of your Germany, the wholly uninfluential exiles are not to be blamed or credited for that. The widespread notion to the contrary among your fellow countrymen is totally benighted, and it would be a good thing if you opposed it." In explaining his point of view, he wrote:

> No, I do not regard the new Germany (but can it be called new? it
> is simply that the same forces which have oppressed and

threatened us for more than ten years have now achieved absolute autocracy) through any distorting medium. Rather, I see it as I am accustomed to see things, with my own eyes. I know its thoughts and works, its style of speaking and writing, its bad—in every sense of the word—German, its base moral and intellectual level proclaimed with astonishing frankness. I know all this, and it suffices. I am sure that you too occasionally find this level an embarrassment, however fiercely you may deny it. But I use far too facile a word for things that are ultimately mortally serious. (*Letters*, p. 206)

And last he tried to talk Bertram into taking a trip to Switzerland: "We will be able to talk about the 'landslide of the century' with the requisite manly control." The meeting never came to pass, however. Bertram put his lectures on the spirit of the "new Germany" and the "national revolution" ahead of his conversations with Mann.

A few months later, in one of his letters to a friend, Mann wrote: "My old friend Bertram recently gave a speech in honor of Schiller, in which he called him 'a Doric' German-Frederickian man.' Those people have really lost their minds. It almost tempts one to warn them: 'Children, consider how this will look in a few years.' " To Bertram he wrote bluntly:

I have been reading your essays with all the response that your upright and judiciously intelligent Germanism has always aroused in me. That you are capable of confounding this Germanism with its basest travesty and taking the most repulsive scarecrow begotten by world history for the "savior" of whom your poet speaks— this is a constant grief to me, a grief that often enough all but converts into its opposite the feeling of which it ultimately is an expression. I am surely not speaking with exaggerated solemnity when I remind you that if I had followed your well-meant and insistent advice I would today—the probability is so great that it may just as well be called a certainty—no longer be alive. What would that matter, you will say, compared with the "historical creativity" now in progress? Of course it would not matter. And yet I sometimes think that this certainty, simply in view of your nature, should slightly modify your credulous support of the powers from whose grasp a merciful fate has preserved me.

"We shall see," I wrote to you a good while back, and you replied defiantly: "Of course we shall." Have you begun to see?

No, for they are holding your eyes closed with bloody hands, and you accept the "protection" only too gladly. The German intellectuals—forgive the word, it is intended as a purely objective term—will in fact be the very last to begin to see, for they have too deeply, too shamefully collaborated and exposed themselves. (*Letters*, p. 222)

One must know Thomas Mann's prose and essays well, one must continually remember his cultural refinement, the reticence of his feelings, and his fascination with German spirituality and zealous World War I patriotism to truly understand how much these words must have cost him.

How differently he related good news! In a letter to his brother Heinrich written two years later, he described a miraculous meeting: "Out of the house, like a ghost, Dr. Fiedler came to meet us. He escaped from a police prison in Würzburg, jumped over two walls, he himself cannot explain how he did it; some brave Tell transported him across the lake in a boat. . . . Now we are pampering and coddling him."

But he didn't coddle the Nazis for an instant.

4

The invective in Thomas Mann's letters of those years says the most about his mood. This paragon of impeccable manners used a gamut of unparliamentarian epithets in characterizing the Nazis. He wrote about "the ruling gang," "idiots," and "hoodlums"; about "the repulsive clown" and "the miserable wretch"; about "the excrescence" and "villains," "obscurantist cretinism," "grim farce," "base servility," and "spiritual castration." Why did he lose control of his tongue?

In simplest terms, he was enraged because his moral sense had been offended, because those closest to him had been hurt. This answer, however, is unsatisfactory. It does not explain why an inner voice told him to respond to the "landslide of the century" with the linguistic landslide of his private correspondence. Let us repeat the question: why did he write about the legal government of the German state, recognized by all foreign capitals, in the language of a barroom brawl?—he, the epitome of German patrician courtesy.

Thomas Mann had been a patriot of the German state. In contrast to his brother Heinrich, he always kept his distance from the formulas of the international left. Revolutionary criticism in the name of supranational values was alien to him. He followed in the footsteps of Luther and Goethe, which for him meant a program of loyalty to the German nation and state. This was the world of his values; if there was room here for opposition to the government, then it was only in a language of loyalty toward the law and an ironic distance to the pressure of historical events. This "apolitical man" was clearly afraid of being sucked dry by politics, with its one-dimensionality and inescapable fanaticism. And by the language of politics in which arguments are replaced with words of abuse. Why then did he reach for invective?

He was a writer who was familiar with the ambivalence of human destiny. He knew that every right has its counterright, that every conclusion is an oversimplification, that a natural and splendid feature of human existence is openness, ambiguity, and the multiplicity of values. He knew that only irony and friendly appraisal of all the formulated positions allow harmonious participation in culture. He knew this better than any other German writer. Why then did he reach for invective?

He loved his nation and his state. He knew how to look with unjaundiced eye upon the gentry, the middle class, and the rebels; the emperors and Bismarck; the generals and Social Democrats. He was able to discern the authentic values in each of these spiritual stances. It was only in regard to the Nazis that he could not. Here he gave up discursive language, friendly appraisal, dialogue in the name of understanding. Here he reached for invective. Why?

We are trying to understand why he felt it was impossible to conduct polemics with the Nazis.

To a friend he wrote: "So-called National Socialism has no place at all within any European and ethical framework. It stands in opposition not just to 'liberalism' and 'Western democracy,' but also to civilization in general" (*Letters*, p. 226).

This is how he assessed the devastation of the natural environment of pluralism. This meant that a man in Germany, subject to the pressure of terror and totalitarian propaganda, lost the capacity to distinguish good from evil, truth from falsehood; he lost the elementary power of recognizing the contours of reality and the causal ties governing it. Such a man cannot be a partner in dialogue, for dialogue is by its very nature the privilege of people who are free. A German repeating Goebbels's formulas about Jewish domination is as sensitive to arguments as the fanatic who believes two plus two is five. Self-stupefaction and self-imposed blindness result in—this was Mann's intuition—the inefficacy of reasoned persuasion. Instead one needs a sharp, piercing shout and coarse words that can disturb the internal order of the self-infatuated mind.

After all at stake was—the very soul of the German people. Thomas Mann had a clear idea of what could be lost in the struggle. He labeled nazism barbarism and used his authority to defend democratic order and the frail humanism that was growing weaker day by day. In the essay "Goethe and Tolstoy" already mentioned above, he wrote:

> The question is put today whether this Mediterranean, classic, humanistic tradition is commensurate with humanity and thus coeval with it, or whether it is only the intellectual expression and appanage of the bourgeois liberal epoch and destined to perish with its passing.
>
> Europe seems to have answered the question already. The anti-liberal rebound is more than plain, it is palpable. It finds political expression in a disgusted turning away from democracy and parliamentary government, in a beetle-browed about-face toward dictatorship and terror. (*Essays*, pp. 170–71)

That is what he wrote during the period of the Weimar Republic. Amid the ruckus of Hitlerite *Parteitags*, humanism was losing. And with it, the German people were losing, and he, a German writer. He saw this clearly: barbarism was going to triumph for many long years. And what was worse, this triumph was not just the victory of force; it was also the introduction of *new rules*. Nazism was being recognized by Germans and by European democracies. Hitler's Reich was becoming a full-fledged member of Europe.

And he was powerless. He—a Nobel laureate, a man who talked with premiers and with presidents, the crown jewel of the most exclusive European elites—felt completely helpless. And it is this helplessness that lends the letters of this titan of German literature their unconventional ethical resonance. That is why he turned to invective: out of helplessness and the pain of clairvoyance.

5

For he saw clearly, and perhaps that is why he wrote about Germany in a way that to this day may arouse the distaste of aesthetes. He was not satisfied with distinguishing between the Nazi regime and the German people ("Germans reduced to the notion those idiots have created! What an absurdity!"); he also launched a brutal attack on German compliance with the Nazis. "This vile excrescence must first be removed, so that something decent and possible for the world and human beings can arise." He recalled the words uttered by Alexander von Villers in 1870—"I am so fed up with the gleeful and belabored platitudes of the nation that out of repugnance I have broken a thousand ties linking my soul to Germany"—and added, "Yes, yes." "Unhappy, unhappy nation! I have long ago reached the point of begging the World Spirit to liberate this nation from political life, to dissolve it and disperse it in a new world like the Jews, with whom so much kindred tragic destiny links it" (*Letters*, p. 222)

In formulating his thoughts so sharply, he had no doubt that his countrymen would accuse him of contempt for the people, of treating them "like mud." He also knew why he was so afraid of German consent to nazism. He knew that the condition for effective Nazi terror was the spiritual capitulation of the terrorized. He was after an inner gesture of resistance (an external one would be heroism), after some psychological protest to barbarism. Every sign of resistance bolstered his faith, but he did not conceal his pessimism. In an April 1934 letter he wrote:

> But the German people are great at taking what comes, and since they do not love freedom but feel it rather as a form of neglect (for which reason it actually does become a kind of negligence for them), they will in spite of harsh disillusionments feel even better and happier under the new grimly disciplinarian constitution than under the Republic. Added to that is the regime's vast apparatus for deceiving, stupefying, and brutalizing them. The intellectual and moral level long ago sank so low that the spirit necessary for a real uprising simply cannot be summoned up. And at

the same time they have, in that debased state, the heady sense of representing a new world—which indeed it is; a world of debasement. We are aliens in it, and ultimately can do nothing but resign ourselves. (*Letters*, p. 217)

How could he feel like anything but an intruder when he read the German papers brimming with the mental acrobatics of German intellectuals?

In a September 1934 letter to Ferdinand Lion he wrote:

> The fact that German writers are really no smarter than they are allowed to be there is a happiness thanks to which they do not feel how restricted they are. . . . This is due to the concept of "the nation," which is the center and common denominator of various philosophical and artistic directions, as Hellpach announced at the congress of philosophers in Prague—which, of course, outraged the congress; Swiss newspapers defend Hellpach, however, because supposedly he was always a "democrat." Can one believe such idiocy? As if today talk about the "nation" was a manifestation of one's "democratic leanings" and not, to a considerably greater degree—servility and miserable renegation. I refer here to your statement that "never were we a nation in such minute degree." This deceit, this swindle infuriates me so much it almost kills me.

Mann looked with equal horror upon the blindness of Western democracies. In a December 1933 letter in which he reflects on the rumors of Hitler's plans for Austria, he writes:

> But would the annexation of Austria really be tolerated internationally? Granted, the weakness and perplexity is vast, and I fear that this gang may put Europe into its pocket by "legal," "democratic" methods—without war, that is. The fact is that their present propagandistic claims of pacifism are a complete fraud—simply the counterpart in foreign policy of the pose of legality which they used on the domestic front in order to come to power. We had better arm ourselves with the equanimity of the cynic in the event that they succeed. (*Letters*, p. 205)

In the meantime, "they" were doing quite well: using a method that was part request and part threat, the carrot and the stick, military blackmail and declarations of peace, Hitler's people were making a fool of Europe. They used slogans advertising neutrality and thereby gained acceptance for whatever they did.

They plucked one opponent after another and did them in individually, with the silent approval of the whole world, which believed that each successive victim procured peace everlasting on the continent. In August 1936 Mann wrote: "The 'naive' are at the top today, that is, those who shamelessly give priority to their own interests without regard for moral considerations." Even Nazi brutality aroused fascination: there were more and more notables who expressed themselves on Hitler's side. "What incomprehensible crudity!" wrote Mann about Knut Hamsun's pro-Hitler declarations. Oh yes! The Nazis were cunning and treacherous. "This is what they are like," he wrote in November 1935. "They send the half-Jew Lehwald to Zurich to give a lofty humanitarian propaganda speech on the Olympics, full of claptrap about human dignity, the brotherhood of nations . . . and so forth—in the name of the Third Reich! This is how they are. There are no baser swine under the sun!"

During Thomas Mann's visit to Vienna (in the summer of 1936), the Nazis threw stink bombs into the opera to sweeten the writer's stay. The stench was so bad the actors were vomiting during the performance: "That, too, is an experience worth having; now at least I know exactly what Nazism smells like: sweaty feet to a high power" (*Letters*, p. 252).

Poor Thomas Mann.

6

What is so strange about having a normal European receive the news of normalization in Germany without anger? Who likes to poison his moral complacency with news of someone else's misfortune? Can it strike anyone as strange that the European gladly believed Adolf Hitler's declarations of peace? Who likes to think that war, with its cruelties and victims, is inevitable? Who does not crave everlasting peace, as long as the gates of a concentration camp do not stare him in the face?

Did Thomas Mann want war? It is impossible to answer the question put this way. Its very construction conceals a style of reasoning characteristic of people like Goebbels. No, Mann did not long for war, misfortune, slaughter, or tears. But he did understand that if the Nazis were not removed from power, war would be unavoidable. That is why he repeated that "one cannot and should not help the current rulers and destroyers of the country." One should help Germany in only one way: by helping them get rid of the Nazi dictatorship. Hence his extremely negative view of pacifism, which—often unintentionally—rendered European democracies defenseless against brown totalitarianism.

On his lips, invective became a symbol. It documented the conviction that, in relations with the Nazis, comportment based on models of democratic culture was suicide. It was a desperate warning formulated about Germany and the world. One Nazi publicist called Mann's statements "the view of one who has been overthrown." In spite of its malicious intent, this was an accurate observation. In fact, Mann was the defender of a losing humanism. From this perspective he told the Germans that the current rulers would lead them to ruin. He was of the opinion that a nation that approves the rule of bandits armed with a nationalist ideology commits an act of self-degradation.

Invective, therefore, was the way this most German of all German writers expressed his loyalty to the national environment. The German state, Thomas Mann seemed to be saying, has ceased to exist. The Nazi state—the "pitiful prison," "idiotic military camp called Germany"—does not deserve to be called a "state" in the European sense of the word (just as a gang of bandits does not deserve to be called a legal organization). People are not obliged to be loyal to gangsters. ("I am not afraid of the revolt; rather, I desire it, for anything is better than this," he wrote.) There can be no talk of compromise with Nazis. A compromise is possible only as a result of clearly delineated fields of understanding; it requires the sobering light of day. It is different with nazism: "Hitler's stars shine only during the darkest night."

A citizen's and a German's duty, therefore, is unconditional resistance to nazism. One must wish this "national revolution" defeat. Whosoever labels such a position betrayal of the "national cause" or "cause of peace" betrays the human cause. For this German mixture of "sentimentality and force" can bring nothing but catastrophe to Germany and the world.

For at bottom I am much too good a German for the thought of permanent exile not to weigh heavily indeed, and the breach with my country, which is almost unavoidable, fills me with depression and dread—a sign that it does not fit my nature, which has been formed by elements of the Goethean tradition of representation, so that I cannot feel I was destined for martyrdom. For me to have been forced into this role, something thoroughly wrong and evil must surely have taken place. And it is my deepest conviction that this whole "German Revolution" is indeed wrong and evil. It lacks all the characteristics which have won the sympathy of the world for genuine revolutions, however bloody they may have been. In its essence it is not a "rising," no matter how its proponents rant on, but a terrible fall into hatred, vengeance, lust for killing, and petit-bourgeois mean-spiritedness. I shall never believe that any good can come of it, for either Germany or the world. (*Letters*, p. 198)

He was aware that in proposing the candidacy of the imprisoned Carl von Ossietzky for the Nobel Peace Prize, he was throwing his writer's authority onto the political scales. When it was pointed out to him that he was discarding his writer's ethic of irony and distance, he answered that "a defender of Pure Literature seems almost pathetic to himself," and that the "political struggle in current circumstances" is at times more important, decisive, and worthy of recognition "than all of poetry."

This is what he wrote to Eduard Korrodi in the open letter mentioned at the beginning of these reflections.

7

It was all brought on by a trifle. Korrodi had publicly attacked a German emigrant publicist for claiming that "all of contemporary literature has transferred abroad." But he did not stop at pointing out the exaggeration. He also wrote that the majority of those who found themselves abroad—with the exception of a few literary graphomaniacs or so—were Jews.

Mann agreed the claim that "all of contemporary literature" had transferred abroad was an exaggeration and overstatement. "I do not want to call anyone to the Gestapo's attention, but in many cases purely mechanical rather than intellectual reasons may be decisive, and thus the boundary between exiled and nonexiled German literature is not so easy to draw; it does not coincide so precisely with the boundaries of the Reich" (*Letters*, pp. 244–45).

By introducing the term "Gestapo" into the discussion, Thomas Mann was fixing its ideological horizons. He could also admit that the exaggerated claim about "all of German literature" could "arouse the ire of a neutral" such as Korrodi.

> But neutrality remains a difficult art even for people who have such long practice in it as you Swiss! How easily the neutral, in combatting one injustice, falls into another. The moment that you raise objections to the identification of exile literature with the whole of German literature, you yourself set up an untenable equation. For, curiously, it is not the error itself that angers you, but the fact that a Jewish writer commits it; and even as you conclude from this fact that once again literature of Jewish origin is being confounded with German literature (the old complaint of the Fatherland fanatics), you yourself confound exile with Jewish literature. (*Letters*, p. 245)

In response, Mann named an entire list—"which I would never have thought of compiling"—of writers who were "pure" German. He explained that the presence of the "Jewish element" among the emigrants followed from "the sweeping nature of National Socialist racial philosophy and from the revulsion which the Jewish spirit feels for certain state institutions of our times."

But was the thesis—that the work of writers labeled "Jewish" did not belong to German literature because of its international qualities—tenable? Mann was of a different opinion:

> The "international" qualities of Jews are nothing more nor less than their Mediterranean-European qualities. And these are at the same time *German;* without them, Germanism would not be Germanism, but a totally useless sluggishness. That is precisely what the Catholic Church—which today is in straits that make her revered once again even by a product of Protestant culture—is defending inside Germany when she declares that only after the Germans accepted Christianity did they enter the company of civilized nations. (*Letters*, p. 248)

Mann unveiled, with great precision and consistency, the antihumanist ground common to Nazi anti-Semitism and anti-Christianity. He also showed its anti-German edge:

Being voelkisch is not being German. But the Germans', or the German rulers', hatred of the Jews is in the higher sense not directed toward the Jews at all, or not toward them alone: it is directed against Europe and all loftier Germanism; it is directed, as becomes increasingly apparent, against the Christian and classical foundations of Western morality. It is the attempt (symbolized by the withdrawal from the League of Nations) to shake off the ties of civilization. That attempt threatens to bring about a terrible alienation, fraught with evil potentialities, between the land of Goethe and the rest of the world.

And then he concluded:

Countless human, moral, and aesthetic observations support my profound conviction that nothing good can possibly come of the present German regime, not for Germany and not for the world. This conviction has made me shun the country in whose spiritual traditions I am more deeply rooted than the present rulers who for three years have vacillated, not quite daring to deny me my Germanism before the eyes of the world.

After Mann's letter to Korrodi, the Nazis no longer vacillated—they stripped the writer of his citizenship in the German Reich.

Why had Mann pulled up his visor at this precise moment, when there had been plenty of important events before? It is impossible to answer this question. Sometimes it takes only a straw to break the proverbial camel's back. Shortly afterward Mann wrote:

Sooner or later I had to speak out, and I chose a moment when someone was insidiously attempting to draw a line between me and the exiles, and with the feeling moreover that unpleasant half-and-half notions of my relations to the Third Reich prevail in some parts of the world. But in addition, simply from inner, psychic reasons. It was in good part a temperamental act, a natural reaction to all the insults and outrages that daily come raining down upon us all. It was also the real and deep conviction that this mischief will mean the doom of the whole continent if it continues, and that I must oppose it here and now, so far as my feeble strength permits, as I have already opposed it at home. (*Letters*, p. 250)

8

Let us repeat nevertheless, Mann was far from being an opti-
mist. In a Nazi world, he wanted to be Don Quixote. This was the
spiritual strategy he formulated. He wanted to show solidarity with
the victims; he felt that he had become one of them. In a private
November 1935 letter to Korrodi he wrote that only one thing
linked him to other German exiles:

> All of its members are victims of this regime (this is an honor that
> is not becoming to all) and . . . I cannot understand . . . the re-
> pugnance that can clearly be felt in your attitude to this category
> of people. Isn't there a certain mean-spiritedness concealed in the
> statement "A man who has quarreled with his government is a
> man who arouses fear in decent people" and shouldn't one cor-
> rect it? What kind of government are you talking about? The label
> of political exile has been an honorable title in times that provided
> fewer moral justifications than today's! What has happened to
> this world!

Mann's fear was free of rhetoric; he knew that in "this world"
he could only be a renegade or a Don Quixote. He looked around
aghast:

> Someone who himself has fascist inclinations has an easier time of
> maintaining calm and an attitude of repugnance to the desperate
> hatred of exiles. Generally speaking, the world is somehow inca-
> pable of understanding what is happening to people in Germany
> and this lack of understanding allows it to maintain its phlegm
> and disinterest. I have observed this astounding phenomenon on
> several occasions. People do not understand what is happening
> and even if they condemn it, they remain indifferent in their
> souls, because they lack the authentic experience. Expressing this
> in words is truly impossible. All of this moves well beyond poli-
> tics. Fascism, the government of the proletariat, dictatorship—
> none of these terms render the incredible excrescence that rules
> there.

Only one person—an English bishop—used words that seemed
appropriate. He said that he went "blind with rage" when he
thought about Germany. Mann, too, an intruder in the Nazi
period who recognized himself as a "relic of a bygone cultural
epoch," went blind with rage. He kept repeating, though, that

"there is nothing more beautiful than glorious skirmishes during a retreat."

When in late spring 1934 he sailed to the United States to receive an honorary doctoral degree from Harvard University, he took with him Cervantes's novel. The losing Don Quixote had Mann's complete sympathy—he became mental shorthand for Mann's own dilemmas. The main one was, How does one make a value out of being a "relic"? The "relic" loses, and just like Don Quixote falls under the "wheels of the speeding vehicle of history." But so what? Is it better to forgo courage and give up being noble? "But what would a Don Quixote at the other extreme be like? Anti-idealistic, sinister, a pessimistic believer in force—and yet a Don Quixote? A brutalized Don Quixote?"

No!

> Agitated times like ours always tend to confound the merely epochal with the eternal—as for instance liberalism with freedom— and to throw out the baby with the bathwater. Thus each free and thoughtful person, each mind which does not flicker in the wind of time, is forced back upon the foundations; driven to become once more conscious of them and to base more solidly upon them. (*Essays*, p. 454)

One should not, he claimed, flatter an epoch whose grace one wins at the price of trampling "reason and civilization." "To be able to look into the future one must indeed be of the time. But not only in the sense of actual movement, in which every donkey partakes, bursting with pride and scorn against liberal reactionaries of a different stripe" (*Essays*, p. 456). One must have the whole epoch in oneself, in all its complexity and contradiction; one must know how to interpret one's own crisis as a fragment of the world crisis. This is the only way to freedom: "Freedom has worth, it confers rank, only when it is won from unfreedom, when it is the process of becoming free." This kind of struggle for freedom, which "mingles cruel humiliation and moving nobility of soul," is Don Quixote-ism, a challenge made to the world.

This Don Quixote of the Nazi era has a few ideas worth noting.

First: "Do not worry about the future—this is the only possible life strategy in today's times."

Second: "Immerse yourself in innocent and internally equanimous work—this is the only thing that can help us deal with this nightmare." Create one's work calmly and persistently amid the "upheavals, coups, and threats."

Third: "Be one's own signpost when there are no other signposts."

Fourth: Know how to "wait and endure"; know how to create decent works in "sad, wicked, barrenly resistant times."

Fifth: "Maintain the bravery and the patience that Schopenhauer so beautifully associated with courage."

Sixth: Call "baseness, base."

9

Immediately after being deprived of his citizenship, Mann wrote to a friend, "I simply do not believe this can possibly last for long." He also passed on the rumors from Germany that "the Nationalist Socialist adventure is in its final stage," that it was a matter of weeks or months. "I tell myself that either the war will come in a year and a half or two years, or conditions within this period will change so much that our books, too, will again be permitted in Germany."

The war broke out in three years—his calculations were off by just a single year.

In reading these letters after forty years, you wonder, Polish reader, if their author could have decided differently. Could he have returned to Germany and with his, even silent, presence legalized the totalitarian government? Could he have participated, as so many others did, in academic meetings and traveled to international congresses as a representative of the culture of the Third Reich? Could he have—at the price of tolerance for his books—served as an argument for the propaganda claim about "normalization in Germany"? Could he have—in the name of praiseworthy neutrality and objectivity—publicly noted his recognition of the political successes, of which there was no dearth? Could he have convinced himself that he was choosing the realism of participation against the exaggerated high-mindedness of the emigrants' refusal?

It is true that these questions have no bearing on an understanding of history. They do help, however, to get at its moral roots. We who love Mann's books and look in them for a way to face up to fate, our hearts command us to say, no, no he could not have acted differently. Reason, however, tells us to put down a question mark. The biographical adventures of twentieth-century intellectuals do not allow us to answer unequivocally.

I have called Thomas Mann's life—as recorded in his *Letters*—a *Bildungsroman*. What did I want to learn from this novel? In reconstructing one of its chapters I did not intend at all to tell the story of the author's attitude to nazism—I am putting off this fascinating topic to another time. I was interested in only one subject. I wanted to get at the dominant feeling that dictated the most risky decisions of his life. And I think I did—it was disgust.

Mann's attitude to nazism was saturated with an instinctive revulsion; it was only later that he wrote his penetrating analyses of the devil concealed in the legacy of German culture. It was the aesthetic abhorrence, and not the intellectual afterthought, that compelled Mann to choose a position of integral opposition. It was revulsion that allowed him to see instantly and clearly everything that others would see only during the war. But let me say this differently: Mann's life was a striking microcosm of the modern history of European humanism, its isolation in the face of totalitarian forces. The helplessness of the German writer-expatriate became an augury of Europe's destiny, a Europe whose fragments were shortly to fall, one after the other, "beneath the armed feet of alien might."

Hitler's totalitarian state applied the same technique toward isolated individuals that it did toward isolated nations: the appearance of legality and paragraphs of inhuman penal codes concealed brute force. The invective and insults in Mann's letters were a desperate attempt to shatter conventions, within the framework of which nazism was treated as an "interesting experiment." ("The scholastic apotheosis of German events without seeing reality is not just a bad joke for someone who has come to know the benefits of this 'spirit' on his own hide. This is not for me!") How quixotic Mann is in his attitude toward the Gestapo. Yet . . .

The educational value of the letters from the years 1933–36 as read today is the awareness of the *pointe* which Mann could not know when he decided to break with the German state. You, Polish reader, know the finale: Berlin in flames, the Nuremberg trials, the division of Germany. So you know that this German Don Quixote turned out to be a more farsighted realist than the devoted functionaries of brown-shirt propaganda; that this solitary exile powerlessly dispensing invective turned out to be stronger than the mighty totalitarian regime he was assailing. Can there be a more heartening argument in favor of conviction, that in being defeated—like Mann forty years ago—one might at the same time win? This is probably what you are thinking, Polish reader, and it is difficult to call this conclusion unreasonable. But this is not a story as optimistic as you and the author of this essay would like. Thomas Mann paid the highest price for his decision—the price of estrangement. The estrangement that allowed him later to speak to Germans via American radio and write *Doctor Faustus* but would not allow him to return to his homeland after the war.

For a country does not like those who were prematurely right against it, and it never forgives this premature rightness. Remember this, too, Polish reader, in reading Thomas Mann's old correspondence today. For—and this is the important moral of reading the *Letters*—a great writer is inaccessible to us only when we live with his work. Only then does he inhabit the stellar regions, off-limits to us ordinary mortals. Nevertheless, when he rises from his desk and puts down his pen he is once again one of us: weak and full of doubts, anxious and susceptible to the temptations of practicality. And, like each of us, he is reluctant to break with habits, comfort, and a feeling of safety. Yet life lived in truth and dignity, though difficult and full of complications, has something truly addictive to it. Whoever has once tasted it has a hard time getting rid of such fatal addictions.

That is why the Berlin ukase banishing Mann strengthened him. Something had ended, something was beginning, the ambivalent period was over. Now came the days in which Thomas Mann's public invective saved Germany's honor, days that testified to the conscience and sovereign dignity of a great German culture. Mann wrote: "I would be a scoundrel like the authors of that ukase if I were to regret anything. God knows, I was not born for hatred, but I hate those bloodthirsty fools and corrupters of humanity from the bottom of my heart and fervently wish them the dreadful end they deserve" (*Letters*, p. 257).

10

And you, Polish reader, remember these words well, because Thomas Mann formulated a moral obligation in them—for you as well. If you feel a bond with something like an international republic of humanists, you must be aware of the consequence of such a choice. Namely: when you read, hear, and say that on your native land Germans pronounced themselves supermen and propagated an architecture of concentration camps, pillaged and slaughtered, destroyed human bodies, and depraved human souls in the name of a millennial Reich, you, Polish reader, have the obligation to remember and repeat that there was a certain German Don Quixote, a helpless writer, who, nauseous with disgust, wished defeat to the Nazi executioners long before they invaded your country; who put human solidarity in humanist values above tribal discipline in the name of nationalist doctrines.

Thus when you remember, Polish reader, the fate of Polish writers and professors of Polish universities transported to death camps and executed in the streets, you are to repeat stubbornly, through clenched teeth, as a sign of solidarity and communion in pain: Thomas Mann, Thomas Mann, Thomas Mann . . .

Barczewo Prison, January 1986

TRANSLATED BY LILLIAN VALLEE

Notes on Contributors

STANISŁAW BARAŃCZAK (1946–) was born in Poznan. A poet, literary critic, and translator, he taught at Poznan University until he was fired in 1972 for political reasons. He is the author of eight collections of poems, eight books of literary criticism, and many volumes of translations into Polish of English, American, and Russian poetry. His poems and essays have appeared in *Encounter, Salmagundi, The New Republic,* and elsewhere. Since 1981 he has been a professor of Polish language and literature at Harvard University.

JAN BŁOŃSKI (1931–) is a literary critic, translator, and editor who teaches at the Jagellonian University in Krakow. He has translated Artaud and Genet into Polish and is the author of several essays on Gombrowicz and Witkiewicz. His major publications include *Zmiana warty* (1961; "A changing of the guard") *Odmarsz* (1978; "Marching off"), and *Kilka mysli co nie nowe* (1985; "A few thoughts on well-worn themes").

JÓZEF CZAPSKI (1896–) is a painter and art critic. Born in Prague, he studied in Krakow and in Paris. During the war he was interned in the Soviet Union, and from 1941 he served with the Polish Army in campaigns in Egypt and Italy. In 1945 he settled in Paris. Influential as an art critic and a postimpressionist painter, he has exhibited widely and written extensively on literary, political, religious, and artistic subjects. His works include collections of essays: *Oko* (1960; "The Eye"), *Tumult i widma* (1981; "Tumult and specters"), and *Patrzac*

(1983; "Seeing"); studies of painters: *Jozef Pankiewicz* (1936) and *O Cezannie i świadomości malarskiej* (1937; "On Cezanne and painterly Consciousness"); and autobiographical writings.

WITOLD GOMBROWICZ (1904–69), novelist and playwright, was born in Małoszyce and died in Vence, France. When the war broke out in 1939, he was on a trip to Argentina, and he did not return to Europe until 1963. His major novels are *Ferdydurke* (1937; Eng. trans., 1961), *Trans-Atlantyk* (1953; Eng. trans., *Trans-Atlantic*), *Pornografia* (1960; Eng. trans. 1966), and *Kosmos* (1956; Eng. trans. *Cosmos*, 1966). His plays include *Iwona, księżniczka Burgunda* (1938; Eng. trans., *Ivona, Princess of Burgundia*, 1969); *Slub* (1947; Eng. trans., *The Marriage*, 1969); and *Operetka* (1966; Eng. trans., *Operetta*, 1971). His three-volume *Diary* is published by Northwestern University Press.

JERZY GROTOWSKI (1933–) was born in Rzeszow. A theater director and theorist, he graduated from the Moscow State Institute of Theater Arts. His productions and theories, particularly the concept of a "poor theater," have had a major impact on the avant-garde in Europe, America, and Japan. He is the founder of the Theater of 13 Rows (1959–65 in Opole, Poland), later known as the Laboratory Theater (from 1965 in Wroclaw). His major productions include *The Constant Prince, Acropolis,* and *Apocalypsis cum Figuris,* his last work for the theater. He is the author of *Towards a Poor Theatre* (1968). Having left Poland in 1981 he now runs the Centro di Lavoro di Jerzy Grotowski in Pontedera, Italy.

ZBIGNIEW HERBERT (1924–), a poet, playwright, and essayist, was born in Lvov, where he attended a clandestine gymnasium during the war and joined the underground. After the war, he studied philosophy and history of art in Warsaw, where he now lives. His first book of poetry appeared in 1956 during the post-Stalin "thaw." Herbert's poetry has steadily gained international recognition and has been translated into many languages. Recent English translations include *The Selected Poems* (1986) and *Report from the Besieged City* (1985).

GUSTAW HERLING (1919–) is a short-story writer, essayist, and literary critic. Born in Kielce, he studied Polish literature in Warsaw. He took part in the 1939 September campaign and was deported in 1940 to a Soviet labor camp. After the war he lived in Rome and London and now lives in Naples. His *Inny świat* (1953), an account of his experiences in the labor camp, appeared in many languages (Eng. trans., *A World Apart*, 1951), as did many of his short stories (*The Island, Three Tales*, 1967). *Dziennik pisany nocą* (A diary written at night), a series of essays, appears regularly in the Polish monthly *Kultura* in Paris, to which he has contributed since 1948.

JAROSŁAW IWASZKIEWICZ (1894–1980) was born in Kalnik in the Ukraine. A poet, novelist, playwright, and essayist, he studied law and music in Kiev. From 1918 until his death he lived in Warsaw. He was a member of the prewar group of poets associated with the literary magazine *Skamander* and also held diplomatic posts. In the postwar period he was president of the Polish Writer's Association for many years and the editor of *Twórczość*, a literary monthly. His major works include several volumes of poetry (beginning in 1915 with *Oktostychy*); novels: *Czerwone tarcze* (1934; "Red shields"), *Sława i chwała* (1956–62; "Fame and glory"), *Lato w Nohant* (1936; Eng. trans., *A Summer at Nohant*, 1942), a play about George Sand and Chopin; essays on literature and music; and biographies and memoirs. Many of his writings appeared in French and German translations.

KONSTANTY JELEŃSKI (1922–87) was born in Warsaw. An art and literary critic and translator, he was educated in England. During the war he served with the Polish Army in France and England and took part in the invasion of Normandy. In 1952 he settled in Paris, where he died. His essays and criticism have appeared in major European literary magazines. He was the editor of *Antholgie de la poésie polonaise* (1981) and the author of the collection of essays *Zbiegi okoliczności* (1962; "Coincidences") and *Witold Gombrowicz: Theater* (1976).

WOJCIECH KARPIŃSKI (1943–) was born in Warsaw. A literary critic, he has lived in Paris since 1981. Recent books include *Chusteczka Imperatora* (1983; "The Emperor's handkerchief"), *Cień*

Metternicha (1983; "The shadow of Metternich"), *Amerykańskie cienie* (1983; "American shadows"), and *Herb wygnania* (1990; "The blazon of exile").

ANDRZEJ KIJOWSKI (1928–80) was born in Krakow and died in Warsaw. A literary critic and writer, he was on the editorial staff of the literary monthly *Twórczość*. His publications include collections of short stories, film scenarios, and essays, including the posthumous *Tropy* (1986; "Traces").

LESZEK KOLAKOWSKI (1927–) was born in Radom. A philosopher, essayist, and playwright, he taught modern philosophy at the University of Warsaw. Active in the opposition movement, he was expelled from the Polish Communist party in 1966, and two years later deprived of his chair at the university. He has lived in England since 1969. He teaches at All Souls College, Oxford, and the University of Chicago. Recent publications include *Religion* (1982), *Bergson* (1985), and *Cywilizacja na ławie oskarżonych* (1986; "Civilization on Trial").

JAN KOTT (1914–) was born in Warsaw. An essayist and a literary and theater critic, in 1969 he was dismissed from the University of Warsaw for political reasons. Since then he has lived in the United States. His *Shakespeare, Our Contemporary* has appeared in over twenty languages. Recent publications in English are *The Theater of Essence and Other Essays* (1984) and *The Bottom Translation* (1986).

ZYGMUNT KUBIAK (1929–) was born and lives in Warsaw. A literary critic, editor, and translator, he writes for many literary magazines and is known for his translations of poetry from classical and modern languages. His collections of essays include *Półmrok ludzkiego świata* (1963; "Twilight of the human world"), *Wędrówki po stuleciach* (1968; "Journeys through centuries"), and *Jak w zwierciadle* (1985; "As in the mirror").

STANISLAW JERZY LEC (1909–64) was born in Lvov and died in Warsaw. A poet, satirist, and aphorist, he studied in Lvov. During the war he was in a German concentration camp, from which he escaped to join the underground Polish People's Army. His aphorisms first appeared in a number of literary journals; only after the 1956 "thaw" were they published in book form, under the title *Myśli nieuczesane* (1957; Eng. trans., *Unkempt Thoughts*, 1962).

Stanisław Lem (1921–) was born in Lvov. A science fiction writer, he studied medicine in Krakow, where he has lived since 1946. During the Nazi occupation he worked as a garage mechanic and took part in the resistance movement. Since the mid-fifties, his works have appeared in twenty-five languages. In his essays *Summa Technologiae* (1968) and *Filozofia przypadku* (1968; "The philosophy of chance") he discusses the cultural and moral implications of science and technology. His most recent works published in America include *The Masters Voice* (1983), *Microworlds: Writings on Science Fiction and Fanatasy* (1984), *One Human Minute* (1986), and *The Hospital of Transfiguration* (1988).

Adam Michnik (1946–) was born in Warsaw. A historian and publicist, he was a prominent figure in the Solidarity movement and spent over six years in prison (the last time in 1986). At one time the editor of two Warsaw underground journals, *Krytyka* and *Zapis*, he is currently the editor of *Gazeta wyborcza* and a deputy to the Sejm. He lives in Warsaw. His recent publications include *Z dziejów honoru w Polsce: Wypisy więzienne* (1985; Eng. trans. *Letters from Prison and other Essays*), *Takie czasy—rzecz o kompromisie* (1985; "Times like these, or making compromises"), and *Polskie pytania* (1987; "Polish questions").

Bolesław Miciński (1911–43), born in eastern Poland, was a poet and literary critic. He is known for his collection of essays, *Podróże do piekieł* (Journeys to the underworlds), published in 1937—a wide-ranging comparative study of the interrelations among the arts and an exploration of the subconscious in literature. After the outbreak of World War II, he went to France, and later died in Laffrey, Switzerland.

Czesław Miłosz (1911–) was born in Sztejnie, Lithuania. A poet, novelist, and translator, he left Poland in 1951. Living in the United States since 1960, he is the winner of the 1980 Nobel Prize in Literature. His recent American publications include

Unattainable Earth (1988), *The Separate Notebooks* (1988), and *The Collected Poems 1931–87* (1988).

BRUNO SCHULZ (1892–1942) was born in Drohobycz. A writer and graphic artist, he studied architecture in Lvov and fine arts in Vienna. His two collections of short stories, *Sklepy cynamonowe* (1934; "Cinnamon shops"; Eng. trans., *Street of Crocodiles*, 1963) and *Sanatorium pod klepsydrą* (1937; Eng. trans., *Sanatorium under the Sign of the Hourglass*, 1978) have gained him recognition as one of the most important prose writers between the wars. Schulz was killed by a German officer on a street in Drohobycz.

JERZY STEMPOWSKI (1894–1969) was a literary critic and essayist. Born in Krakow, he studied humanities in Krakow, Munich, and Zurich. In 1939 he emigrated, settling in Switzerland, where he died in Bern. The undisputed master of the Polish essay, he contributed regularly to the Paris émigré monthly *Kultura*. His work appeared as "Meditations of an Unhurried Wanderer," under the penname Paweł Hostowiec. His collections of essays include *Eseje dla Kasandry* (1961; "Essays for Cassandra"); a posthumous collection, *Od Berdyczowa do Rzymu* (From Berdyczowo to Rome); *A Journal of Travel to Germany and Austria* (1946); and *La terre bernoise* (1954).

STANISLAW VINCENZ (1888–1971), born in Słoboda Runguska in eastern Galicia, was a writer, folklorist, and philosopher. He studied in Vienna. When World War II broke out, he escaped first to Hungary and then settled in the French Alps. He died in Lausanne. He was the author of essays on Dante and ancient Greece, and of memoirs. His principal works are *Na wysokiej połoninie* (1936; Eng. trans., *On the High Uplands*, 1955), a collection of the lore and sagas of the Hucul country (the Carpathian Mountains) interspersed with numerous tales of the Hasidim; *Tematy żydowskie* (1973; "Jewish themes"); *Listy z nieba* (1974; "Letters from heaven"); and *Powojenne perypetie Sokratesa* (1985; "Socrates' adventures after the war").

ALEKSANDER WAT (1900–1967) was born in Warsaw. A poet, editor, translator, and literary critic, before World War II he was one of the founders of the Polish futurist movement. Later he embraced Marxism. From 1939 to 1946 he spent long periods in Soviet prisons and in deportation in Soviet Asia. From the late 1950s he lived in Italy and France, and he died in Paris. His major works are a collection of short stories and parables, *Bezrobotny Lucyfer* (1927; Eng. trans., *Lucifer Unemployed*, 1990); *Wiersze Śródziemnomorskie* (1962; Eng. trans., *Mediterranean Poems*, 1971); a memoir and commentary on literary life and politics, *Mój wiek* (1977; Eng. trans., *My Century*, 1988); and a collection of poems, translated into English by Czesław Miłosz and Leonard Nathan, *With the Skin* (1989).

STANISLAW IGNACY WITKIEWICZ (1885–1939) was a painter, playwright, novelist, and philosopher. He was born in Warsaw but grew up and spent much of his life in Zakopane. He went with Bronislaw Malinowski to Australia in 1914 and served as a officer in the Czarist army from 1914 to 1917. He was active in Poland as an artist and writer until his death. Among his best known plays are *Wariat i zakonnica* (1925; Eng. trans., *The Madman and the Nun*) and *Szewcy* (1933; Eng. trans., *The Shoemakers*); his novels include *Pożegnanie jesieni* (1927; "Farewell to autumn") and *Nienasycenie* (1930; Eng. trans., *Insatiability*).

JÓZEF WITTLIN (1896–1976) was born in Dmytrow in the Ukraine. A poet, novelist, essayist, and translator, he studied philosophy and linguistics in Vienna. Before the war he was affiliated with the expressionist group *Zdrój* (The Source). He emigrated in 1940, and from 1941 he lived in New York, where he died. He was the author of an antiwar novel, *Sól ziemi* (1936; Eng. trans., *The Salt of the Earth*, 1939); a book of memoirs, *Moj Lwów* (1946; "My Lvov"); a collection of essays, *Orfeusz w piekle dwudziestego wieku* (1963; "Orpheus in the inferno of the twentieth century"); and translations of Homer.

ADAM ZAGAJEWSKI (1945–) was born in Lvov. A poet and fiction writer, he is one of the representatives of the "Generation of 1968." His poems, novels, and short stories have appeared in many languages. His recent publications include a selection of poems in English, *Tremor* (1985), and *Solidarność i samotność* (1986; Eng. trans., *Solidarity, Solitude*).